CW00942924

ALASTAIR DENNISTON

Code-breaking From Room 40 *to* Berkeley Street *and the* Birth of GCHQ

ALASTAIR DENNISTON

Code-breaking From Room 40 *to* Berkeley Street *and the* Birth of GCHQ

Joel Greenberg

Frontline Books

ALASTAIR DENNISTON:
Code-Breaking From Room 40 to Berkeley Street and the Birth of GCHQ

First published in 2017 by Frontline Books,
an imprint of Pen & Sword Books Ltd,
47 Church Street, Barnsley, S. Yorkshire, S70 2AS

ISBN: 978-1-52670-912-7

CIP data records for this title are available from the British Library

For more information on our books, please visit
www.frontline-books.com
email info@frontline-books.com
or write to us at the above address.

Printed and bound by Gutenberg Press Ltd.
Typeset in 10.5/12.5 point Palatino

For Robin Denniston and Margaret ('Y') Finch

Contents

Foreword

Alastair Denniston was not only my favourite uncle but also a very special godfather. How lucky I was that my Mother, always deeply proud of her brother, asked him to undertake this extra duty! It made us especially close.

This special warm relationship began when I was shipped off to school in Kent at the age of 13. At the beginning of each term he would meet a very fearful child off the train from Leeds at King's Cross and take me quietly across London to the 'school train' at Charing Cross. In spite of the heavy burden he must have been carrying at this time, 1936–38, he appeared to me to have all the time in the world for a very nervous homesick youngster, chatting warmly about his very special sister (my mother) and all our family 'doings', and telling me of the holiday escapades of his beloved son and daughter, my cousins Robin and Y.

I remember once he told me that he had decided to swap birthdays with his son Robin, who was born on Christmas Day. He and his wife had decided that a small boy should not have to cope with birthday and Christmas Day on the same day, so that was why Robin should always celebrate his birthday on 1 December. He would be very happy to have his on Christmas Day, and so it was until Robin was grown up.

Holiday times often brought the two families together, either with us up in Yorkshire or in the South. I was invited down to their cottage at Barton-on-Sea. Uncle Alastair met me again in London and the drive down was yet another chance to get to know each other. He said to my mother after one trip that getting me past Walls Ice Cream 'Stop Me and Buy One' bicycles was like getting a dog past lamp posts! I remember that the sun always shone at Barton!

Perhaps one of the happiest and most recent memories of Uncle Alastair was well after the war when he would come up to Yorkshire to stay with my parents in Upper Nidderdale. My father had a grouse moor and shooting days were full of expectation and excitement. Beaters sent out to drive the birds forward were an integral part of the organisation. Uncle Alastair, who had no wish to use a gun, lined himself up with the beaters with his white flag and stumped across the heather. Everyone loved him and you could hear the other beaters call, 'Come on Uncle Alastair!' or 'Are you alright there Uncle Alastair?' Everyone really enjoyed his company, not remembering that he had won the war for us, but because he was such a genuine quiet loveable person.

Libby Buchanan

Preface

I first came across the name of Alastair Denniston and a photograph of him while reading the *Sunday Telegraph* on 21 July 1974. I had just been awarded a PhD in Numerical Mathematics by the University of Manchester and had a passing interest in codes and ciphers. I was immediately drawn to a headline in bold capital letters which said 'DEEPEST SECRET OF THE WAR'. The paper contained edited extracts from a new book called *The Ultra Secret* by F.W. Winterbotham. The author had set up the first Scientific Intelligence Unit in his Air Section of the Secret Intelligence Service (SIS) in offices in Broadway near Victoria. Two floors below were the offices of an organisation called the Government Code and Cypher School (GC&CS). According to Winterbotham, it consisted of 'a dedicated team of highly intellectual individuals under the control of Commander Alastair Denniston'. Denniston was a veteran of the British Admiralty's codebreaking team during World War One (WW1) and had set up GC&CS. Winterbotham went on to say that when the British discovered that Germany had adopted a cipher machine known as 'Enigma', to disguise its operational communications, 'it was Denniston himself who went to Poland and triumphantly, but in the utmost secrecy, brought back the complete, new, electrically operated Enigma cypher machine which we now knew was being produced in its thousands and was destined to carry all the secret signal traffic of the great war machine'. While Winterbotham's account of Denniston and the work of GC&CS would later prove to be inaccurate and somewhat fanciful, little did I know that over 38 years later I would meet Denniston's family and agree to write his biography.

Denniston's career in intelligence had begun on the outbreak of war in August 1914 when reservists were called up, and all members of the Royal Navy (RN) began their wartime duties. RN coastal wireless stations began to intercept and forward to the Admiralty wireless traffic of the Imperial German Navy and the task of making sense of this traffic was given to Sir Alfred Ewing, the Director of Naval Education. He gathered together a group of German-speakers who were given Room 40 in the old Admiralty Building to work from. One of his first recruits was Denniston who had been teaching French and German at Osborne Royal Naval College since 1909. At the end of WW1, he was chosen as the RN candidate to head the new GC&CS which had been formed under Admiralty control on 1 November 1919 by a merger of Room 40 and its Army counterpart MI1(b). In the process that followed he was preferred to the Army's candidate and duly appointed Operational Director of GC&CS.

It seems that the Director of Naval Intelligence during WW1, Admiral Hall, and Admiral Sinclair, Hall's successor in 1919 and subsequently Chief of the Secret Intelligence Service (SIS) from 1921, felt that Denniston had the right set of skills to manage, encourage, support and develop a set of individual and idiosyncratic staff involved in work which few outsiders understood. He was tasked with producing the vital intelligence which the Prime Minister, the Foreign Secretary and the Secretary of State for War would come to rely on. In 1921, GC&CS became subordinate to the Foreign Office and from 1923 was administered by Sinclair as its Director. During the interwar years, Denniston's organisation was probably the most effective cryptanalytic bureau the world had ever seen. However, in Denniston's eyes: 'Beyond a salary and accommodation vote GC&CS had no financial status; it became in fact an adopted child of the Foreign Office with no family rights, and the poor relation of the SIS, whose peacetime activities left little cash to spare.' In fact, GC&CS was treated much better than most other branches of government because of the value senior politicians and officials placed on its output.

In the years that followed the publication of Winterbotham's book, more information emerged about the activities of GC&CS while based at its war station at Bletchley Park (BP). Denniston had run the operation from 1939 until early 1942 at which point he had been removed from overall command and sent to London to run its much smaller Civil side based in offices in Berkeley Street. However, there was little information in the public domain about Denniston's Berkeley Street operation. Most authors seemed to concentrate on the period from 1938 to 1945 and activities at BP with a passing reference to the work done by Denniston's organisation between the wars. The picture that emerged of him was of a man who had set up the BP operation and allowed innovation to flourish, but ultimately, was unable to effectively run it as its requirements for more staff and equipment became increasingly urgent. The circumstances of his removal as Operational Director of GC&CS seemed somewhat obscure. Early accounts were charitable and Ronald Lewin, writing in his book *Ultra Goes to War* in 1978, said that 'If it was difficult for Denniston in the early days, it was an even more formidable task for his successor Commander Edward Travis who took over in 1942 after illness caused Denniston, now a veteran warhorse, to be transferred to quieter fields.' By 1998, GC&CS wartime documents had been released into the public domain and author Michael Smith, in his book *Station X,* wrote that, 'No doubt influenced in part by this [problems in the management of Hut 3] and in part by the discontent that had led to the joint letter to Churchill [the famous 'Action This Day' letter], Menzies [Head of the SIS and Director of GC&CS] decided that Denniston had neither the political nous nor the force of personality to control the rapidly growing organisation. In order to resolve the problem, he moved him to one side, putting him in charge of diplomatic and commercial codebreaking as Deputy Director (Civilian) with the more dynamic Travis as Deputy Director (Services) in charge of the military sections.'

In his new role, Denniston established a diplomatic and commercial organisation in Berkeley Street which in effect recreated the GC&CS of the interwar years. This played to his strengths, that of running a smaller group in a very personal and collegiate way. Others could be left to run the codebreaking factory at BP which he had played a key role in creating with the help of colleagues. As German military wireless Enigma traffic diminished in the last few years of the war, diplomatic and commercial traffic continued to increase so that the Berkeley Street operation became a key part of Britain's signal intelligence (Sigint) effort. American visitors to Berkeley Street produced reports for Washington full of praise for what Denniston was achieving with a small number of staff, both in terms of its scale and quality.

Ultimately, Denniston's strategy for consolidating all British Sigint under GC&CS succeeded and by 1944, the organisation had won the right to be in total command of it. Their success from 1940 and onwards won them this right. Therefore, it must have been a bitter pill for Denniston to swallow that he was not allowed to share some of the fruits of this success, given how fundamental his contribution had been. A reorganisation at the end of World War Two (WW2) had made Sir Stewart Menzies (Sinclair's successor) Director General, with Travis as Director. There was no part for Denniston to play in the future of the organisation which emerged out of GC&CS. He was encouraged out before VJ Day with a pension much smaller than he had expected. He left London and, after a brief spell teaching French and Latin at a prep school in Leatherhead, he retired with his wife to a cottage in the New Forest.

Denniston died in 1961 at the age of 79 and was buried in Burley in the New Forest. Much to the chagrin of his family, his death was ignored by obituary writers of all the major British newspapers and no acknowledgement was forthcoming from Government Communications Headquarters (GCHQ), the organisation that was born out of his own GC&CS. In 1982, his son Robin decided that the time had come to write a book about his father's long and distinguished career in intelligence. While former colleagues were keen to contribute, the response from GCHQ and the Defence, Press and Broadcasting Committee was at best, lukewarm. Fighting his failing health, Robin pressed ahead and in 2007, finally published his book, *Thirty Secret Years, A.G. Denniston's work in signals intelligence, 1914-1944.*

In 2009, by now hospitalised, Robin was approached by GCHQ's Departmental Historian, Tony Comer, who was researching his father's work during the interwar period. On 6 November 2011, a special memorial service for Denniston was held at St John the Baptist Church, Burley. His grandchildren and other members of the family had organised a short service of rededication in the churchyard at Burley where Denniston was buried. Comer gave the eulogy, in which he summarised Dennison's achievements as follows:

> His memorial is that he built the UK's first unified cryptanalytic organisation and developed the values and standards which made it a world leader, an organisation which partners aspired to emulate; and that he personally worked tirelessly to ensure an Anglo-American cryptologic alliance which has outlived and out grown anything even he could have hoped for.

I first met the Denniston family at an event held at BP on 1 December 2012. As part of the ongoing restoration of the site, it had been decided to recreate Denniston's office in the Mansion and the family had kindly agreed to donate artefacts to help with the 'dressing' of the room. I was asked to take the family on a tour of BP after a short ceremony marking the official handover of the artefacts and a talk by Tony Comer. I had just completed a biography of Gordon Welchman, a Denniston appointment and key member of the GC&CS management team. Welchman had not been treated kindly by the intelligence community after publishing, in 1982, his own account of the work at BP. Both Welchman and Denniston were unknown to the general public and it seemed to me that there was a common theme running through both their lives. On 4 December 2013, Denniston's family formally opened the exhibition in his old 'office' at BP. At that event, it was announced that I had agreed to write the biography of Alastair Denniston with the support of his family and GCHQ.

Alastair Denniston's career in intelligence spanned two world wars and ran from the pioneering work of Room 40 to the triumph of BP and the success of Berkeley Street. Between lay the creation of the world's first cryptanalytic organisation capable of operating on an industrial scale, the famous meeting at Pyry in Poland when French, British and Polish collaboration led to the defeat of Germany's Enigma cipher system and, arguably, the start of the special relationship between the United States and Great Britain. Yet in the end, something was missing. Those who enter the world of intelligence generally commit to a lifetime of secrecy and anonymity. However, an honours system and other 'perks' have been historically used to reward people who have committed a lifetime of service to their country. While some honours came his way, he remains the only Head of GCHQ not to receive a knighthood. He ultimately received scant reward for his many years of service to his country.

It is my hope that this book brings Alastair Denniston's remarkable career and the story of Sigint to the attention of the general public. While his legacy to the UK and its allies is the organisation that he built, it ultimately outgrew him and, in many respects, he was a victim of his own success.

Joel Greenberg

Acknowledgements

It was a great honour to be entrusted by the family of Alastair Denniston with the task of telling the story of his life and career in signals intelligence. I would like to thank them all, particularly his niece Libby, for their support and providing me with documents and photographs. AGD's son Robin had researched his father's career for a number of years. I am grateful to Robin's son Nick for providing me with all of his father's research material which he had faithfully kept. When I began this project, Tony Comer, the GCHQ Departmental Historian, offered his support. I am grateful to Tony for reviewing an early draft of the book and providing an official statement on behalf of GCHQ as well as several previously unpublished photographs. I would like to thank my daughters for their ever-present support and love. Finally, I would like to thank the woman in my life for making every day worth living.

Abbreviations

AD(C)	Assistant Director (Civil)
ADIC	Assistant Director of the Operational Intelligence Centre
Adm	Admiralty
ADMI	Assistant Director of Military Intelligence
AEF	American Expeditionary Force
AI	Air Intelligence (Directorate)
ASA	Army Security Agency (US)
ATB	Advisory Committee on Trade Questions in Time of War
BEF	British Expeditionary Force
BJs	'Blue jackets' (nickname for GC&CS reports)
BOT	Board of Trade
BP	Bletchley Park
BSC	British Security Coordination
'C'	Chief of the Secret Service
Cab. Cons.	Cabinet Conclusions (minutes of Cabinet meetings)
CAS	Chief of the Air Staff
CBME	Combined Bureau Middle East
CID	Committee of Imperial Defence
CIGS	Chief of the Imperial General Staff
COMINT	Communications intelligence
COMINTERN	Communist International organisation
COMSEC	Communications security
CNS	Chief of the Naval Staff
COS	Chiefs of Staff
CSS	Chief of the Secret Service
CTO	Central Telegraph Office
D & R	Distribution and Reference (Office)
DCAS	Deputy Chief of the Air Staff
DCIGS	Deputy Chief of the Imperial General Staff

DCOS	Deputy Chiefs of Staff
DD(C)	Deputy Director (Civil)
DDI	Deputy Director of Intelligence (Air Ministry)
DDMI	Deputy Director, Military Intelligence
DD(S)	Deputy Director (Service)
DID	Director of Intelligence Division (Admiralty)
DMI	Director of Military Intelligence
DNI	Director of Naval Intelligence
DOD	Director Operations Division (Admiralty)
DRC	Defence Requirements Committee
DSLTB	Defence Services Lines Telecommunications Board
D/F	Direction finding
ELINT	Electronics intelligence
FECB	Far East Combined Bureau
GAF	German Air Force
GC&CS	Government Code and Cypher School
GCHQ	Government Communications Headquarters
GHQ	General Headquarters
GPO	General Post Office
HVB	*Handelsverkehrsbuch*
IE	Intelligence Exchange
ISK	Intelligence Services, Knox
ISOS	Intelligence Services, Oliver Strachey
ISSIS	Interservice Special Intelligence School
JCC	Joint Committee of Control
JIC	Joint Intelligence Sub-committee (of the COS)
JIG	Japanese Imperial Government
JPC, JP	Joint Planning Sub-committee (of the COS)
MEW	Ministry of Economic Warfare
MI	Military Intelligence (Directorate)
MI3	German Division, Military Intelligence Directorate
MI5	Security Service
MI6	Secret Intelligence Service (SIS)
MSS	'Most Secret Source' – original designation for 'Ultra' material
NID	Naval Intelligence Division
NSA	National Security Agency
OD	Operations Division (Admiralty)
OIC	Operational Intelligence Centre (Admiralty)
OTP	One-Time Pad
PWE	Political Warfare Executive
RN	Royal Navy

RNVR	Royal Naval Volunteer Reserve
RSS	Radio Security Service
Sigint	Signals intelligence
SIS	Secret Intelligence Service (MI6) (British)/Signal Intelligence Service (US)
SKM	*Signalbuch der Kaiserlichen Marine*
SOE	Special Operations Executive
SSA	Signal Security Agency (US – formerly SIS)
TNA	The National Archive, Kew, London
VB	*Verkehrsbuch*
WO	War Office
WOG	Wireless Observation Group (Army)
WW1	World War One
WW2	World War Two
W/T	Wireless telegraphy
WTI	W/T intelligence

Chapter 1

A Life in Signals Intelligence

The ability to acquire and apply knowledge and skills, commonly known as intelligence, is invaluable in all walks of life. It is of particular value in political and military affairs. Military intelligence on its own does not win or shorten wars but it does help to shape their course and in unusual ways. It provides information which may improve the 'number of chances' at a commander's disposal.[1] E.T. Williams, head of intelligence for the 21st Army Group during WW2 noted that:

> Perfect Intelligence in war must of necessity be out-of-date and therefore cease to be perfect. We deal with partial and outmoded sources from which we attempt to compose an intelligible appreciation having regard to the rules of evidence and our soldierly training and which we must be prepared constantly to revise as new evidence merges. We deal not with the true but with the likely. Speed is therefore of the essence of the matter.[2]

Intelligence, in a military sense, aims to minimise uncertainty about the enemy and at the same time, maximise the efficient use of one's own resources. So the challenge for intelligence services is to provide current, reliable and effective information which commanders in the field can add to their own knowledge. This information typically emerges from an intelligence chain, which starts with the interception of the enemy's communications or signals. This is followed in turn by decryption, translation, analysis, distribution and action. This process can be flawed at any point in the chain and pieces of intelligence are usually fragmentary and controversial, with their value never entirely clear. They can generate debate as much as information, and inferences drawn from a number of messages have to be combined into an assessment which can then generate a strategy for action. In the end, its effectiveness depends on a military organisation able to exploit it.

During WW1, the intelligence branch at General Headquarters (GHQ) in Iraq noted that 'the mass of information received by GHQ almost always came in in disconnected fragments of very varying value, fragments were the general rule, and the bulk of intelligence work at any GHQ really consists in putting together a gigantic jig-saw puzzle from innumerable little bits, good, bad and indifferent.'[3] Commanders wished to gather information on all aspects of the enemy. However, their most fundamental needs were to determine the intentions and movements of their enemy. Walter Kirke, a senior member of the intelligence branch at GHQ in France during WW,1 termed this 'the bed-rock of all intelligence work', to uncover the enemy's order of battle, that is, the locations, strength and organisation of its troops.[4]

William Frederick Friedman was arguably the leading American expert in the field of signals intelligence during the first half of the twentieth century. In a series of lectures, serialised in the *NSA Technical Journal* from 1959 to 1961, Friedman attempted to define the various components of signals intelligence and its historical origins.[5] In his view, signals intelligence (Sigint) has two main components: communications intelligence (COMINT) – information derived from the organised interception, study and analysis of the enemy's communications, and electronic intelligence (ELINT) – information obtained from a study of enemy electronic emissions such as homing or directional beacons, radar, recording data of an electronic nature at a distance. Not only do most countries seek to obtain Sigint even during peacetime, most also invest heavily in protecting their own communications. Friedman defined this latter activity as communications security (COMSEC) – the protection resulting from all measures designed to deny to the enemy information of value that may be derived from the interception and study of such communications. A few other definitions are needed at this time: *cryptology* is the science that is concerned with all of these branches of secret signalling, *cryptography* is the science of preparing secret communications and *cryptanalysis* is the science of solving secret communications. So in summary, Sigint involves the interception of messages, traffic analysis – the study of unencrypted information contained within the messages such as the identity of the sender, recipient, etc. – and the solution of codes and ciphers.

All messages sent through a communications system start off life in so-called *plaintext,* usually the language of the sender. They are converted or transformed by following certain rules, steps or processes to disguise them. For the purposes of this book, the conversion or transformation is called *encryption* and the reverse process, *decryption*. In general terms, the resulting disguised text can be called a *cryptogram*. This terminology is often confusing for new readers because some authors prefer to use *encode* or *encipher* instead of encrypt and *decode* or *decipher* instead of decrypt. The reason for this is that encrypting and decrypting are achieved by means of *codes* and *ciphers* which lay at the heart of Sigint and COMSEC systems. It is important to understand the difference between the two. In cipher or cipher systems, cryptograms are produced by applying specific rules, steps or processes to individual letters of the plaintext. These types of cryptograms can be said to be in *cipher text*. In code or code systems, cryptograms are produced by applying specific rules, steps or processes generally to entire words, phrases and sentences of the plaintext.

The earliest reliable information of the use of cryptography in connection with an alphabetic language dates from about 900 BC. Use was made of a device called a scytale, a wooden cylinder of specific dimensions around which was wrapped spirally a piece of parchment or leather. The message was written on the parchment, unwound and sent to its destination by a safe courier. The recipient would have the same device to wind the parchment on, thus bringing together properly the letters representing the message. However, exact details of how this device worked in practice are unknown.

There are number of examples of ciphers in the Bible and one of the more interesting ones involves the mention in *Jeremiah* 25:26 and *Jeremiah* 51:41 of a place called Sheshakh. This was unknown to geographers and historians, until a coding system was discovered using the Hebrew language. If you write the twenty-two letters of the Hebrew alphabet in two rows, letters 11 to 1 in one and letters 12 to 22 in another, you have a substitution alphabet where you can replace letters with those opposite. This is called ATHBASH writing where aleph, the first letter, is replaced by tech, the last letter; beth, the second letter by shin, the next-to-last, etc. This revealed that Sheshakh actually translates as Babel, the ancient name for Babylon.

However, the world of signals intelligence that Alastair Denniston would serve for thirty years really began in 1653. The first regular interception and cryptanalytic organisation in Britain was born with the establishment of the postal monopoly and the Secret Office in 1653. In 1657, Parliament passed the first Post Office Act and the separate Inland and Continental postal offices were united into a General Post Office. This provided a legal basis under which the power of the Secretary of State to issue warrants was recognised, and authorised the Postmaster General to open and examine correspondence. Postal rates were fixed and John Thurloe[6] became the first Postmaster General. Throughout the eighteenth century, the Post Office transmitted, collected and created intelligence. This was achieved by the simple expediency of opening, detaining and copying correspondence and then sending it on to the Secretaries of State. The Post Office Act of 1711 guaranteed a regular source of material from the Post Office's monopoly of the mails, supplemented by occasional captures of documents in war time, or from the activities of secret agents.

Inland post was examined in the Private Office while foreign post was examined in a special office known as the Secret Office. The Private Office of the Secretary of the Post Office was responsible for the execution of warrants to intercept inland mail in connection with political and criminal investigations. The Secret Office was tasked with opening, reading, copying and re-sealing letters and dispatches, and sometimes deciphering those in simpler codes or ciphers. It was located in Post Office premises but was responsible to the appropriate Secretary of State. Eventually, it dealt almost exclusively with foreign mail and was responsible to the Secretary of State for the Foreign Department. It had no official existence and was headed by the Foreign Secretary. Its first manager was Isaac Dorislaus,[7] who was known intriguingly as the Secret Man. The Foreign Secretary was responsible for supervising the opening and copying of foreign correspondence and sending it on to the Secretaries of State in packets marked 'Private and Most Secret'. Those in plain text were sent directly to the King while those in cipher were passed on to another department known as the Deciphering Branch.

The Deciphering Branch was responsible for cryptography and translation and, from 1762, also undertook experimental work. It had no specific location, formal organisation or head. However, one of its most successful operatives was Dr John Wallis, a famous mathematician who can lay claim to being the father of British cryptography.[8] Wallis' assistant was his grandson, William Blencowe, an undergraduate at Magdalen College, Oxford. On Wallis' death in 1703, Blencowe became the first official Decipherer. The branch was staffed by two or three experts working on their own as research specialists to investigate new ciphers and, if possible, solve them. From a staff of around five or six in the early years, it eventually grew to about twelve in number.

There are numerous examples of the Post Office's intelligence work helping to guarantee the safety of the British Empire. One example was intelligence which warned the British forces at Philadelphia of the arrival of the French fleet in 1778 during the American Revolutionary War. Foreign correspondence from many countries was read, including that of the courts of France, Prussia, Austria, Russia, Spain, Sardinia, Holland and Sweden, and intercepts averaged two or three per week. The Hanoverian government which ruled the United Kingdom from 1714 to 1837 maintained a 'secret bureau' of openers and deciphers at Neinburg (a district in Lower Saxony, Germany). Interceptions were sometimes obtained from agents or foreign postmasters in Brussels, Danzig, Hamburg, Leyden and Rotterdam. The security of the Post Office's intelligence operation depended on the skill of its operatives, restricted knowledge, loyalty and the absence of Parliamentary criticism. The distinction between the Private Office, Secret Office and Deciphering Branch, along with a short distribution list of intelligence, helped to maintain secrecy. A system of recruitment and training was put in place, based on patronage and nepotism. This served to provide suitably motivated and reliable individuals from a small number of family dynasties for both the Secret Office and the Deciphering Branch.

In June 1844, the Government faced criticism as some of its intelligence activities became known. At the end of June, it stopped the interception of diplomatic correspondence in the Secret Office. This was done on the basis that the act of 1711 only authorised express as opposed to general warrants for the opening of post. However, the Home Secretary of the day, Sir James Graham, had signed a warrant for the interception of the correspondence of Giuseppe Mazzini. He was an Italian nationalist living in Britain and the Austrian Ambassador was concerned that he was conducting subversive activities. Mazzini's letters were intercepted between March and June 1844 and sent to the Foreign Secretary. Mazzini discovered that his letters had been intercepted and complained to a Member of Parliament. The issuing of general warrants could not be defended by the Government and in February 1845, the Home Secretary announced the department formally maintained in the Post Office by the Secretary of State for the Foreign Office had been abolished and that no similar establishment was maintained by the Home Office. As public opinion against such activity mounted, in August the Government abolished the Secret Office and in October, the Deciphering Branch. The last official Decipherer was Francis Willes, who worked alone apart from an assistant from 1825 until the branch was abolished. The Private Office gradually became less important, as the attitude of the day was that England 'does not stand in need of such expedients for her safety'.[9] It was abolished along with the Deciphering Branch in 1844.

Under the Hanoverians (from George I in 1714 to the end of Victoria's reign in 1901), British Sigint provided technical assistance in opening and re-sealing dispatches, provision of staff, and a service of deciphered product from the King's Hanoverian Sigint organisation. It had considerable success in solving the diplomatic ciphers of many European countries and provided a service of decrypts of the diplomatic dispatches for the King and his most senior ministers only, providing support to managing affairs of state and the conduct of diplomacy.

It does seem that the British Sigint organisation was broken up and abandoned in 1844, and the expertise lost, much to the detriment of British cipher security. While telegrams could legally be intercepted, this could be done only by individual warrants to investigate political or criminal matters. Remarkably, most Victorian statesmen maintained strict moral codes of gentlemanly conduct and there appears to be no evidence in either GCHQ or other archives of British Sigint activity between 1844 and 1914.

***

The telegraph was first developed by Samuel F.B. Morse, an artist-turned-inventor who conceived the idea of the electric telegraph in 1832. Several European inventors had proposed such a device, but Morse, working independently, had by the mid-1830s built a working telegraph instrument. In the late 1830s, he perfected Morse Code, a set of signals that could represent language in telegraph messages. In May 1844, Morse inaugurated the world's first commercial telegraph line with the message 'What hath God wrought', sent from the US Capitol to a railroad station in Baltimore. Within a decade, more than 20,000 miles of telegraph cable criss-crossed the country. The rapid communication it made possible greatly aided American expansion, making railroad travel safer as it provided a boost to business conducted across the great distances of a growing United States.

The idea of a transatlantic communications cable was first raised in 1839, following the introduction of the working telegraph by William Fothergill Cooke and Charles Wheatstone. Morse threw his weight behind it in 1840, and by 1850, a link had been laid between Britain and France. The same year, construction began on a telegraph line up the far north-east coast of North America – from Nova Scotia to the very tip of Newfoundland. Cyrus West Field, a businessman and financier from New York City, took up the idea of extending the east-coast cable across the Atlantic to Britain. In 1857, after several attempts had failed, two ships, the USS *Niagara* and HMS *Agamemnon*, met in the centre of the Atlantic on 29 July 1858, and attached the cables together. This time there were no cable breaks, and the *Niagara* made it to Trinity Bay in Newfoundland on 4 August, and the *Agamemnon* arrived at Valentia

Island off the west coast of Ireland on 5 August. Over the following days, the shore ends were landed on both sides using a team of horses, and tests were conducted. On 16 August 1858, the first message was sent across the Atlantic by telegraph cable, reading 'Glory to God in the highest; on earth, peace and good will toward men'. The transmission marked the culmination of nineteen years of dreams, plans and hard work, bridging the economic and political systems of both the UK and the US. The reception across the cable was terrible, and it took an average of two minutes and five seconds to transmit a single character. The first message took 17 hours and 40 minutes to transmit. On 3 September 1858, the cable failed. In an attempt to increase the speed of transmission, the voltage on the line was boosted from 600V to 2,000V, and the insulation on the cable couldn't cope. It failed over the course of a few hours, and it would be another six years before the capital was raised for another attempt. By the end of the nineteenth century, the British Empire was self-sufficient in its cable infrastructure. All parts of the Empire could be reached with British-owned cable with sufficient redundancy built in.

By 1869, telegrams were treated like letters and could be legally intercepted if political or criminal activity was suspicious. However, there was really no Sigint in the UK before 1914 and the Royal Navy and Army had given it little, if any, thought. During the Victorian era, some analytical activity was carried out, but on an ad hoc basis. There was no permanent intelligence infrastructure in place, despite there being a legal framework to permit it. Countries such as France, Russia and Austria-Hungary did have effective Sigint operations in place before 1914. Russia regularly read British diplomatic ciphers between 1854 and 1917. Around 1890, a UK cipher committee was formed to consider the use of new cryptographic machines.

Technological developments which would shape Sigint through two world wars came to fruition before the end of the nineteenth century. It had been claimed that either the British physicist Oliver Lodge or the Soviet scientist Aleksander Popov invented wireless radio. However, it was the Italian Guglielmo Marconi who arrived in England in 1896 and filed his first patent on wireless telegraphy. Marconi's work was timely because on 5 August 1914, in the early days of WW1, Britain sent the General Post Office Cable Ship *Alert* to cut five German telegraphic cables. These ran down the English Channel to connect with France, Spain, Africa and North and South America. Later in the war, missions by the Cable Ship *Telconia* and other ships eliminated the remainder of Germany's cable network. In some instances cable was reeled in and re-laid for use by Allied powers. Britain also destroyed the German cable station in Lome in West Africa and the remaining German cable link, the German-American line to Liberia and Brazil, was cut in 1915. Germany retaliated with troops raiding a number of British and French cable stations, ones on the East African coast and Baltic Sea and also cutting cable links to India. While the cutting of German cables in 1914 was probably for strategic reasons unconnected with Sigint, when Sigint did start up again it was not in the Foreign Office, but in the Admiralty and War Office, which provided the true forebears of the Sigint organisation of today. The Army did maintain an interest in cryptanalysis after the invention of wireless radio and for the Navy it at least became a practical proposition. Both had an interest in exploiting captured documents.

Modern signals intelligence would be born during WW1 when Sigint techniques started to become more sophisticated. This was due to the emergence of wireless radio as the main form of communication and the ability of countries to intercept and read messages. However, no army really appreciated the cryptological consequences of using wireless radio and they expected effective field communications to be maintained through telegraph, telephone and dispatch riders. Sigint would prove to be a constant battle between codebreakers and codemakers, the latter continually having to balance security and usability.[10] During WW1, armies tended to prioritise usability, which was understandable given the problems posed by the systems at their disposal. In one instance in 1918, experts using the British Army's 'field cipher' spent thirteen minutes in enciphering and deciphering a fourteen-word message.[11]

In military conflict, commanders deploy techniques which aim to create confusion in the mind of the enemy. Signal security, surprise and deception play a crucial role in achieving this objective. Each side needs to conceal its order of battle and movements at an operational level to achieve surprise. Enemy traffic analysts can be thwarted by effective security and misleading information can be disseminated through deception. According to the historian John Ferris:

> Although in 1917 all armies sought to improve their signals security, it seems that only those of Britain and Germany seriously linked this practice to one of deception. Throughout the last 18 months of the war these two belligerents alternately led the world in this endeavour, with the scales of the technical balance between them wavering continually, first towards one and then the other. Their techniques became increasingly sophisticated; indeed not until 1943 would any army in the world begin to surpass the quality of the British and German policies of signals deception of 1918.[12]

So, as in day-to day-life, intelligence affects all human endeavours. It can be used for good and for bad and can influence world events. Sigint would play a vital role in affecting the outcome of two world wars and Alastair Denniston would be destined to play a defining role in its evolution over thirty years.

***

John Denniston was a farmer who worked on Devol Moor in Kilmalcom, a village and parish in the Lower Ward of Renfrewshire in Scotland. His grandson, Archibald, was born in 1814 and eventually settled in Greenock, a historic industrial town by the Firth of Clyde, 25 miles west of Glasgow. Archibald's son, James, was born on 5 June 1854 and after studying at Edinburgh, he moved to Glasgow where he was awarded an M.D. degree in 1875. He found it hard to get into the smart practices in Edinburgh and became an impoverished country doctor in the Argyll seaside resort of Dunoon. He first mooted the idea of erecting a cottage hospital there and, after working tirelessly on the project, the new hospital was opened in October 1885 by H.R.H. Princess Louise. He was also on the staff of the Stafford House Committee which sent doctors, nurses and supplies to war stricken Turkey. During the Russo-Turkish War of 1877–8, he was one of the surgeons sent out by Lord Blantyre and attached to his sections in Asia. He became the chief surgeon of the British Hospital in Erzurum, treating wounded Turkish soldiers who were fighting their ancestral enemies, the Russians. He was present at the siege of Erzerum working under Red Crescent Movement[13] auspices for the civilian and service wounded. He received several honours[14] from the Sultan and had a street named after him in Erzerum. His heroism was acknowledged by colleagues as he had to deal with thousands of sick and wounded patients under terrible conditions.

James Denniston began courting Agnes Buntin Guthrie before going abroad and continued his courtship through letters after he arrived in Turkey in late 1877. He returned to London in May 1878 and Agnes and he were married in 1880. He acquired the practice of Dr Reid in Dunoon where he worked as a general practitioner. In the following years, the Dennistons had three children who were raised and educated in Dunoon. Alexander Guthrie was their first born on 1 December 1881, followed by another boy, William (known to family as Bill), and a girl, Elizabeth (known to family as Biddy), born in 1890. James had contracted tuberculosis as a result of his work with wounded and dying Turkish soldiers and his health suffered from the damp Scottish climate.

Much to his regret and that of his family, they moved to Bowden, Cheshire, and apparently a better climate. He was even advised to take sea voyages for his health and travelled as a ship's doctor across the world. He died from pneumonia during one of these voyages in 1892, on board the Royal Mail Steamer *Tongariro* on its homeward-bound trip from Australia. His wife Agnes, a notable cook, was left to raise their children.

His son Alexander was known as Alastair and in later years AGD, which is how he will be referred to for the rest of this book. AGD went to Bowden College, Altrincham, where he won numerous prizes before moving on to London University, where he was awarded a BA in 1902. He enrolled as a student of philosophical sciences at Bonn University on 28 April 1903 and remained there until he received a certificate of departure on 30 July 1904. He also seems to have spent some time studying at the Sorbonne, but little is known of his days at these European universities. However, Bonn University records show him taking courses in old high German languages and literature, middle high German, middle English grammar, history of the German language, German art and literary history as well as the sounds of German and French. The experience clearly strengthened his abilities in the classics and languages, particularly German and French. After returning to the UK he took a post as a Modern Language teacher at Merchiston Castle School, Edinburgh in 1907 under the headship of George Smith, a graduate of Edinburgh and Oxford Universities. The school had been founded in 1883 in Merchiston Castle[15] as an academy for boys and AGD took an active part in the school's games programme. This was not surprising as he was a talented athlete and had played field hockey for Scotland. The team competed in the first Olympic field hockey tournament in the 1908 Olympics and shared the bronze medal with Wales. He had a single-figure handicap for most of his golf-playing life. Six years after winning his Olympic medal, AGD's career in intelligence would be launched by the man who ran the Admiralty's training programme.

In January 1903, Alfred Ewing,[16] a Professor of Mechanical Engineering at Cambridge University, was invited by the then First Lord of the Admiralty, Lord Selbourne, to become Director of Naval Education. Selbourne and Admiral Fisher,[17] the Second Sea Lord, had just launched their New Scheme of Naval Education, under which all naval cadets were to receive, as an essential part of their training, a serious grounding in the principles and techniques of engineering. Ewing took on the role of adviser and inspector of the educational work in the training establishments, the dockyards and the Fleet. He was based in the Admiralty and after investigating the method of naval selection, both Osborne and Dartmouth were established under his direction. Osborne was intended to serve as a 'junior' college for the first two years of cadet training before they moved on to Dartmouth for a further two years.

The Royal Naval College at Osborne, Isle of Wight, opened in September 1903 with seventy-four cadets beginning their studies there.[18] The minimum age was twelve and a half years initially but was increased to twelve years and nine or ten months in 1906 and eventually, in 1913, to between thirteen years and four to eight months to bring it in line with the age of entry to public schools. While its focus was on practical science and engineering, Ewing stated that 'During these four years the boy receives a broad and liberal education in the subjects of a modern side at a public school.' However, he went on to say that 'not only does the curriculum include a certain amount of teaching in seamanship and navigation, but the boys are under naval discipline and breathing a naval atmosphere throughout their course'.[19] So while Osborne was very much a naval training establishment, it was providing a more general education which would require non-naval academic staff to deliver it. Shortly after his appointment, Ewing began recruiting staff for Osborne, and a senior science master at Harrow School, Cyril Ashford, was appointed headmaster. Captain Rosslyn Wemyss was appointed overall head of the college and when the first cohort of cadets moved on to Dartmouth, Ashford and Wemyss moved with them to ensure continuity.

Ashford was replaced at Osborne by the mathematician Charles Godfrey and Wemyss remained in overall command of both colleges. Upon opening, Ashford had a staff of nine masters under his command. Building work was not complete so the civilian masters had to 'live out' although they did have a common-room next to the headmaster's office. As the College expanded, more staff was needed and among the recruits in late 1909 was twenty-one year old Alastair Denniston. His name first appears both in the Osborne and Navy Lists as a Modern Language Master in January 1910.[20] He was welcomed to the college in the Editor's Notes in the September 1910 edition of the *Osborne Magazine*.[21]

AGD's linguistic talents were put to good use at Osborne. The subject of the examinations which were held over two days in December, March and July give a clear indication of the emphasis on languages, with papers on English, French, German and Latin. They were prepared by the Oxford and Cambridge Universities Examination Board, and the French and German examinations included 'an oral examination to which importance will be attached'.[22] Cadets were grouped in 'tutor sets', each of which was associated with a particular master who advised them in all aspects of their study. AGD was expected to tutor up to twenty cadets at any one time and he taught French, of which he was a fluent speaker, and German.

Given his own athletic prowess, AGD enjoyed the various sporting activities undertaken by cadets during the afternoon. Officers and Masters (O. & M.) frequently took part in team sports alongside the cadets, as well in teams of their own. AGD showed himself to be an all-rounder at cricket, frequently batting, bowling and taking catches. In a match against the Staff College Camberley he scored forty-eight runs and took four wickets in a winning effort. He turned out for the O. & M. rugby team, surprisingly, given his size, as a forward. Given his field hockey prowess, it is not surprising that AGD featured as a halfback in the O. & M. hockey team. He played fullback for their football team and at 10st 7lbs, rowed at stroke for the rowing team. AGD also took part in the college's annual Christmas pantomime. The Osborne College magazine lists him featuring as a Pirate Boatswain named Dick Deadeye in the 1910 production, as one of two villains called Francis in the 1911 production of *Dick Whittington* and as Count Zogitoff, The King's Chamberlain, in the 1912 production of *Jack and the Beanstalk*.

Apart from the civilian masters such as AGD, naval officers acted as Term Lieutenants, and their Engineer Officer second-in-command taught the cadets seamanship and oversaw their engineering education. Petty Officers acted as cadet mentors and physical training instructors. Experience of working with naval officers on a day-to-day basis would serve AGD well through two world wars. A 1912 Education Inspectors' Report noted that the thirty-four civilian masters were on the whole 'extremely competent' and the average teaching skills were 'high'; several were 'brilliant'.[23]

***

On 4 August 1914, Admiral Oliver, Director of Naval Intelligence Division (DID) and a friend of Ewing, showed him a number of telegrams sent via wireless radio in cipher by Germany from German ships and land stations. These had been intercepted by listening stations belonging to the Navy, the Post Office and the Marconi Company. Ewing had previously talked to Oliver about his interest in mechanical methods for enciphering and deciphering messages. Oliver asked Ewing to see whether he could make any progress with them and eventually Oliver arranged for all such messages to be sent to Ewing, numbers sometimes exceeded 2,000 per day.

Ewing proceeded to examine code books held by Lloyd's, the General Post Office and the British Museum. He also contacted the manager of the Marconi Company to arrange for more systematic interception of enemy signals. He agreed to set up a new 'section' in the Admiralty and began recruiting staff, placing an emphasis on people with both a good working knowledge of German and discretion. One of his first ports of call was the Naval Colleges at Dartmouth and Osborne, and one of his first recruits, initially on a temporary basis, was AGD. Other Osborne and Dartmouth schoolmasters, such as the Headmaster of Osborne, Charles Godfrey,[24] were recruited and served until the colleges restarted towards the end of September 1914. Other early recruits included R.D. Norton, an ex-member of the Foreign Office and company promoter, of whom little is known, and Lord Herschell, son of one of Gladstone's Lord Chancellors. Staff numbers were small in the early days, although some help was provided by naval instructors Parish and Curtis and by Professor Henderson, a scientist and mathematician from Greenwich Naval College. The majority chosen were classicists, the exceptions being Ewing, Henderson, Russell Clarke and Hopkinson, who had mathematical minds. Less skilled people were added who knew German, such as ladies with a university education and wounded officers unfit for active service. Typists were also essential with skills in sorting, filing and analysing.

AGD and a few of the other early recruits quickly identified one distinct class of messages; military messages using transposition ciphers, suitable for use in the field. The German Navy used code books and one signal book for ordinary fleet signals and confidential orders. Different keys[25] were used with each and they dominated the traffic sent to Ewing. With a small number of staff now in place, collaboration was established between Ewing's section in the Admiralty and the War Office and Ewing sent AGD over as his representative and to act as a liaison officer. The first elements of a real cryptographic section within the War Office began to emerge and AGD, Norton and Herschell were seconded to this section as watchkeepers.[26] At this stage, AGD had been working without pay during his vacation but as the amount of work increased, he obtained leave from Osborne. Eventually the War Office informed the Treasury that he and several others had been employed in the general intelligence section of the Directorate of Military Operations and that it may be necessary to at least cover their out-of-pocket expenses.[27]

Ewing's staff now consisted of Naval Instructors Parish and Curtis, and Professor Henderson when their other duties permitted them, and, as watchkeepers doing night duty in the War Office, AGD, Hershall and Norton. According to AGD: 'The first three knew something of mathematics and little of German; all six were singularly ignorant of cryptography, but they were becoming expert analysers, filers and translators of German military telegraphese.'[28] They had to use Ewing's small office in the Admiralty as their base and move to his secretary's even smaller office when Ewing held meetings in his capacity as Director of Naval Education. The first six weeks were devoted to research without any results, and work was confined to messages being sent from the German high power station at Nauen to German West Africa and elsewhere. The staff had little expertise in wireless telegraphy (W/T) but with the help of the manager of the Marconi Company, Mr Bradfield, they began to identify enemy call signs.[29] They were able to collect the code books of German commercial firms but little was learned other than that Germany was communicating with its representatives abroad and others. The Army section was also having little success and military cipher messages were often confused with naval codes. After a few weeks, codes and ciphers could be separated and with the help of the French, who provided the key and method of the German military cipher, real decryption work became possible for the first time by the War Office's naval secondees in their role as the 'War Office Watch'. AGD would later write that 'the signs of jealousy were not absent even in this small section of men drawn from many branches of civil life'.[30]

It is unlikely that when AGD accepted Ewing's offer of some work without pay during his vacation, he could have imagined that it would set him on his career path for the next thirty years. However, events in continental Europe would soon put him on that path.

Chapter 2

British Signit in World War One

On 28 June 1914, the Archduke Franz Ferdinand, heir to the throne of Austria-Hungary was visiting Sarajevo on the final day of his trip to Bosnia. Early in the morning his motorcade was attacked and a Bosnian Serb named Gavrilo Princip shot and killed the Archduke and his wife. Immediately following the assassination, Britain and Germany remained united until Germany backed Austro-Hungarian action against Serbia. On 26 July, Britain proposed a peace conference to try to avert war in the Balkans. However, by 3 August, Germany had declared war on Russia and France, and when Belgium refused to allow German soldiers to cross its borders, the die was cast. The following day, Britain declared war on Germany.

When war broke out, the Admiralty wireless intercept (also known as Y) stations intercepted a number of German messages and passed them to the Admiralty. They were programme messages sent out by the German high power W/T station, Norddeich, and consisted mainly of weather and intelligence reports. These were the messages that Oliver had shown to Ewing on 4 August. Early in September, Russell Clarke, a former student of Ewing, told him that he and his friend Colonel Hippiseley, a wealthy landowner, had been intercepting German messages on their own receiving sets in London and Wales. Clarke was a prominent amateur W/T expert and Hippiseley was an amateur mechanic with an interest in W/T. It is remarkable that the police had not confiscated their equipment, but Clarke was a barrister and well connected. They told Ewing that there was a considerable amount of German naval W/T signalling going on at a lower wavelength than that being used for the Norddeich traffic. They offered to provide the Admiralty with enough German signals for it to study the movements and plans of the German High Seas Fleet. To do this, they only required access to the appropriate facilities, which Ewing provided, and permission was granted for them to install their equipment at Hunstanton Coast Guard Station. This was a sensible choice as it was already equipped with W/T and was ideal for interception in Flanders and Northern France. They involved another amateur in the work, Leslie Lambert, and the new station was able to keep a continuous watch on German field stations. As they grew more successful, additional radio masts were added. In all the intercept stations, each aerial had an assigned range of wave length to monitor and it was arranged to take down every message in two separate locations. Each was connected to the Admiralty by telephone line to a telegraph office in the basement. From there, messages went by pneumatic tube to Ewing's section, where they fell into a waiting basket.

By the end of the war, Clarke presided over four stations at Hunstanton, and one at Slough, Ashford, Lizard and Ballybunion which were manned by General Post Office (GPO) operators as well as Lambert. Traffic was worked on in the Admiralty and War Office during the day and by the night watch in the War Office overnight. Additional intercept facilities were provided by the Marconi Company using its own operators. In all, over 200 wireless stations were in use in England during WW1.[1]

Within the first four months of the war, the Admiralty was in possession of all three principal code books of the German Navy. The first was captured from the German-Australian steamship *Hobart,* which was seized off Port Philips Heads, Melbourne. The haul included the *Handelsverkehrsbuch* (HVB), the code used by the Admiralstab (German Admiralty) as well as the High Seas Fleet. It reached the Admiralty by the end of October 1914 and remained in use until March 1916. On 26 August, the German light cruiser *Magdeburg* ran aground in thick fog on the Island of Odensholm off the coast of Russian Estonia in the Gulf of Finland. Before confidential papers could be removed and the ship blown up, two Russian cruisers attacked her as the fog lifted. The Russians seized the ship and captured two copies of the *Signalbuch der Kaiserlichen Marine* (SKM), the current key, a copy of the German naval gridded chart for the Baltic, the bridge log and the ship's War Diary. According to Winston Churchill, the First Lord of the Admiralty at the time, the SKM code book was found in the arms of a German signalman whose body washed ashore a few days after the *Magdeburg* ran aground.[2] The Russian Naval Attaché met with Churchill on 6 September. The Russian Admiralty had successfully used the cipher and signal books but felt that the Royal Navy, as the leading naval power, ought to have them, along with the charts.[3] Churchill ordered a ship to be sent to Alexandrov to transport two officers of the Imperial Russian

Navy to Britain. He duly received them in person on 13 October at Scapa Flow. The Naval Attaché, Captain Wolcoff, delivered the code book to the Admiralty on 17 October. The book only worked on unimportant messages because the rest used a key along with the code book. It continued to be used by the Germans until May 1917. Its code consisted of groups of letters, usually three to a group. The usual process of keying consisted of substituting each letter for another letter based on a prescribed plan.

At the end of 1914, the 'tool set'[4] of Ewing's section was enhanced when an English trawler, fishing in the North Sea, hauled up a collection of German books and documents. They were forwarded to DID in the Admiralty and included a naval signal book, not previously available, as well as confidential papers and charts. They came from a German destroyer which had been sunk in the North Sea off the Dutch coast on 17 October 1914. Among this treasure trove was a most secret code book, the *Verkehrsbuch* (VB). On 3 December 1914, Ewing was given a parcel of books which had arrived from Lowestoft. The Germans applied keys to the VB so these still had to be found. This was achieved later the same day while Ewing dried the code book by his fire! Some days earlier, two versions of a message had been sent out independently from separate German stations. One was encrypted completely using the VB book and easily read. The second was identical, except for a few words which had been encrypted using another code. Comparing the two messages allowed Ewing's section to discover the key to the new book. This would be known at GC&CS years later as a 'kiss'. According to AGD: 'The VB was found to be of the greatest immediate value in dealing with the German cruiser fleet, while the fact that it was solely used for the correspondence with the Naval Attachés abroad, especially in Madrid, escaped notice for some months.'[5]

By the middle of October, a naval officer, unknown to Ewing's team, had taken over the office of Ewing's secretary, Mountstephen. He was Fleet Paymaster Rotter at the time, the head and principle German expert of the Intelligence Division. Rotter had spent four or five years prior to the war trying to persuade the Admiralty to take cryptanalysis seriously but had failed. He had been placed at Ewing's disposal and was investigating the assertion of the Russian naval attaché that the SKM book was the one now in force in the German Navy and that any naval intercepts in the Admiralty's possession could be decrypted with it. Within a week, Rotter had identified the German procedure of numbering messages and the re-encrypting of the numbers, and this provided him with a good starting point. The weather reports came from the bcok and were then subjected to a simple substitution cipher.

The messages were a numbered series sent out by Norddeich (K.A.V.) to all ships (A.S.). The Germans had re-encrypted the numbers of the messages, which provided a simple and certain way into their re-encryption tables. Clarke claimed that he could intercept hundreds of such messages on short wave, which would provide the daily movements of the German fleet. Rotter eventually produced the key to the captured book and with Clarke proving true to his word, the Hunstanton traffic flowed into the Admiralty and on to Ewing's team.

It was now clear that the Admiralty cryptographic section under Ewing had found its niche and expansion was necessary. The section was formally known as NID 25, being part of Naval Intelligence Division (NID). AGD, Herschell and Norton returned full-time to Ewing's team and Rotter was formally transferred to the section. In early November, additional office space in the Admiralty was obtained and the section moved into a 24ft by 17ft room on the first floor of the Old Building of the Admiralty. The number on the door of their new accommodation was 40 and gradually the section became known as Room 40 OB or just Room 40 and ultimately would be considered by many historians to be the birthplace of modern British Sigint.[6] By 6 November, Rotter, Henderson, Curtis and Parish were working as day men and AGD, Herschell & Norton as watchkeepers. Room 40 was expanded to around fifty staff, and new recruits included Claud Serocold, a stockbroker; Lord Monk Bretton, a former private secretary to the Liberal politician Joseph Chamberlain; H.A. Morrah, former President of the Oxford Union; W.H. Antsie, a Dartmouth schoolmaster; H.W. Lawrence, an expert on furniture and art; and Commander Fremantle, a member of a famous naval family.[7] Of two others, Hooper and Bond, little is known.

Ewing and his counterpart in the War Office had continued to cooperate in attacking the military ciphers but once Room 40 started to solve naval ciphers, Ewing could no longer help the War Office team. Ewing also took on responsibility for diplomatic traffic. In the early days of the war he visited the Eastern Telegraph Company to discuss monitoring German wireless stations in Africa which were receiving signals from the Nauen transmitter. They provided old material sent on this link. The main concern of the Admiralty was to solve the enemy's naval cipher used to communicate information and orders by wireless from ship to ship or from shore stations, often conveying the orders of the Commander-in-Chief of the German Admiralty. The number of intercepts increased thanks to the work of the Post Office, the Marconi stations, the single Admiralty 'police' station at Stockton and Clarke's Hunstanton operation. Hunstanton and Stockton became the core of

Britain's Y Service and along with the Post Office and Marconi intercept stations, eventually recorded almost every German naval, diplomatic, commercial and consular wireless message transmitted.

Secrecy was paramount and apart from Ewing, his staff and a few responsible officials, there was no knowledge of Room 40's work, even amongst the admirals at sea. To quote Ewing:

> Within the small circle of initiated persons the mysterious agency thus set up was called 'Room 40'. The origin of the same was that when the staff of deciphers first overflowed the tiny limits of my private room, a large room numbered 40 in the old building of the Admiralty was assigned to us. Later more spacious quarters and room after room was added, but the original title stuck – a title that suggested nothing and stirred nobody's curiosity. Lord Balfour, after he took office as First Lord, sometimes used another piece of camouflage by calling us 'the Japanese' – perhaps in tribute to the impenetrability of the oriental mind. Mr Churchill has told how, while he was having a fateful interview with the Prime Minster in the political crisis of 1915, he was summoned by telephone to come back to the Admiralty at once because 'very important news of the kind that never fails' had just come in. It was an agreeable periphrasis, 'news of the kind that never fails'.[8]

The Admiralty made a number of changes to its hierarchy in the latter part of 1914. On 30 October, Admiral John ('Jacky') Fisher was appointed as its professional head and First Sea Lord. One other key change was the appointment of the 50-year-old Rear-Admiral H.F. Oliver as Chief of the War Staff (COS).[9] According to Churchill:

> The decision to recall Lord Fisher to the Admiralty was very important. He was, as has been here contended, the most distinguished British Naval officer since Nelson. The originality of his mind and the spontaneity of his nature freed him from conventionalities of all kinds. His genius was deep and true. Above all, he was in harmony with the vast size of events. Like them, he was built upon a titanic scale. But he was seventy-four years of age. As in a great castle which has long contended with time, the mighty central mass of the donjon towered up intact and seemingly everlasting. But the outworks and the battlements had fallen away, and its imperious ruler dwelt only in the special apartments and corridors with which he had a lifelong familiarity. Had he and his comrade, Sir Arthur Wilson,[10] been born ten years later, the British

> naval direction at the outbreak of the Great War would have reached its highest state of perfection, both at the Admiralty and afloat.[11]

Oliver had been Director of the Intelligence Division (DID) and his replacement was Captain Reginald Hall[12], who had had to give up his previous command as captain of the new battlecruiser *Queen Mary* due to ill health. Hall's nickname was 'Blinker', apparently because of a chronic facial twitch. It was only when he took up his position that he became aware of the small section working for Sir Alfred Ewing[13] on intercepting German naval wireless signals. They were successful enough to be supplying the Operations Division with information about German fleet movements.

Herbert Hope, a commander at the Admiralty, was given charge of the activities in Room 40. He was to keep the Operations and Intelligence Divisions informed of the activities of the German fleet from the Section's cryptographic work. They had expanded and nine rooms were now assigned to them. Hope was responsible for receiving decrypted messages and attaching remarks to them before and taking them to Hall, who in turn took them to the First Lord (Churchill) and then to the COS (Admiral Oliver). Ewing's section became part of Hall's Naval Intelligence Division but Hope was kept away from the cryptanalysts in Room 40 and this isolated position was a problem. On 16 November 1914, he became Hall's representative in charge of the staff of cryptanalysts in Room 40.

Hall was not prepared to simply sit back and oversee this successful operation. It was his job, he believed, to find out everything he could about possible future theatres of naval operations and to be ready for any future conflict involving Germany. He strengthened his staff and Claud Serocold became his PA. Others new recruits included Lord Herschell, Lord Abinger, Mr Vaughan-Williams, Ralph Nevill, 2nd Lieutenant Leeson of the Middlesex Regiment – who had been invalided out of the Army in France – James Randall, a City wine merchant, L.G. Wickham-Legg, a Fellow of New College, Oxford, George Prothero, editor of the *Quarterly Review*, Algernon Cecil, a distinguished historian, Harold Russell, a barrister, Gerald Fitzmaurice, Dragoman at the Constantinople Embassy, Thomas Inskip, KC and Sir Philip Baker Wilbraham, Fellow of All Souls, Oxford and Chancellor of the Diocese of Chester. All had specific tasks. Wickham-Legg and Leeson, for example, prepared the summaries of intelligence that were issued to the Fleet twice a week. Hall also took the unusual step of recruiting women, something quite new in a department undertaking secret work. The criteria for selection was that candidates needed to have naval connections, know at least two foreign languages and be able to type. They became known as 'Blinkers' Beauty Chorus' and in this way he was able to expand the establishment of Room 40. AGD continued to be on loan to Room 40 from Osborne until September 1915, when he makes his last appearance in the Osborne Lists as 'Serving at Admiralty'. Interestingly, his last appearance on the Navy List as a member of an educational establishment is April 1915.

Soon after taking up his post, Hall turned his attention to the organisation which was in place for the censorship of telegrams, cables and wireless traffic and for the censorship of all incoming, outgoing and transit mails. He initiated discussions with Colonel Cockerill (later Sir George Cockerill) who soon after became Director of Special Intelligence at the War Office. They agreed to set up a private censorship organisation which would open all foreign mail coming into the main post office at Mount Pleasant. Hall took on the task of finding the manpower and money to do so. Hall won over Churchill to his proposal and within a few days the new department was hard at work. Eventually the Foreign Secretary, McKenna, and Prime Minister Asquith supported Hall's proposal and a permanent department, a War Trade Intelligence Department, was set up in the War Office to carry out the work.

***

In 1914, like every army in Europe, the British Army was badly prepared to acquire and exploit intelligence from its enemy's communications. Before 1914, European armies assumed that communications would be based on telegraph, telephone and despatch riders and no army developed effective cryptographic systems which exploited wireless radio with an acceptable level of security. However, intelligence was available through other channels such as reconnaissance, the capture of prisoners and documents as well as networks of agents. As the use of wireless radio increased between 1896 and 1914, enemy communications could be intercepted and there were more opportunities to attack new cipher systems as they were introduced by the enemy. After the Boer War ended, the next significant British Sigint effort was established in 1906 as part of the Intelligence Branch of the Indian Army's headquarters at Simla, today the capital of the northern Indian state of Himachal Pradesh. A single cryptanalyst, George Church and one linguist, Captain Gerald Palmer, were employed and, by 1912, they were producing decrypts from Russian, Persian, Chinese and Tibetan communications.[14]

In the early 1900s, the 'Special Section' was set up within the Department of Military Intelligence. This organisation eventually helped to give rise to the Security Service and the Secret Intelligence Service, better known to most as MI5 and MI6. It housed any cryptographic and cryptanalytic activity within the War Office. Although activity was minimal, it did cover cryptography, cryptanalytical training, planning for war and foreign relations. Colonel George Macdonagh, head of the 'Special Section', attended the International Wireless Conference in London in 1912 and established a working relationship with Commandant Francois François Cartier, chief of the French War Ministry's cryptanalytical bureau. By the start of WW1, the French understood from their peacetime work the German Army's wireless cipher system.[15]

Most of the modern techniques for gathering and exploiting Sigint had to be developed during WW1. At the beginning of the war, the British Army had a radio service of mediocre efficiency and primitive signals security procedures. However, it did have an elementary grasp of cryptanalysis techniques along with some expertise in solving the codes and ciphers of other countries. As cipher systems were cumbersome, most countries were sending radio signals in unencrypted form (known as 'clear') and this would have a significant impact on the early campaigns of WW1. According to the historian John Ferris:

> During September-November 1914 French and British forces intercepted at least some 50 radio messages in plain language from German divisions, corps, armies and army groups. These provided otherwise unavailable insights into the collapse of enemy command and the yawning gap in its line during mid-September 1914. Victory on the Marne was no miracle. Over the next two months similar en clair transmissions (combined with solutions of encrypted German traffic) warned the British Expeditionary Force of the precise time, location and strength of six full scale attacks on its front, each involving four or more German corps. Without this material, the BEF might well have lost the race to the sea, or even have been destroyed. At no time in this century has signals intelligence affected campaigns more significantly than at the very hours of its birth, in 1914.[16]

Another problem facing the British Army, as well as its enemies, was that secure cipher systems were slow to implement. As late as 1918, experts using two different versions of the British Army's 'field cipher' required four and thirteen minutes respectively to encrypt, transmit and decrypt a message of fourteen words.[17] Therefore, most armies opted for usability over security.

While the Admiralty ran the naval war from London, the Army made operational decisions in the field by commanders there with their own staff. Military intelligence, consisting of both interception and cryptanalysis, was therefore a widely distributed function, with practitioners both in London and at GHQ. The War Office played a strategic role, providing training, a central repository of information and longer-term backup to units in the field. Ewing had visited the War Office in early August 1914 to see what steps they were taking, if any, to deal with military wireless traffic.[18] Intelligence was part of the Directorate of Military Operations and he found that a new War Office group, MO5(e), had been set up in early 1914 shortly after the creation of Room 40. It had been done with the cooperation of Colonel. F.J. Anderson of the Royal Engineers, who had been involved in reading ciphers during the Boer War[19], and Major G.R.M. Church who was in charge of cryptographic duties at Simla. In 1912, Macdonagh had established very close relations with Commandant Cartier, head of the Bureau des Chiffres of the French Ministry of War. Anderson offered his services to the War Office in August 1914. He was ordered to set up a subsection of MO5 to deal with and decipher intercepted German wireless messages, and initially he had four civilian assistants. MO5(e) became MO6(b) in April 1915 and MI1(b) in January 1916.

However, there was very little exploitation of wireless traffic for military purposes, or even a tradition of military interception and cryptanalysis in the War Office. The German Army had expanded its use of wireless telegraphy for command and control during its rapid advance through Belgium and Northern France in the opening months of the war. The War Office unit was also helped by the more experienced French War Ministry Sigint team, which cracked the main German military code used on the Western Front early in October 1914 and passed the solution to the British. The French, following early American work, also broke the new German cipher in June 1918.[20]

In April 1915, MO5 section became a sub-directorate entitled 'The Directorate of Special Intelligence'. From January 1916 onwards, a completely separate Directorate of Military Intelligence was established. Initially MO5 handled censorship and cryptanalysis and was headed by Macdonagh, who at the beginning of the war departed to GHQ along with most of the staff.[21] MO5(d), under Colonel A.G. Churchill, the Chief Cable Censor handled censorship, and MO5(e), under Anderson, investigated enemy ciphers.

Censorship was introduced in August 1914 and all enemy telegrams were stopped and private codes banned. This included cable traffic in transit between Europe and the Americas but the coded telegrams of Allied governments and neutral ones were allowed to pass. MO5(d) became MO8 in April 1915 and MI8 in January 1916. Postal censorship (later MO/MI9) had by March 1916 extended to the scrutiny of mail in transit on the high seas on neutral ships intercepted by RN ships. This would later prove useful to Room 40's work on diplomatic Sigint.

The group collaborated with the American Military Intelligence Division in France and the British, French and Americans exchanged technical information and results with a limited division of tasks. When MO5b was formed, Ewing had sent AGD, Norton and Herschell as watchkeepers and there was initial collaboration. This ended in October 1914 when Churchill showed Kitchener, his opposite number at the War Office, the contents of a military intercept before his own section had managed to get the information through to him. Liaison was not resumed until the spring of 1917, when limited cooperation in the form of exchanges of decrypts was resumed.

MI1(b)[22] consisted of only four staff by the end of 1915, with Major Malcolm Vivian Hay[23] in charge. Thirty-four years of age and the grandson of the second son of the seventh Marquess of Tweeddale, Hay was educated at Beaumont College and joined the Gordon Highlanders as a captain at the outbreak of war. He suffered a head wound and was captured by the Germans. He was left partly paralyzed and eventually repatriated, being unfit for military service. After learning to walk with the aid of a stick, Hay was promoted to major and put in command of MI1(b). Hay seems to have taken over from Anderson sometime between March 1916 and early 1917. His recollection was that it was 1916:

> In the Spring of 1916, I began to realise the potential value of the enormous mass of encoded messages from all over the world which was accumulating in certain War Office cupboards. And about this time I had an interview with the [Deputy] Cable Censor, Lord Arthur Browne, who arranged for copies of all diplomatic cables to be sent to my office. In 1916 information about what was going on in Greece was badly wanted and I decided to make a start with the Greek code. No one in this country had hitherto succeeded in breaking a diplomatic code book without what we called a 'crib'.[24] The problem was undertaken and solved by Mr. John Fraser, who is now Professor of Celtic at Oxford. … In June Fraser sent me a telegram: 'Pillars of Hercules have fallen'.[25]

In July 1916, a new section, MI1(e), was split from MI1(b), initially for work in the UK against air raids. By autumn 1916, MI1(b) had ten staff but MI1(e) shared the same offices and some MI1(b) staff had to move temporarily to 2 Whitehall Court, which also housed SIS. The original members of MI1(b) were: J. St. Vincent Pletts, a radio engineer from Marconi's Wireless Telegraph Company; J.D. Crocker, a Cambridge scholar; and Oliver Strachey of the Indian Civil Service. Hay started recruiting new members from the universities, with a preference for language scholars. They included John Fraser, 32, later professor of Celtic as a fellow of Jesus College, Oxford (and Hay's chief assistant); Arthur Surridge Hunt, 45, then and later Professor of Papyrology at Oxford and a world expert on ancient writing; David Samuel Margoliouth, 58, professor of Arabic at Oxford and later president of the Royal Asiatic Society and author of many books on Arabic literature and history; Zachary Nugent Brooke, 34, then lecturer in history at Cambridge, later professor of medieval history there and an editor of the *Cambridge Medieval History*; Edward Thurloe Leeds, 39, then assistant keeper of the department of antiquities of the Ashmolean Museum; Ellis H. Minns, 42, then and later lecturer in palaeography at Cambridge; Norman Brooke Jopson, 26, from Cambridge and later professor of Comparative philology there; George Baily Sansom of the embassy in Tokyo; and Henry E.G. Tyndale, 28, later a housemaster at Winchester College.

At the end of 1914 MO6(b) started to look at 'the great volume of diplomatic code messages sent by cable routes which, owing to the censorship, were now for the first time accessible.'[26] According to Hay:

> In 1914 and 1915, before my appointment to M.O.6(b) some progress had already been made by Messrs. Strachey and Pletts with the American diplomatic code. I am not able to say definitely how this code was first broken. I was told that some clear texts were obtained which facilitated solution. Until the beginning of 1916 the work of the War Office cryptographic section was limited to reconstruction of the American Diplomatic code books.[27]

America was an obvious target, given the amount of material available. Three code books were solved and super-enciphering tables recovered, so some convalescent officers were temporarily attached to the sub-section to help in decoding although they did not tackle 'the more technical work'.[28] During 1916, MI1(b) broadened its work and

> the section successfully attacked and solved the current Greek, Swiss and Spanish code books. The Greek book was of the greatest interest;

> very long messages which were passing in great numbers between King Constantine of Greece and Berlin had, owing to the presence of Allied forces at Salonika, to be sent by wireless between Athens and Sofia and were duly intercepted. The solving of the code in which these messages were being sent proved of the very highest importance.[29]

It was not until 1917 that there was any exchange between Room 40 and MI1(b), and this was restricted to results. Ironically, MI1(b) exchanged technical information as well as results with the French military bureau and the American Military Intelligence Division in Paris. Room 40 received Mediterranean intercepts from the French Ministre de la Marine, collaborated with the Italians in the Adriatic and established liaison with and shared information with the Russians before the revolution. However, much could be learnt from the primitive but pioneering work of WW1 Service Sigint as it comprised the four main elements of Sigint – Interception, Traffic Analysis, Cryptanalysis and Intelligence (operational and research).[30]

According to AGD: 'Room 40's work was principally German naval, latterly a certain amount of diplomatic enemy and neutral, only using material obtained by interception of W/T by stations under Admiralty control.' MI1(b) worked on 'principally German military and some neutral and later even Allied diplomatic, the material for the latter being obtained from Cable Censorship under War Office control' and that 'only from 1917 was there any exchange' between Room 40 and MI1(b) and even then 'principally of results'. [31]

The diplomatic work of MI1(b) and Room 40 was quite complimentary, given the different initial sources of material. Room 40 concentrated on Germany while MI1(b) monitored every other country. MI1(b) relied on censorship while Room 40 relied on radio and physical interception of diplomatic material from enemy states, mainly Germany. In September 1916, Room 40 discovered how Germany was evading interception of their diplomatic telegrams. Those to their missions in the Americas were going through Sweden's Foreign Office and sent as Swedish telegrams. Also, the US State Department sometimes laundered German telegrams to and from Washington and MI1(b) had not spotted this. De Grey wrote to Hall on 21 September, noting:

> It is now abundantly clear that telegrams are passing to Washington not intercepted by us [as postal mail] and not transmitted via Buenos Aires [as Swedish]. Neither can the telegrams omitted from our series be fitted into the wireless messages from Sayville or Tuckerton

> [US radio stations] – their number is by no means large enough. I consider it likely that they are sent via the State Dept. and the USA Embassy and might consequently be interceptable there.[32]

This kindled Room 40's interest in cable censorship, which had been the preserve of MI1(b) and perhaps established collaboration between the two departments. The earliest communication is a note from AGD dated 15 October 1916 and by late December the bureaux were exchanging technical details of Greek and Spanish code book recoveries and usage.[33]

Room 40's interest in cable censorship continued to grow and, from the end of September 1916, it received 'American'/German telegrams from censorship. This inevitably led to cooperation between Room 40 and MI1(b). The earliest known contact is a note from AGD dated 15 October 1916. On 26 December, AGD mentioned, in a note about Greek keys, that 'I am very glad this opportunity to avoid duplication of work has arisen and hope it may be carried through successfully.'

MI1(b) was brought together again in offices at 5 Cork Street Piccadilly, in the latter half of 1917. They had two outside telephone numbers and twenty-one extensions off the main War Office switchboard.

'At Cork Street a private line had been installed from Major Hay's office to the Admiralty and Sir Reginald Hall. Malcolm greatly admired the efficiency of this man, though he was of the opinion that he could be almost entirely ruthless, especially in what he considered to be the execution of his duty.'[34]

Staff numbers grew throughout 1917 as they solved the diplomatic codes of Argentina, Brazil, Denmark, Italy, Japan, the Netherlands, Norway, Persia, Sweden, Uruguay and the Vatican. By the end of the year, forty-three out of the fifty staff were working on diplomatic codes according to the official history. This compares to below ten in Room 40. Correspondence between AGD and Crocker continued through the year, with the last available example dated 30 October. During 1918, MI1(b) solved the code books of France, Peru and Romania.

By the end of the war, MI1(b) had eighty-four staff including thirty women and they were mainly based in a private house requisitioned by the War Office several streets away from its main building in Whitehall. Hay was very security-conscious and instigated an elaborate entry procedure which prevented visitors from wandering around the building. MI1(b)'s work was helped by keys and techniques for German military ciphers provided by the French. Intelligence from MI1(b) to army command soon started to flow.[35] The unit broke the German Army political section's cipher which was used to communicate to agents.

Through this source and resumed liaison with its Admiralty counterpart, the navy sunk a German submarine in the Mediterranean carrying arms for Arab nationalists in North Africa.

An Admiralty memorandum in May 1918 says that the Director of Naval Intelligence (DNI) and the Director of Military Intelligence (DMI) each received all the available information from their own Service's work and then communicated it 'to whom they think fit'. MI1(b) is reported to have solved fifty-two diplomatic codes during WW1 and seems to have done most of the work on the American diplomatic telegrams for the period 1916–18, from which the British authorities learned about American attitudes to the war in Europe and the state of their relations with Germany. Again, AGD later noted that the diplomatic codes of the period were 'most elementary', only the German Foreign Office was using 'hatted' books and reciphering methods.[36] All others were arranged alphabetically. Codes were being read from Japan, Greece, Spain and Scandinavia.

Hall had set up a diplomatic annex of Room 40 in 1915, reporting directly to him and headed by Sir George Young, a former diplomat. By 1917, Room 40 was receiving copies of German diplomatic telegrams from the War Office censorship as well as from the Admiralty's intercept stations. Their work was helped by the acquisition of a German diplomatic code book retrieved from the baggage left behind in Persia by a German consul, Wassmuss, and acquired by Hall from the India Office in 1915. By 1916, Room 40 was reading German telegrams between Berlin and the German Embassy in Washington. From these, Hall learned of plans for German assistance to the Irish nationalists in an armed uprising. He then arranged for the navy to intercept a shipment of arms on 21 April 1916. This enabled the authorities to capture Roger Casement, an Irish nationalist, activist and diplomat who was plotting an uprising with the help of Germany, within hours of him landing from a U-boat on the Irish coast at Tralee Bay. He was subsequently tried for treason and executed on 3 August 1916. Hall's source of intelligence on the Irish problem dried up when the German Embassy in Washington closed in February 1917, the US having broken off diplomatic relations over Germany's declaration of unrestricted submarine warfare.

MI1(b) never developed into an integrated military Sigint centre like the Admiralty section would become but it did have all of the hallmarks of an integrated diplomatic Sigint centre. It had little control over intercepts and poor interaction between cryptanalysts and linguists. However, Sigint activities were carried out in the field in France in support of the BEF. It achieved results of some value from decryption, traffic analysis and direction finding. Sections on each front could break the codes being used by its opponents. Results were sent to the Intelligence Branch of the General Staff. William Friedman, at the time a lieutenant with the American Sigint unit, G2A6, in France, was of the view that in 1917, very little cipher work was done at British GHQ 'as they depended more or less on their offices in London for this'. During the static trench warfare on the Western Front, both sides obtained Sigint through the interception of line telegraphy and telephone conversations. Poor British security allowed the Germans to make a transcript of an entire British operational plan read out over the telephone in 1916 and inflict significant casualties. In early 1917, the Germans introduced a number of special code books as they extended wireless telegraphy in more forward positions.[37]

Until June 1917 the British Army's overseas Sigint service, both in terms of operations and intelligence, existed as a separate though parallel branch of the Army Signal Service. Afterwards, the intelligence sections were transferred to the newly formed special branch of the Intelligence Staff at GHQ, Section I9e at Le Touquet, headed by Captain O.T. Hitchings. Its success was measured for the first time as a force multiplier, in this case, the equivalent of four divisions. The Army also supplied intelligence for the Royal Flying Corps, enabling early warning of enemy attacks. While GHQ had a Wireless Observation Group (WOG) monitoring the traffic of German radio stations behind the lines, interception of tactical communications was covered by other WOGs, each with around fifty personnel. WOGs were also established in other operational theatres. The first, No. 2, was formed in Egypt in 1916 to cover operations in Palestine. Later that year, No. 3 was started in Salonica and No. 4 in Mesopotamia, covering Southern Russia and Anatolia. They worked closely together, exchanged intercepts, traffic analysis reports, cryptographic data and translations. They shared a cipher with MI1(b) to which they supplied data and material. While detailed information about the operation of these groups is unknown, their legacy would be seen in WW2.

***

The existence of Hall's cryptographic section came to the attention of Churchill, in his capacity as First Lord, but his interest was greeted with some scepticism by AGD. Writing in 1919 he said:

> The First Lord, Winston Churchill, now took official note of the existence of the Section and issued its charter. As is seen, he laid

> down certain instructions for the distribution of the translations. One is bound to confess that the First Lord's view of the possibilities of cryptography appear now distinctly limited. To have carried out his instructions literally would, no doubt, have safeguarded the secret but must also have nullified the value of the messages.[38]

Churchill dictated his 'charter' to his personal secretary Edward March on 8 November 1914 and initialled it 'WSC' in red ink. It was addressed to Ewing and Fisher, who initialled it 'F' in green ink. The charter document[39] said:

> An officer of the War Staff, preferably from the I.D., should be selected to study all the decoded intercepts, not only current but past, and to compare them continually with what actually took place in order to penetrate the German mind and movements, and make reports. All these intercepts are to be written in a locked book with their decodes, and all other copies are to be collected and burnt. All new messages are to be entered in the book, and the book is only to be handled under direction from COS.
>
> The officer selected is for the present to do no other work.
>
> I shall be grateful if Sir Alfred Ewing will associate himself continuously with this work.

Fisher passed it on to Hall, who replied the next day:

> I have consulted with Sir Alfred Ewing and propose that Fleet Paymaster Rotter be detailed exclusively for this work (he discovered the code). The system at present in force is as follows. All intercepts are decoded immediately they are received. The original intercept is then filed and kept under lock and key. The translation is entered in a book which is kept under lock and key. Two copies are made out of the translation – one sent by hand and given personally to COS, the other given to DID. This system ensures that the information is given at once to the responsible people, the COS to act as necessary, the DID to compare with information from other sources. DID's copy is kept under lock and key and is seen by no one but DID. In future, the envelopes will be marked 'To be opened only by – - -.' I would point out that to carry the book round will entail much delay and will not save copies being taken as so many messages are being received. I would therefore propose that the work be continued under the direction of Sir Alfred Ewing on the lines indicated above.

AGD's assessment of Churchill's charter document proved to be correct, as his insistence on security proved unhelpful. It only served to cut off Room 40 from the rest of Naval Intelligence and hence limited the impact that its work might have had. Churchill's 'charter' seemed to make Ewing and Room 40 responsible to Oliver as COS. However, given Oliver's workload, it in effect meant that Ewing was not responsible to anyone, a situation which was unlikely to sit well with Hall. Oliver would later record that 'only the First Lord, the First Sea Lord, the Second Sea Lord, the Secretary [of the Admiralty], Sir Arthur Wilson, me and Hall, the DOD [Director Operations Division], the Assistant Director and my three Duty Captains were supposed to be aware [of Rooms 40's work] in the Admiralty. Churchill may have told the Prime Minister but I never had any evidence that the rest of the War Cabinet knew.'[40]

The Operations Division was also sceptical due to two unfortunate incidents which occurred even before Ewing's staff moved to Room 40. It stemmed from the fact that any signal that could be read was circulated without proper analysis or comment. According to AGD:

> Owing to poor interception and lack of knowledge on the part of the staff, a signal was circulated alleging that the *Ariadne* was proceeding to the Jade. The Operations Division knew that the *Ariadne* was sunk in the Heligoland Bight[41] action. Worse than that, a message was circulated on two or three successive evenings purporting to order destroyers to patrol the Inner Gabbard. The COS took counter-action and, at some considerable trouble and expense, English destroyers also patrolled that spot and never found the enemy. Subsequently it was found that the German destroyers had merely been ordered to proceed to Heligoland, an island which could only be distinguished from the Inner Gabbard by the bar over the letter 'A' which had escaped the notice of the inexperienced and geographically ignorant watchkeeper.
>
> Further, any signal which could be read was circulated without comment and for reasons best known to W/T experts, many of those emanating from Bulk were among the best intercepted and hence most easily read. The poor watchkeepers had the haziest of notions as to the whereabouts of Bulk but the Operations Division cannot be blamed for the lack of enthusiasm for the times at which the Kiel barrier was opened. The watchkeepers knew nothing of the German Fleet, very little of the geography of the German coastline, while their ignorance of English and German naval phraseology was profound. Hope did his best for them while Lord Fisher pointed out

> that warships did not 'run in' and begged the staff to adopt the word 'proceed'.[42]

British Sigint was truly born in November 1914 and AGD was at the heart of the action. Room 40 consisted of Ewing in charge, Commander Hope and Fleet Paymaster Rotter dealing respectively with the intelligence and cryptographic sides of the work, Herschell, Denniston and Norton as watchkeepers, and Russell Clarke and Hippiseley at the Hunstanton intercept station. This was supplemented by the educational staff, Naval instructors Parish, Curtis and Professor Henderson. Their 'tools' consisted of a copy of the German Navy Signal Book (additional copies were made) and the HVB which had been captured by the Australians. It was used by the whole German High Sea Fleet, submarines and airships, albeit in re-encrypted form, until March 1915. It proved invaluable, particularly in gaining advance warning of air raids. They also had the VB book which DID had handed over to Ewing when it arrived in the Admiralty. Herschell was moved to DID to head up a team to deal with the translation of the mass of secret papers recovered along with the VB book. The watches were brought up to two-man strength with the addition of Monk Bretton, Hopkinson, Fremantle, Lawrence and Morrah in December. According to AGD:

> They knew ordinary literary German fluently and they could be relied on. But of cryptography, of naval German, of the habits of war vessels of any nationality they knew not a jot. Their training was of the shortest before they were sent off onto watches of two men each and given the responsibility of looking after the German Fleet. Worse than that, they had to learn the intricacies of the office routine. They probably had more than their fair share of log writing, they had to sort and circulate. They had to turn the German squared chart into latitude and longitude of which they had not heard since the geography class of their school days. There was no traditional routine to be followed. New methods had to be evolved to meet new problems.[43]

Gradually during November, Ewing's team had succeeded in translating intelligible portions of various German naval messages. Most were routine, such as: 'One of our torpedo boats will be running out into square 7T at 8 p.m.' According to Churchill: 'Admiral Oliver has the foresight to begin setting up directional stations in August 1914. The Admiralty 'thus carried to an unrivalled and indeed unapproached degree of perfection our means of fixing the position and, by successive positions, the course of any enemy ship that used its wireless installation.'[44]

By the beginning of 1915, Russell Clarke's new Y stations were intercepting most German signals and Room 40, having mastered the SKM and HVB codes, was reading all of them. Room 40's decrypts let them keep a watch on German ship movements as well as important inferences to be drawn regarding such things as the composition of the enemy squadrons, the presence of new ships, the position of minefields, etc. Deducing such information from these messages required specific expertise, which was why Rear-Admiral Hope was lent to Room 40 from the Intelligence Division to help with this work.

AGD recorded Room 40's daily routine in November 1914 as follows:

> Hope and Rotter were present daily from 9am till 7pm, the former dealing with the translated messages, the latter working on the many fragments and examining the unknown. The man on watch had to sort, decode and translate the new.
>
> Hunstanton, Stockton Leafield and Hall Street had direct lines to the Admiralty. There was a never-ending stream of postmen delivering bundles of intercepts. In a few months these men were replaced by an automatic tube which discharged the goods into a basket with a rush which shook the nerve of any unwitting visitor and very much disturbed the slumbers of a night watchman taking his time off.
>
> In the very early days every message which appeared to give sense to the man on duty was 'logged' and 'sent'. That is, the translation was written in the current log book and three copies were made for circulation, one for the COS and one for DID and one for Hope. With luck, there were three or four copies of every message from the various stations. These had to be pinned together and stacked in the file of logged messages. But still there were a vast number of fragments, of messages which failed to satisfy the fastidious German taste of the watchkeeper, or messages in unknown codes and languages. All these were bundled into a tin on which was printed 'N.S.L.'. It was a very important tin, nearly always very full in those days, but to explain it to the many newcomers was one of the most complex points in a very complicated system. Truly N.S.L. only meant 'neither sent or logged'. When the war was finished there was still a box called N.S.L. when there had been no log for the last two years. N.S.L. was a living thing with a specific meaning, and it recounted how a night

> watchman woke trembling in a sweat – he had dreamt he had been sent to the N.S.L. and got lost.
>
> The log became an object of hatred before long. The First Lord had called into being that particular form of filing the current work and it was over two years, when its originator was elsewhere, before a more labour-saving and less soul-destroying method was allowed to replace it. In the days when a watchkeeper averaged 12 messages it could be written up, though even then it was the fashion to let the messages accumulate and allow the new watch to write up the log, and thus appreciate the situation! But it was beyond a joke when naval actions were pending or zepps fluttering and the watchkeeper had 12 to 20 pages of the book to write up.
>
> For two months at least the night man had a lonely time, though he was probably too busy to note it. It was no good bringing pyjamas in those days or hoping the Admiralty would provide a bath. All that was needed was plenty of sandwiches. Tastes in drinks varied and only one man is alleged to have worked throughout the night with a revolver at his elbow.[45]

By 1915, all German naval signals which could be intercepted were read and circulated since almost all German communications were encrypted using one of the three books in the possession of Room 40. The disposition (strength as well as general location) of its High Seas Fleet was known, along with information about its submarines and airships. In January 1915, Hope began submitting a daily return to Churchill, Fisher, Wilson and Oliver which set out the last known position of every U-boat mentioned in decodes. He had built up an accurate idea of the total operational strength, of the location and state of readiness of every individual boat if in port, and when and if it put to sea. However, at this stage Room 40 was not an intelligence centre. It was not allowed to keep a plot of British warships or merchant ships, so could not know whether a decrypted U-boat position posed a risk.

According to AGD:

> No attempt was made to develop any intelligence side of the work, beyond Hope's duty of instructing the authorities on the real meaning of certain signals. The request that 40 OB should be allowed to keep a flagged chart of the German coastline was vetoed as an unnecessary duplication of the work in the Operations Division. (In May 1917 this request received sanction). But all naval signals were read even without intelligence. True it is that in certain cupboards there were increasing piles of 'stuff' which was not read

> but it was not naval German. The art of reading other peoples' telegrams was still in extreme infancy; no one then imagined that all those piles contained telegrams possibly of the greatest interest which could be read and, in 1915 it may be said, read without extreme difficulty.[46]

However, intelligence was not always accepted from NID without questions, as shown by this note from Churchill to NID on 7 November 1914:

> With reference to your report of yesterday, apparently attaching credence to a statement that from 100 to 200 small submarines have been manufactured secretly in Germany, have you considered how many trained officers and personnel this important flotilla would require? What evidence is there at your disposal to show that the Germans have trained this number of submarine captains and officers? I have always understood that their flotilla of submarines before the war did not exceed 27. There are no personnel that require more careful training than the submarine personnel. All the experience of our officers shows that a submarine depends for its effectiveness mainly upon its captain. The function of the Naval Intelligence Division is not merely to collect and pass on the Munchausen tales of spies and untrustworthy agents, but carefully to sift and scrutinize the intelligence they receive, and in putting it forward to indicate the degree of probability which attaches to it. It appears to me impossible that any large addition to the German submarine force can be made for many months to come. Even if the difficulties of material were overcome those of personnel would impose an absolute limit. It is very likely that a few small portable submarines have been prepared for coast work.

In early 1915, Room 40 was clearly understaffed and Ewing and Hall both began looking for suitable new recruits. Two naval schoolmasters, Edmund Green and G.L.N. Hope, were brought in first, followed by B.F. Talbot, P.A. Somers-Cocks and George Young from the Diplomatic Service. On the academic side, Dilwyn 'Dilly' Knox may have been the first recruit. He was a 31-year-old Greek scholar and Fellow of King's College, Cambridge.[47] Knox started off 'learning the ropes' as a watchkeeper but quickly demonstrated a flair for cryptanalysis. He was given Room 53, a cubbyhole of a room which housed a bath for the use of men on the night watch. This was no problem for Knox and legend has it that he did his best work in a hot bath.[48] Knox shared a house in

Chelsea with another King's fellow, Frank Birch,[49] seven years his junior, who arrived at the end of 1915 or early 1916. He specialised in the analysis and assessment of the intelligence, rather than in cryptanalysis. As a serving Royal Naval Volunteer Reserve (RNVR) officer, Birch was one of the few men working in Room 40 who wore naval uniform. He was active in the theatre and apparently played the Widow Twankie in professional pantomimes at Christmas. A third King's man joined them, Frank E. Adcock, lay dean of the college.[50] Adcock did not share the eccentricities of his King's colleagues and stayed true to his chosen field of Ancient History. In contrast to the King's men, the Rev. William Montgomery[51] came from Westminster Presbyterian College, Cambridge, and contributed linguistic skills. Also arriving in 1915 was Edward Bullough from Caius College, Cambridge and another linguist, along with Professor L.A. Willoughby, a German specialist from London University.

Hall personally recruited Nigel de Grey[52], who had joined the RNVR and become an observer in the Balloon Section of the Royal Naval Air Service in Belgium. In mid-1915, Hall formed a separate Diplomatic Section with George Young as its head and early members including de Grey, Flaudel-Phillips and Montgomery. It occupied Room 45 but retained the name Room 40. They struggled to break German diplomatic codes, which were far more complex than those used by the Imperial Navy until a copy of their codes was captured. W.F. Clarke,[53] a barrister, arrived in early 1916, having secured a commission as an Assistant Paymaster RNVR at the beginning of 1915. Further recruits were drawn from wounded Army officers such as Lionel Fraser, a friend of Serocold. Benjamin Flaudel-Phillips was another Serocold recruit and he succeeded Young as head of the Diplomatic Section.

Room 40 assumed that eventually a change in cipher key would occur and, in early January, the evening watch was unable to read a batch of signals delivered to them. Through a concerted effort by all available staff, the new key was obtained by the next morning. Churchill called to offer his personal congratulations. Ironically, subsequent work during the day revealed that the key had not been changed but just modified slightly, something that should have been detected quite quickly. Room 40 kept the information to itself to avoid embarrassment, and when the key did actually change a few days later, it was solved in a few hours without fanfare. By 1917, the key was changing every night at midnight. The number of intercepting aerials controlled by Clarke and the Marconi Company increased during the spring of 1915 and this led to a very large increase in intercepted traffic. The operators were starting to discover different frequencies being used by different

German communication networks. AGD summoned up their increasing expertise:

> But the intercepting officers were now learning a lot about the methods of German naval W/T and it was possible to allot aerials to various wavelengths and even districts. Thus the operators soon realised that the Baltic and North Sea Fleets were on different circuits and under different controls. The submarines formed a separate group and the small outpost craft in the Bight yet another. 40 OB learnt these things too and, even at this period, Baltic messages received scanty treatment.[54]

Room 40 had a number of noteworthy successes during WW1, during which it broke most of the German naval keys. The German Navy had produced charts which divided up the North Sea into numbered squares to identify the position of its ships. Room 40's first success was reading a message which showed that a German auxiliary ship had been ordered to search for missing torpedo boats in a particular area. Ewing took the information to Oliver (COS), and a cruiser was dispatched and confirmed that the information was correct. Rotter discovered the key being used for the private messages of the German Commander-in-Chief. Messages were telegraphed over a private wire from the intercept stations to the Admiralty and delivered to Ewing's office. They were then decrypted, translated and if deemed of importance brought at once to the notice of the War Staff. They often led to direct action by the British fleet.

The German High Seas Fleet was usually kept in the safely-guarded river estuaries of the Heligoland Bight behind a minefield and only came out into open waters from time to time for raids. Room 40 had advance notice of most of the actions of the German fleet: messages would order minesweepers to clear certain channels, a lighthouse would receive orders to show its lights for a certain period, orders would be issued for barrier booms to be opened or for aerial reconnaissance. Orders would also be read from the German Commander-in-Chief to squadrons and flotillas giving the composition of the force and its time of departure.

In December 1914, German battlecruisers bombarded Scarborough and Hartlepool. On the afternoon of the 14th, Room 40 had intelligence that the German fleet would come out the next day. Due to bad weather, effective contact was never made by the British fleet, but it convinced the British authorities of the effectiveness of Room 40. Churchill later wrote:

> Naturally there was much indignation at the failure of the Navy to prevent, or at least to avenge, such an attack upon our shores. What was the Admiralty doing? Were they asleep? Although the bombarded towns, in which nearly five hundred civilians had been killed and wounded, supported their ordeal with fortitude, dissatisfaction was widespread. However we could not say a word in explanation. We had to bear in silence the censures of our countrymen. We could never admit, for fear of compromising our secret information, where our squadrons were, nor how near the German raiding cruisers had been to destruction. One comfort we had. The indications upon which we had acted had been confirmed by events. The sources upon which we relied were evidently trustworthy. Next time we might at least have average visibility. But would there be a next time? The German Admiral must have known that he was very near to powerful British ships, but which they were, or where they were, or how near he was, might be a mystery. Would it not also be a mystery how they came to be there? On the other hand, the exultation of Germany at the hated English towns being actually made to feel for the first time the real lash of war might encourage a second attempt. Even the indignation of our own newspapers had a value for this purpose. One could only hope for the best. Meanwhile British naval plans and secrets remained wrapped in impenetrable silence.[55]

Admiral Hugo von Pohl, Chief of the German Admiralty Staff, made a number of proposals to the German Emperor. They included a submarine attack on merchant shipping and 'sending airships to attack England in the months of January and February, when the weather is suitably calm and cool'. Churchill wrote, 'So excellent was our Intelligence Service that reports of what was passing in the minds of the German Naval Staff reached us even before Admiral von Pohl's memorandum had been laid before the Emperor.'[56] Churchill's note to the Cabinet on 1 January 1915 attributed the information to a 'trustworthy source'.

During 1915 and 1916, Room 40 was able to watch the German fleet and its movements. On Saturday, 23 January 1915, Room 40 read a message from the Commander-in-Chief, Admiral von Ingenohl to the commander of the battlecruisers, Rear-Admiral Hipper, sent at 10.25 am ordering him to scout on Dogger Bank.[57] 'First and Second Scouting Groups, Senior Officer of the Destroyers and two flotillas to be selected by the Senior Officer Scouting Forces are to reconnoitre the Dogger Bank. They are to leave harbour this evening after dark and to return tomorrow evening after dark.'[58]

They were to proceed to sea that night and to return the next evening after dark. Subsequent decrypts identified the flotilla's orders regarding the lighting of buoys, the channel to be used to bypass minefields and orders for aerial reconnaissance. Oliver and Sir Arthur Wilson informed Churchill that day and orders went out to the Grand Fleet to prepare to sail. Wilson's conclusions from the intercepted messages and other intelligence sources were that 'All the German fast vessels were putting to sea at dark, and a raid upon the British coast was clearly to be expected.'[59]

A telegram was sent to the Commander-in-Chief with the Grand Fleet at Scapa, to Admiral Bradford with the Third Battle Squadron, to Admiral Beatty with the battlecruisers at Rosyth, and to Commodore Tyrwhitt with the light cruisers and destroyers at Harwich with deployment orders.

They were to meet at a point which would intercept the German fleet before it could reach the Heligoland Bight. The operation wasn't entirely successful but one ship, the *Blücher*, was sunk. As each message came in, Ewing delivered it to the War Room of the Admiralty where Churchill, Lord Fisher, Admiral Wilson and Admiral Oliver awaited developments. Early the next morning, Churchill, Fisher, Wilson and Oliver were in the War Room when signals were received that the enemy had been sighted. In the action that followed, according to Churchill: 'The moment the German Commander discovered himself in the presence of numerous British warships, including the battle-cruisers, his decision was taken. He collected his ships, turned completely round, and ran for home with the utmost possible despatch.'[60]

At 3.45 pm on the 24th, Churchill sent the following letter to the Prime Minister:

> This morning Beatty with 5 battle-cruisers and a superior force of light cruisers and destroyers, met *Derfflinger, Seydlitz, Moltke* and *Blücher* with light cruisers and destroyers in the middle of the North Sea. The Germans ran for home immediately, and a fierce pursuit ensued, producing a severe action between the battle-cruisers on both sides.
>
> The *Lion* is damaged, but is returning home at 12 knots. Beatty has shifted his flag to the *Princess Royal.*
>
> The *Blücher* (15,500 tons, 25 ½ knots), practically a battle-cruiser, though with 12 8.2 inch guns and 880 men [she actually had 1,200 men on board] is sunk. Two other German battle-cruisers reported seriously injured. Deserting the *Blücher,* the Germans managed to

> make good their escape into their own torpedo area, where we thought better not to follow.

He concluded with the comment that '*Blücher* is a heavy loss to the German cruiser fleet – she was only five years old.'

Room 40's achievement in the Dogger Bank action was summed up by Churchill as follows:

> The victory of the Dogger Bank brought for the time being abruptly to an end the adverse movement against my administration of the Admiralty, which had begun to gather. Congratulations flowed in from every side, and we enjoyed once again an adequate measure of prestige. The sinking of the *Blücher* and the flight, after heavy injuries, of the other German ships was accepted as a solid and indisputable result. The German Emperor was confirmed in the gloomy impressions he had sustained after the action of August 28, 1914. All enterprise in the German Admiralty was again effectively quelled, and apart from submarine warfare a period of nearly fifteen months halcyon calm reigned over the North Sea and throughout Home Waters. The neutral world accepted the event as decisive proof of the British supremacy at sea: and even at home the Admiralty felt the benefit in a sensible increase of confidence and goodwill.[61]

Ewing later reflected on the action from a Room 40 perspective: 'But on that memorable Sunday of the Dogger Bank action we, who in this strange way were spectators, were left in no uncertainty as to the progress and the issues of the drama. When it was over, the workers of Room 40 could reflect with satisfaction on the contribution they had made.'[62]

After Dogger Bank, the High Seas Fleet rarely came out until the spring of 1916 when the command had passed to Admiral Scheer, who adopted a bolder strategy. On 25 April, the battlecruisers bombarded Lowestoft but returned to base before the British fleet could intercept them. This and other activity culminated in the Battle of Jutland. Enemy messages, intercepted on 30 May, made it clear that the German fleet was about to set to sea in force. On the afternoon of the 31st, the vanguard of the German fleet encountered, to their surprise, battlecruisers under Beatty and the battle began. At 3.45 pm on 31 May, 1916 Admiral Hipper's battlecruisers fired the first shots. Intercepted German signals had enabled Room 40 to inform Admiral Sir John Jellicoe, the position, course and speed of the German battle fleet after it had broken off the action. At 9.50 pm, he was told that three destroyer flotillas had been ordered to attack him during the night and at 9.58 pm he was told the position of the rear ship of the enemy battle fleet and that the fleet was on a southerly course. However, this was contradicted by the position he knew the fleet to be in. It turned out that the mistake was made by the cruiser *Regensburg,* which incorrectly reported its position in the message read by Room 40. But it made Jellicoe nervous about using Room 40's reports. Further messages renewed his confidence, but an important message from the German Commander-in-Chief was not passed to Jellicoe. The officer who received the intelligence from Room 40 had very little experience of German operational signals and German naval procedure and was not aware of its significance. This was a direct result of Room 40 being restricted to operate as a cryptographic bureau rather than as an intelligence centre. Further decrypted signals flowed to Jellicoe throughout the night. Ironically, they included the disposition of Jellicoe's forces as seen through German eyes!

In 1916 the Germans changed the key of the principal naval signals every night at midnight, so the night watch played an important role in Room 40. They frequently had solved the new key within several hours, taking advantage of routine messages which provided easy material to aid solution of the key. Another group of stations at Lowestoft, near York, at Murcar on the coast of Aberdeenshire and later at Lerwick provided direction finding information by taking down the bearing of a signal and sending it to Room 40. A big chart would be used to pinpoint the position of the ship that sent the signal. When the Germans started to use the same technique to guide their Zeppelins, Room 40 could use the same information in the intercepted messages to locate them. The technique also helped mask the cryptographic success of Room 40. This was the beginning of naval traffic analysis which, along with military traffic analysis, would prove such a crucial tool for the Allies during WW2.

Given the difficulty of distributing new code books, the Germans relied on keys alone to secure their communications, which proved to be a flawed strategy. Count von Bernstorff, the German Ambassador in Washington, gave evidence about ciphers to a Committee of Enquiry of the National German Assembly after the war and, speaking of the German correspondence with Washington, said: 'The cipher was not changed as often as would have been the case under normal conditions ... To the extent that it was possible to do so, we operated the existing ciphers by means of keys; but I learnt later that the British decoded all our telegrams.' Hall had feared that the Germans would realise that their signal books were compromised but they failed to change them.

Russell Clarke was now controlling an increasing number of intercept stations. With Marconi-controlled stations also intercepting German signals, the number of messages coming into Room 40 was increasing daily. The civilians operating these stations were placed in a special section of the RNVR called the Shore Wireless Service (SWS). Following a meeting with Captain Round of the Marconi Company, Hall encouraged W/T directional apparatus to be installed in a number of locations to fix the position of a ship or airplane. This enabled Room 40 to obtain by cross-bearings the position of every German ship that sent out a signal. In April 1915, Hall received a copy of the German diplomatic code book. It was used for messages between Berlin and Madrid, and Berlin and Constantinople. The Germans sent messages to their diplomats in North, South and Central America through Madrid. A large number of messages, constructed differently to naval messages, had been previously received by Room 40 and put to one side. By the summer of 1915, progress in reading them was being made. Hall's political section recruited further staff, with George Young remaining in charge. Young had a wide knowledge of foreign affairs and a flair for cryptography. By October, Young was able to pass on intelligence to Hall about the efforts of the German Government to encourage revolution in India and Afghanistan, both under British rule, and about sabotage in America and the Far East. Hall also became aware of the activities of German agents in the US through these diplomatic messages. One message in April from Arthur Zimmermann, the German Foreign Secretary, to the German Minister in Buenos Aires was a good example of sabotage plans:

> It would be desirable to render useless certain particular cargoes of corn, an operation which can be effected, without danger to human beings, by means of doses of KOKODYL or MERKAPTAN contained in GELODORAT capsules. Experiments made here have demonstrated that the capsules can be made to look like grains of corn. They would for this purpose be mixed with the corn when the latter is being shipped from the silos. Two or three capsules would suffice to render 100 kilogrammes of corn offensive to the smell. There is no result until the corn is ground in a mill. You should report whether it is possible to get supplies of the above and to carry out the project.

On 6 May 1916, Ewing was offered the Principalship of Edinburgh University and handed over complete control of Room 40 to Hall. The relationship between the two men appears to have been difficult, caused in part by Hall's greater understanding of the potential of Room 40. However, Ewing was the founding father of Room 40, the first to recruit staff and through his friend Russell Clarke, responsible for the creation of the Y stations in a very short time.[63]

In light of German plans to defeat Britain by an unrestricted submarine campaign against merchant shipping, in the autumn of 1916, the operations of submarines became the main concern of Room 40 and the German section under Brandon and Trench. U-boat intelligence was gathered from cryptography, directional wireless plotting, agent reports on the activities in German dockyards, reports of sightings and attacks from convoys and hunting squadrons and interrogation of prisoners. Every shred of evidence was sifted and collated by Room 40.

Room 40 continued to be beset with problems throughout 1916. There was a shortage of staff and while Hope started compiling a card index, assisted by Clarke and Birch, there were no office aids and no typists. However, the main difficulty lay in the separation of its activities from that of Intelligence Division. Ever since the Battle of Jutland, Hall was not happy with the existing system of passing intelligence from Room 40 to the naval Operations Division without comment. However, Operations Division could not be expected to agree readily to intelligence reports from professors and schoolmasters who did not understand the meaning of naval messages. The fault lay in the system in place, in which the senior naval figures such as Oliver, Wilson and Jackson formed their views solely on raw decrypts. Hall managed to convince naval staff that Intelligence Division would benefit from having direct access to Room 40. This was finally put in place at the beginning of 1917. A war diary was compiled and sent daily to the Commander-in-Chief Grand Fleet. Sir David Beatty and individual intercepts were sent with reasoned assessments. The French Admiralty and the Russians (up until the Revolution) were regularly briefed and wounded officers were provided by the War Office to provide administration support. Finally, as the war spread to new territories, Hall invited Professors Dickson (Reading), Calder (Manchester), Stevenson (Glasgow) and Henry Marden to prepare handbooks with information about individual intercepts. Room 40 developed special sections dealing with cryptography, the Bight, the Baltic, minesweeping, U-boats, directional, etc.

Staff shortages were addressed at last with the arrival of new staff, including Ernest Harrison, a classical tutor of Trinity College, Cambridge; J.D. Beezley from Oxford; Dr E.C. Quiggin, lecturer in German from Cambridge who then recruited W.H. Bruford and C.W.

Hardisty; Edward Bullough, a lecturer in German; L.A. Willoughby, a Taylorian Lecturer in Oxford; G. Waterhouse, a Professor of German from Trinity College, Dublin; F.E. Sandbach from Birmingham; C.E. Gough from Leeds; D.L. Savory, a Professor of French at Belfast; Gerald and Patrick Lawrence, both actors; Desmond McCarthy, an author; G.P. Mackerson, a caricaturist; Father Ronald Knox, Dilly's brother; Francis Toye, a music critic and author; Edward Molyneux, a couturier; and Frank Tiarks, a banker from Schroeders. Clarke later commented on the new secretarial help provided by carefully-selected young women who were all recommended by an existing member of staff:

> Miss Tribe, secretary to Hope, Welsford who insisted on joining up again in 1939, Jenkin now [1953] famous in the BBC programmes, Nugent who went to Chatham House, Mrs Denniston [AGD's wife Dorothy], Spears, Henderson, daughter of Willie [later Admiral Sir Wilfred Henderson and one of the organisers of the convoy system], Mrs Bailey, who rather upset things with her love affairs, Hudson who came as my secretary and used to embarrass us by her early arrival [when the night watch were still bathing] and was a sister of Hudson, later in the Conservative government and daughter of the soap king, Lady Hambro, as efficient as her husband in the City, who startled Hope at one of our dinners by smoking a large cigar. Curtiss who in my view was the most useful of them all, Joan Harbey, daughter of the Secretary to the Bank of England. Surprisingly there was only one romance. Miss Reddam, who spent most of working time in a bathroom, which we had some difficulty persuading the authorities to install. She married Dilly Knox [she was his secretary] and shared his somewhat bizarre office.[64]

In July 1916, Hall received a telegram from Room 40 which provided an insight into Germany's view of US/Mexican relations.

> From: – Washington
> To: – Berlin
> July 25th, 1916
>
> The Mexican question has again reached the stage of diplomatic negotiations and may for that reason be regarded as settled for the moment. It becomes clearer and clearer that the American Government has drawn back from a rupture because her military resources are not sufficient to face a war with Mexico. On every hand

> there was an absence of the first necessities of war. For that reason the decision of the Mexican question again rest with Carranza and Villa. If no new incident occurs, no breach will take place.
>
> Wilson has no reason to be satisfied with the developments of the last few weeks. The pacifists praise him, but their friendship is ever with him. In all leading American circles Wilson is still blamed for his Mexican policy. To judge from certain American symptoms, it looks as if Wilson could not hope to be re-elected unless he succeeds in bringing about peace in Europe.
>
> As regards our relations with the United States, the improvement which was begun makes slow but certain progress.
>
> The English black list has evoked general resentment and will force Wilson to take steps directed against England.

Hall was concerned that Germany intended to deploy its submarines against merchant ships of all nationalities. If the US did eventually enter the war, it would be too late, as British and French supplies would be depleted. He wrote to Commodore Gaunt, Britain's Naval Attaché in Washington, at the end of September 1916:

> You will have seen by Lloyd George's speech that for once in our lives we hold the same views. It has been a struggle to get our Ministers out in the open and say exactly what the people of England think. The Germans, I think, will start their submarine warfare within the next few weeks. They have tried for their armistice with neutrals and failed. I think they are now trying to secure an armistice direct and will fail again, and, when convinced that we mean war, they will go all out.

By October, 200 submarines were ready, having been refitted and their crews trained. Hall hoped that US patience would be exhausted but President Wilson had no intention of going to war unless all States supported it. In England there was a shortage of men and food and the Government, along with the Admiralty was under fire. At the end of November, Sir John Jellicoe handed over command of the Grand Fleet to Sir David Beatty and replaced Sir Henry Jackson as First Sea Lord. Less than a week later, Asquith resigned as Prime Minister and was replaced by Lloyd George, with Sir Edward Carson appointed First Lord and his predecessor Arthur Balfour as Foreign Secretary.

At the end of December, Room 40 decrypted a 'code letter' from Heinrich von Eckardt, the German ambassador to Mexico, to Chancellor Dr Theobold von Bethmann-Hollweg.

> 8th March
> The Swedish Chargé d'Affaires, here, Herr F. Cronholm has, since he has been here, made no concealment of his sympathy for Germany and placed himself in close connection with this Legation. Since the closing of the Brazilian and Guatemalan Legations in August last year he is the only neutral diplomat through whom information from the enemy camp can be obtained. Further, he arranges the conditions for the official telegraphic traffic from your Excellency. In this connection he is obliged every time, often late at night, personally to go to the telegraph office to hand in his dispatches … Herr Cronholm has not got a Swedish order but only a Chilean one. I beg to submit to your Excellency, if your Excellency approves, that Herr Cronholm should be recommended in the proper quarter for the Kronenorden of the 2nd class.
>
> In order to raise no suspicion on the side of our opponents, it would be more advisable to treat the decoration if it be granted, as a secret matter till the end of the war, and only to inform the recipient and his Government of it, and then only under the seal of promise not to publish his investiture until after the end of the war.

This proved that in certain quarters diplomatic privileges were being misused and the mail on all neutral ships should be examined. In particular, Swedish Foreign Office cipher telegrams needed to be brought to the Admiralty, as the Eckardt letter implicated the Swedish Chargé d'Affaires in Mexico, F. Cronholm, in handling illicit traffic. Examination of the Swedish cables revealed German code groups following a few Swedish groups in the messages. By January 1917, the Swedish Foreign Office had become, in effect, an integral part of the German diplomatic organisation. This was further confirmation of what Room 40 had discovered in September 1916, the two routes which Count Johann von Bernstorff, the German ambassador in the United States was using to communicate with his Government while by-passing British censorship. Room 40 was soon providing most of Bernstorff's dispatches and the replies of his government. On 1 September 1916, Eckardt telegraphed Berlin: 'The Swedish representative fears English suspicion and complains in Stockholm on account of his frequent telegrams. He suggested that for the future his reports about ships might be allowed to lapse.'

In an October dispatch, Eckardt was asking why he had not had a reply about Cronholm's decoration and reported on the attitude of President of Mexico General Venustiano Carranza: 'Carranza, who is now openly friendly to Germany, is willing to support, if necessary,

German submarines in Mexican waters to the best of his ability'. An even more important dispatch, sent on 12 November, said that:

> The Imperial Government proposes to employ the most efficacious means to annihilate its principal enemy, and since it designs to carry its operations to America with the object of destroying its enemy's commerce, it will be very valuable to have certain bases to assist the work of the submarines both in South America and in Mexico, as for example, in the State of Tamaulipas. Accordingly, the Imperial Government would see with the greatest pleasure the Mexican Government's consent to cede the necessary permission for the establishment of a base in its territory, on the understanding that any arrangements completed will not involve the slightest damage to the dignity or integrity of Mexico, since that country will be treated like the free and independent nation which it is. The Imperial Government being perfectly acquainted with the special circumstances through which Mexico is passing at the current time – in that period of reconstruction in which being a young nation she finds herself – would like to know what advantages Mexico would find suitable on her part, especially in the financial and economic crisis through which she is passing, if she agrees to the desires of the Imperial Government

On 16 January 1917, an encrypted telegram was sent by Arthur Zimmermann, the German Minister of Foreign Affairs in Berlin, to Ambassador von Bernstorff in Washington. It was to be forwarded on to Eckardt in Mexico. The telegram would forever be known as the Zimmermann Telegram.[65] The following day, Room 40 received from Cable Censorship two copies of the telegram and by the end of the day had partly decrypted it. It would prove to be one of the most significant Sigint events in the twentieth century and Room 40's greatest success.

One had been sent to Washington through American diplomatic channels. It was in a new two-part code known as Code 7500[66] which had been recently introduced and which Room 40 had not broken.[67] The second had been sent via the Swedish Minister in Berlin to Stockholm, Sweden. From there it had gone via cable to Buenos Aires, Argentina, and from there via cable to Washington and then on to Mexico City. The telegram had been encoded using an old German one-part code, known as Code 13040.[68] Most but not all of this code had been recovered by Room 40.[69] This method became known as the 'Swedish roundabout'.

During the morning of the 17th, Knox and De Grey recovered a 'skeleton version' of the text. In the event of war with the US resulting from the unrestricted submarine warfare which Germany would be beginning on 1 February, Eckardt was instructed to invite Mexico to join in the conflict. In turn it would receive the territories of Arizona, New Mexico and Texas. De Grey knew that this proposal could change US policy with regards to the German threat and overcome President Wilson's reluctance to go to war. He showed it to Hall, by-passing Ewing who was still nominally in charge of Room 40. De Grey later wrote that, 'Blinker Hall was always accessible to the lads of Room 40, at least he was to me at the time, because I was getting him all the news from diplomatic Germany and Hall had made a compact with a few of the research party that if ever we dug out anything of real importance we were to take it to him without showing it to Ewing, whom he mistrusted as a chatterbox (and rightly).'[70]

De Grey showed Hall the partially-deciphered message on 17 January and it read:

> Berlin to Washington
> W.158. 16 January 1917.
>
> Most Secret for Your Excellency's personal information and to be handed on to the Imperial Minister in (?) Mexico with … by a safe route.
> We propose to begin on 1 February unrestricted submarine warfare. In doing so, however, we shall endeavour to keep America neutral … (?) If we should not (succeed in doing so) we propose to (?Mexico) an alliance upon the following basis:
> (joint) conduct of war
> (joint) conclusion of peace …
> Your excellency should for the present inform the President [of Mexico] secretly (that we expect) war with the USA (possibly) (… Japan) and at the same time to negotiate between us and Japan …(Indecipherable sentence meaning Please tell the President) that … our submarines … will compel England to peace within a few months. Acknowledge Receipt.
>
> Zimmermann

Hall would later give his own account of first seeing it:

> I am not likely to forget that Wednesday morning, 17 January 1917. There was the usual docket of papers to be gone through on my

arrival at the office, and Claud Serocold and I were still at work on them when at about half past ten de Grey came in. He seemed excited, 'DID,' he began, 'do you want to bring America into the war?' 'Yes, my boy,' I answered, 'Why?' 'I've got something here which – well, it is a rather astonishing message which might do the trick if we could use it. It isn't very clear, I'm afraid, but I'm sure I've got most of the important points right. It's from the German Foreign Office to Bernstorff.'[71]

In 1918, Hall testifying before a Commission investigating an explosion in New Jersey, claimed that: 'The German cipher book covering this system [Code 13040] of enciphering is in our possession, it having been captured by the British authorities in the baggage of a German consul named Wasmuss who was stationed at Shiraz while Wasmuss was engaged in an endeavour to cut a British oil pipe.'

Hall's account is now considered to be at best a case of faulty memory. British intelligence may well have recovered copies of telegrams with the code text along with the corresponding plain text. This would have been of great assistance to Room 40 in reconstructing the 13040 code book. However, the more likely explanation is that Hall instinctively knew that it was better for the Germans to believe that 13040 had been captured rather than reconstructed by Room 40 cryptanalysis.

Hall had a number of problems to solve: should he make use of the telegram; if its disclosure was essential, he needed a complete and accurate text; and he needed to protect its source, Room 40; he needed to find a way to present the information to the President so that he and the American public were convinced by its authenticity; what should they do if Zimmermann denounced the telegram as a forgery? As De Grey recalled:

He asked for the best version that we could produce – in fact, we had got only a little further with the help of Rotter. He then discussed with me again the pros and cons. Obviously we had two fears. The first and by far the greatest was that we should 'blow' Room 40 – a crazy risk to run when it is remembered that we read the German naval codes operationally and always currently. Secondly we did not want to risk the fact that we took drop copies in London off the cables or reveal that we had bowled out the Swedes in a non-neutral act. The first would have lost us an invaluable source of intelligence if the coup with America failed, the second would have created an unpleasant situation at a pretty

> critical moment of the war. I remember him saying to me 'Our first job would be to convince the Americans that it's true – how can we do that? Who would believe? Is there any Englishman, whom they will believe? I've been thinking and the only person I think they would believe is Balfour. To all Englishman at that time Balfour stood head and shoulders above the politicians as the wise man, the elder statesman. Indeed I have always thought that Blinker's use of Balfour as his mouthpiece was a stroke of genius (such as he used to exhibit from time to time).

Hall's first problem was solved by 10 February when he had an almost perfect transcript of the Zimmermann telegram. It had been translated into English as follows:

> Washington to Mexico
> 19 January 1917
> We intend to begin on 1 February unrestricted submarine warfare. We shall endeavour in spite of this to keep the USA neutral. In the event of this not succeeding we make Mexico a proposal of alliance on the following basis: make war together, make peace together.
>
> Generous financial support and an undertaking on our part that Mexico is to reconquer the lost territory in Texas, New Mexico and Arizona. The settlement in detail is left to you.
>
> You will inform the President of the above most secretly as soon as the outbreak of war with the USA is certain, and add the suggestion that he should on his own initiative invite Japan to immediate adherence and at the same time mediate between Japan and ourselves. Please call the President's attention to the fact that the ruthless employment of our submarines now offers the prospect of compelling England in a few months to make peace.
>
> ZIMMERMANN

Hall ordered that all copies except the original and one decrypted copy be destroyed, given its obvious importance. He was not convinced that Germany's intention to begin unrestricted submarine warfare on 1 February would persuade President Wilson to declare war. Publication of the telegram in the US would force his hand but this could compromise the work of Room 40. He was even reluctant to pass it to the Foreign Office for security reasons. However, if he could acquire a copy, he could claim that it was one of the messages passing from Washington to Mexico and that it had been decrypted by the American Intelligence Service. Hall showed the telegram to Lord Hardinge, the

Permanent Secretary at the Foreign Office on 5 February and explained that the dispatch had not been in Europe and at worst, he could disclose its origins in secret to the American Government. At the same time, Hall secured from his agent in Mexico, copies of all telegrams sent by Bernstorff to Eckardt since 18 January.

On 8 February, Room 40 decrypted a second telegram from Zimmermann to Mexico:

> Most Secret. Decypher personally.
> Provided there is no danger of secret being betrayed to USA, you are desired without further delay to broach the question of an Alliance to the President. The definite conclusion of an alliance, however, is dependent on the outbreak of war between Germany and the USA. The President might even now, on his own account, sound Japan.
>
> If the President declines from fear of subsequent revenge you are empowered to offer him a definite alliance after conclusion of peace provided Mexico succeeds in drawing Japan into the alliance.
>
> ZIMMERMANN

Hall decided that the best solution was for President Wilson to release the telegram and say that it had been obtained and decrypted on American soil by Americans.

Hall consulted Balfour, the Foreign Secretary, who knew of Room 40's activities, having been First Lord of the Admiralty from 1915 to 1916. He knew that Zimmermann had asked Bernstorff in Washington to send on to Mexico the text he had received, and that this would probably be in the same one-part code used for the direct transmission by the Swedes. This was likely, as it was the only code held by the mission in Mexico. Hall telegraphed the Naval Attaché in New York on 5 February, asking him to get hold of all telegrams sent to the German Embassy in Mexico since 18 January. On 10 February, he received a copy of just what he needed, the version of the telegram sent on from Washington to Mexico, in the one-part code that Room 40 could read. This was said to have been acquired somehow from the Mexican telegraph office by the British Mission and could prove the telegram was authentic without compromising Hall's true sources.

Hall needed to approach the Americans while at the same time, protecting his source, Room 40. He elected to speak to Edward Bell at the American Embassy. Bell had been posted to the US Embassy in London as Second Secretary on 1 September 1913, and had quickly established good relations with Hall and his staff, particularly Herschell and Serocold. He had the confidence of the US ambassador to Britain, Walter Hines Page[72], who had taken up his post in 1913 and was much more pro-British than President Wilson. Bell provided a trusted link between the US and British Intelligence. Hall preferred to deal with Bell, as the US was neutral so their Naval Attaché, Captain Powers Symington, and his five assistants could not be given detail of British intelligence activities. Germany was active in the US through the activities of Ambassador Bernstorff, which included subsidising anti-British German-American and Irish-American organisations, stirring up trouble in India by funding Indian nationalists, organising the cutting of the Canadian Pacific Railway, sabotaging American factories working for the Allies and planting bombs on British merchant ships sailing from US ports. The American security services were not equipped to deal with these problems. Apart from Bell, Hall liaised with the British Ambassador in Washington, Sir Cecil Spring-Rice and made use of one of the British Naval Attachés in Washington, Captain Guy Gaunt. He kept Gaunt and his colleagues well informed, and wrote to them personally. He also liaised with Mr (later Sir) William Wiseman, a British businessman and Wall Street banker who became head of the British Secret Service in the US.[73]

Hall waited until 22 February to show the telegram to the Americans, presumably because he wanted to have a fully recovered text which would seem to have been acquired from an original text version, rather than through interception and decryption. On 23 February, Balfour handed the text of the Zimmermann Telegram to Walter Page, the US ambassador, and the following day, Page cabled President Wilson and the Secretary of State, Robert Lansing, and it reached Washington at 8.30 pm. His cable read:

> Confidential for the President and Secretary of State
> Balfour has handed me the translation of a cypher message from Zimmermann, the German Secretary of State for Foreign Affairs, to the General Minster in Mexico, which was sent via Washington and relayed by Bernstorff on January 19th.
>
> You can probably obtain a copy of the text relayed by Bernstorff from the cable office in Washington. The first group is the number of the telegram, 130, and the second is 13042, indicating the number of the code used. The last but two is 97556, which is Zimmermann's signature.
>
> I shall send you by mail a copy of the cypher text and of the decode into German, and meanwhile I give you the English translation as follows:-

> [Here follows the text as printed above.]
>
> The receipt of this information has so greatly exercised the British Government that they have lost no time in communicating it to me to transmit to you in order that you may be able, without delay, to make such dispositions as may be necessary in view of the threatened invasion of our territory.
>
> The following paragraph is strictly confidential.
>
> Early in the war the British Government obtained possession of a copy of the German cypher code used in the above message and have made it their business to obtain copies of Bernstorff's cypher messages to Mexico, amongst others, which are sent back to London and decyphered here. This accounts for their being able to decipher this message from the German Government to their representative in Mexico and also for the delay from January 19 until now in their receiving the information.
>
> This system has hitherto been a jealously guarded secret and is only divulged now to you by the British Government in view of the circumstances and their friendly feelings towards the United States. They earnestly request that you will keep the source of your information and the British Government's method of obtaining it profoundly secret, but they put no prohibition on the publication of the Zimmermann telegram itself.
>
> The copies of this, and other telegrams, were not obtained in Washington, but were bought in Mexico.
>
> I have thanked Balfour for the service his Government has rendered us and suggest that a private official message of thanks from our Government to his would be appreciated.
>
> I am informed that this information has not yet been given to the Japanese Government but I think it is not unlikely that, when it reaches them, they will make a public statement on it in order to clear up their position regarding America and prove their good faith in their allies.

On 28 February, Page informed Hall that he was instructed to thank Balfour for the information and that the telegram would be revealed on 1 March. Later that day, Bell gave Hall three messages from 17 January from Bernstorff to German legations in South America. In Lansing's absence, Frank Polk, a counsellor for the State Department, brought it to the attention of the President on 27 February. Wilson wanted to publish it immediately but Polk persuaded the President to await Lansing's return. The following day, Polk obtained a copy of the original message filed by Bernstorff in Washington to the German Minister in

Mexico City. Lansing then communicated a paraphrased version of the text of the Zimmermann Telegram to the Associated Press at 6.00 pm for release after 10.00 pm. On 1 March, the English text was published in the morning papers in the US and then discussed in Congress. Following questions about the telegram's authenticity, Lansing cabled Page the same day as follows:

> Some members of Congress are attempting to discredit Zimmermann message charging that message was furnished to this Government by one of the belligerents. This Government has not the slightest doubt as to its authenticity, but it would be of the greatest service if the British Government would permit you or someone in the Embassy to personally decode the original message we have secured from the telegraph office in Washington and then cable to Department German text. Assure Mr. Balfour that the Department hesitated to make this request but feels that this course will materially strengthen its position and make it possible for the Department to state that had secured the Zimmermann note from our own people.

The State Department had found the telegram in the Washington cable office and wanted to assure the American public that it possessed and deciphered it. On 1 March, Page wrote to the Secretary of State:

> The question of our having a copy of the code has been taken up, but there appear to be serious difficulties. I am told actual code would be of no use to us as it was never used straight, but with a great number of variations which are known to only one or two experts here. They cannot be spared to go to America. If you will send me copies of B's cypher telegrams the British authorities will gladly decipher them as quickly as possible, giving me copies as fast as deciphered. I could telegraph texts or summaries in matters of importance and send the others by pouch. Neither Spring Rae nor Gaunt knows anything about this matter.

It was eventually agreed that the Washington cable office version of the Zimmermann telegram would be deciphered in London by Edward Bell with the assistance of De Grey. Bell used the part solution of German diplomatic code 13040 to decode the first part of the message, partly to satisfy himself that the solution was genuine. He then handed over the tedious job of decoding the entire message to De Grey.[74] On 2 March, Page sent the following message to Lansing:

> Bell took the cipher text of the German messages contained in your 4494 of yesterday to the Admiralty and there, himself, deciphered it from the German code which is in the Admiralty's possession. The first group, 130, indicates Bernstorff's number of telegram number ...The second group, 13042, indicates the code to be used in deciphering the cipher telegram. From the third group onwards, message reads as follows: [German text followed]. Punctuations are given as in German text. I am sending decode into German, group by group, by tomorrow's pouch.

The text of the Zimmermann Telegram was given to the Associated Press's Edwin M. Hood and appeared in the American press nationwide on 2 March. Not surprisingly, it caused a sensation in America. The German-American press said it was a fraud but a senator offered a resolution in the Senate asking the President to give assurances that it was genuine. He duly issued a statement through Lansing saying 'I have the honour to state that the Government is in possession of evidence which establishes the fact that the note referred to is authentic and that the evidence was procured by this Government during the present week.'

The following day, Zimmermann admitted that the communication was authentic and Germany officially admitted that the telegram was genuine. His justification was that 'it was not only the right but the duty of our Government to take precautions in time, in the event of a warlike conflict with the United States, in order to balance if possible the adhesion of our enemies to a new enemy. The German Minister in Mexico was therefore, in the middle of January, instructed, should the United States declare war, to offer the Mexican Government an alliance and arrange further details.'

On 21 March, Wilson recalled Congress and it met on 2 April. In his speech, the President commented that 'the intrigues of the German Government had played their part in serving to convince us at last that that Government entertains no real friendship for us, and means to act against our peace and security at its convenience. It means to stir up enemies against us at our very doors; the intercepted Note to the German Minster at Mexico City is eloquent evidence.' On 6 April, shortly after 13.00 hours, the American Congress declared the existence of a state of war with Germany. American reaction to the telegram is best summed up by a message from Gaunt to Hall on 6 March when the chairman declared that 'the Zimmermann note was a forgery, and was practically unanimously supported by the whole bunch.' Gaunt goes on to say that

> I then told them that information has been conveyed to me by US authorities, that I was satisfied that the note was correct, and a little surprised that they should cross-examine me on it instead of accepting the word of their President. That carried the day completely. The above is an illustration of the way it was received over here, nineteen out of twenty men believed it was a forgery, and had not Zimmermann come out with his statement on Saturday, I think it would have done us a great deal of harm.

Hall now needed to ensure that the Germans did not discover the truth behind the exposing of the Zimmermann Telegram. To do so, a number of fanciful stories were put about and while they did not prevent the Germans from trying to discover the truth, they continued to use the same code, thus enabling Hall to follow their every move. A communication from Berlin to Mexico on 4 April 1917 confirmed the German view that no betrayal took place in Mexico and that the theft had taken place in Washington. The Germans continued to negotiate with Mexico, using the same compromised cipher and each deciphered telegram was passed by Hall to the American Embassy and then on to Washington. Once the US declared war, Mexico decided to remain neutral.

Hall's brilliant plan had worked and all the countries involved assumed the Americans were responsible for the discovery and decoding of the Zimmermann Telegram. In fact, attacks on the British Government and its Intelligence Service appeared in the British press, saying that their secret service was inferior to that of the Americans. Page acknowledged Hall's contribution in a note to the President on 17 March 1918, but really he was, without realising it, praising the efforts of Room 40, the inner workings of which he knew very little:

> Hall is one genius that the war has developed. Neither in fiction nor in fact can you find any such man to match him. Of the wonderful things that I know he has done, there are several that it would take an exciting volume to tell. The man is a genius – a clear case of genius. All other secret service men are amateurs by comparison. If there be any life left me after this war and if Hall's abnormal activity and ingenuity have not caused him to be translated, I wish to spend a week with him in some quite place and then spend a year in writing out what he will have told me. That's the shortest cut to immortality for him and for me that has yet occurred to me. I shall never meet another man like him: that were too much to expect.
>
> And (whether it becomes me to say so or not) Bell and I have his complete confidence and that fact entitles us to some special

> consideration in the esteem of our friends. For Hall can look through you and see the very muscular movements of your immortal soul while he is talking to you. Such eyes has the man! My Lord! I do study these men here most diligently who have this vast and appalling War-Job. These are most uncommon creatures among them – men about whom our great grandchildren will read in their school histories; but, of them all, the most extraordinary is this naval officer – of whom, probably, they'll never hear. He locks up certain documents 'not to be opened till 20 years after this date.' I've made up my mind to live twenty years more. I shall be present at the opening of that safe.

Page had written to Hall on 24 October 1917 congratulating him on the award of his KCMG as had the advisor to the American President, Colonel House[75] on 22 September 1917. The Zimmermann Telegram affair has been described as one of the greatest intelligence coups in history by some historians and linked to Hall's name forever. According to the doyen of American cryptography, William Friedman: 'Among the official cryptograms which have been intercepted and translated by governmental authorities other than those for whom they were intended, the most important of all time, either in war or peace, is undoubtedly the one deciphered by the British Naval Intelligence which is known to historians as the Zimmermann Telegram.'[76]

While AGD was not directly involved in work on the Zimmermann Telegram, as a senior member of Room 40 he was party to all stages of it. What a mentor Hall proved to be for AGD and he certainly served as an inspiration for his future career in intelligence. AGD was able to witness at first hand the master at work in deploying intelligence to best effect. He also saw the benefit of establishing trust with foreign intelligence officers. While the American Edward Bell played a crucial role in the Zimmermann Telegram affair, little has been written about it.[77] Yet it was his relationship with British naval intelligence, supported by his superior in the State Department, Leland Harrison,[78] which facilitated the successful deployment of the Zimmermann Telegram and was, arguably, the start of the special relationship between the US and Britain intelligence matters.

So who was Edward Bell? Born in New York City on 9 October 1892 into a well-established family, he attended Harvard University and became a close friend of one of his classmates, Franklin (later President) Roosevelt. The two men visited Britain during their junior year at Harvard and both graduated in 1904. After serving two years as vice and deputy consul general in Cairo, Bell joined the Foreign Service, serving in Tehran and Cuba. His post of Second Secretary in the US Embassy in London was obtained at his own request. Harrison had been obtaining copies of all of Bernstorff's cables and would then get Bell to ask for them to be decoded by Hall's 'people'. As Bell built up a trusted relationship with Room 40, he dealt directly with the key codebreakers, including Serocold and Herschell and even Montgomery, generally considered to be Room 40's whizz. Correspondence between Bell and Harrison[79] demonstrates the clandestine nature of their relationship. For example, on 20 September 1917 Bell wrote to Harrison as follows:

> My dear Harrison:
> The Intelligence Department of the Admiralty are trying to keep in as close touch as possible with affairs in Mexico on account of the German intrigues there. Their interest is due in part of course to the fact that German intrigues anywhere require watching, and also because of the great importance to the British and Allied Mexico cause generally of keeping the Tampico oil wells safe.
>
> Since Hohler left Mexico about a year ago the British Government has had practically no representative there, except some stray Consuls, and the Legation is, I believe in the hands of a Chargé des Affaires who has no diplomatic quality. The Foreign Office have apparently left Mexico out of their calculations for some time past and as a result none of the reports from diplomatic officers which would ordinarily be available for the Admiralty's Intelligence Service now come from Mexico.
>
> The Director of Intelligence at the Admiralty has assigned one of his officers to the duty of making a comprehensive study of Mexican affairs, and this officer has asked me if I could obtain information for him on the subject of which I attach a list. If you could at an early date let me have the information he desires I should be greatly obliged to you, as we are so much indebted to the Intelligence Department of the Admiralty that anything I can do to meet their wishes in return I am only too anxious to do.
>
> The officer in question, with whom I had a talk yesterday, says they understand that some sort of an expedition in the nature of a raid against our territory is planning in Lower California, and that a good deal of gun-running is going on there in which Japanese and Austrians are implicated. The arms for this adventure will have to come from either Spain or South America, and there is an impression here that since the lifting of our embargo against the import of munitions of war into Mexico a good deal of arms and ammunition have come in from Spain to Vera Cruz on the ships of the Compania

> Transatlantico. German officers are also involved and the attempt may also extend to the Tampico district.
>
> If you could let me have the information in question piece meal, if this is more convenient than sending it all at once, it would do equally well. In any case I hope you will be able to do as I request, and I don't think the British Authorities have any desire to poach on our preserves. But as you are aware they get a great deal of information here and in Spain about what is going on in Mexico and they want to be in a position to check up their information intelligently.

On 30 October 1917 he wrote:

> My Dear Harrison:
> I hasten to acknowledge with thanks the receipt of your letter of October 15th in reply to mine of September 20th transmitting the Mexican questionnaire. I should be indeed grateful if you would let me have some information as soon as convenient for I am under such obligations to the Admiralty for services rendered to our Government that I must do everything I can to meet their wishes.
>
> With reference to the last paragraph of your letter, the British authorities are not waiting to get information from us before giving us what they have regarding Mexico, as I think our telegrams No, 7242 of September 24th, 5 P.M., No. 7405 of October 12th, 11 A.M., and No. 7546 of October 27th, 4 P.M. will show. All the information contained in these telegrams came from the Admiralty.

Another interesting example is found in correspondence from Bell dated 15 February 1918 in which he enclosed a letter from an Irishman in New York to his brother, a priest in Dublin, which contains interesting information about the Irish situation and Irish organisations in the US. There are numerous examples of code words being used such as this exchange: Harrison from Bell on 14 January 1919: 'My letter No. 22, January 6th. Charlie will arrive tomorrow night and has more golf balls for you. Please have him met.' Harrison from American Mission in Paris to Bell on 18 January 1919: 'Golf balls satisfactory and we can use them at once.'

Following the public release of the Zimmermann Telegram, intelligence continued to flow between Britain and the United States. On 31 August 1917, Page informed President Wilson that:

> Admiral Hall has given me a number of documents comprising German cipher messages between German diplomatic officers and

> the Berlin Foreign Office, chiefly relating to the Argentine and definitely implicating the Swedish Government. In view of the negotiations now going on between Germany and the Argentine, the British Government hope that you will immediately publish these telegrams asking that their origins be kept secret as in the case of the Zimmermann Telegram. I have the cipher originals and sending them to you by a trustworthy messenger [Wiseman] who will deliver them into your hands about 12–15 September. These telegrams will prove that Sweden has continuously user her legations and pouches and her code to transmit official information between Berlin and German diplomatic offices.

Hall would share diplomatic and naval intelligence with the Americans when it was to the Allies' advantage, but he would not share cryptographic expertise or assist them in their own efforts in the field despite representations from the State Department and the Office of Naval Intelligence. The US War Department set up a cipher bureau in June 1917 and recruited Herbert O. Yardley as its head. The US Navy tended to defer to Yardley's group and Hall supplied an out-of-date HVB book used by the German High Seas Fleet until March 1915. Meanwhile, the US continued through Bell to provide Room 40 with intercepted messages, some old and some new from Stockholm and other neutral countries. By July 1918, Harrison was pressing for complete cooperation and exchange of information. Yardley visited London in August 1918 and later claimed[80] that Hall refused to give him the VB code but did give him that of a neutral country and promised to send a two-volume German naval code to Washington for his use. This claim is considered unlikely by most historians.[81]

***

By 1917, interception was almost 100 per cent complete for North Sea traffic. Later in the war, the British tried to organise more systematic interception. De Grey led a small cryptanalytical team to Italy (Otranto and Rome) to work on Austrian naval codes but the Austrian fleet made little use of W/T. A separate unit was set up in Malta to work on the German U-boat codes in use in the Mediterranean. Room 40 reached its peak towards the end of the war and kept pace with successive innovations and complications introduced by the enemy. Early traffic analysis and direction finding became increasingly important and kept the intelligence flow going while new systems were being overcome.

According to Admiral Sir William James, writing in December 1936:

> It is extremely unlikely that we will enjoy all those remarkable advantages in another war. The whole of the movements of our main Fleet and the defence of our trade were to a great extent dependent on this particular form of intelligence which was hatched in Room 40. But a point that is very often forgotten is that … it was during the last year of the War that a system was introduced whereby an intelligence section, thanks to careful study of everything that came their way, were actually able, at one period, I remember, to keep up a flow of intelligence when there was no cryptography which was very little different from that which was being issued when we enjoyed 100 per cent of cryptography.[82]

The large number of translated decrypts soon swamped Operations Division (OD) and Room 40 began to weed out unimportant communications. This was necessary as OD did not have the capability to thoroughly analyse all of the traffic coming through. Recording and research devolved to Room 40. And from February 1916, their selected and annotated decrypts were supplemented with a daily summary. Room 40 gradually comprised carefully selected, trained and experienced intelligence officers and by the summer of 1918, the organisation was operating effectively. From 1 July 1918, a branch of Room 40's Intelligence Section 'was set apart to survey and examine all wireless messages as they arrived and to report from time to time as necessary on the development of the situation'.[83] Another unit, divided into parties specialising according to area or type of vessel, carried out intelligence research. It could be said that Ewing's small cryptanalytic of 1914 had developed by 1918 into a full-blown naval Sigint centre.[84]

All Sigint organisations have to deal with problems, both personal and political, and Room 40 was no different in this regard. According to Frank Birch, the official historian of British Sigint from 1914 to 1945:

> [The] Admiralty's failings in dealing with Sigint were due in part to Oliver's overwork and a reluctance to delegate as COS. He slept in the War Room, rarely left it and insisted on drafting reports based on Sigint himself. Beatty complained that Room 40 gave Oliver 'priceless information which he sits on until it is too late for the Sea Forces to take action. What it amounts to is the War Staff has developed into a One Man Show. The man is not born yet who can run it by himself.'[85]

The un-naval language of the civilian cryptographers annoyed navy personnel. Even AGD, despite years of teaching German at Osborne, translated an early decrypt as 'The Fleet will proceed into harbour athartwise'. One of his colleagues produced an equally bizarre translation: 'Fisherman have reported that a destroyer with a bulwark over the sternpost rammed and sank a submarine.' Through Hope's efforts, Room 40 staff increasingly used correct naval jargon.[86] Traditional naval men such as Rear Admiral Thomas Jackson (DOO) were annoyed by professors dressed in RNVR uniforms but who forgot to salute, mislaid parts of their uniform or wore their cap back to front.[87]

William Clarke later wrote of Jackson: 'Admiral Thomas Jackson displayed supreme contempt for the work of Room 40. He never came into the room during the writer's time there except on two or three occasions, on one of which he came in to complain that one of the locked boxes in which the information was sent him had cut his hand, and on another to say, at a time when the Germans had introduced a new code book, "Thank God, I shan't have any more of this damned stuff!"'[88]

Hope left Room 40 in early 1917 to serve at sea, was awarded the DSO and became a Rear-Admiral after the war. He was replaced by Admiral Sir William James[89] who had been Hall's executive officer aboard the *Queen Mary*. James decided that all those not already in uniform should receive commissions as lieutenants in the RNVR. While some of the senior civilians in Room 40 were not keen on the idea, AGD was not one of them and duly received his commission as a lieutenant commander on 8 July 1917.[90]

By the autumn of 1917, the battle with the U-boats was turning in favour of the British as Room 40 continued to locate German submarines and forecast their intentions. It was working smoothly and seemed to be able to handle anything which came its way. Even when the Germans introduced a more frequent change of key and some new ciphers, apart from the odd delay, Room 40 was able to keep a steady flow of intelligence to OD and the Commander-in-Chief up to the end of 1917. In April 1918, it became clear that the Germans were trying to maintain wireless silence. By November, there were indications that the High Seas Fleet was sailing but then Room 40 became aware that the German sailors were refusing to put to sea. Hall's work was done as the war wound down and from July 1914 until November 1918, he had not had a day off. While some thought of him as a future Foreign Secretary, he had also made enemies. He had crossed swords with the press barons and by-passed regulations to get things done and therefore was not liked by the civil staff who felt they had lost control of the Navy. He had hoped to attend the peace conference as Head of the Intelligence Bureau but was told that he was not going. He also received no post-war honours.[91]

Writing after the war, Churchill gave his view of the contribution of British naval Sigint:

> Our Intelligence service has won and deserved world-wide fame. More than perhaps any other Power, we were successful in the war in penetrating the intentions of the enemy. Again and again the forecasts both of the military and of the naval Intelligence Staffs were vindicated to the wonder of friends and the chagrin of foes. The three successive chiefs of the Naval Intelligence Division, Captain Thomas Jackson, Rear-Admiral Oliver and lastly, Captain Hall, were all men of mark in the service, and continuously built and extended an efficient and profound organization. There were others – a brilliant confederacy – whose names even now are wrapt [*sic*] in mystery. Our information about German naval movements was principally obtained (1) from the reports of secret agents in neutral and enemy countries and particularly Germany, (2) from the reports of our submarines, which lay far up in the Heligoland Bight in perilous vigilance, and (3) from a special study we had made of the German wireless. In this we were for a time aided by great good luck.
>
> The Admiralty thus carried to an unrivalled and indeed unapproached degree of perfection our means of fixing the position and, by successive positions, the course of any enemy ship that used its wireless installation.[92]

German histories after the war concurred with this assessment and according to Vice-Admiral Reinhard Scheer, Commander-in-Chief of the German High Seas Fleet from 18 January 1916:

> The English received news through their 'directional stations' which they already had in use, but which were only introduced by us at a much later period. In possessing them the English had a very great advantage in the conduct of the war, as they were thus able to obtain quite accurate information of the locality of the enemy as soon as any wireless signals were sent by him. In the case of a large fleet, whose separate units are stationed far apart and communication between them is essential, an absolute cessation of all wireless intercourse would be fatal to any enterprise.[93]

The use of intercepted traffic by Allied forces during WW1 to determine the enemy's order of battle, played a vital role in their ultimate success. This early form of traffic analysis, which would prove so effective for

Allied Forces in WW2, had a major impact on the land war in Europe during WW1. According to the head of intelligence of the American Expeditionary Force (AEF) in 1917–18, 'frequently, as many as two-thirds of the identification of enemy divisions along the front became known due to the ability of the Allies to decode intercepted wireless messages'.[94]

It is hard to determine exactly how many encrypted (using either codes or ciphers) German messages on the Western Front were broken during 1917–18. From the Spring of 1917 until the end of the war, the radio monitoring personnel of each British Army intercepted around 150–200 German messages per week. On occasion, individual Allied stations intercepted 120 German radio messages each day.[95] In 1917 alone, British codebreakers solved several hundred encoded German messages.[96] In that year according to Friedman, 'the text of one week was sufficient to break into a new [German] code, and by the end of three weeks, messages were being read by us as quickly and almost as completely by the code-officers as by the enemy'.

The French reconstructed some thirty front-line codes of the German Army during the war. In 1918, the Americans, British and French together continually penetrated one of the two main German trench code systems, had much success with the other, and sometimes solved both of the two main systems used near the front lines. Ferris estimates that the British codebreaking effort probably yielded in terms of text, up to twelve stencilled pages per day.

Between January 1915 and July 1916, the British Army paid little attention to Sigint but from July 1916, it was recognised as an increasingly valuable and reliable form of information. By 1918, the British Second Army noted that the,

> special nature of wireless intelligence called for very close liaison between I(e) and the personnel responsible for assessing the enemy's order of battle. At the same time, according to a well-informed American source, British GHQ regarded signals intelligence on the enemy's dispositions and order of battle as being 'always correct and, … by far the most valuable identification of divisional positions and intentions outside of capture of a prisoner. They are even more valuable in a way because they anticipate coming events before prisoners can be obtained'.[97]

According to Ferris, a reasonably efficient system emerged during WW1 in which Sigint was collected by signals personal who were generally controlled by intelligence officers. It was assessed by the latter before distribution to operations staff and commanders. The British Army handled Sigint as well as any other army during WW1. Sigint staff grew from seventy-five in mid-1916 to 13,300 by the end of the war. In 1917–18 around 250 men served with listening sets, 600 served in the eleven WOGS in the field and around 200 in the War Office.

Apart from Room 40 and MI1(b), there was a branch of the Intelligence department of the Indian Army as well as agencies at the GHQs of the army in the field. In December 1917, Hindenburg's Chief of Staff, Erich von Ludendorff, warned the army commanders that:

> From a map issued by the British Intelligence Service (that is, by the British General Headquarters (GHQ) in France), captured at CAMBRAI, it appears that the enemy was completely informed regarding the distribution of our forces in the line and the divisions which had been withdrawn. On the other hand, he was almost completely in the dark regarding the divisions newly brought into back areas of the Army. Judging from the military situation at that time, it is to be supposed that the enemy obtained part of his information from prisoners' statements. The larger part, however, he undoubtedly obtained from his Intercepting Service. The enemy, and particularly the British, installs his mobile intercepting stations even under the most difficult conditions. The fact that our signal discipline is completely wanting, particularly on battle fronts, plays directly into the hands of the enemy's Intelligence. The fighting troops must understand the necessity for this discipline, otherwise there is grave danger that the enemy will prematurely learn our intentions, which are calculated on surprise and will be able to take counter-measures accordingly.[98]

Little is known of AGD's personal work during WW1. While he would later document the work of Room 40, he always resisted the temptation to describe his own work. There is no record of his activities apart from examples of decrypts bearing his initial. (see Appendix 4). However, as a senior member of the Watch, he would have had a full workload. Despite this, AGD found time for romance. A watchkeeper had been working in Room 40 from 1914 to 1917 as a linguist with good French and German. Dorothy Gilliat was one of five children of a successful Leeds businessman, Arthur Gilliat. Known as 'D' to her sisters, she was born in 1891 and read English at Lady Margaret Hall (LMH), Oxford from 1911 and was known to all her friends there as DG. AGD's sister, Biddy, was one of her year at LMH. She graduated in 1914 and did clerical work in Leeds Military Hospital. She was remembered by friends there as:

> Very pretty and attractive with blue eyes, her ready and sympathetic smile, and a quizzical, rather deprecating lift of an eyebrow. She had poise and elegance, she loved social life, and worked the dons hard in those days of the chaperons. But there was another side. D.G. was a fine student who used her excellent brain, but with no parade of industry. Under her charm and a gentle mocking façade was a serious attitude to life. In anything she did she was utterly reliable and competent; she was never shattered by disaster, but undaunted in every crisis. To her friends her sympathy was unfailing.

AGD began courting Dorothy and in 1917 finally asked her to marry him. In a telegram to her parents in Leeds, she sought their approval: 'Greatly surprised. Deeply thankful. Please may I marry Alastair. Wire reply to D R, 5 War Office Annexe Whitehall Place.' Their response was positive and AGD and Dorothy were married the same year. The following year, on 7 January 1918, AGD was appointed an Officer of the Order of the British Empire (OBE), an honour which had been created in 1917 by King George V.

At the 11th hour on the 11th day of the 11th month of 1918, WW1 came to an end. At 5.00 am that morning, Germany, now lacking manpower and supplies, facing imminent invasion and revolution at home, signed an armistice agreement with the Allies in a railway carriage outside Compiégne in France. The war left nine million soldiers dead and 21 million wounded, with Germany, Russia, Austria-Hungary, France, and Great Britain each losing nearly a million or more lives. In addition, at least five million civilians died from disease, starvation or exposure. Vast crowds gathered in London's Trafalgar Square to celebrate but the joyous mood was short-lived. Post-war Britain was facing a range of political, economic and social problems.

In December 1918, a month after the Armistice, the Room 40 team celebrated their wartime success (some 15,000 German messages decrypted and read) with a concert party in Chelsea. AGD and a colleague composed and sang a duet for their team:

> While some say that the boche was not beaten by Foch
> But by Winston or Ramsey MacDonald
> There are others who claim that the *coup de grace* came
> From the Knoxes (our Dilly and Ronald)
>
> It was Tiarks and Thring who with charts and with string
> Gave the U-boats their oily quietus

Yet without the Lord Mayor in his diplomat's lair
The Huns *might* have managed to beat us.

There are Zeppelins about, the key isn't out
And Lord knows what's afoot in the Bight now
When the tube basket's crammed and each message is jammed
Operations want all the news right now ....

There was also a performance of a parody of *Alice's Adventures in Wonderland,* written by Frank Birch and Dilly Knox. This party marked the end of Room 40 as most of the staff were returning to their pre-war lives. It would be left to AGD to keep Britain's cryptanalytical capability alive for the next twenty years, as the gathered group would hear at the end of a song near the end of the show:

No more delights like these for us
But *Denniston* will *never*
Desert his solitary post.
He will go on for ever.

As evidence of the high regard which AGD was held by his Room 40 colleagues, they saw fit to present him and his wife with a silver salver.

The very existence of Room 40 was kept secret until 1925, when former American ambassador in London, Walter Page, published some letters in a magazine article, telling how these had been discovered through the Intelligence Division of the British Navy. Lord Balfour, Chancellor of Edinburgh University, revealed to Prime Minster Stanley Baldwin, at a university lunch, that the university's Principal, Alfred Ewing, had been head of an organisation responsible for the vital decrypts. Two years later, at the request of Balfour and in response to general pressure, Ewing agreed to give a lecture in the university's Assembly Hall to an audience of 1,500. Given the Admiralty's misgivings, Ewing agreed not to publish the text. It was eventually published by the Royal Society of London.[99] As for AGD, his work in signals intelligence had only just begun.

Chapter 3

Between the Wars

True to the words in the Room 40 ditty, AGD did indeed 'go on', and at the conclusion of hostilities, he was sent to Scapa Flow to interpret for Admiral Sir David Beatty, Commander-in-Chief of the Grand Fleet, at the surrender of the German fleet. He would later document his time at Scapa Flow[1] and the problems that he faced:

> I was a landsman on board a battleship, and a lot of my time was taken up in trying to conform to the life therein, no easy matter if you remember that it is really a foreign land where the inhabitants have a distinctive mode of life, even a distinctive language and very distinctive habits which to learn in a few days is not an easy matter for a visitor to this foreign land. My impressions of this particular foreign land have nothing at all to do with the matter in hand, namely the surrender of the German Fleet and the end of the motive power which has driven the British Navy for the last twenty years and made it such a wonderful machine. First of all I should like to confess that for the last four years I considered myself, and the department in which I worked, a very important cog in the machine; now for the first time I ran across the 'business end' of the weapon and I realised most strongly what a little cog we were. Practically no one I met had any idea of the existence of such a cog, which was satisfactory to know, as we had tried to conceal our identity. I had to keep a straight face, and lie right well to many an old friend from Osborne days whom I met up there, who wanted to know what my job was. On the whole I fancy I gave myself and my department a highly sensational appearance, such as would rejoice the readers of William le Quex.[2]

On arriving at Rosyth, AGD went directly to HMS *Queen Elizabeth,* Beatty's flagship, to find out what duties were assigned to him. He met an old friend by the name of Spickerwell, who was secretary to the admiral. He actually had no interpreting to do but instead was to act as an intermediary between Beatty, who was concentrating on general policy and his opposite number, the commander-in-chief of the German High Sea Fleet. This dialogue was conducted by means of wireless. AGD was not impressed with Beatty, whom he regarded as 'a very wilful man, and has no mercy on a man or nation he despises'.

They set sail around 2.00 am on 21 November and when *Queen Elizabeth* approached the location of the German fleet, action stations was sounded. AGD reported to Beatty on the signalling bridge and the German ships were spotted at 9.30 am. Beatty informed the Admiralty that he had taken them over and told AGD that he would rather have been able to report that he had sunk them instead. The British fleet then escorted the German fleet into the Firth of Forth.

After completing his duties with Beatty, AGD was transferred to HMS *Lion,* the flagship of the Battle Cruiser Fleet, to escort the German battlecruisers to the Orkneys. Once in Scapa Flow, he boarded the German flagship, *Seydlitz,* to oversee the voyage. AGD felt sorry for the senior German officers:

> They were keen efficient men, who had learnt their work, and made the German Navy their career, and this was the end of it. We knew that many of them had fought a gallant action at Jutland, in fact, the Commodore, a fine looking old norseman with now a very sad expression had been captain of the *Seydlitz* at Jutland where she had been very badly hit. Only fine seamanship in his part had got her home, and now he had to save his ship for this end.

The rest of AGD's stay at Scapa was, in his words, 'dull beyond words'. On returning home, AGD would soon be asked to apply for a job which would shape the rest of his career.

***

In November 1918, along with his scheme for an amalgamated Secret Service, the DMI, William Thwaites, proposed to his naval counterpart, Admiral Hall, that their signals intelligence sections should be united into a single 'School'. Calling the new unit a School would provide cover by stressing the organisation's positive side, for example by studying ways to achieve secure communications.[3] Thwaites had succeeded General Macdonagh, DMI at the War Office from 1916 to 1918, who had been promoted to adjutant-general. Colonel C.N.

French, a senior figure in the Military Intelligence Directorate in London, had left the War Office as well and been replaced by an officer from GHQ, Malcolm Hay. Hay believed that Sir Henry Wilson[4] was responsible for breaking up the staff of Military Intelligence at the War Office and that it was a great blunder. The reorganised Intelligence directorate was now composed almost entirely of officers from GHQ and Hay felt that:

> Thwaites had no previous experience of Intelligence work, and no obvious qualifications for the position, or for the difficult task which it now involved of acting as military adviser at the Peace Conference. Sir George Macdonagh had acquired some useful knowledge about the political situation of Europe, his successor had none. The loss of Colonel Charles French was irreparable; he was perhaps the one man in the Directorate of Military Intelligence during the war who was indispensable.[5]

Hall agreed with Hay's assessment and offered rooms in the Admiralty for the military side to merge 'brain power'. French opposed a rapid amalgamation and argued that during the peace negotiations, the information produced by MI1(b) would be as, or perhaps more important than it had ever been during hostilities. Furthermore, the temperamental nature of the cryptographers meant that their move from Cork Street to the Admiralty could cause problems. Hay was unhappy with the proposed changes as well as the management of the Honours List:

> The distribution of foreign decorations seems to have been successfully controlled at GHQ. An order was issued in 1915 that no officer would be allowed to wear any foreign decoration unless it had been personally presented to him for some specific service. A growing disgust with the traffic in medals was noticeable among soldiers during the latter period of the war. People in the War Office and at GHQ who stood, as the saying was, 'nearest to the bag', always seemed to secure the lion's share of the spoil.[6]

On 10 December 1918, French proposed that a combined cryptographic unit be set up as part of a joint intelligence organisation.[7] Hall was opposed to this but by mid-January 1919 he had been replaced by Commander Hugh Sinclair,[8] who was more cooperative. A new unit would need to be responsible for the construction of British governmental codes and ciphers, work against foreign codes and ciphers and be able to secure a supply of raw material to replace the wartime censorship regime, which would expire with the Government's emergency powers as soon as the peace treaty was ratified.

In January 1919, Lord Curzon (acting Foreign Secretary while Balfour was at the Paris Peace Conference), stated that the Foreign Office was 'the proper place for the new school to be housed'. Sinclair disagreed and argued that it should be located in the Admiralty, as the Service Ministries had the required expertise and 'all the arrangements as regards deciphering messages were already in existence in the Admiralty building'. He went on to say: 'Without wishing to disparage the Foreign Office in the least, it is considered that the atmosphere of calm deliberation which characterizes that department is not suited to an organisation such as the proposed Code and Cypher School, which, above all things, must be a "live" undertaking, especially in connection with the "breaking" of codes and cyphers.'

By 27 February the Admiralty, War Office, Air Ministry and Foreign Office were agreed that there should be a new 'Code and Cypher Department' comprising a code-making 'Code and Cypher School' of about twenty-five people with a budget of £5,000–£6,000 per year and a codebreaking 'secret sub-section' with a budget of £10,000 per year. The War Office drafted a clause for the new Official Secrets Bill which required cable companies to provide all telegrams to the new organisation. In March, the War Office proposed that the new organisation should be headed by Hay with twenty-six staff and a budget of £8,250–£13,400 per year.

In a memo to Lord Drogheda of the Foreign Office dated 28 March 1919, Churchill, now serving as Secretary of State for War and Secretary of State for Air, gave the Admiralty's view of the proposed Code & Cypher School:

> Private and confidential
>
> March 28, 1919,
> Dear Lord Drogheda,
> I had a few minutes conversation with Lord Curzon yesterday on the subject of the new Cypher Department which it is proposed to establish, and concerning which a memorandum is now in his hands, containing the views of the Admiralty and the War Office.
>
> Lord Curzon told me that he hoped to summon a conference at the Foreign Office one day next week to consider the matter, when I should have an opportunity of stating my opinions, and he asked me to send you in advance a memorandum of the points I wished to

raise. I therefore send you herewith the following notes of matters which the Admiralty consider essential in any scheme that may be adopted.

We have in the Section of the Naval Intelligence Department which has dealt with enemy wireless during the war, a great deal of material, some of which is worked out and filed for reference or historical purposes and some of which will require further study. We also have a small remaining nucleus of the expert staff which has done this work during the war. If the Admiralty is to join the new Department, we regard it as essential that this material and staff should be kept together.

Wherever the new Department may be located in peace time, we should have to stipulate that on the outbreak of war the naval portion of its staff should immediately be mobilised and take up their work in the Admiralty. Our experience has proved that in war the deciphering staff must be in the closest possible proximity to the War Staff. We have had to work day and night all the year round, and as immediate action has often had to be taken in consequence of the information which we have supplied, no avoidable delay in transmitting the information to the Operations Division can be allowed.

We should only consent to pool our staff with that of the War Office on condition that Commander A. G. Denniston is placed in charge of the new Department.[9] I do not say this on account of any jealousy of the War Office, or any reluctance to accept a War Office man, but because no one who has not been trained in the conditions under which we have to work could meet the requirements of the Admiralty in time of war. Our work has been done in the face of the enemy and always against time. The messages we have had to decipher were from ships at sea, engaged in actual operations, or from airships also operating. We have had to master a new key every morning before we could begin to read the messages, and sometimes we have had to grapple with two keys in one day!

This has of necessity developed a particular kind of aptitude for the work, which depends for its success more on a study of the psychology of the persons sending out the messages and a sort of instinctive 'flair' for the kind of things they are saying, than upon careful study and analysis for which there is no time.

In the War Office they have dealt with cables which are far more accurate than wireless, and have never had to work against time, and the aptitude they have developed is different from – I do not for a moment suggest it is inferior to that of which the conditions of our

> work have produced. Denniston is not only the best man we have had, but he is the only one we have left with special genius for this work. We shall not be able to retain him in a subordinate capacity, and no advantages of concentration and cooperation with the War Office would compensate us for the loss of his services. If the War Office people are not willing to accept this condition, we should prefer to retain our staff in the Admiralty, but should of course cooperate with them in every other way that is possible.

A conference was held at the Foreign Office on 28 April 1919 to consider the question of the proposed new Code & Cypher School. Present were The Right Hon. Earl Curzon of Kedleston, KG (Chairman), The First Lord of the Admiralty (Walter Long); The Secretary of State for War and Air (Winston Churchill); The DNI, Admiralty; The Deputy Director, Military Intelligence (DDMI), War Office; Captain W.M. James, Deputy Director, Naval Intelligence (DDNI); Captain R.L. Nicholson, Director of Signals Division; Major H.E. Franklin DSO, MC, Secretary; The Earl of Drogheda, Foreign Office. It noted that:

> The Chairman summarized briefly the recommendations of the Inter-departmental conference which recently met to consider the matter, and said that the main question now before the meeting was the housing of the new department, with the establishment of which everyone in principle agreed. In his opinion the arguments in favour of housing the new department in the Admiralty in time of war were unanswerable, but we were providing for its establishment under peace conditions, and in time of peace he thought that the fact that the interest of the intercepted telegrams was practically entirely political indicated that the new department should be housed in the Foreign Office.

It was decided that Curzon, as acting Foreign Secretary, should receive all intercepted telegrams and be responsible for passing them on to the Prime Minister or other Cabinet Ministers concerned when they were of sufficient importance.[10]

A further meeting was held at the Admiralty on 8 May 1919 to further consider the formation of a Code & Cypher School. Present were the DNI, Commodore H.P. Sinclair CB, RN; the Earl of Drogheda, Foreign Office; Captain R.L. Nicholson DSO, RN, Director of Signals Division; Captain W.M. James, DDNI; Lieutenant Colonel W.E. Wynn OBE, Air Intelligence; Commander B. Buxton DSO, Admiralty; Mr. A.P. Waterfield, Treasury; Major M.V. Hay, Reserve of Officers; and Major

H.E. Franklyn, DSO, MM. It agreed that the new unit would be staffed by a head (salary of £1,200), senior assistants (salary of £600–£800 plus war bonus), junior assistants (salary of £200–£500), translators (salary of £200–£300) and clerks (salary in accordance with ordinary gradings).

The question of who would head the new organisation was yet to be decided, with AGD being the Admiralty candidate and Hay that of the War Office. A meeting was held at the Admiralty on 5 August 1919 to resolve the issue.[11] The meeting was chaired by Sinclair, with James, Drogheda, Major-General Bartholomew (DDMI), Colonel Dick (Assistant Director of Military Intelligence, ADMI) and Franklyn in attendance. Sinclair and Bartholomew had interviewed the two candidates. Hay had made it very clear that he would only serve as Head and while he would accept AGD as part of his team, he didn't rate him or want him on it. AGD on the other hand, would work as head or for Hay 'at all events for a time'. Bartholomew thought it was 'intolerable' that Hay 'should attempt to dictate his terms of service in such a manner'. Franklyn noted of Hay and AGD that 'when they were together they could not agree' and was of the view that MI1(b) workers at Cork Street didn't like AGD. James replied that everyone at the Admiralty 'had the highest respect amounting to affection' for AGD. Drogheda thought that Hay was probably cleverer but AGD was a better administrator.

After due consideration, it was agreed that AGD would head up the new organisation.[12] While no official statement of the reason for this decision exists, AGD was probably regarded as a safer pair of hands who looked upon Hall as a father-figure and the Royal Navy as his home. He could be trusted to know his place in the hierarchy as a subordinate to DNI and provide leadership to the cryptanalysts. The words 'Denniston will never desert his solitary post' would prove to be prophetic. Hay, on the other hand, clearly had strong views and pressed for independence from DNI as long as he 'produced the goods'. His notes[13] show him to be a prickly individual who 'for many years after the war refused even to speak to a General'. He refused the OBE offered to him on 12 December 1919.[14] His attitude is perhaps best summed up after he departed quickly on 21 August 1919 by his one-sided view of WW1 codebreaking successes:

> Before decoding the messages, [we] had to reconstruct the code books … All these difficulties were overcome. Cork Street was never defeated … Some publicity has been given to the fact that German Naval messages and German Diplomatic wireless messages between Berlin and Washington were intercepted by the Admiralty

> and read by a section of Naval intelligence housed in Room 40 O.B. All or nearly all of these German intercepts were in code. Various stories are current about the way copies of the German code books were obtained. I do not know which of these stories is the true one. But it is certain that these encoded messages were not read by reconstructing the code books without some outside assistance.

On 24 October 1919, R.R. Scott wrote to the Secretary, War Office; The Secretary, Air Ministry; The Under Secretary of State for Foreign Affairs, Foreign Office; The Under Secretary of State for India, India Office; The Secretary, Ministry of Munitions; The Secretary, Ministry of Food; The Secretary, Ministry of Transport; The Secretary, General Post Office; and the Under-Secretary of State for the Colonies, Colonial Office, making the following points:

> That the War Cabinet has now given approval for the formation of a Government Code & Cypher School under the control of the Director of Naval Intelligence, and that it is proposed that it should commence its duties on the 1st November, 1919.
>
> It has been decided to appoint Commander A.G. Denniston, O.B.E., R.N.V.R. as Head of the Government Code & Cypher School, which will be accommodated in Watergate House, Adelphi, W.C.I. The duties of the Code & Cypher School will be as follows:-
>
> To compile and be responsible for printing all codes and cyphers used by the British Government Departments with the sole exception of those mentioned in paragraph 5 below (this refers to Signal Books and purely Departmental Codes of the three fighting services. However, GC&CS was to advise on the general principles of their construction and the limitation of their 'life'. GC& CS would decide on what is classified as Departmental Codes after consulting relevant Department).
>
> To examine all the British Government Codes and cyphers now in force and the purpose for which they are used, mainly with a view to ascertain and, where necessary, increasing their degree of security; but also so as to ensure that messages shall be free from ambiguity and undue delay ensuing from mutilation in transit, and that they shall be coded in the most economical manner possible.
>
> To maintain the closest liaison with all British Government Departments using codes and cyphers, and to advise them generally in matters relating thereto.
>
> To instruct as large a proportion of Officers as possible who may be employed at any time in coding or cyphering.

> To assist in the preparation of any hand-books or instructions relating to coding or cyphering, or of those concerning the handling of code and cypher messages in general.
>
> It was suggested that the following departments appoint a Liaison Officer with GC&CS: War Office, Air Ministry, Foreign Office, India Office, Colonial Office, Ministry of Munitions, Ministry of Food, Ministry of Transport, General Post Office.

AGD's new organisation was formally called the Government Code and Cypher School (GC&CS). The name itself was invented by Courtney Forbes, a member of the Communications Department of the Foreign Office. Publicly it was 'to advise as to the security of codes and cyphers used by all Government departments and to assist in their provision'. However, its secret directive was 'to study the methods of cypher communications used by foreign powers'. Pressure from DNI and others forced the inclusion in the new Official Secrets Act of a clause instructing all cable companies operating in the UK to hand over for scrutiny copies of all cable traffic passing over their systems within ten days of despatch or receipt. The discussions in 1919 made it clear that the Foreign Office and Lord Curzon recognised the potential of the diplomatic decrypts from GC&CS.[15] Interestingly, the three services were expressly excluded from needing GC&CS's advice.

GC&CS was up and running very quickly and its first decrypts were issued two days after its formation. The new organisation was housed as agreed in Watergate House in the Adelphi in London. Lieutenant-Commander Edward Travis[16] was appointed to run the Construction Section and act as Deputy Head. Travis had experience of naval code book construction, so he took responsibility for cipher security while AGD supervised cipher-breaking. Travis also advised the Admiralty on communications security. However, GC&CS had no authority to advise on good security practice, so his role was limited. This may have led to his losing interest in security, hence the two Admiralty security staff assigned to GC&CS ended up working as cryptanalysts. In the end, the advice from GC&CS to the Admiralty about code and cipher security was very poor.

By December 1919, the GC&CS staff included five seniors (three from MI1(b), two from Room 40), seventeen juniors (ten from MI1(b) and six from Room 40, one from the Foreign Office), three female translators from MI1(b) and thirty female clerks for the Construction Section. Almost all of the traffic being dealt with was of a diplomatic or commercial nature, and it is estimated that between 1 November 1919 and 21 January 1920, 900 decrypts were distributed as follows: Argentina, Denmark, France, Italy, Japan, Norway, Persia, Romania, Sweden, United States, Uruguay: 54.3 per cent; Austria, Chile, Germany, Russia: 14.6 per cent; Greece, Spain: 26.8 per cent; Kingdom of the Hejaz, Poland, Syria: 4.3 per cent.[17]

In mid-1921, Curzon had succeeded Balfour as Foreign Secretary and described the work of GC&CS as 'by far the most important branch of our confidential work. The decrypted telegrams of foreign Govts., are without doubt the most valuable source of our secret information respecting their policy and actions. They provide the most accurate and, withal, intrinsically the cheapest, means of obtaining secret political information that exists.'[18] In February 1921, Walter Hulme Long, who was interested in intelligence matters, was replaced as First Lord at the Admiralty by Arthur Hamilton Lee. On 25 April 1921, Lord Curzon, who had previously argued for GC&CS to be in the Foreign Office, wrote to Lee:

> I think I mentioned to you a little while ago that I proposed with your assent that the Code and Cypher School, which during the war was for very good reason placed under the Admiralty [Curzon seems to have forgotten about MI1(b)], should now be taken over by the Foreign Office, to which nine-tenths of its work appertains.
>
> I was the Chairman of a Conference just two years ago ... at which it was decided to continue the Code & Cypher School in existence [*sic*], and to house it, at any rate for the present, in the Admiralty. The reasons for this decision were that it would be undesirable to deprive the School of the shelter which the Admiralty buildings afforded, that the vote would be more likely to slip through the House of Commons if it came under the Admiralty disguise, and that the Foreign Office might feel more compunction if through the interviews of the Secretary of State with foreign Ambassadors and Ministers he were to profit by information which his own Department had secretly acquired [this rather obscure point does not appear in the minutes].
>
> These reasons struck me at the time as very flimsy – nor did I entertain any of the qualms described in the last paragraph. I deferred however, to the representations of my colleagues ... I now realise that [the arrangement] is both illogical and indefensible.
>
> It is wrong in principle ... the sphere of the activity of the School is now purely political, and the intelligence procured has, except in very rare cases, no relation to, and can be of no value to, the Admiralty.

> In some cases, as you may know, our possession of the ciphers has been detected by foreign Powers, and in the consequent change of ciphers by them we have lost almost immeasurably.
>
> I cannot doubt that there will be an increase in efficiency if the School is brought under the Foreign Office, since the greater part of its work ought to be done in the closest cooperation with us, and our experience of the matter is now very considerable.
>
> Even the argument of the Admiralty 'cover' has ceased to apply; for whereas I was led to believe, two years ago, the Department was likely to be housed in the Admiralty building, it is now domiciled in separate quarters, as detached from one Office as from the other.
>
> What has terrified me most has been the too generous and careless distribution of the material under the existing system. I have already been obliged to resume the powers conferred upon me by the Cabinet Committee of deciding to whom the intercepted telegrams should go, and the danger of a profuse or undiscriminating distribution, I hope, no longer exists.

In May, Lee, who had little interest in intelligence, agreed with Curzon's views and Sinclair did not object. Another factor might well have been the proposed cuts in public expenditure which were aimed mainly at the armed services. These were introduced in 1922 and became known as the 'Geddes Axe'.[19]

On 23 July 1921, the Foreign Office told the Treasury it was taking over GC&CS from the Admiralty along with its staff of eighty-seven and operating costs of £31,464 per year. The change was effected on 1 April 1922 for Treasury budgetary reasons. Sinclair returned to Intelligence as Head of SIS following the death in June of Mansfield Cumming, the Service's first head.[20] By September, he had arranged for GC&CS to come under his control. To appease the Service Ministries, who had complained vigorously in April 1923 that GC&CS had lost its interdepartmental character since it had come under the Foreign Office, the Foreign Office agreed to return five named individuals to the Admiralty in the event of war.[21] The Permanent Under-Secretary at the Foreign Office, Sir Eyre Crowe, devised the compromise of AGD reporting to Sinclair as both Head of SIS and Director of GC&CS but in turn, Sinclair would report to the Foreign Office.[22]

Sinclair and his successor would remain both Head of SIS and Director of GC&CS for more than twenty years. While the armed services kept some intelligence-gathering expertise in the field,[23] SIS in effect acquired monopoly control over British Sigint. This proved to be an effective strategy, and GC&CS provided Whitehall with a constant stream of intercepted and decrypted foreign governments' telegrams. It read the communications of France, Italy, the United States and Japan, and that of many smaller countries. The historian John Ferris later noted that 'the GC&CS was one of the world's largest code-breaking agencies, perhaps the biggest; as effective as any other, better than most, possibly the best on earth between 1919 and 1935'.

AGD's organisation had moved to Queens Gate in 1921 and when Sinclair took over in 1923, he brought SIS and GC&CS together. By 1925, they occupied the third and fourth floors of the Broadway Buildings. This move was opposed by Lord Curzon as it was in Kensington, two miles from Whitehall,[24] but according to AGD, in Kensington 'we were more comfortable rather remote from other departments'.[25] At the end of 1923, GC&CS's staff numbered ninety-one and Sinclair told the Foreign Office that he wanted to reorganise the Service to meet the demands of war.[26] The burden of keeping GC&CS afloat fell on the shoulders of AGD and he regarded his organisation as 'an adopted child of the Foreign Office with no family rights, and the poor relation of the SIS, whose peacetime activities left no cash to spare'. In reality, GC&CS's funding was comparable to other parts of Sinclair's Service. However, he rarely complained since his dogged fidelity as a public servant was equalled by his dislike of publicity. AGD's problem was that because of the secrecy, few in Whitehall knew of the war-winning work of Room 40 and AGD's organisation had few supporters. He was not in a strong position to fight for funds and staff in the lean interwar years. He and his colleagues worked on a shoestring and in a kind of Civil Service limbo. Most Whitehall insiders thought that Room 40 had been wound up at the end of WW1 and were unaware of AGD's new organisation.

Sinclair met with AGD in January 1924 and confirmed that he wanted to integrate the work of GC&CS with that of SIS.[27] GC&CS would be responsible for cryptography and SIS for the distribution of intelligence derived from them. SIS would also supply intelligence and criticism to GC&CS to assist cryptography. Section I of SIS was to 'supply GC&CS with a list of general subjects on which to concentrate . . . Armed Forces Sections of SIS to collaborate'. GC&CS was to 'have full access to SIS records'. By June 1924, because of the large volume of 'intelligence product' available, AGD was told to distribute it directly to GC&CS's customer departments and send copies to Sinclair. However, SIS kept overall control of the distribution of 'Sigint product'.

In 1924, the Cabinet appointed a committee, with General Romer as chairman to advise on the anti-aircraft defence of the UK. One of its recommendations was that the control of the 'Wireless Interception Service' should be taken over by AGD 'at the request of the Fighting

Services and with the consent of the Foreign Office'.[28] To oversee formal coordination within the intelligence services, the 'Cryptography and Interception Committee' (later the 'Co-ordination of W/T Interception Committee') was set up.[29] Sinclair chaired the committee, with membership drawn from the three Service Ministries and GC&CS. The Secretary was an SIS officer, Colonel Arthur Peel, who had previously been Assistant DNI to Sinclair during his tenure as DNI. Peel helped develop a relationship between GC&CS and the Metropolitan Police during the 1920s. In the late 1930s, he helped coordinate the development of wireless intercept service in the Dominions.[30] The Committee's remit went beyond interception and covered cryptanalytic training and war planning, although it never had a controlling role, only one of coordination. While the police interception work was initially intended for suspected illicit wireless transmitters in Britain, from 1927 they began to intercept diplomatic wireless traffic for GC&CS.[31] A sub-committee was set up initially under Peel and then AGD from the mid-1930s. As it only met every two years, it was agreed in July 1928 to form a standing sub-committee which 'should concentrate on formulating definitive recommendations, and should in future prepare agenda for the main committee'. This new 'Y Sub-Committee' as it became known, met fortnightly under AGD and included representatives from the three Services, Scotland Yard, the GPO and the Head of the W/T Board.

GC&CS had to handle its own telegram collection service with an SIS car collecting material from the General Post Office and commercial communications companies daily and delivering them to Broadway, where they were copied and returned within twenty-four hours. The Cable Intercept Section, under Henry Maine, controlled the collection effort. Similar collections took place in India, Tehran, Haifa and Jerusalem. Between 1920 and 1927, GC&CS was producing on average 3,500 reports annually. These were known as 'flimsies' or 'BJs' (the file covers used to circulate GC&CS reports in the Foreign Office were blue, hence 'blue jackets'. Confusingly, in the early 1920s, army reports were referred to as 'black jumbos'.)

The GC&CS reports were verbatim transcriptions of decrypted messages, translated unless the original was in English or French, in which case the customer would be able to read it for himself. GC&CS did not attempt to provide context or explanation apart from cross-referencing them with related reports. AGD told colleagues within GC&CS that their role at this point was simply decryption. This was openly opposed by some in GC&CS such as William Clarke of the Naval Section, a veteran of Room 40. He firmly believed that GC&CS should be producing intelligence reports, as its predecessor Room 40 had done.

However, Sinclair and AGD knew that customer departments regarded intelligence assessments as their domain and would have resisted any attempt by GC&CS to overstep agreed boundaries.

The distribution of 'BJs' changed from a restricted circulation of Admiralty, Foreign Office and War Office to include the Prime Minister, Lord Privy Seal, Colonial Office, India Office, Air Ministry and the Home Office 'Directorate of Intelligence'. GC&CS's Naval Section was the first in GC&CS to be dedicated to military matters, and worked against specific foreign navies.

It was the only GC&CS military section funded by GC&CS and the only one to use non-cryptanalytic techniques such as traffic analysis. When GC&CS had moved to Foreign Office control, Clarke became one of GC&CS's liaison officers to the Admiralty and eventually head of the new Naval Section in GC&CS. Sinclair, as a former DNI, took a personal interest in their work and Clarke frequently bypassed AGD. However, from 1925, Sinclair, AGD and the Admiralty put constraints on the overzealous Clarke.[32]

***

With his heavy workload, AGD found it difficult to find time for friends and family. His wife Dorothy worked regularly at the Chelsea Day Nursery and at the Infant Welfare Centres in Chelsea and Shadwell and would continue to do so until 1939. The couple were very much in love and he talked freely to her about his work. When she became pregnant in 1924, they called the child 'X', assuming it was male. When their daughter Margaret was born instead on 21 May 1925, they called her 'Y'. The much anticipated son Robin was born 19 months later on Christmas Day 1926. AGD was a good father, even though he was so busy, as Robin remembered:

> Through all this my father was perhaps the most important part. When I fell downstairs during a party (at age four) I was brought down, screaming with pain and fear, to my father sitting alone in the drawing room, on plumped up cushions; and he read me Winnie the Pooh to our mutual delight until the panic was over. He went with me to fetch the car from the garage in King's Street, and was interested to note that I noted that the steering did not work well, thanks to there being a puncture in one of the front tyres. He drove a snub-nosed Morris with great care, particularly down to Barton-on-Sea for the summer holidays, where we had a small bungalow and rented a bath hut. Modest family picnics, sea bathing, some

agreeable adult company including several from the Office; the beginnings of golf and tennis.

Robin had a nanny called Sheila. She was young and the daughter of a sergeant-major at Camberley. She was followed by a number of governesses, who he despised, until Dorothy decided to look after her own son, unusual in those days for those of their social standing. He attended nursery classes in Tedworth Square and then a day school called Mrs Spencers (an early form of elementary school, usually taught by women in their own homes) in South Kensington. 'Y' also went there and AGD would walk them to school every morning before catching the Underground from Gloucester Road to St James' Park and his office at Broadway. AGD worked long hours, six days a week but took a few weeks off in the summer. As war came nearer, his holidays were frequently interrupted. He was a benign presence who obviously enjoyed family life. He often went to play golf or tennis but preferred if the family came with him. The family attended King George V's funeral in January 1936, and Robin was the bearer of a bouquet for Mrs Stanley Baldwin when she visited Shadwell Infant Welfare Centre where Dorothy did volunteer work.

***

In April 1927, information from a Chinese raid on the Soviet Embassy in Peking reached London. It revealed that Arcos, the official Soviet trading organisation in London, was a centre of Soviet espionage in Britain. On 12 May 1927, several hundred policemen raided the Arcos offices in 'Soviet House' at 49 Moorgate in London. Over several days, police and intelligence officials removed numerous documents. Considerable intelligence was obtained of interest to both Britain and the US. However, to justify the raid, the Government revealed to Parliament that the intelligence obtained demonstrated Russia's hostile intentions with regard to diplomatic and trade relations. Remarkably, the Prime Minister revealed that Britain could read the most secret Soviet cipher traffic. This was to provide proof to the Government's parliamentary opponents that the intelligence was accurate. However, it was done despite lobbying from AGD and Stewart Menzies,[33] Assistant Director for Special Intelligence in SIS. As AGD later noted: 'The only real operational intelligence came from our work on Soviet traffic. We were able to attack their systems step by step with success from the days of Litinov's first visit to Copenhagen, of Kamenev as their first representative in London followed by Krassin.'[34] The Soviet reaction to the Prime Minister's statement was immediate: 'Until the famous Arcos Raid in 1927 when HMG found it necessary to compromise our work beyond any question. From that time the Soviet Government introduced OTPs [one-time pads][35] for their diplomatic and commercial traffic to all capitals where they had diplomatic representatives.' However, Soviet diplomatic traffic continued to be read by GC&CS for some time.

By the mid-1920s, GC&CS staff numbered twenty-five officers (one head, six senior assistants, eighteen junior assistants) and about twenty-eight clerical staff (six typists, twelve clerks for code construction and ten traffic sorters and slip readers[36]). AGD began recruiting staff from the universities as early as 1925. Initially, those brought in were classicists, linguists and papyrologists, and the establishment increased to ten seniors and twenty juniors. As there was virtually no difference between the work of good juniors and seniors, in the early 1930s the balance was changed to fifteen seniors and fifteen juniors. The services also contributed staff and from 1923, the Admiralty's interest in Japanese diplomatic and naval attaché traffic led to the permanent placing of a Japanese interpreter officer in GC&CS.

The War Office established a station at Sarafand in Palestine, with an intercepting and cryptographic unit which had close links to GC&CS. In November 1925 AGD visited Sarafand to research the setting-up of wireless stations there. He arrived on 7 November and wrote to Dorothy every few days. 'Y' was almost six months old and AGD was clearly missing his family, ending one letter 'Good night dearest D.G. & kiss wee Y on the brow for me'. He carefully restricted himself to general descriptions of life in the areas he visited. While much of his time was spent travelling to potential wireless station sites in Egypt and Palestine, he still managed to fit in the odd game of tennis and round of golf. He boarded a ship, the *Maloja*, on Sunday, 22 November, at Port Said and arrived in Marseilles on Friday, 27 November. He then took the train to Paris and the boat train from Calais, arriving home the following day.

The War Office also sent officers to GC&CS for training before being posted abroad. Pre-eminent amongst these was John Tiltman,[37] who would remain a close friend of AGD for the rest of his life. Older specialists were drawn from the original Room 40/MI1(b) staff, such as Ernest Hobart-Hampden, former consul in China and Japan, and Ernst Fetterlein,[38] a former Tsarist cryptanalyst.

On 29 July 1926, AGD's deputy, Edward Travis, in his role of protecting British codes and cyphers, received a note from R. Hume, probably from the embassy in Berlin. The Admiralty wished to purchase two Enigma encryption machines which were commercially available in Germany. Hume informed Travis that a new machine was under development which was cheaper, simpler and more fool-proof, although not available for ten months. The existing large machines cost 2,000 marks (less than £100) while the smaller machine was 600 marks (less than £30). Travis replied by telegram in September, saying 'Am proceeding Prague to inspect machine for War Office. Admiralty wish me to break journey at Berlin and ascertain particulars of new Enigma.' Travis duly travelled to Berlin and purchased one machine for the British Government and brought it back to London.[39] It survives to this day and is on display in alternate years at Bletchley Park and GCHQ.

The Armistice which marked the cessation of hostilities on the Western Front had seen the end of military wireless traffic. This had enabled Lord Curzon to argue successfully for the move of GC&CS to the Foreign Office. Over the following years, the focus of AGD's organisation was very much on diplomatic traffic. Some elementary work had been carried out from 1914–18 by both Room 40 and MI1(b). AGD had taken a small Admiralty party to Paris in April 1919 to work with the French on German material during the Peace Conference and stayed until the signing of the Peace of Versailles. He regarded the trip as 'useless though pleasant', the latter because the party included Dorothy.[40] The Germans came to the conference with new code books and methods, not surprisingly following the Zimmermann Telegram episode. In 1919, only a small number of staff had any real cryptography expertise and most were linguists. The reconstruction of code books being used by various governments and the translation and editing of the resulting text was GC&CS's primary function in the early years of its existence. Fetterlein, Strachey and Knox were the key men initially, along with Turner as master-linguist and Hobart-Hampden in charge of Japanese work.

Code books, known as 'hat books', were used by the Germans and within one year of GC&CS's inception, they could be solved by one good linguist. The work was based on a method used by Ernst Fetterlein for many years in this type of work in Russia. John Tiltman joined Fetterlein's team in the summer of 1920 and later recalled their work:

> I worked as one of a group of from 5 to 7 persons on Russian diplomatic ciphers under the direction of Ernst Fetterlein. Fetterlein had been Chief Cryptanalyst of the Russian Czarist Government and held the rank of both admiral and general; he had practiced cryptanalysis since 1898 or earlier. At the Revolution he walked out of Russia across the Finnish frontier and was specially naturalized on arrival in England.

At the time of my arrival, Fetterlein's small section was entirely occupied with the solution of the current Moscow-London and London-Moscow diplomatic traffic intercepted in the cable office. All messages were enciphered by simple columnar transposition of Russian plain text conventionally transliterated out of Cyrillic characters, As each message was transposed on a different key, all messages had to be individually solved. The average delay, was I believe, 1 or 2 days.[41]

The traffic of two British allies was also read, as AGD recalled:

The Americans celebrated the advent of peace by introducing a new hatted diplomatic code recyphered with tables changing quarterly. The solution of the first of these tables was a year's work and thereafter the American Section had to be expanded for the increased task of breaking the tables and reconstructing the code. Good progress was made and the section was able to be of some assistance during the Washington Naval Conference of 1922.

The second really big task was to make a concentrated attack on French Diplomatic cyphers, which had received no attention during the war.

A large number of hatted books of 10,000 groups were used and with the constant practice of reconstruction of such books they never presented any difficulty. Given sufficient traffic, legibility appeared with a month of birth. Many recycled books also appeared and after the initial struggle to obtain the general system the constant change of tables presented little difficulty.

The reading of this traffic during the years of peace and intrigue did from time to time produce very interesting if not invaluable intelligence. But the proximity of the two capitals did mean that a great deal passed by bag.[42]

Only the Soviet traffic yielded operational intelligence. According to AGD:

The Revolutionary Government in 1919 had no codes and did not risk using the Czarist codes which they must have inherited. They began with simple transposition of plain Russian and gradually developed systems of increasing difficulty. The presence of Fetterlein as a senior member of the staff and two very competent girls, refugees from Russia, with a perfect knowledge of the language, who subsequently became permanent members of the staff, enabled

> us to succeed in this work. We were also able to borrow certain British Consuls who could not return to Russia.[43]

A major effort was made on Japanese diplomatic traffic and was largely productive. It was led by Hobart-Hampden who had thirty years of service in Asia. While no more than 20 per cent of the intercepted traffic was read and circulated, the Section was able to provide the views of the Japanese Government in advance of major conferences. Hobart-Hamden was joined by another former member of the British service in Japan, Sir Harold Parlett, in 1926.

A watch was kept on all former enemy countries, and it was known that Germany was using OTPs and a second method nicknamed 'Floradora', which was eventually broken during WW2. Austrian traffic was read in 1918–19, thanks to work by Fetterlein. Knox successfully read some Hungarian traffic and, building on work in MI1(b) and Room 40, traffic was read from Greece, Spain, Italy, Scandinavia and Persia. Targets were driven by the politics of the day so new sections looked at various South American republics, Portugal, Brazil, the Balkans and Near East.

AGD summarised GC&CS's effort on diplomatic traffic over its first twenty years as follows:

> To sum up the cryptographic effort of twenty years on diplomatic traffic: we started in 1919 at the period of bow-and-arrow methods, i.e., alphabetic books; we followed the various developments of security measures adopted in every country; we reached 1939 with a full knowledge of all of the methods evolved, and with the ability to read all diplomatic communications of all powers except those which had been forced, like Germany and Russia, to adopt OTP.
>
> The authority who sanctioned our Establishment in 1919 clearly never envisaged a complete reading, translation and issue of every telegram received by us.
>
> Such was a physical impossibility for the thirty specialists who composed the main body of the staff employed on the work.
>
> Hence from the outset sections did exercise their own discretion as to what they translated and submitted for circulation. They got guidance from the D and R who in turn received intelligence directives from the Foreign Office, the circulating sections of SIS and the officers who used our material in the Service and other large departments.
>
> During the thirties we did supplement our daily issue by a daily 'Summary of telegrams decoded but not circulated', for the benefit

> of SIS, Admiralty and War Office (occasionally the Foreign Office) and it is noteworthy that it was only a very small percentage that were ever asked for in complete form.
>
> With personal satisfaction I maintain that GC and CS did during those twenty years fulfil its allotted function with success, with exiguous numbers and with an absence of publicity which greatly enhanced the value of its work.[44]

Apart from the diplomatic traffic, unusual transmissions were picked up around 1930 which turned out to be a worldwide network of clandestine stations controlled by a station near Moscow (the Comintern network). The police station at Denmark Hill[45] in South London obtained German diplomatic traffic broadcasts in 1937–8 from an unlisted station in Germany to unknown recipient call signs as well as obvious replies from unknown stations. Interception, traffic analysis and direction finding helped in these early days to map the traffic between German embassies, legations and consulates.

GC&CS had no W/T intercept facilities of its own and was totally dependent on the Admiralty and War Office for material to work on. Sinclair had persuaded the Admiralty to retain its intercept stations at Scarborough and Pembroke at the end of WW1. The Military Directorate in the War Office had also agreed to retain its station at Chatham. While there was little German naval traffic in the early 1920s due to the fact that Germany had no real navy, GC&CS's Naval Section was probably set up in 1921 when Clarke joined after completing a naval history of WW1. What German naval traffic there was could not be read and, by the mid-1920s, this could well have been early Enigma traffic. Italy did have a navy, however, and its traffic was read by reconstructing their main naval code book. This work was helped by the Italians' habit of enciphering long political leaders from the daily press. Around 1934, Italian naval traffic increased, albeit in a more secure form, so GC&CS's naval Italian section continued to grow to keep pace with it. Their reports kept DNI well informed about Italian naval plans. During the Spanish Civil War between 1936 and 1939, the Italians introduced the commercial Enigma machine for all of their secret naval communications. Hitler had issued an order for ten Enigma machines to be sent to Franco in October 1936, so it is likely that some were also provided to Mussolini at the same time. This gave GC&CS and a team led by Knox and including William Bodsworth, its first opportunity to research machine encryption. This pioneering work would prove invaluable in the years to come and it was Bodsworth who broke Enigma traffic between Franco's navy and the Italian Navy, the

Regia Marina, in late April 1937.[46] By 1936, a large amount of German naval traffic started to appear in the Mediterranean. Knox made some progress but by 1937 the security of the German naval Enigma machine had been significantly enhanced with an attachment known as the steckerboard.[47] The Germans also added code books as part of the daily Enigma setup procedure and Knox made no further progress. The only source of intelligence came from an early form of traffic analysis which looked at the origins of traffic and plotted the routes that it followed.

A start was also made on Japanese naval traffic, and while there was no interception in Britain, a steady flow of material was delivered by bag to London. A small bureau for interception and cryptography was established, initially in Hong Kong and then Singapore in 1939. AGD summarised the situation in 1939 as follows: 'To sum up the situation of the Naval Section in 1939, including the Japanese branch in Hong Kong: they exercised a very fair measure of control of all Italian and Japanese naval cyphers; they had only seen German signals by the Enigma machine and this they could not read; they had started an intensive professional study of raw German traffic with a view to extracting any available intelligence.'

Many of the foundations of a united Sigint Service were laid in the post-WW1 arrangements, but the Service Ministries seemed to regard them as peacetime arrangements only. War Office policy was summarised in 1925 as follows:

> On the outbreak of war the War Office will be responsible for intercepting the enemy's field wireless sets, and for collecting all information obtainable from this source. For this purpose it will provide, from officers on the active list and on the reserve, the necessary personnel for wireless intelligence and cryptography.
>
> At this stage the help of the GC&CS will only be required in the event of the enemy using a cypher which cannot be broken by the cryptographers in the field. Should this occur the GC&CS will be provided with the necessary material and asked to break the cypher. When this has been done, the results will be handed over to the cryptographers in the field who will thenceforth decipher the messages.[48]

The Navy also intended to run its own 'show', and as the DNI wrote in November 1927: 'On the outbreak of war, the entire naval section of the Government Code and Cypher School will be transferred to the Admiralty, who may require it to go abroad. This transfer may be called for in an emergency other than war, and the Admiralty will always decide when the transfer is necessary. The naval section will then come entirely under the orders of the Admiralty.'[49]

The RAF was still happy, in the event of offensive warfare abroad, to 'obtain its intelligence either from the Army or Navy, therefore GC&CS needs take no steps in this matter'. It assumed that it was responsible for erecting W/T and direction finding (D/F) stations to locate enemy aircraft and that: 'The best solution [to the cryptanalytic problem] would be for the Air Force to possess a small nucleus of officers who had received training in simple cryptography. These trained Air Force officers would be attached on the outbreak of a European war to Air Defence headquarters, and they could be reinforced, if necessary, either by one or two members of the GC&CS or by the recruits called up by the GC&CS.'[50] The higher authorities in the RAF had no WW1 Sigint experience and as AGD wrote in 1932 'the higher authorities were frankly very sceptical about the value of wireless interception and intelligence obtained therefrom'.[51] In 1927, following recommendations by the Romer Committee in 1924, an Air Ministry Y station was erected near Waddington. Initially dealing with diplomatic traffic, by 1932 it was processing enough Russian air material to appoint a cryptanalyst and when he died in 1934, two others were appointed and stationed with GC&CS. In 1936, with the threat of war looming, the Air Ministry intelligence authorities felt that they needed their own experts, so a cryptanalytic Air Section was attached to GC&CS under J.E.S. (Josh) Cooper. He had been a member of GC&CS since 1925 and was transferred from the Foreign Office to the Air Ministry Civil Establishment. By 1938, the section had been expanded and Waddington transferred to Chatham to provided foreign air traffic to GC&CS. The RAF also recruited a former Royal Signals NCO who was promised a commission. A station was set up at Mere Branston and then moved to Cheadle in 1937.

The Army opened a Y station at Fort Bridgewoods, Chatham in 1926 and made progress thanks to Lieutenant-Commander (later Lieutenant-Colonel) M.J.W. Ellingworth. The War Office had been sending serving Army officers to GC&CS for training ever since GC&CS was formed, but this resulted in the Military Wing in GC&CS not being as cohesive as its Naval and RAF counterparts.

A separate GC&CS Military Section was not set up until after 1930. It was established under Tiltman, although he remained on the payroll of the War Office. F.A. Jacobs, a recently retired Army captain, joined him as deputy along with eight staff, including at least two civilian cryptanalysts. Experience had modified War Office policy and all Sigint stations overseas were not regarded as being under the control of AGD and the Committee. Furthermore, 'the GC&CS should be responsible for the control of the interception of traffic by permanent stations, and the War Office for expeditionary force traffic'. Also 'the War Office would certainly require a section of GC&CS to continue foreign military intelligence as well as a cryptographic staff with the expeditionary force'.[52]

Military Intelligence had maintained an interest in interception and cryptography, which is why they sent officers to GC&CS for training. The Admiralty would lend officers to GC&CS to assist in producing results. The War Office had maintained posts abroad and set up a permanent intercept station in the Middle East in the early 1920s and in 1923 at Sarafand, with three officers attached to No. 2 W/T Company there. GC&CS's Military Section worked closely with the intercept station at Chatham, which produced the first army and air force material and German police transmissions in 1937. Knox led the attack on the German military Enigma, having failed to make progress on their naval Enigma traffic.

Commercial work was not in the original GC&CS mandate but in 1938, Sinclair and DNI agreed that in the event of political turmoil in the Far East, the Japanese might enhance the security of their diplomatic and service traffic. Therefore, the communications of large Japanese companies might provide useful intelligence. A small section was set up under Hope in 1938 to investigate commercial traffic, telegrams of large Japanese firms, less likely to be enciphered than Japanese diplomatic and service material.

While initially set up as a 'School' to study world-wide cryptographic methods and practices, events led GC&CS to develop a dual role as a Sigint 'Centre', tasked with extracting as much intelligence as possible, as quickly as possible from communications which were of interest to the British Government and relevant departments. The original sanctioned staff consisted of twenty-five cryptanalysts and around thirty support staff. As many as ten Service officers were loaned to GC&CS until the Military and Air Sections were established. Clearly, the size of GC&CS meant that it could not cover all of the diplomatic and commercial traffic circulating around the world. AGD, as Head was responsible for allocating tasks, directing all branches of work and line managing all subordinate Section Heads. This remained the model for diplomatic work both between the wars and during WW2. He had a registry for correspondence and a small number of administration staff. Travis, as his deputy, was responsible for advising on the security of British codes and ciphers and assisting on their provision. He was eventually assigned a junior assistant and clerical staff which formed the nucleus of the Cipher Security Department. On 2 January 1933, AGD received another honour in his capacity as the head of a department of the Foreign Office. He was appointed a Companion of the Order of the British Empire (CBE).

Diplomatic 'product' did not require much comment or interpretation. It was processed by a Distribution and Reference Section which was led by a senior officer with cryptanalytic expertise. The section became a reference library which was indexed for research and editorial ease. It never exceeded five staff, including support staff. Unlike the rest of GC&CS, which allocated tasks to a team of cryptanalysts, the Diplomatic Section assigned tasks to one senior cryptanalyst who possessed wide linguistic expertise, thus bypassing the 'country section' organisation which was in place. This suited the 'country section' model of flexibility and variability of size. For example, during the Italian-Ethiopian War in 1935–6, Italian diplomatic traffic could be exploited so the Italian Section was increased from five to twenty. This was done by passing the work to experienced cryptanalysts and their support staff in other sections such as the French, Romanian and Scandinavian.

In the early days of GC&CS, several experienced cryptanalysts with mathematical expertise were used on more difficult problems such as the German OTP or when a country section was unable to make progress. A senior linguist was also employed in this way and these men reported directly to AGD. At that time there were a number of small country sections, including French, Belgian, Japanese, Italian, Spanish, Near Eastern, Balkan States, Scandinavia and Greek. Not all countries could be covered due to a shortage of staff. The Heads of all of these country sections reported to AGD. The Head of each section selected which deciphered material should be translated and submitted for circulation. The Distribution and Reference Section, by its contacts with the user departments, became the conveyer to the country sections of current priorities; and its Head, by continuity of experience and knowledge of current needs, had become a guide to the exploiting sections in this matter. No more formal 'priorities' machinery existed. During the Ethiopian and Spanish Civil wars, the Diplomatic Sections gained valuable experience about the value of its product in supporting military, naval and air operations. It also realised that standard commercial coded traffic might be of considerable value to 'Economic Warfare'. In 1938, a special Commercial Section' was set up. Therefore, the Diplomatic and Commercial Sections were already operational and experienced in their work at the beginning of WW2. While the organisation would have to expand to provide full cover as required by their 'customers', they would never face the expansion, evolution and exploitation problems faced by the Service Sections. It was able to retain its pre-war structure throughout the war.

GC&CS continued to deal with Japan's diplomatic and naval attaché communications which could be intercepted at home. Consular, military and naval traffic was handled by outstations in the Far East. Copies of translations were sent to DNI and intercepts to GC&CS, which used them as training material or for cryptanalysis on unbroken systems. There was an agreement between DNI and AGD that in the event of war, GC&CS's Naval Section would transfer to the Far East theatre.[53] A Far Eastern Bureau was considered necessary and it would be inter-service in nature. In the Spring of 1934, the bureau was set up on Stonecutters Island in Hong Kong. By June 1935, it was completely staffed and while intelligence was handled on an inter-service basis, apart from five RAF staff the cryptanalysts and interception staff were from the Navy.[54] From 1935 to 1939 there was a shift in Sigint concern from the Far East to the Middle East and from the Mediterranean to Western Europe. There was still no Army or RAF presence at the Hong Kong Bureau (Hong Kong Combined Bureau or Far East Combined Bureau [FECB]). The Army was waiting for preliminary cryptanalytical research in the Military Section of GC&CS to facilitate local exploitation. By 1939, progress at GC&CS was sufficient for two Army officers and one RAF officer to be sent to FECB. Up until 1938, GC&CS's Naval Section and the FECB were successful in reading Japan's diplomatic and naval attaché machine cipher. FECB reported being able to be 'in the happy position of being able to read all Japanese Naval cypher messages'.[55]At the end of 1938, Japan rapidly changed its cryptographic systems. Its fleet introduced a five-figure subtractor cipher[56], while diplomatic and consular traffic used a new electrical cipher machine, called the 'Purple Machine' by the Americans. Little progress was made against the Japanese fleet system, called JN25, by FECB staff, but it was broken by Tiltman (he had made the earlier break into the main military cipher) and the first decrypted messages were dispatched to FECB in September 1939. By then plans were in place to move FECB to Singapore. GC&CS had provided FECB with JN25 codebreaking material in September 1939, which was used on 75 per cent of Japanese naval traffic. However, GC&CS made virtually no contribution to anti-Japanese Service Sigint from 3 September 1939 until the outbreak of war with Japan in December 1941. The Japanese Diplomatic Subsection translated and did minor research on Japanese diplomatic ciphers.

In early 1934, Italian naval Sigint became of interest as Italy seemed to be on a war footing and communications contained operational intelligence. By the end of 1937, GC&CS's Naval Section (eighteen-strong excluding Japanese staff)) was engaged almost entirely on Italian Sigint. Encrypted traffic was provided by intercept stations at Flowerdown, Malta and Gibraltar. The Military Section was also concentrating on Italian work by 1936, with seven officers involved, supported by six female clerks. By 1938, with six current Italian code books and much of the traffic being read, Tiltman complained about the lack of resources. Encrypted traffic was provided by the intercept station at Chatham and abroad from Sarafand in Palestine and detachments from there. Tiltman's section also tackled Italian air ciphers.

The Air Ministry was finally stirred into action with the resurgence of the German Air Force (GAF) in 1935, and a section, A.I.1e, was formed to scan, translate and summarise plain text intercepts. In July 1938, it was suggested to AGD that coordination could best be achieved in Malta by a small inter-service Y Intelligence Centre in which intelligence officers from the three Services would produce intelligence from intercepts, direction finding bearings and ciphers broken in GC&CS. AGD proposed the creation of a Combined Bureau in the Middle East, similar to FECB, to perform all Sigint functions, including cryptanalysis. Each Service favoured its own main station: Malta for the Navy, Sarafand for the Army and Cairo for the Air Force. In the end a Middle East Intelligence Centre was set up in Cairo in the summer of 1939, receiving decrypts direct from Sarafand and via the War Office, from GC&CS. NID got Board approval for an Operations Intelligence Centre in Malta and AGD reluctantly agreed in July 1939 to supply, for local exploitation, 'any broken cyphers used unrecyphered by the Italians since such books can be used without the assistance of a skilled cryptographic staff'.[57]

In May 1938, a German subsection of the Naval Section at GC&CS was set up to analyse traffic, consisting of one officer and one lady clerk. However, German military W/T activity was suspended at Chatham in 1935. The study of German Army systems did not even rate a mention in the Military Section report of July 1938.[58] Even though the Air Ministry was aware of the growth of GAF activity in 1935, it was a low priority of the Air Section in 1936[59] and Italian traffic remained its main concern.

The general view within the British Service and intelligence communities in the mid- to late 1930s was that the likelihood of solving Enigma was 'not yet sufficient to justify real confidence in eventual success'.[60] German diplomatic traffic was unreadable, and even low-level German Army transposition and stencil systems had not been broken and no effort was being made on naval Enigma until military Enigma was solved. The Air Ministry believed that Enigma was not being used by the GAF. AGD himself seemed to be pessimistic 'as to the possible value of cryptography in another war'[61] and Sinclair was concerned after the Munich crisis 'that as soon as matters become serious, wireless silence is enforced, and that therefore this organisation of ours is useless for the purpose for which it is intended'.[62] The Naval Section of GC&CS wrote to AGD in February 1938 saying that 'D/F will certainly be our only real source of information as to enemy movements by sea, land and air in the early and therefore probably the most important days of a modern war'.[63] However, Service Ministry thinking was starting to change and, increasingly, their view was that in the event of war, the Sigint effort shouldn't be split between them. The Main Committee recommended the interconnection of all intercept and D/F stations in the UK to GC&CS by telephone and teleprinter and the formation of a 'joint Inter-Service Operational Intelligence Section at the GC&CS'.[64] But the Ministries preferred to keep 'operational intelligence' under their control and the section was never formed. However, it did speed up the expansion and improvement of D/F facilities and the communications needed to combine the stations into a network. All Y stations were linked to GC&CS and a Defence Services Lines Telecommunications Board (DSLTB) created by the Director-General of the Post Office, with representatives of all Services and AGD. The teleprinter and telephone lines converged on a special room at the Central Telegraph Office (CTO) in London, which was connected by a private cable to GC&CS in the Broadway Buildings, to operate the system from another centre such as GC&CS's war station at BP. It was only necessary to switch the system over from the CTO room to the new site.

The RAF needed Sigint to be delivered swiftly and a test was carried out in March 1938 to demonstrate the advantages of decentralised cryptanalysis. Italian and Spanish Nationalist Air Force traffic was sent to Waddington where Cooper and two other cryptanalysts, supported by a colleague at GC&CS, spent three days decrypting and reporting on the traffic. This convinced the Air Ministry that a cryptanalysis section should be located at the central Y station in peace or war. The role of the GC&CS Air Section would be restricted to cryptanalysis and training new personnel. Meanwhile, the Admiralty set up an Operational Intelligence Centre in 1937, but Operational Intelligence was another name for traffic analysis which was really carried out in the Naval Section of GC&CS. The new centre collated intelligence from non-Sigint sources or decrypts from GC&CS.

By 1938, it was increasingly clear to AGD that he was going to have to expand his organisation. With Sinclair's backing, he asked two former Cambridge dons, Frank Birch and Frank Adcock, both veterans of WW1 codebreaking, to trawl through the staff and student lists at both Oxford and Cambridge and other universities. They were looking for men who were deemed suitable for secret intelligence work within the Foreign Office. While the WW1 cryptanalysts did not have much time for mathematicians, GC&CS had recruited one before 1935 and was already putting a Cambridge mathematician through preliminary training in London. A second was recruited from Oxford in February 1939. Through the Chief Clerk's Department, AGD got the Treasury to sanction fifty-six senior assistants at £600 per year and thirty women with a graduate's knowledge of at least two of the languages required at £3 per week.

According to AGD: 'It was naturally at that time impossible to give details of the work, nor was it always advisable to insist too much in these circles on the imminence of war. At certain universities, however, there were men now in senior positions who had worked in our ranks during 1914–18. These men knew the type required.'[65] One such recruit was E.R.P. Vincent, a Fellow of Corpus Christi and a professor of Italian. He had learned German during his internment in Germany during WW1. He later recalled dinner with Adcock in the spring of 1937:

> We dined very well, for he was something of an epicure, and the meal was very suitably concluded with a bottle of 1920 port. It was then that he did something which seemed to me most extraordinary; he went quickly to the door, looked outside and then came back to his seat. As a reader of spy fiction I recognised the procedure, but I never expected to witness it. He then told me that he was authorised to offer me a post in an organisation working under the Foreign Office, but which was so secret he couldn't tell me anything about it. I thought that if that was the case he need not have been so cautious about eavesdropping, but I didn't say so. He told me that war with Germany was inevitable and that it would be an advantage for one of my qualifications to prepare to have something useful to do.[66]

Vincent was summoned by telephone to Broadway Buildings in London shortly afterwards and returned periodically until war was declared. He was able to learn something about cryptographic problems and he 'picked up the jargon and got to know some of the people'.

Another recruit in 1938 would certainly make his mark during the impending war. Alan Turing was identified by either Adcock or Birch as having the right skills for GC&CS and he was invited to a training course at GC&CS's offices in London in the summer of 1938. He attended another course at Christmas and then visited every two or three weeks to help with the work. He was attached to a team led by Dilly Knox and worked alongside Peter Twinn,[67] the young mathematician who had been recruited from Oxford in February 1939.

Throughout the 1930s, Sinclair had become concerned that his intelligence organisations were based in Central London, which would make them vulnerable in the event of war. He started to look for somewhere outside of London to establish a war station for intelligence activities. In early 1937, it was brought to his attention that the remains of a large Victorian estate, located around 50 miles from London, was on the market.[68] Its 55 acres would provide ample space for a growing intelligence organisation. Furthermore, it was only five minutes' walk to a railway station, which sat on the main line from London to the North. Also close by was the main north/south arterial road. Sinclair initially leased the property and, on 9 June 1938, he purchased the property, called Bletchley Park, for £6,000. This was done using his own initiative and many authors believe that he was following a Service tradition by paying for it out of his own pocket. The Official History of MI6 is less certain:

> The relevant property transaction documents show him personally as the sole owner, and after he died in November 1939, apart from legacies of £3,500 to each of his two sons, his sister Evelyn inherited the remainder of his property, with a total value of £21,391. In April 1940 Evelyn (as personal representative of 'Sir Hugh Sinclair deceased') transferred BP to William Ridley and Percy Stanley Sykes [the Service's Finance Officer] for ten shillings [40p]. In their turn, on 3 March 1947, Ridley and Sykes transferred the property to the Ministry of Works, again for ten shillings, all of which strongly suggests that the original purchase money had come from public, if not also SIS, funds.[69]

Engineers from the GPO began installing telecommunications equipment and by the autumn, enough was in place for Sinclair to order a dress rehearsal at his new intelligence war station. As the Head of GC&CS's Air Section, Josh Cooper, remembered:

> In Autumn 1938 GC&CS had no administrative staff and the Admiral (who appears to have taken the decision to move unilaterally) put Captain Ridley RN of SIS in charge. All personnel of every grade were accommodated in hotels in Bletchley and surrounding towns and villages. The Admiral sent out an excellent

> chef from London and we all sat down to lunch together at one long table in the House. All this was simply paid for out of SIS funds; Captain Ridley was not concerned with Civil Service regulations. A large room on the ground floor of the House had been set aside for Air Section. Tables and chairs had been provided but there were no cupboards and I remember coming into a scene of chaos with a great mound of books and papers piled on the floor. After Munich we all trooped back to London.[70]

The rehearsal at BP revealed a number of shortcomings in accommodation (work and billeting), in staff and in efficiency of communication. So while GC&CS staff returned to London after the signing of the Munich Agreement[71] on 30 September 1938, work continued on preparing BP for war and improving arrangements for accommodation and catering.

By the end of 1938, the Air Ministry not only recognised its responsibility for the air defence of Britain, but also that it couldn't live off the work of other Services. A Section at GC&CS would have to be engaged in cryptanalytic research and training and would work with a W/T and direction finding complex centred at Cheadle. For the War Office, MI8 would take over Sigint responsibility in September 1939 and 'the collection, correlation and dissemination of all Military Intelligence obtained from the study of foreign military intercepted communications, for the plotting and identification of foreign enemy wireless stations, the breaking of foreign code call systems and the measure of the enemy's wireless activity'.[72] Chatham was concerned with purely strategic interception work and the Military section of GC&CS, like its Air Force counterpart, with higher-grade cryptanalysis and training. At this stage, the Air Ministry was concerned about the defence of Britain and had made no provision for strategic interception, on the basis that there was no such traffic. The War Office was concerned with Sigint in the field and their Chatham Y station alone intercepted GAF Enigma traffic. The Army and Air Ministries controlled their respective sections at GC&CS, while the Admiralty did not, following the removal of its GC &CS's sections operational intelligence work.

GC&CS was changing from two groups working on diplomatic cryptographic systems as a sideline to their Service work, to one which developed Service sections as an adjunct to its diplomatic work. Traffic Section was responsible for the intake and sorting of intercepts. Distribution and Reference Section edited and distributed decrypts translated by cryptanalysts and kept in contact with users to assess their needs. The Civil side in 1939 outnumbered all of the Service sections combined and consisted of a large number of cryptanalytic units, ranging from one to fifteen staff. The Head of each continued to report directly to AGD. Some of the units carried out cryptanalytic research and others operated as a centre for the production of decrypt intelligence and unit boundaries were flexible. A Commercial Section with six staff was set up in 1938 to scan and select from a mass of intercepted correspondence, mainly in plain language or public commercial codes. This was passed to a centre in London which eventually became the Ministry of Economic Welfare. However, the civil side of GC&CS was functionally far more limited than the military side. Its sole functions were cryptanalysis and translation. It had little involvement with traffic analysis or intelligence and even interception presented few problems, as the most reliable source of supply were the copies of cable traffic that had been handed in for transmission and held by the Post Offices and Cable Companies after they had been sent.

***

On 7 December 1931, a representative of the Polish cipher department met a French intelligence officer at the Central Station in Warsaw. The officer, Captain Gustave Bertrand, carried with him operational instructions for the Enigma machine being used by the German military. The *Gebrauchanleitung für die Chiffriermaschine Enigma* also contained four drawings of the machine. A further document in his possession, the *Schlüsselanleitung*, provided vital information about the various settings of the machine. His source for these documents was a German by the name of Hans-Thilo Schmidt, who had first contacted the intelligence representative at the French Embassy in Berlin on 8 June 1931. Through his brother Rudolf, Schmidt had been given a job in the German Defence Ministry's Cipher Centre, the *Chiffrierstelle,* known as the *ChiStelle.* Rudolf Schmidt had been the previous head of the *ChiStelle* and, ironically, had approved the Enigma machine for use by the German Army. This was the very machine which his brother had now betrayed for no other reason than money to fund his lavish lifestyle. The Deuxième Bureau's Service de Renseignements had assigned one of its operatives, Rudolf Lemoine, to make contact with Hans-Thilo and they duly met on 1 November 1931 at the Grand Hotel in Verviers, a town in eastern Belgium around 15 miles from the German border. Bertrand attended a subsequent meeting on 8 November, along with a photographer. As well as the two Enigma documents, Schmidt produced an organisation chart of the *ChiStelle,* an army hand cipher and a memorandum on poison gas. Schmidt was duly paid 10,000 marks (about £41,000 today) and Bertrand returned to Paris. He handed them to Colonel Bassières, a top French cryptanalyst who, after analysing them for two weeks, told Bertrand that they were of little use to French intelligence. Bertrand now turned to British intelligence and on 23 November, handed copies to their Paris representative, Wilfred (Bill) Dunderdale. Three days later, Dunderdale also rejected the documents, as they would be of little use in decrypting Enigma messages. Thus it was that Bertrand got permission to offer the material to Polish intelligence and was subsequently greeted by them with open arms.[73]

Polish intelligence's interest in the material from Hans-Thilo Schmidt was understandable, given the difficult historical relationship between Poland and Germany. At the end of WW1, the newly-reborn Polish state had taken part of Silesia, Pomerania and territory around Poznan, as it had been part of Poland before the partition by Frederick the Great. This was a cause of considerable anger in Germany, and an atmosphere of enmity and continual tension persisted, fuelled by the long history of numerous and bloody wars between Poland and Germany. The re-born Polish state felt seriously threatened by its neighbour to the west. On 15 July 1928, Polish radio-monitoring stations in Starogard, Gdanski, Poznan and Krakow-Krzeslawice had intercepted the first German messages which were in a machine-generated cipher. The following year a course in cryptology was started at the University of Poznan for twenty of its most advanced mathematics students who could also speak German. The course was set up at the initiative of the radio intelligence department and some of their specialist officers would give lectures to the students, the most gifted of whom would be asked to volunteer to continue their studies within Military Intelligence. Throughout 1931, a cipher bureau was created which was an amalgamation of the radio intelligence and cryptography sections. The new bureau was headed by Major (later Lieutenant-Colonel) Gwido Langer. As the new bureau was being organised in 1931, the course at Poznan was coming to an end, and three students had frequently managed to solve the German ciphers that had been set for them on the course. It was decided to set up a small section of the department for them in Poznan. Their names were Marian Rejewski, Hendryk Zygalski and Jerzy Różycki.

The German military had introduced a new version of an Enigma machine with a plugboard at the beginning of June 1930 and, the following year, the Poles purchased a commercial model on the open market in Germany. At the beginning of September 1931, Rejewski,

Zygalski and Różycki were employed by Section BS 4 (German intelligence) of the Cipher Office of Department II of the General Staff in Warsaw. This section was under the command of Captain (later Major) Maksymilian Ciez'ki. Rejewski was the most advanced academically of the three young students, having just been awarded his degree in mathematics. He had also spent a further year studying the subject in depth at the University of Gottingen in Germany. He began work on his own in October 1932 with the commercial Enigma machine which had been purchased earlier. He was also receiving several dozen messages daily which had been encrypted on the military version of the Enigma machine. By December, he had a photograph of the military machine, user instructions for it and a schedule of daily keys for September and October 1932. Remarkably, by the end of December 1932, Rejewski had reconstructed the internal connections within the Enigma machine and identified the indicator system[74] currently being used by the German Army. He had done it entirely using a mathematical technique called permutation theory. Along with significant contributions from Zygalski and Różycki, the first breakthrough in solving the German military Enigma machine had been achieved. The three young Polish cryptanalysts handed to their superior the first completely decrypted Reichswehr[75] signal which had been encrypted using the military Enigma.

In early 1933, Rejewski, Zygalski and Różycki began working together and were successful for a number of years in reading encrypted German Army messages. After the GAF introduced Enigma at the end of 1934, they grouped radio operators who worked alongside Enigma operators into different radio networks. The number of these grew rapidly and the Poles had to monitor an increasing amount of traffic. By 1 February 1936, the Germans had introduced significant changes which improved the security of the Enigma machine. Each radio network had its own setting of the machine which changed every twenty-four hours. The following year, the Polish General Staff transferred their German cryptographic section BS4 to a camouflaged and high-security new headquarters in the Kabacki Woods near Pyry outside Warsaw. They developed technologies such as the Zygalski sheets, the cyclometer and the bomba to help work out the Enigma settings being used by operators on different networks. Up until December 1938, GAF and Army Enigma operators had three wheels for their Enigma machines. They would change the order of the wheels in the machine each day, and as each wheel was wired uniquely, this would in effect change the wiring in the machine. This meant that there were six possible wheel configurations and the Poles had built six bombas to speed up their work. On 15 December, the Enigma operators were given two additional wheels and could now choose three from a set of five uniquely wired. This increased the number of possible wheel configurations to sixty and the Poles would need a bomba for each additional configuration. They simply did not have the resources to build fifty-four more machines. To make matters worse, the Germans had introduced a plugboard at the front of the Enigma machine with twenty-six sockets and a number of letters were plugged together. When they also increased the number of plugboard connections to ten, working out the daily settings of the Enigma machine became a daunting task indeed!

The deployment of the Enigma machine across all of its services was becoming an increasing concern to AGD. From 1937 onward, it was obviously desirable that British naval, military and air intelligence should get in very close touch with their French colleagues for political and military reasons. Sinclair had always been keen to maintain a close liaison between SIS and GC&CS and had established links with the French intelligence agency the Deuxième Bureau de l'État-major général, directed by Colonel Maurice-Henri Gauché. Sinclair's deputy, Menzies, had a close relationship with Colonel Louis Rivet, the head of the French Army's '2ième Bureau' (the *Services de Renseignements et de Contre-Espionnage militaire*). Bertrand worked under Rivet but AGD believed that it was Dunderdale, although he had little knowledge of cryptography, who urged the British to liaise with the French on a technical level.[76]

AGD was concerned about how far he could go in collaborating with the French. He wrote to Sinclair on 2 November 1938, asking for guidance.

> Liaison with the French
> I should like to have your guidance as to the limits to which this liaison should go.
> We have received about 100 documents of varying types and varying value:-
> Three photographs of codes of which one might well have had great value in the event of war with Germany last month.
> Photographs of documents relating to the use of the Enigma machine which did increase our knowledge of the machine and have greatly aided our researches.
> Studies of the German Military and Air services.
> A full description of the German Y Service.
> Reconstructed German and Italian codes (unrecyphered).
> Considerable amount of German and Italian intercepted telegrams.

The results of French D/F work.

We have given them purely cryptographic assistance in the shape of :-

Our reconstruction to date of the Italian recyphered and unrecyphered books.

Copies of two Italian recyphered books on which they set great store.

We propose to give them results of our Y work in the shape of:-

German Naval Call Signs.

A complete study of the German Air Force.

A complete study of the German Military.

It appears to us that their cryptographic work is less ambitious than ours. They have worked on the German and Italian unrecyphered codes with success and on the German Military hand cypher (double transposition).

As to their Y Service it appears:-

That the Navy works separately. I was informed by a Naval Officer liaison officer with ? that they relied entirely on their station at Dunkerque for interception and D/F.

We have received no Naval intercepts but the French version of situation report of the German Navy from time to time through? We have reciprocated with our version through Section III.

That the army, Y and D/F service is considerable; M/F interception is more productive that ours.

The Military Section report that the organisation is not so complete as here, no night watch being kept and no work done on Sundays.

That the Y watch on German Air Force is very poor (vide Air Section report).

That they have an organisation for watching N. Italy, Libya and to a certain extent Eritrea (vide reports from Italian Diplomatic Section and Military Section).

It is <u>very remarkable</u> that we have received no example of any interception in Spain, either German, Italian or Spanish, work which occupies a large part of our staff. It occurs to me that this may have been a special study for the Navy who will no doubt watch the Mediterranean and Bay of Biscay.

This may also account for the entire absence of reference to Italian Naval Cyphers. On my own work on French Naval Cyphers during the last two years I have come across references to interception, etc. which lead me to suppose that it is the French Navy and the Bureau de Chiffre of the Marine who carry out this side of the work.

> Our main reason for seeking this liaison in the first place was the desire to leave no stone unturned which might lead to a solution of the Enigma Machine as used by the various German services. This is of vital importance for us and the French have furnished us with documents which have assisted us but we are still doubtful if success can be obtained without further documents. During the coming meetings we hope to show Mr. X. the lines on which we are working and make clear to him what other evidence we need in the hope that his agents may produce it.
>
> We also hope to obtain from him more material prior to September 15th, 1938, as there was a slight prospect of a break-in on the military machine before their mobilisation change.
>
> We shall continue to work on the machine and will naturally give Mr. X. any results we obtain.
>
> An interchange of current intercepted material may be necessary, unless the French prefer to put the onus of research on us.
>
> We can also continue to cooperate on the reconstruction of the two Italian codes. As yet there has been no discussion on Italian Naval and Military cyphers and on this question I should like to receive orders in view of the fact (a) that I suspect that the Italian Naval is being worked in another branch in Paris and (b) that the Foreign Office considered that cooperation on the Italian Military telegrams between Spain and Rome was, at that time, undesirable.[77]

In early January, Bertrand asked AGD to come to Paris to meet some Polish experts in cryptography. In the hope that such a meeting would help GC&CS with work on German and Soviet ciphers, AGD attended meetings on 9 and 10 January along with Tiltman, Knox and Hugh Foss.[78] In attendance on the Polish side were Langer and Ciez'ki; on the French side Bertrand and a French cryptanalyst, Henri Braquenie. The meeting was shrouded in secrecy and mystery and began with a presentation by Ciez'ki on the results of the Polish research into the Enigma machine as used by the German services. The British delegation was not impressed, as Ciez'ki gave a long and pedantic account of results which Tiltman had already achieved in an hour's work. AGD and his colleagues felt that the Poles had little to contribute and Knox went further, claiming that the Poles' knowledge of the Wehrmacht Enigma was 'nil'.[79] Writing of the meeting in May 1948 (see Appendix 5), AGD soon realised that in fact the Poles had been vetting the British, and had instructions not to disclose any of their real work on Enigma unless the British and French could demonstrate that they had made comparable progress and were prepared to share it with them.[80]

While nothing more was heard from the Poles for six months, tensions between Poland and Germany were close to breaking point. In the middle of July, Langer sent an invitation, through Bertrand, for AGD and his colleagues to come to Warsaw. The invitation specifically included Knox, as both the Poles and the French knew that he was working on the Enigma machine as used by the German military. AGD was very reluctant to take Knox with him, given his temperamental nature. However, Sinclair instructed him to do so and after discussions with the DNI, AGD was also told to include Commander Humphrey Sandwith, Head of the Admiralty's interception service, in his group.[81] He wanted to talk to the Poles about placing a site in Poland to help with British direction finding efforts. Bertrand proposed that the second tri-lateral meeting be held in Warsaw from 24–27 July. Bertrand and Sandwith travelled by air to Warsaw but AGD and Knox travelled by train as they wished to see Germany, possibly for the last time for quite some while. The latter arrived on the 24th and were met by Bertrand and the Poles. They were lodged at the Hotel Bristol while the French stayed at the Hotel Polonia.

The Poles entertained their visitors to lunch at the Hotel Bristol and ironically the fairly banal conversation was conducted in German as it was the only common language of all in attendance. On Wednesday, the 27th, the Poles called for AGD and Knox at 7.00 am and drove them to a clearing in the Kabacki woods about 20 kilometres from Warsaw. About a kilometre from the small town of Pyry, a clearing had been made and here lay the Polish *Biuro Szyfrow*'s secret headquarters which was partly underground. It was in the shape of a square with sides of about 200m surrounded by a high wall enclosing two brick buildings. The smaller of the two served as an air-raid shelter and radio station which was serviced by aerials which could be lowered to avoid detection.

The Poles had exploited a weakness in the Germans' procedures for Enigma in the 1930s. Hendryk Zygalski had devised a method which exploited this weakness to help work out some of the settings used in the Enigma machine for any given day. It was based upon a catalogue of perforated sheets and it had the huge advantage that it was not compromised by the plug connections on the Enigma machine. As there were only six wheel orders in operational use at this time (the operator could mix up his three wheels in six ways), a complete catalogue contained twenty-six perforated sheets, one for each of the possible ring settings[82] on the right-hand wheel. Thus, 6 x 26 = 156 sheets had to be manufactured. When the Germans introduced two additional wheels in December 1938, the number of wheel orders had increased from six to sixty and 1,560 sheets were required. The Poles had also developed two machines to help with their work. The cyclometer helped with the task of constructing a card index system containing information about all possible Enigma start positions that could have been used. The bomba had three pairs of Enigma wheel systems driven by an electric motor and exploited the same weakness as the Zygalski sheets. However, the increase in possible wheel orders and lack of resources meant that the bomba could no longer be used.

Ciez'ki proceeded to demonstrate, with the assistance of an Enigma machine which included a plugboard, how the Poles had gone about working out the daily setting of the machine. Once this was known, they could read the messages by simply typing the encrypted text into their Enigma machines. The British and the French attendees were then shown the Zygalski sheets, cyclometer and bombas. Knox, in his position as the British expert, stood close to the machines during the demonstration. During a break for tea after three hours, and then afterwards, AGD's worst fears about Knox's attendance at the meeting were realised. He maintained a stony silence throughout the meeting and was clearly upset by what he was hearing. Matters came to a head when they got into a car to leave, as AGD later recalled:

> It was only when we got back in the car to drive away that he (Knox) suddenly let himself go and assuming that no one understood any English raged and raged that they were lying to us now as in Paris. The whole thing was a pinch he kept on repeating – they never worked it out – they pinched it years ago and have followed developments as anyone could but they must have bought it or pinched it.[83]

Knox probably knew more about the Enigma machine than anyone in Britain at the time of the Pyry meetings. While he had some success in breaking versions of the Enigma machine which were similar to the early commercial version, he had been unable to break the new military version with the plugboard. His problem had been the connections between the keyboard and the entry drum inside the machine. On the models of Enigma machines that he had successfully broken, the connection pattern followed the order of the keys left to right, row by row and alphabetically around the entry drum. So the Q key was connected to A, W key to B, E key to C, R key to D, etc. On the model of Enigma in mass use by the German Army and Air Force, the connection pattern had been changed and Knox's team (which included Turing) could not work out the new pattern. This problem had also stumped Rejewski initially, and he described his solution in a paper written in 1980:

> What, then, were the connections in the entry drum? It turned out later that they can be found by deduction, but in December 1932, or perhaps in the first days of 1933, I obtained those connections by guessing. I assumed that since the keyboard keys were not connected with the successive contacts in the entry drum in the order of the letters on the keyboard, then maybe they were connected up in alphabetical order; that is, that the permutation caused by the entry drum was an identity and need not be taken into account at all. This time luck smiled upon me. The hypothesis proved correct, and the very first trial yielded a positive result.[84]

When Knox met Rejewski he had quickly asked him: 'What are the connections to the entry drum?' Knox was furious when he heard the answer; '*A, B, C,* —'. In other words, the Germans had wired it up in the simplest possible way, the Q key to Q, the W key to W, the E key to E, the R key to R, etc. He remained aloof and alone over dinner and gave the impression that he had a grudge against the Poles. AGD spoke with Bertrand and Sandwith and it was decided to return to Warsaw as soon as possible. The next day, Knox met with Langer, Ciez'ki, Rejewski, Zygalski and Różycki. According to AGD, Knox was 'his own bright self & won the hearts & admiration of the young men with whom he was so much in touch'. Ever the loyal colleague, AGD explained Knox's behaviour as follows: 'If only that first day of formal disclosure could have been avoided & pompous declarations by senior officers had been omitted. Knox's mind & personality in touch with men who really knew their job would have made that visit a very real success. They were all simple & straightforward.'

AGD and Sandwith left on the 28th to return to home and he was back in London by Sunday the 30th. The following day he wrote to Bertrand:

> My dear Colonel,
> Our party returned safely if with difficulty. Mr. Knox's papers were not quite in order and he had to spend the night in Posen, but arrived safely 24 hours later.
>
> I wish again to assure you our extreme gratitude for all that you did for us and our appreciation of your very fine achievements. I

have reported the matter in brief to my Chief who also expressed freely his appreciation of your work as I described it. He empowers me to repeat our invitation for you and the Major to visit us.

I trust such a visit may be in the near future, but the next few weeks are unusual with us owing to manoeuvres, and I also think it might be a good thing to get our cooperation started on the lines we outlined before you came, in order that any weak points might be noted and eliminated.

In accordance with the desire of your staff I hope to send by an early courier our intercepts of the T.G.D. group and these I will continue to send by each courier via our mutual friend Captain B. I am also sending our interception of the Naval material during the month of May 1937, as our experts felt that the additional material at that period might prove of great value to them.

Mr. Knox is now organising his staff to continue investigations on the Military material on the lines suggested by your experts.

I shall be grateful, my dear Colonel, if you will convey to Colonel S. and Colonel M. our gratitude and in the hope that our close collaboration may achieve further useful results.[85]

AGD had agreed with the Poles that the British, with greater resources at their disposal, would produce the Zygalski sheets.[86]

Knox's passport had been wrongly stamped for a return journey through Germany. Instead, he had to travel to Poznan to get a visa from the British Consul there. AGD's patience with Knox must have been sorely tested when he received a letter from him, written on Hotel Bristol notepaper and dated 30 July:

My Dear Alastair
Let's get this straight.

The Poles have got the machine to Sept 15th 38 out by luck. As I have said only Mrs B.B. had seriously contemplated the equation A = 1 B = 2. Had she worked on the crib we should be teaching them.

They must have done very well to determine the two new wheels. How they did it might be important. I have not discussed this.

Their machine for determining all ciphers (O.S.) and SSD (n.s.) may be good. If we are going to read them we should be given a detailed study: if not, we only want the broadest outline of its electrical principles.

Military (?) Sept 15 – ?? April 1 ??. Here they seem to have failed badly Mathematically the data are more not less than with the other cipher (if there be over 300 messages). If we are to attempt this we should examine their system and statistics (if any) with considerable scepticism*. Why have they failed on an astronomical but simple calculation.

April 1st (??) to now. The whole basis of diagnosis may have changed though doubtless the machine remains.

Before deciding anything we must settle

Whether we are going to give a miss to the S.S.D. stuff

Whether they have got the right system for the other.

I am fairly clear that Schessky [Knox is referring to Ciez'ki] knows very little about the machine & may try to conceal facts from us.

The young men seem very capable and honest.

A.D.K.

Finally (f) It cannot too strongly be emphasised that all successes have depended on a factor (the machine coding of indicators) which may at any moment be cancelled.

Even the principle of electrical selection must be viewed with distrust.[87]

It is typical of Knox that he ends his rant against the Poles with kind words for Rejewski, Zygalski and Różycki. He was also correct in pointing out the weakness in the Polish methods, i.e. their dependence on the machine coding of indicators. This was indeed cancelled in early May 1940, rendering the Polish methods useless.[88]

Despite being friends with Knox since their Room 40 days, AGD revealed his exasperation in a remarkably candid letter to Bertrand, dated 3 August 1939. It was written on the same Hotel Bristol note paper that Knox had used:

My dear Bertrand,

I have finally had a day off and I take this opportunity to write to you a very personal letter, 'from the heart', which seems necessary to me.

I have seen D;[89] in his opinion I may have said something bad about you and that is why I wish to emphasise that we owe everything solely to you and I look forward to the cooperation of our trio and, that to reach our goal you must remain in the leading position. In Warsaw it was you who advised me to return and think about it – and you were right.

Maybe you understand my problem in the shape of Knox. He is a man of exceptional intelligence, but he does not know the word cooperation. You surely must have noticed that off duty, he is a

> pleasant chap loved by all. But in the office his behaviour is different.
>
> In Warsaw I had some deplorable experiences with him. He wants to do everything himself. He does not know how to explain anything. He can't stand it when someone knows more than him. Unfortunately, I cannot do without him, he knows more about the machine than anyone else in the country. He built a machine of the type used by the Spanish, and frequently by the Italians in Spain, which is not to be sneered at, even if not so much has been done as has been done by our friends in Z.
>
> You must forgive me for being so keen to keep him, but I will tell you in all sincerity, that I will never take him to a conference again if I can only avoid it. From now on, we must establish the rules of our cooperation in order to avoid unnecessary effort.

The Pyry meeting came just in time because on 1 September, Germany invaded Poland and two days later, Britain declared war on Germany. By 10 September 1939, German forces were rolling relentlessly across Poland and their armoured columns broke through near Warsaw. The Polish Cipher Department was ordered to leave the capital and the Pyry Centre as soon as possible and move its essential equipment. However, the advance of the Red Army into Poland on 17 September made the Poles change their plans. The cryptanalysts were forced to destroy all traces of their equipment and documents, retaining several Enigmas. The military and civilian sections of the Cipher Department split after they crossed the border into Romania. On 20 September Bertrand delivered a replica Enigma to Menzies in London as a gift from the Poles. The Polish contribution to the early success of BP would prove to be significant. They had recognised in the late 1920s that the age of machine cryptography had begun and that mathematicians would be effective as cryptanalysts.

While it is likely that Knox came away from the Pyry conference with the missing link in his attempt to construct the Enigma machine itself, AGD clearly saw the bigger picture, and on returning to Britain began to recruit more mathematicians for GC&CS. The Poles had demonstrated to the British that encryption machines like Enigma could be broken, if the right mathematical minds were allowed to concentrate on the problem. With the prospect of many years of war ahead, AGD's knowledge and experience of Sigint and its effectiveness in military conflict, would certainly be put to the test.

Chapter 4

Bletchley Park

AGD and his family had moved to Ashtead in Surrey in 1937. They enjoyed their tall, thin house at 48 Tedworth Square, Chelsea, and AGD had a twenty-year lease on the property. They also had a bungalow, called Greengates, in Fairfield Road, Barton-on-Sea, Hampshire, where they spent the summers. They went to the beach twice a day and AGD enjoyed building sandcastles and paddling in the shallows. He also played golf nearby with his son, but AGD was not good at small talk and conversation was restricted to golfing matters. The move was prompted by Robin's poor health and the same year they holidayed in St. Malo and Dinard in France. The Dennistons were a nuclear family and AGD usually partnered his daughter 'Y' when they played bridge, while his son Robin partnered his mother. The family played tennis in Chelsea and used public courts in Bletchley and Ashtead, Robin describing AGD as being 'small but nippy and devious and could do spin shots which the straightforward players of those days found hard to return'. AGD and Dorothy talked endlessly about the children in the evenings. In 1938, they went to Scotland, borrowing a disused cottage half-way up Loch Striven in South Argyllshire, only a few miles from where AGD's father had practised medicine. Their cottage could only be accessed by boat. AGD loved boats and the sea, having been brought up amongst them at Dunoon. Their party included a German, Ian Schiller, who had 'adopted' the Dennistons and made 'Y' his 'honorary' goddaughter. Although partially lame, he was adept on boats, which was helpful, given that all of their holiday effects needed to be transported to their holiday cottage by boat. AGD had to hurry back to London, leaving the family in Schiller's care. In 1939, the family spent several weekends at Barton-on-Sea, having sold the bungalow in Fairfield Road. That summer they were holidaying in Fowey in Cornwall when, once again, AGD had to suddenly rush back to London.

On 1 August 1939, Sinclair had ordered the Service sections of GC&CS to take up their war stations at BP. The Diplomatic and Commercial Sections were ordered to move to BP on 15 August. At the time of the move to BP, the number of cryptanalysts had grown to around eighty-five and support staff had also increased, with staff numbers totalling around 200. In anticipation of the move, AGD wrote to all his staff on 11 July:

> The War Station is to be manned from 15th August, unless otherwise ordered, in order to carry out a test mobilisation and to test war communications. Combined Navy and Air Force exercises are to take place from 15th to 21st August in which G.C.&C.S. may possibly take part.
>
> Detailed orders for the move of the first wave will be issued later.
>
> Leave arrangements are not to be interfered with. Heads of Sections should inform Commander Travis by 1st August which members of their sections will be on leave in order to assist the billeting and catering department.
>
> With regard to railway fares, petrol allowances and subsistence allowances, the position should be cleared up now with the various departments concerned. It is to be hoped that similar arrangements to those of September 1938 should obtain, namely, Departments to pay full subsistence rates and the staff, being in receipt of lodging and food, should pay over two-thirds and retain one-third with a maximum of 5/- a day.
>
> Mr. Clarke should clear up this question for Naval officers, Captain Tiltman for Military officers, Mr. Cooper for RAF officers and Commander Travis for members of the Foreign Office.[1]

He sent a further communication the following day:

> In order to carry out communication tests the war site will be manned a.m. and p.m. 15th August by those detailed in G.C. & C. S. 1st wave who are not on leave at the time.
>
> [Follows with instructions for those travelling by train or car.]
>
> There will be no travelling allowances for those who do not make use of billets.
>
> The official address for letters will be Room 47 Foreign Office and the telephone No. Whitehall 7947 but no private message is to be made from B. without authority.
>
> The staff are warned against any conversations regarding the work with other members of the staff whilst in their billets. If

> occasion should arise as to what you are doing the answer should be that you are part of the aerial defence of London.

All leave was cancelled and Travis led the first wave of around seventy-four staff to BP and was in charge. He was joined by many of the Section Heads including Clarke (Naval), Miss Milne (Spanish Naval), O'Callaghan (Italian Intelligence), Craufurd (German Intelligence), Westall (Call Signs and Movements), Tiltman (Military), Jacobs (Italian), Cooper (Air) and Knox (Research). AGD himself led the second wave of around thirty-three staff a week later, along with some late arrivals. Hotels in Leighton Buzzard, Bletchley, Bedford, Buckingham and Newport Pagnell were used for accommodation, and there were separate lists for men and women.

Office space was limited at BP and AGD and his section heads were assigned rooms in the old house on the site. AGD's office was on the ground floor in what had been the pre-war owner's morning room. Here, he would personally welcome new staff members when they reported for work. AGD decided that it was time to strengthen the organisation by recruiting the men who had agreed the previous year to undertake secret work for the Foreign Office in the event of war. On 3 September 1939, AGD informed T.J. Wilson of the Foreign Office that they had been obliged to recruit men from the emergency list at the rate of pay agreed by the Treasury:

> For some days now we have been obliged to recruit from our emergency list men of the Professor type who the Treasury agreed to pay at the rate of £600 a year. I attached herewith a list of these gentleman already called up together with the dates of their joining.
>
> I will keep you informed at intervals of further recruitment.'[2]

The first intake arrived between 15 August and 2 September and included R. Bacon, L.W. Forster, Professor G. Waterhouse, Professor W.H. Bruford, N. de Grey, R. Gore Brown, Professor E.R. Vincent, Professor R.J.H. Jenkins and Professor T.S.R. Boase. On 7 September, AGD wrote to Wilson again with a list of the second intake, which included A.T. Hatto, Professor F. Norman, J.R.F. Jeffries, W.G. Welchman, Professor F.E. Adcock, Professor A.H. Campbell, Professor H.M. Last, A.M. Turing, F.L. Birch and Admiral H.W.W. Hope. They arrived between 4 and 6 September. Finally, L.P. Wilkinson and E.J. Passant arrived on 18 September. These twenty-one 'men of the Professor type' formed the vanguard of the vast expansion of GC&CS staff which would follow. Six of them had worked in Room 40, and only three, Jeffries, Turing and Welchman, were mathematicians. Six of the men were linguists, four were historians and eleven were or would become professors.

AGD had organised a short course in London from 3 to 6 January 1939 which was attended by M.P. Charlesworth, P.E. Charvet, D.W. Lucas, L.P. Wilkinson, A.M. Turing, H.M. Last, G.R. Driver, T.F. Higham and C.H. Roberts. Further recruits were put through a course from 20 to 23 March and from 27 to 30 March 1939. They were all earmarked for specific sections at BP on mobilisation and AGD gave a short historical sketch at the beginning of each course.

As more staff began to arrive, the logistical problems which had been identified during the 'dress rehearsal' the previous year, had still not been resolved. AGD wrote to Menzies on 12 September 1939:

> My dear Menzies,
> I am sending you herewith a memorandum which Travis and I have drafted as I had the Admiral's permission to discuss administrative details with you. The whole question will shortly become so acute that it will have to be laid before him for decision, but in the meantime I wish to make you fully aware of the present position and of future requirements.
>
> In addition to the present policy which has forced G.C. and C.S. into disintegration which I have always held to lead to a real loss of efficiency, I take the opportunity of repeating to you the discontent, in the staff of G.C. and C.S. which is now becoming increasingly vocal, with the actual conditions of work.
>
> The contention is that G.C. and C.S., a Civil Service organisation, was moved out of London by orders of the Admiral and not by orders of the Foreign Office (our administrative head) and that therefore the G.C. and C.S. must receive equality of treatment with S.I.S. who were also moved by the Admiral's order.
>
> Travis and myself and the Senior Assistants now occupy fairly senior positions in the Service and many of our recruits are men of considerable distinction and it is definitely felt that in the allocation of accommodation such facts should be taken into account. It appears to me improper to invite such as these to try to do work requiring a high degree of concentration in overcrowded rooms.
>
> Again the question of billeting, which Captain Ridley has carried out with such tact in the face of difficulty, has forced the staff to live many miles from their work and the question of transport is involved. It is felt that official cars can be made available for members of S.I.S. but G.C. and C.S. has had to raise a force of

volunteers from among its own members and ask them to give their time and their cars to help their colleagues. In fine weather it is hard for a man who has had a heavy day to forego his leisure for this – in the dark evenings to come it will be even harder. If there are not sufficient official cars to do this duty would it not be possible to engage the W.V.S. to deal with the transport of the staff between office and billets?

I have done a great deal and will do all I can to maintain a spirit of cooperation. But there is a real spirit of discontent growing among my colleagues. I have congratulated them on the good work that is being done under very trying conditions and the natural reply is improve our conditions and you will get more results.

The few days that have elapsed since the outbreak of war are sufficient to show that we may hope very soon to contribute intelligence of a definite military value to the Fighting Services. If however we are to function efficiently we must be reasonably housed. These are the main considerations.

Cooperation between the three Service Sections is essential.

All sections should be in close proximity to the Teleprinter Room, for a great part of the raw material used by all sections is transmitted from the Y stations and some of the Cable offices. It should be remembered that The Foreign Office agreed to spend £4000 a month to ensure this rapid means of communication for its own ultimate advantage.

I have always viewed with very grave concern the fact that the Military Section has been moved to the garden to make room for a mess which is used for one hour per day, and the Air Section is also being moved away from the teleprinters to make way for a registry. The Air Section should be right on top of the teleprinters and the Naval Section, with whom it may have to confer urgently and frequently.

The Section working on the machine problem is in No. 3 Cottage and development there is becoming much more hopeful and here again they require very close cooperation with the section with whom they are working. The Diplomatic and Commercial Sections are in Elmers[3] School. Although these sections are called Diplomatic certain of them require collaboration with the Service sections and produce matter of military importance. Twenty minutes spent walking backwards and forwards on a dark winter's afternoon is not going to make for efficiency.

Further, the Naval Section is now grossly overcrowded and we have to remember that we have added to our staff volunteers of

> very considerable standing and the research work they will undertake is of extreme national importance and one which calls for some degree of comfort in their surroundings in order to get the best out of them.
>
> It must be remembered that the three weeks we have been here have been remarkably fine and the walking about has been pleasant. With dark afternoons and evenings and cold conditions, people will hesitate to walk out in the open considerable distances to confer with colleagues. In our overcrowded state the use of the telephone, never satisfactory, is impossible.
>
> It seems that there is not room to house SIS and GC&CS in Bletchley Park efficiently. The only alternative therefore is to separate. It appears to be most difficult to move the teleprinters and provide lines for them, and it therefore remains to examine whether alternative accommodation can be found for some or all sections of SIS.[4]

On 14 September AGD received a reply from Sinclair:

> Colonel Menzies has reported to me the results of his interview with yourself and Travis, yesterday. I understand that some temporary arrangement of erecting further huts is contemplated, which it seems to me will not meet the case.
>
> Now that the dug-out in the basement of Broadway Buildings is approaching completion, which will accommodate up to 500 people, is there any reason why the Diplomatic Section and the Commercial Section (2nd Wave) should not return to Broadway Buildings, so that the situation at the War Station, which I understand you describe as unbearable, may be relieved?
>
> If you concur that this is desirable, in the interests of efficiency, arrangements should be made for the Second Wave to return to Broadway Buildings as soon as conveniently possible. If, however, you do not concur, I shall require from you the fullest and most convincing reasons as to why this should not be done.
>
> Pending an immediate reply from you, I shall not give orders in regard to this matter. I understand that, in any case, the teleprinters will not be required to be transferred from the War Station, as I have gone very carefully into this matter, and I find that the material can be obtained direct from the Censors and Cable & Wireless.

Sinclair wrote again to AGD the following day after consulting with the DNI:

> It is quite apparent to me that the Commercial Section of the G.C. & C.S. will require large additions to the staff, in order to enable it to cope with the work with which it is confronted.
>
> As it is quite impossible to accommodate such individuals at Bletchley, arrangements should be made for the early return of the whole of this Section to London, in order that the work may be properly dealt with.

AGD had always believed that all of GC&CS should remain at BP and he made his case most strenuously in a note to Sinclair on 16 September:

> In my private letter to Menzies I did not describe the position as unbearable and I was careful to raise in the annex only matters affecting the efficiency of the Service Sections. The transfer of the Diplomatic Sections to Broadway would not affect this problem, nor would it be possible to separate the Service Sections by housing one of them in the School.
>
> Although I have no doubt that our personal safety would not suffer by return to Broadway, and personally I should much prefer to be near my home, I do feel that that the possibility of hours spent on a crowded public shelter and the time wasted in putting work away and getting it out again would render any real work by the Diplomatic and Commercial Sections quite impossible.
>
> Suburban rail and road transport is difficult at present and it may become considerably worse, in which case it will be extremely difficult to put in a full day's work.
>
> The work of the G.C. & C.S. as a whole is bound to suffer if we are split into two sections e.g. as a first step in the coordination of the scrutiny of the mass of German traffic from all sources I have established under my own control a central German Coordination Section and would be difficult to determine whether this should be in Broadway or Bletchley.
>
> My submission therefore is that the whole of the G.C. & C.S. including the Commercial Section should remain at Bletchley.
>
> Captain Ridley is now arranging to remove the private furniture from the school and to have the lighting and heating put in order, when this has been done the working conditions in the school will be greatly improved. The large schoolroom is at present practically empty and I propose to transfer the Commercial Section there; it will accommodate about 30. If and when it were found necessary to expand this Section further, it should be possible to transfer the staff engaged on decoding legible commercial codes to a place near M.E.W.

> There has been no question of the erection of huts for the Diplomatic and Commercial Sections.
>
> There is now under consideration a plan for the erection of huts just outside the grounds of BP to house the Service Sections including their necessary expansion, thereby facilitating the necessary expansion of various sections of SIS. It would be necessary to connect these huts with the Teleprinter Room by pneumatic tube.
>
> Finally I shall be personally very greatly relieved when these administrative difficulties are settled as I am most anxious to take my share of the work on the increasing numbers of cryptographic problems confronting us.

Crucially, for the ultimate success of BP, AGD won the day and by 29 September 1939, the huts were under construction.

AGD had kept in contact with Bertrand and in September, a party of French intelligence officers including Bertrand and Henri Braquenie visited BP. Knox was tasked with looking after them, and true to form, was soon writing to AGD about the matter:

> My dear Denniston,
>
> I think it is time we settled on one or two points of general principle.
>
> Entertainment. It has been a great pleasure to me, though somewhat testing to my knowledge of French, to bear-lead Captain B. from 8 a.m. to 10 p.m. I have taken the line, though he offered to pay generously, that entertainment is une affaire de bureau: that is, from my angle, that I should get a billeting allowance from you or Ridley and that you or he should deal with the French. Drinks and transport other than that to or from the Office (for which I get an allowance) I treat as private liability. I trust that this view has been right and will continue, since I don't like making special charges.
>
> Machinery material and Statistics (Liaison).
>
> We can also continue to cooperate on the reconstruction of the two Italian codes. As yet, there has been no discussion on Italian naval and military cyphers and on this question I should like to receive orders in view of the fact (a) that I suspect that the Italian Navy is being worked in another branch in Paris, and (b) that the Foreign Office considered that cooperation on the Italian military telegrams between Spain and Rome was, at that time, undesirable. I assume that Commander Travis handles any questions of finance arising from price of machinery or material (paper for 'Netz (Filets)' or wood or cardboard for rods).

Statistics. (Up to present). I take it that we have been making statistics at our own expense and Travis charges the material to the French.

As regards labour, then we should keep a check, if at all, only on time spent in reduplication which may be considerable as we may have to mark, punch and cut holes twice. It is easy to keep a check on time spent in this way. The French would get their stuff at about a quarter of what we would pay. I don't see how they can actively help as they are a very long time behind and we should have to fly over heavy machines and quantities of paper, or, if they did help, risk everything being out of gauge.

At present I am talking only of Jeffrey's 'Netz (filets)', (reduplication will begin in a few days), where I made some rather conditional offers, without, of course, mentioning finance. I think, however, we could only charge here for reduplication.

In the matter of sex-statistics there is no precise arrangement as yet either as to methods of as to finance, since all progress has been made since B's departure (see my letter of the 26th Sept.). If my estimate of my new machine with Travis's and H.-M's improvements is correct we could either:

handle the whole affair on a fifty-fifty basis, or

Charge for necessary reduplications as suggested for Jeffrey's 'Netz (Filets)'.

If you can give any definite ruling as to whether:

We make no charge for labour.

We charge only for extra labour of reduplication.

We charge fifty-fifty.

I will institute a simple system of checking if necessary.[5]

On 4 September, two Cambridge mathematicians who were on AGD's list arrived at BP and would prove to be fundamental to its ultimate success; Alan Turing, aged 27, from Kings College, and Gordon Welchman, aged 33, from Sydney Sussex. Both were greeted separately by AGD and then told to report to Knox, who had moved along with his small team into one of three cottages in the stableyard behind the house. Knox already knew Turing, as he had done some part-time work for GC&CS in 1938. Welchman had attended the courses in London in March but would later write that he had no recollection of meeting Knox at that time. While Turing remained in 'The Cottage' with Knox, Welchman was moved to the former Elmers School. It lay outside of the grounds of BP and had been acquired by GC&CS to provide additional office accommodation. While primarily tasked with analysing specific information included in every Enigma encrypted message,[6] Welchman had other ideas forming in his mind.

When AGD and Edward Travis came together in 1919 in the newly-formed GC&CS, AGD had taken responsibility for cipher breaking, and Travis for cipher security under him. This separation of roles continued in the early days at BP, even though the cipher 'Construction Section' was now based in Oxford. Travis had been made responsible for the Service Sections of GC&CS in 1938. AGD was very busy coping with the administrative problems arising from the move to Bletchley and the subsequent expansion and as a result did not spend much time out of his office. Travis did make it a habit to get out of the office to see the work on the ground and talk to the staff. So Travis was in effect responsible for the 'Enigma Section', though Dilly often continued to write straight to AGD. Travis also had a direct interest in the security of Enigma as at this time he was concerned with the deployment in the British Services of the Typex machine, which was designed on very similar lines.

Working away in Elmers School with another member of Knox's team, Tony Kendrick, Welchman was seeing something in the intercepted traffic which had escaped others. As he later recalled:

> Previously I suppose I had absorbed the common view that Cryptanalysis was a matter of dealing with individual messages of solving intricate puzzles and of working in a secluded back room, with little contact with the outside world. As I studied the first collection of decodes, however, I began to see, somewhat dimly, that I was involved in something very different. We were dealing with an entire communications system that would serve the needs of the German ground and air forces. The call signs came alive as representing elements of those forces, whose commanders at various echelons would have to send messages to each other. The use of different keys[7] for different purposes, which was known to be the reason for the discriminants, suggested different command structures for the various aspects of military operations.[8]

While analysis of the enemy's wireless traffic was undertaken both by Room 40 and MI1(b) during WW1, what no one at BP seemed to have recognised was that a considerable amount of intelligence could be obtained from intercepted German messages by analysing the traffic as a whole. Welchman drew up a comprehensive plan calling for the close coordination of radio interception, analysis of the intercepted traffic, breaking Enigma keys, decrypting messages on the broken keys and extracting intelligence from the decrypts. It is likely that as Travis was a more visible presence at BP in the early days, Welchman decided to present his plan to him and he immediately saw the urgent need to act on it. Welchman convinced Travis that a large scaling-up of the effort would be needed when the methods of breaking Enigma, outlined in his plan, produced results. He was in effect proposing a system of mass production which was completely at odds with the approach taken by Knox. In his world, the various tasks of decryption, translation and writing the resulting out-going message were all performed essentially by one cryptanalyst. Welchman and now Travis realised that this approach would simply not be able to handle the volumes of intercepted traffic envisaged. It would have to be replaced by a clear division of labour amongst a team of experts. Travis won AGD over to the idea and then remarkably, persuaded Whitehall to back this gamble, even though not one German Enigma message had ever been broken in the UK either before or since the war began.

Welchman's plan was soon the subject of discussion around BP and not surprisingly, Knox was not happy with it. His view was that research was all important and that 'Bletchley Park should be a cryptographical bureau supplying its results straight and unadorned to Intelligence Sections at the various Ministries. At present we are encumbered with "Intelligence Officers" who maul and conceal our results, yet make no effort to check up on their arbitrary corrections.'

He was questioning the whole intelligence distribution chain which was being proposed for BP. The following letters reveal Knox's views and AGD's patient attempt to explain the rationale for Welchman's plan.[9]

On 6 October 1940, Knox wrote:

> My dear Denniston,
> This Italian business has now diverted large proportions & takes almost all our time in the cottage & very much work is done in the hut. While I expressed myself willing to decode occasionally for the Naval Section, I am bound now to raise the question of circulation. Apart from consideration of our position – why should the largest & most important section not use its own existing mouthpiece? – the Enigma results are of an order of certainty differing wholly from the products of most other intelligence sections.
>
> On personal grounds I find that I have been ?? to our arrangement of Dec 5th etc. Had I appreciated at the time the sense in which you now take it – I should have gone to any lengths to oppose it.

I must ask you to deal at once with the question. I have no intention of continuing to work as an obscure subordinate of Commander Clarke.

Yours faithfully

A.D. Knox

On 8 October 1940, AGD replied:

My dear Knox,

Here is my view of what happened. If there are any discrepancies – we can clear them up.

The meeting of December 5th decided on the division of Enigma work into Research and Production. When on January 24th the first current solution was obtained the section known as FJ (now Hut 3) was formed to translate and circulate this traffic and to study. It accepted the cover of S.I.S. and all results are attributed to Secret Service reports. That is the existing mouthpiece of the German Air – Army Enigma.

When in January the solution of the Spanish Naval Attaché Enigma messages was obtained, circulation was controlled and continues to be controlled by the Spanish Naval Section.

When the research party broke into the Naval Enigma for certain days in April, the circulation of results was made through the German naval section.

When the machine used by the German Railways was fixed early in August results were circulated from the military section.

If, as I hope, you obtain the solution of the machine used by the German Secret Service I anticipate that Strachey's section will handle the circulation, as they have already dealt with so much traffic in other cyphers.

As far as the Italian Naval Enigma is concerned (the subject of your letter), I cannot understand why you should wish for an alteration of the practice.

Clarke deals with the circulation of all this traffic of which the Enigma forms a part. He dealt with it pre-war days when you first broke into the machine.

If the duty were given to Hut 3 it would be necessary to find Italian speaking staff to work there and to study the contents, in fact to duplicate the work which Clark's section already does.

So far as the personal side is concerned I hope you do not underrate your own position. From the above it is obvious that the Research side of Enigma, which you direct, has met with very considerable success

> and it must be perfectly clear to you, to all those concerned in G.C. & C.S. and to the recipients of the decodes that without the Cottage and Huts 6 and 8 there would be no enigma traffic.
>
> That is my view: I cannot, therefore, see any reason why the existing methods of circulation should be changed.

AGD had always had a cordial working relationship with Sinclair, who as DNI had been part of the Committee which had appointed AGD to his post. Sinclair had been suffering from cancer of the spleen and was taken to hospital in late October 1939. Characteristically, he sent a message to a friend on the morning of 4 November saying 'First bulletin: Nearly dead'. He died at 4.30 pm on the same day. Stewart Menzies was Sinclair's deputy and the day after Sinclair died, he gave Lord Cadogan, Permanent Under-Secretary for Foreign Affairs, a sealed letter written by Sinclair two days earlier. In it Sinclair strongly recommended that Menzies should succeed him.[10] After a delay of three weeks, Cadogan noted in his diary on 27 November: 'Tiresome letter from Menzies, with whom I sympathise. Am trying to binge up H. [Lord Halifax] to get decision [on Sinclair's successor] tomorrow. M. [Menzies] is in a difficult position, and it's silly of everyone to go on funking Winston.'

It seems that Churchill favoured Admiral John Godfrey, who had succeeded Sinclair as DNI. However, he had been a battleship admiral and only had some ten months in the intelligence service. The following day, at a meeting attended by the Prime Minister and the service ministers, Cadogan wrote that Lord Halifax 'played his hand well and won the trick'. It was unanimously agreed that Menzies should have the job and on the 29th, Halifax duly offered it to him. There was a caveat that there should be 'some enquiry' into the organisation of the Service.[11]

On 18 November 1939, AGD received the following memo:

> <u>Commander Denniston.</u>
> Now that we may with some hope look forward to the state when we shall be able to deal with some of the German Enigma traffic, I think we must consider how best the traffic could be deciphered with the minimum loss of time.
>
> If conditions remain as at present, I understand the position to be such that when the 'Netz' are complete we shall be able to decipher traffic from several groups which use the Standard Indicating System. When this becomes a fact I should like to see Research divorced from Production and the work organised on the following lines:-

> Research Section who should investigate the still unknown problems such as the Naval and T.G.D. This should be done by Knox, Kendrick, Turing, Miss Nugent, and such of the clerks as Knox requires.
>
> The production section requires dividing into several subsections as follows:-
>
> Receiving, Registration, sorting and W/T Liaison. This section would prepare data for Netz and Bombes. Staff: Welchman, Twinn and 4 clerks.
>
> 'Netz' party. The work of finding machine settings etc., from sheets punched from cyclometer results, Jeffries + X assistants
>
> 'Bombes' machines run by Dawson + 1 assistant.
>
> Decyphering Section. This should include staff to test 'Netz' and 'Bombes' results. They will decipher all available traffic with minimum loss of time and pass to Service Sections for translation. It will require someone (or ones) with good German to scrutinise traffic before passing on for translation. Two female clerks must be trained by R.A.F. to work their machines.
>
> A special hut will be required for the Production section.[12]

The memo itself is not signed and was certainly not written by Welchman, as he would never have proposed himself for any specific role. At the top right of the front page of the memo are the words 'Paper? By EWT'. It is highly unlikely that Travis would have used the words 'I should like to see' to his superior. In all likelihood, it was written by Menzies who was already making his mark on part of his new organisation. It was clearly based on the Welchman proposal[13] for an organisation which would remain basically unchanged throughout the war, with the hut numbers becoming, in effect, the cover name for their activities. The new Production section initially set up shop in the Elmers School and by late January 1940, two new wooden huts were ready for occupation. The Production section moved into Hut 6 and soon became known by that name. The linguists and intelligence officers who would translate and interpret their output moved into the adjacent Hut 3 and soon adopted that as their section name. Their naval counterparts would eventually be housed in Huts 8 and 4. Travis continued to take direct responsibility for the Enigma huts as they came on stream, their staff and the mechanisation programme.

The 'Menzies memo' can be seen as a direct challenge to AGD and his position as Head of GC&CS. He was very much Hall and the Admiralty's man when he took up his post at the end of WW1. He maintained an excellent working relationship with Sinclair but his relationship with Menzies was less certain. Menzies was, after all, an Army man and Hay, the Army's candidate to be Head of GC&CS, had been overlooked in favour of AGD. However, there is no evidence that Menzies was party to the process which saw AGD chosen over Hay. Perhaps AGD's letter to Menzies on 12 September, describing all of the administrative difficulties at BP had planted in Menzies's mind, seeds of doubt about AGD's managerial competence.

***

Both Turing and Welchman had started to think about how machines could help with the work soon after their arrival at BP. First Travis and then AGD had been won over to the potential of machines to speed up the decryption process. Turing's work on a machine solution had reached the build stage by the autumn of 1939 and the British Tabulating Machine Company at Letchworth had been contracted to carry out the work. Their Research Director, Harold 'Doc' Keen needed to be briefed on BP's requirements and one of Knox's team, Peter Twinn, was given the task.[14] By March 1940, the manufacture of the prototype Bombe, a complex electro-mechanical machine, was well under way. The first prototype, named Victory, was installed in Hut 1 on 18 March but did not prove particularly effective. It was only when a second and improved machine was installed in Hut 1 in August that real results were achieved. This machine, named Agnus, incorporated a brilliant design modification invented by Welchman and called the Diagonal Board. Victory was then moved to Wavendon as a training machine, as it was unreliable and six more machines were on order by November. The first of the even more sophisticated models, the Jumbo Bombe, arrived in Hut 11 in March 1941.

Recruitment started almost immediately for the high-quality staff that would be needed after the emergency list that AGD had drawn up the year before was quickly exhausted. A new intake was needed as soon as possible. Welchman returned to Cambridge and began recruiting former colleagues and students, while Travis recruited from the commercial world. A number of young and intelligent women were brought into the fledgling Hut 6. With recruitment came administration to support it and on 10 November, 1939, AGD issued a notice that 'In future Paymaster A.N. Bradshaw R.N. will act as General Administrative Officer for the G.C. & C.S. and all questions in this connection should be referred to him.'[15] On 8 October 1940, AGD informed staff of further changes in the administration of BP: 'By direction of the CSS, the general administration of the War Station B.P. will in future be under the joint management of Captain Ridley R.N.

and Paymaster Commander Bradshaw R.N. who will form a Joint Management Committee (short title J.M.C.).'

During 1940 and 1941 this committee issued notices on subjects such as catering, billeting, addresses, personal security, maintenance/repairs and appointment of administrative sub-sections. It was abolished on 12 May 1941 after the Joint Committee of Control (JCC) was set up in April. It was chaired by the Deputy Chief of the Secret Service (Valentine Vivian) and included Travis, Tiltman, Bradshaw, Earnshaw-Smith, Hope, Cooper, Ridley, Hastings and Woodfield. At its meeting of 5 April 1941, it dealt with the future of Elmers School, catering and the BP recreational club and tennis courts. On 12 April they agreed to recommend building a dining hall with provision for serving 1,000 at each meal. It was agreed to take over extra land if suitable.

Knox continued to be a thorn in AGD's side and usually included a threat of resignation along with his latest complaint. He wrote to AGD on 7 January 1940,[16] reminding him that 'on our journey to Warsaw I promised to assist the Poles and the French in producing statistics'. This had not been done and Knox went on to say, 'My personal feelings on this matter are so strong that unless they leave by Wednesday night I shall tender my resignation.' Surprisingly, given that Knox was supposed to be at the heart of the Enigma work, he closes with: 'I do not want to go to Paris but if you cannot secure another messenger I am actually at the moment completely idle.' In the end Turing was sent to Paris to meet the Poles. On 9 January 1940, unknown to Knox, AGD wrote to Menzies with regards to the Poles:

> Dear Menzies,
> Here are the names of the three young Poles, Jerzy Różycki, Marian Rejewski, Hendryk Zygalski.
>
> If we are faced with a change on the outbreak of war (and we begin to suspect it), the experience of these men may shorten our task by months.
>
> We possess certain mechanical devices which cannot be transferred to France. These young men possess ten years' experience and a short visit from them might prove of very great value.[17]

On 10 January, AGD wrote to Rivet, Bertrand's superior, urging him to allow the three Poles to visit Britain for a short period. They were at that time working at a joint French/Polish intelligence station near Paris called PC Bruno, and the request was denied by the French.

AGD's workload was increasing dramatically and not only was he dealing directly with the three Service Ministries, he was also in regular contact with intelligence chiefs, as the following memo from DNI John Godfrey, sent on 31 October, reveals:

> Clarke has been complaining about delays in sending naval intelligence out to Commanders-in-Chief. He understands that the R.A.F. Section transmit direct to Cairo without reference to the Air Ministry using the R.A.F. High Speed W/T Service. This may be the origin of Clarke's complaint.
>
> He goes on to say that the Chiefs of Staff are instructing the three Commanders-in-Chief to set up a Combined Bureau under Jacob.
>
> He also says 'I am going into the question of setting up an organisation to arrange "pinches", and I think the solution will be found in a combined committee of talent in your department and mine, who can think out cunning schemes.' [18]

On 9 April 1940, the so-called 'Phoney War'[19] ended when Germany invaded Denmark and then Holland on 10 May. A new Enigma military key appeared on 10 April for operational traffic involving all three German services. It was broken daily by Hut 6 from 15 April and as the workload increased, Hut 3 moved to a three-shift system. Intelligence reports, disguised as agents' reports, were passed to the War Office and Air Ministry and they in turn communicated the information in secrecy to commands in Norway. The Admiralty also had a communication channel in place and had been informed as early as 5 January that messages prefixed 'HYDRO' would contain information 'from a very authentic and secret source'. On 15 May, the prefix was changed to 'ULTRA'.[20] Hut 6 had decided to concentrate its limited resources on the general-purpose 'Red' key of the GAF although there was an increasing amount of military traffic. In early May, the Germans changed the Enigma indicator system that the Poles had exploited[21] which meant that no breaks were made again until 22 May. From that point on, success was continuous as traffic increased to 1,000 messages per day. However, the Service channels were by now completely disrupted and by 24 May only one link remained, a SIS mobile unit attached to GHQ

Unfortunately, the Sigint intelligence proved to be of little tactical value at this stage for several reasons. Hut 3 lacked experience and the reference books and maps necessary to assess the information were unavailable. Ministries found it difficult to assess its significance and commanders in the field could only take the intelligence at face value as agents' reports. Furthermore, the intelligence reports frequently arrived too late for action to be taken. Finally, there was no real military capability in the field to act on it in an effective way. GC&CS had, however, put in place a secure method of distributing intelligence to GHQ in France. Signals were typed and then checked by the No. 5 of the Hut 3 Watch.[22] One copy was passed to the SIS Codes Section in BP where the message was encrypted with an OTP. This version was taken by despatch rider to Section VIII at Whaddon[23] for transmission over the SIS W/T channel to the SIS representative in France for decrypting into plain text before delivery to GHQ.

By April 1940, GC&CS's Naval Section had built up a fairly complete picture of the German W/T organisation as part of its work on traffic analysis in support of cryptanalysis. From the beginning of 1940, short reports of operational interest were flowing via teleprinter from German Naval Section to the Admiralty. Some senior staff seemed to resent this intrusion on their 'patch' and thus, at its prompting, the Operational Intelligence Centre (OIC) was sceptical. The sinking of the aircraft carrier HMS *Glorious* off Namsos by *Scharnhorst* and *Gneisenau* on 8 June was a turning point in the OIC view of GC&CS intelligence, as they had ignored several weeks of warnings from GC&CS. The War Office and Air Ministry also showed an increasing confidence in the work of AGD's organisation by placing officers in Hut 3. By the summer of 1940, the RAF intercept station at Chatham started its move to Chicksands.

Thanks in part to intelligence from BP, the British Government realised that the British Expeditionary Force in Europe was in a hopeless position. From 27 May until 4 June, some 338,000 men, of whom 224,000 were British troops, were rescued from the beaches of Dunkirk. The evacuation of Norway was completed by 8 June and on 10 June Italy declared war against France and Great Britain. German Panzer divisions quickly moved across France and the country was forced to surrender on 22 June.

Given that Britain now stood alone and invasion was a real possibility, AGD put together a plan to ensure that his organisation could continue to operate if Britain was overrun. On 26 June 1940, he wrote to Menzies with the details:

> I attach a plan for the disposal of our records and would be glad to know which items of this plan you would sanction in order that I may take early action. My plan does entail certain risks, though risks may have to be taken at this stage. I have not mentioned a more far reaching suggestion namely to contemplate sending skeleton crews of certain Diplomatic Sections to Canada. The difficulty would be that we would obtain very little material and I doubt whether at this

stage such a plan would do more than attempt to preserve continuity for a post war era.

DISPOSAL OF RECORDS

To Canada via D.M. and D.N.I. Ottawa.

Office personal records.
CXFJ records of 1940.
Plans of main machines.
One E machine.

Lloyds Bank Dunstable.

Office personal records.
Copies of main important books.
Sectional records

This because when all is over (a) either we have won or (b) we are defeated.

If (a) we may want to begin again.

If (b) a compromise of our activities will not surprise the victors, should they discover these papers.

In this respect, I blame myself alone for destruction of French naval records which <u>might</u> have been of use today.

Certain Diplomatic sections may be invaluable during negotiations viz. American, S. American, Spanish, Vatican, Turkish, Arabic, Persian, Chinese & Japanese.

If I can disperse these sections in a crisis in the case of trustworthy leaders to unobtrusive unknown private homes with a promise of destruction in the face of danger, these sections could be reassembled and made to function at short notice should it be necessary and should material again become available.

Thus, for example, the American section (Captain Hanly and Miss Curtis) have a little villa in Water Eaton. They could here keep current books and material and rejoin; the Chinese section leader, Colonel Jeffrey, is with Sir Everard Duncombe at Great Brickhill with cellars and security and obviously a country gentleman and nothing more.

> Similarly I might find safe homes for the other important sections. Some risk must be accepted. If we are defeated, what extra harm will be done, if we win we keep the stuff in odd places and start again when we are wanted.[24]

By September 1940, BP's codebreaking efforts were starting to have real impact on the conduct of the war. Hut 6 broke a key which they called Brown I and was used by the GAF Signals Experimental Regiment.[25] An earlier decrypt on 5 June revealed that something called 'Knickebein' was being used by German aircraft with special receiving equipment. It was already known that this was the cover name for navigational beams. No.8 Group (Bomber Command) was formed and became responsible for all radio countermeasures. By October, their success forced the Germans to switch to another system, the 'X Gerãt', used by the pathfinders of KG 100 to locate and illuminate targets for the main bomber force. Hut 6's break of Brown I allowed the X Gerãt transmissions to be jammed by the end of 1940. Good liaison was established between Huts 6 and 3 and Assistant Director of Intelligence (Science) in this work. As Birch wrote in his Official History after the war: 'In 1940 we find only the beginnings of a long story of closely integrated cooperation between operators, log-readers, low and high-grade cryptanalysts, reporting staff and technical intelligence officers that lasted throughout the war and was unique of its kind in the history of British Sigint.'

***

To provide contingency against damage to the six fixed Y stations operational at Denmark Hill, Sandridge, Cheadle, Chatham, Flowerdown and Scarborough, Chicksands was selected as a suitable inter-service site and houses at Wavendon were acquired as a back-up to BP. In case of invasion, quarters were found for around 150 GC&CS staff near Market Drayton. The position by the end of September was grim, with buses providing transport not operable, incomplete billeting accommodation, intercept conditions dubious and a lack of an alternative site evident.[26] AGD did not believe GC&CS could function if it had to move far from BP. By 13 September, German Naval Section inferred from traffic analysis that everything was in place for an invasion but on the 15th, the danger of immediate invasion had receded. This was confirmed from special intelligence at the end of October.

When Italy came into the war, GC&CS was better prepared because of its focus on Italy and Japan between the wars. However, from September 1940, the Italian components of the three service sections at

~~BP struggled to maintain enough staff as many were seconded to~~ locally-based units at Alexandria, Sarafand and Cairo. Some work in the field on Italian ciphers was supported by GC&CS and some at BP as research activity. Middle East military commands wanted more GC&CS staff, claiming that delays rendered its contribution 'of academic interest only by the time it is received'.[27] These claims were rejected by the heads of the Army and Air sections at BP, Tiltman and Cooper.[28]

The Italians had made changes to their high-level code books and ciphers in July and added new ones so that by the end of the year, a multiplicity of new ciphers caused a complete blackout. However, in September Knox broke an Italian machine which had been in use during the Spanish Civil War. While traffic was minimal, it included very important intelligence – most dramatically during the Battle of Matapan.[29] Middle East Control was having success with the East African cipher, while GC&CS struggled against the main Mediterranean cipher which changed frequently. Thus Middle East control pressed for control over all Italian Sigint work. AGD, however, continued to argue for the model of research at home and exploitation in a combined Middle East bureau. A party from GC&CS consisting of one naval, three military, three RAF and two Foreign Office officials[30] left England on 18 July, followed in August by the head of the Italian Military section, F.A. Jacob, and clerical staff. The intention was to set up an inter-service cryptanalytic centre. AGD reported that 'it is not yet known where they will work in Cairo nor under whose organisation'.[31] The three Directors of Intelligence agreed on 29 October that an inter-service cryptographic bureau should be set up under Jacob.[32] The so-called W Committee in Cairo accepted the proposal with certain reservations, as the new Combined Bureau Middle East (CBME) was in effect a cryptanalytical bureau, not a Sigint centre. CBME was supposed to be an inter-service cryptanalytic section reporting to a W Committee. As AGD said 'there is in effect as yet no real inter-service bureau but three components each taking orders from their own Service authorities, Jacob [Lt.-Col Jacob, Director CBME] being allowed to try to co-ordinate their work'.[33]

While the Italian Naval Signals Intelligence Section was making little progress, according to Clarke, Head of the Italian Naval Section at GC&CS,

> it would be a mistake to bring Murray's [Commander J. Murray, Head of SI] party home. Cryptography has its ups and downs, and a little luck might easily change the situation in a moment. The capture of documents might … create the necessity for a decoding

> staff there – there has never been a cryptographical staff. There are plenty of minor ... jobs for them to tackle now – Fleet codes, reporting codes, mercantile codes, etc. Their efforts are wasted, if they try problems too hard for them.[34]

While AGD thought that the inter-service Sigint model should be followed in the Middle East, Birch argued in his Official History that while inter-service was a nice principle,

> at GC&CS itself, although the Sigint work of all three Services was conducted in one place to very great mutual advantage, inter-service fusion of functioning was limited to the use of analytic machinery and to army-air partnership in the solution of and exploitation of German Army and Air Enigma traffic as a result of the originally fortuitous interception of the GAF traffic by a military Y station and the subsequent artificial segregation of this enterprise from all other Sigint activities, and of its subordination not to War Office and Air Ministry but to SIS.

As early as 1937, the cooperation of Commonwealth Allies had been sought to obtain traffic from commercial telegraphy stations. There was wireless intercept cooperation with the navies of Canada, Australia and New Zealand from around 1925, and DNI Ottawa's station at Esquimalt, British Columbia became a useful source of commercial intercepts for GC&CS. As well as Esquimalt on the Pacific, Canadian naval Sigint had Y and direction finding stations at Hartlen Point, Nova Scotia, and St. Hubert, Quebec. Australia also wanted to help and considered it 'desirable to examine the possibility of establishing a nucleus organisation in this country to guard against the contingency of operations in and about Australia and her territories'.[35] However, little was achieved for some time. New Zealand established a 'Combined Intelligence Bureau and Central War Room' in Wellington in September, and exchanged information with FECB in Singapore. South Africa could do nothing officially for political reasons, but discretely, a chain of direction finding stations at Bloemfontein, Durban, Johannesburg, Komatipoort, Port Elizabeth and Simonstown proved valuable.

Other European allies emerged, and the Finnish General Staff offered cooperation with a GC&CS Russian Section and Tiltman obtained from them 'information, copies of documents and intercepted material of very great value'.[36] Just before the French campaign, French Navy and Army cryptanalysts were seconded to GC&CS. However, after the French armistice with Germany on 22 June 1940, they gradually left BP.[37]

Birch summed up the situation at BP at the end of 1940 as follows:

> Dissected thus, G.C. & C.S. as a working organism appears freakish. Its administration was not made easier by the fact that Bletchley Park was at that time the 'War Station' of the S.I.S as well. In November 1939, Commander Denniston had appointed Paymaster-Commander A.R. Bradshaw, R.N. (retd.) as 'General Administrative Officer for the G.C. & C.S.' component but in October 1940 'by direction of the C.S.S., the general administration of the whole War Station was placed under a 'Joint Management Committee' (J.M.C.) consisting of Captain W.H.W. Ridley, R.N. (S.I.S.) and Paymaster-Commander A.R. Bradshaw (G.C. & C.S.). The dual control did not function very smoothly or efficiently, and, what with one thing and another, the administration both of work and for maintenance came in for a good deal of criticism.
>
> The case for the defence is fairly obvious: It is easy to be wise after the event; in a succession of emergencies only hand-to-mouth empirical improvisations are possible. With so many Ministries fingering the pie, each proffering a different solution to every problem and demanding different treatment, no uniform pattern was possible. The unforeseeable contingencies of bombing and invasion made long-term and large scale planning impossible. In 16 months the nominal role of G.C. & C.S. had increased fourfold and, if working accommodation and billets were insufficient and bad, morale was never higher (civilian recruits had all volunteered, and war was not yet routine).
>
> However, these weighty considerations do not entirely dispel the impression of a rudderless vessel buffeted about at the mercy of every wave of circumstance. On the one hand, there is considerable negative evidence of the lack of any adequate machinery for government; on the other hand, there seems to have been some confusion between administration in the sense of governing and administration in the sense of providing ancillary services; so that policy appears unduly conditioned to the convenience of the latter. Such, at all events, were the opinions formed, and expressed more bluntly, in the Service Ministries. Signs of a change of outlook on the part of the G.C. & C.S. management are, however, perceptible in a memorable 'Introductory Remark' to Commander Denniston's 'Report for 1940' to the Director: 'In the past we have fitted the work into the huts as they became available. I believe greater efficiency could be obtained by arranging the huts to suit the work.'

AGD's end-of-year report to Menzies reveals just how busy his organisation had been:

> *Executive Summary:*
>
> I submit herewith a survey of the work of the G.C. & C.S. during 1940, and a report on the position of enemy and neutral ciphers at the beginning of 1941.
>
> I have included a brief resume of the methods of circulation of results to the Departments concerned in case you may wish to make any alterations or expansion.
>
> I have also given details of the staff at present employed on the work, with the estimate from Heads of Sections of necessary increases during 1941.
>
> I have had to ask your sanction for increase of accommodation at the Park during 1940, and it is only my duty to keep you informed of any possible further demands which may have to be made during the coming year.
>
> The increase of staff to meet increase of traffic, and success in tackling new problems, is very closely connected with office accommodation, billeting and transport.
>
> I would suggest that any further building be based on a long-term plan rather than hut-building to accommodate new sections.
>
> In the past we have fitted the work into the huts as they became available. I believe greater efficiency could be obtained by arranging the huts to suit the work.
>
> The ideal (which we can now not attain) would be a star-shaped conclave (to permit expansion) with a D & R (Distribution & Routing) and Teleprinter room in the centre, all interconnects with pneumatic tubes.
>
> The saving of time and staff would well have justified a high initial expenditure.
>
> From the purely cryptographic side of the report certain facts emerge very quickly:
>
> Germans and Russians have taken steps that their diplomatic cyphers shall <u>not</u> be read.
>
> Both these powers have had ample warnings and have profited.
>
> With the introduction, during 1940, of individual tables into our own F.O. service, I am satisfied that at last our own diplomatic authorities have adopted enemy methods and safeguarded our cypher communications.

From a perusal of the reports of our service sections, it seems clear to me that the Naval authorities of the Great Powers pay greater attention to cypher security than their sister services.

Although we employ a large staff of experts on German Naval and Italian Naval work, very few Naval cyphers have become legible since the entry into the war of these powers. French Naval cyphers are legible chiefly because of the capture of the French S/M *Narval*. We had, therefore, been forced in peace to study the new art of W/T Intelligence or Y Intelligence and to assist in its development. I do not, however, intend to include any notes on this subject in this cryptographic report.

The Far East and Near East, who had hoped perhaps that their security lay in language, have been obliged also to tighten up their cypher methods.

We are nearly keeping pace and obtaining solutions but it is only a matter of time until these Powers too produce methods which may make solution more difficult and irregular.

In 1935 I asked Commander Travis to investigate the possibilities of mechanical aids in our work. He started then, but only in 1940 was he able to achieve very considerable success, as is shown in his report.

I consider this success largely due to Travis' intimate cooperation with B.T.M. who have given of their best in staff and equipment, and Travis has known how to utilise it. Thousands of hours and hundreds of staff have been saved by these efforts.

This success has forced us to modify our views on the safety of subtractor tables. Every service using general tables must provide an adequate supply to enable more frequent changes, and must institute safeguards against misuse and overuse of their tables.

Were it not for the loyal cooperation of Colonel Tiltman (Head of the Military Section) and Mr. Cooper (Head of the Air Section) I hardly know how this large interservice office could have been run. Tiltman and Cooper both owe loyalty to their Service chiefs. But they have never failed to back our main duty, attack on enemy cyphers. They are well aware that interservice cooperation as it pertains here is the only way of fulfilling the functions for which we are appointed.

Apart from the normal expansion in the various sections as detailed in this report, I have in mind the development, in which all my senior colleagues agree, of a Service Distribution and Reference office on the same lines as the Diplomatic D. and R. of which Smith is the Head.

Decodes of operational value will continue to be teleprinted direct by the Sections as at present. The distribution of typed copies would however be done by this new Section, who would also distribute them among the Sections here, and maintain all the information from this and other sources in a form for easy reference by the Sections.

If it were possible, this Section should be accommodated next to the Diplomatic D. and R.; but this cannot be so on account of our present accommodation.

The new Section must be in a central part of B/P, and I consider that the senior staff should consist of officers from the Intelligence Divisions of the three Services, who should know the requirements of the general staff and a member of G.C. & C.S. who should know the possibilities of cryptography and the needs of cryptographers. It is in no sense an Intelligence Office except in so far as the needs of the Service Sections of G.C. & C.S. require a centralised Intelligence and File of enemy telegrams which would assist their work.

This Section would have a threefold purpose:

It should be of great assistance to the cryptographers to have a central office to which they could refer for information which may help them in their own problems, or when they can search among contemporary decodes for cribs.

It will meet a need sometimes expressed by the Intelligence Department of the Services for a central office, where all decodes are available for scrutiny by a member of their own Department, and so provide against the loss of anything which might be of interest to them.

It will relieve from the cryptographic sections the responsibility for the distribution of decodes and thus give them more time for their production.[38]

AGD was also keen to establish with Menzies, as he had done with Sinclair, the importance of maintaining a unified cryptography centre as evidenced by this note from him to Menzies on 22 December 1940:

> The Romer Committee in 1919 founded the G.C. & C.S. and directed that all cryptography should be centred there, the Army and Navy to collect the necessary W/T material, of which there was then very little. The G.C. & C.S. was also entrusted with the security of British Cyphers and their construction.
>
> For the first few years W/T interception was kept going with some difficulty owing to the urgent necessity for economy. The R.A.F. came into the picture in 1927.
>
> For cryptography, a military section was started in the G.C. & C.S. in 1932 [?] so that a party would be available for service in the field, and an Air Section was started in 1936. A Far East Joint Bureau was instituted at Hong Kong, administered by the Navy and the Head of the Bureau is paid for by the F.O. A Middle East Joint Bureau has only just come into being.
>
> As you know the fighting services, especially the Army and Air, have been served with intelligence far beyond their expectations during operations in Norway and France and now at Home. The story of this is of some interest in pointing out the benefits of centralisation.
>
> In 1939 (and for some years before) the Army at their Chatham Y Station were intercepting traffic from a very large group of stations in Germany, which were thought to be serving the German Army.
>
> In January 1940, thanks mainly to the S.I.S. and their association with the G.C. & C.S. , this traffic became legible and turned out to be point to point station traffic of the German Air Force. From that moment until fairly recently the Army (MI8) have endeavoured to give up taking this traffic, well knowing that there is no one else to take it and despite the fact that during Spring and Summer it provided Army intelligence of the highest value in Norway and France, but because it emanated from the G.A.F. MI8 have tried to drop it.
>
> The R.A.F. had always maintained that nothing of operational value would come out of point to point traffic and therefore, had made no plans for taking it and did not commence doing so until and are not even now in a position to take it over completely.
>
> In April, it soon became apparent that the Army had insufficient sets and operators to cover the traffic satisfactorily and 18 sets were eventually diverted to this work at the Foreign Office Y stations at

> Sandridge and Denmark Hill, whose proper job is the interception of traffic in commercial routes. Without these additional sets much less of the intelligence would have been obtained.
>
> I maintain, therefore, that if it had not been for our very close association with S.I.S. in the first place, and the fact that G.C. & C.S. were able to pool available W/T and cryptographic resources, much of this very valuable intelligence would have been lost and would not now be obtainable.
>
> This example of the benefits of unification of cryptography in one centre is just additional argument to the many that can be advanced for the advantages cryptographers desire from working in the closest association.[39]

GC&CS continued to grow and by the beginning of 1941, numbers had more than trebled to around 685. The teams working on Enigma had also grown quickly and Huts 6 and 3, which worked on German Army and Air Force Enigma, had ninety-three and sixty staff respectively. Huts 8 and 4 worked on German Naval Enigma and had thirty-seven and forty staff respectively. Knox's Research Section in The Cottage numbered nine staff! Responsibility for recruiting additional scientists and mathematicians was given to C.P. Snow of Christ's College, Cambridge.

***

AGD had moved his family into Stapleford Mill Farm near Bletchley on 13 September 1939, and they would remain there for two years. His son Robin was sent to boarding school at Downsend School between Ashtead and Leatherhead. They regularly entertained friends and GC&CS colleagues and de Grey, Adcock and Birch were frequent visitors. The Dennistons would visit the Knoxs' at their home at Courns Wood, a large ten-bedroom house set in ten acres of private woodland near High Wycombe. Dorothy got on well with Knox's wife Olive but the two men were not close friends. Their battles over control of the Enigma problem at BP had no doubt taken its toll. De Grey would usually appear at Christmas with presents for Robin and 'Y'. These would inevitably be tokens to buy framed Medici prints as he had run the Medici gallery before the war. AGD's circle of friends included Rhoda Welsford whose mother rented Newton Longueville manor house, a mile from BP for the duration of the war. Rhoda worked in the Air Section from September 1939 until November 1944. Christmas 1940 found the family at the farm with a gardener and a cook. Christmas dinner was at the Welsfords at Newton Longueville. The Manor housed 'the Profs' – ERP Vincent, Frank Adcock, Tom Boase and Hugh Last from Kings, Magdalen and Brasenose respectively. All took part in paper games with the Denniston children. Tiltman was also a close friend of AGD, as were their respective wives. On 12 June 1941, AGD was appointed a Companion of the Order of St Michael and St George (CMG), as with his previous honour, in his capacity as head of a department in the Foreign Office.

Ernst Fetterlein and his wife shared at least two Christmas dinners with the Dennistons. Conversation was difficult, as Mrs Fetterlein did not speak English and her husband's only common interest with AGD was work. Robin Denniston remembers Mrs Fetterlein being large and Mr Fetterlein small, formally dressed with boots and a monocle. They always came bearing gifts for the Denniston children.

Ever the frugal Scotsman, AGD kept immaculate records of his finances throughout the year and compiled a month ledger. October showed £155-9-5 received and £155-10-5 paid. November showed his account balanced at £80-7-9.

***

By the beginning of 1941, GC&CS had developed functions other than cryptanalysis and some of these seemed more appropriate for the Signals or Intelligence Departments of the Ministries. At the same time, the War Office and Air Ministry virtually controlled the activities of their respective Service Sections at GC&CS, while the CSS had control of policy over the output of Enigma cryptanalysis. Menzies presided over the Y Board and in effect sat between GC&CS and the Services. In November 1940, Colonel Butler of MI8 approached AGD about moving the seventy members of CIS to BP. The driver for this was to place W/T intelligence (WTI) and cryptography work in one location.[40] AGD's reluctance to take them all was based simply on a lack of space but this was seen as a lack of vision on his part as well as administration inefficiency. It was thought that AGD wanted to preserve GC&CS as a purely cryptanalytical bureau and stop it evolving into a Sigint Centre. The prevailing view of some such as Group-Captain Blandy was: 'I think it is perhaps as well to emphasize that Cryptographers are not intelligence officers, but only exist for providing the material from which Intelligence is produced, and it is as well to keep the intelligence side as far divorced from the cryptanalytical side as possible.'[41]

The Admiralty was quite content with the arrangements at GC&CS, and Captain Sandwith wrote that naval 'cryptography and W.T.I. are both carried out at B.P.'.[42] As far as the War Office was concerned, there should be greater Services control of GC&CS and the Y stations. GC&CS's output had 'greatly exceeded our expectations and pre-war forecasts', and Travis went on to say: 'From 1919-39, the interception services were very definitely run by G.C. & C.S., and it is only since the appointment of senior officers to A.I.1 E and MI8 on outbreak of war that any change has been desired, it is now urged that cryptography is subservient to interception. It is quite obvious that cryptographers will always know more of interception than the interceptors can possibly know about cryptography'.[43] The issue came down to whether or not Y included cryptanalysis. DMI and D's of I said it did, DNI and CSS said not. In January 1941, the latter view prevailed at a meeting of the Y Board: 'The Board discussed at length the definition of "Y" Services and it was ultimately agreed that "Y" indicated interception and the development of all means of interception which might produce intelligence but did not include cryptography and its fruits.'[44]

There still remained the task of defining the relationship between Y and cryptography. On 2 July 1941, a sub-committee of the Y Committee reviewed the issue and concluded that:

> There do not exist two mutually exclusive subjects that can be defined by these names. The two are so inter-related if not very consistent or even, perhaps, legally sound, a compromise which may be expressed (necessarily loosely) thus:

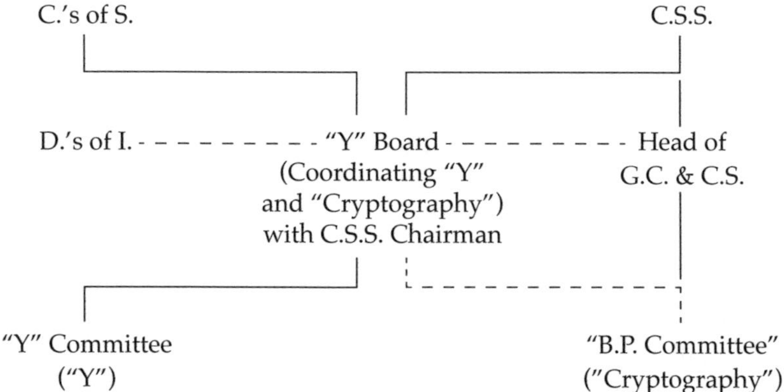

The 'B.P. Committee' was set up and had its first meeting on 25 February 1941, with AGD's objective being 'to bring forward matters concerned with cryptography and anything that might arise there from'.[45] It quickly turned into a GC&CS all-purpose committee and petered out after a few meetings.

At the suggestion of Group Captain Blandy, the Y Committee appointed a special 'E' Committee on 12 March, consisting of military and air force members and Y station commanders with Travis as chair. They met at BP so Travis could pull in staff as required.[46] It confined its work to the requirements for Army and Air Force Enigma traffic and, at its final meeting on 18 November 1941, decided upon an 'E' interception plan for the future, with interception carried out on an Inter-Service basis around four stations – Beaumanor (Army), Chicksands (Air Force) with Whitchurch and Harpenden in support.[47] This was approved by the Y Committee several weeks later.

Y Interception was controlled by a structure overseen by the Chiefs of Staff. AGD sat on the Y Board chaired by CSS and Travis sat on the Y Committee reporting to it, chaired by Air Marshall Sir Philip Joubert. It in turn had Sub-Committees: Technical, Administrative, 'E' and a Noise Investigation Bureau for non-Morse traffic. MI8 still wanted some kind of 'Operational Intelligence Section', but unlike the Admiralty that had OIC, it, unlike MI8, was a Command. All military units engaged on aspects of army-air WTI work were combined into a single group on 25 March 1941 called Intelligence School No. VI or 6 I.S. The exception to this was a group called the Special Liaison Party (SLP) which worked in Hut 3 at GC&CS. 6 I.S. eventually moved to Beaumanor in July along with the War Office Y Group (WOYG) in October. This was compatible with the Board's official ruling that Y did not include cryptography and that the two were indivisible was acknowledged by the appointment of a cryptanalyst from 4 I.S. to command 6 I.S. An MI8 officer was sent to GC&CS to represent MI8(a), the intelligence branch of MI8, and to act as 'the channel through which intelligence from traffic analysis reached the War Office'. He produced a weekly report of the 'changes in the German W/T picture as shown through decodes, and aiming at adding to the fund of intelligence produced by G.C. & C.S'.[48]

AGD had recommended the creation of an 'Interservice Distribution and Reference [D & R] Office' at BP to counter Service dissatisfaction with the apparent lack of uniformity and standardisation in the reporting of Service Sigint products. While diplomatic sections had a uniform and tidy routine through a D & R, naval, military and air Sigint was subdivided among a large number of units, Service, inter-service and partially inter-service with separate outlets to different customers. A Service D & R with a civil head and Service intelligence officers attached to it would 'assure the Directors that their Intelligence

Divisions were fully represented at the centre and their interests in the circulation of the results completely covered'.[49]

The proposal was approved by DMI[50] and DNI[51] and then by the Y Board on 14 February. However, opposing factions within the Ministries and GC&CS caused the proposal to collapse. Part of the problem was that Army and Air Force decrypts were disguised as agents' reports, with all indication of wireless origin removed. According to de Grey 'It would have been difficult to contrive a system more likely to prevent signal intelligence from ever being of the fullest use to its recipients.'[52] The system had worked for Diplomatic Sections because they had little interest in the problems of interception or W/T in general.

In April 1941, de Grey suggested a D & R with two main functions:

> To receive the cryptographic output of the various sections of G.C. & C.S. and ensure that such intelligence as they produced was passed to other sections who might be interested, with a view to aiding cryptography;
>
> To ensure that all information likely to interest the three Service Ministries was passed to the Intelligence Officer of the Service Sections of G.C. & C.S., so that such information may reach the Ministries in as intelligible a form as possible.[53]

AGD reported to the JCC on 14 July that he had set up a new section called the Intelligence Exchange (IE). It was to be headed by de Grey and include an officer from each service. Its remit was to receive and analyse the complete daily output from each Section at BP and include Diplomatic, Naval, Military, Air, Hut 3 (Joint), Russian, French Naval, ISOS (Intelligence Services, Oliver Strachey) and Commercial. They would then be in a position to see that all the Ministries received what might interest them. The exception to this would be Hut 3 as it already served the three Service Ministries and there was no question of re-issuing any of its product. This was not the 'D & R' that the Service Ministries were expecting and,

> only the Admiralty complied, sending an officer from N.I.D., who had no familiarity with and no adherence to Naval Section or to I.E. He proceeded to institute direct reporting from I.E. to N.I.D., so upsetting the principle for which I.E. was then fighting, namely, the unification of the channels of reporting, and the principle for which Naval Section was contending, that Naval Section should be the only channel to the Admiralty. His attachment was of short duration.[54]

The appointment could be seen as an attempt by DNI to safeguard his interests at GC&CS, as unlike the Army and Air Force Section's subordination to their respective Ministries, Naval Section was not subordinated to NID. In any event, DNI had already appointed Captain J.R.S. Haines, RN, as his liaison officer with the title Assistant Director of the Operational Intelligence Centre (ADIC), with the following remit:

> He will visit B.P. frequently to facilitate cooperation between N.I.D. and B.P. and will be responsible to D.N.I. for the coordination of the results of the work of the Naval Section at B.P. and for the action taken by N.I.D. on the material provided by B.P.[55]

This arrangement, according to Birch, 'enduring for the rest of the war and proved an unqualified success'. I.E. became a 'comprehensive up to date library of G.C. & C.S. output' with Naval Section remaining 'its most constant supporter'.[56] With a flood of GAF Sigint pouring in from the Y stations, the Air Ministry's Directorate of Intelligence was upgraded in the spring of 1941.

***

Intelligence obtained from non-military sources was predominant in GC&CS before the war and in wartime continued to be overseen directly by AGD. This part of his organisation operated purely as a cryptanalytical bureau, limited to the decryption and reporting of enemy and neutral diplomatic and commercial communications. The Section had moved to BP from Broadway Buildings (part of Commercial Section) on 26 August 1939, with around ninety staff comprising some thirty on a Senior or Junior Assistant grade (cryptanalysts with varying degrees of experience, in some cases gained in WW1) and some thirty support staff (Higher Clerical Officers, Clerical Officers and Clerical Assistants); the remainder were typists, traffic-handling staff and office keepers. The structure remained as it had been before the war, with AGD as Head with a Registry; the Distribution and Reference Section with its own typists; the Traffic Section; a large number of country sections, each separately responsible to AGD, and some cryptanalysts engaged in specific research problems outside the framework of sections. This last group, consisting of three experienced men and several juniors, was engaged in advance problems such as Enigma (in support of the Services Sections) and the Japanese 'Purple Machine'. The move went smoothly, with no interruption to its output. AGD was based in the Mansion, while the Section occupied Elmers School which provided working accommodation for some sixty people. The Senior Assistant of Distribution and Reference had day to day administration responsibility for sections at Elmers School, while AGD remained in charge of policy and progress of sections whose heads continued to report directly to him.

The Distribution and Reference Section maintained contact with the users but according to Birch 'the producers were not concerned with traffic analysis intelligence or the use of their products and were in general ignorant of even the sources of supply of their raw material'. The key 'country' sections were Italian, Japanese, Near Eastern, Chinese, Balkans, Portuguese and French, which was disbanded in May and reconstituted after the fall of France to deal with Vichy government traffic. The traffic of twenty-six countries had been studied, 70,000 out of 100,000 telegrams received, with 8,495 translated and circulated. At the same time, 135,000 coded or plain text messages had been circulated by the Commercial Section (with thirty-nine staff). There had not been a German section since 1919, because following the publication of the Zimmermann Telegram, German diplomatic ciphers used two very high-grade systems, one of which was an OTP. No breaks had been made and only one cryptanalyst was assigned on a 'care and maintenance' basis.

Seven-day-a-week working was introduced shortly after arrival at BP and a two-shift system was later introduced due to a shortage of space. Adjustments had to be made to the work of the section to take account of wartime priorities. The diplomatic and consular communications of Axis countries could reveal military plans as well as their military and industrial resources. Those of neutral countries who had representatives in enemy countries might reveal similar information as well as their own intentions. It was felt that Allied countries and safe friends did not need to be covered. Work on German diplomatic traffic was treated like a research problem, with German Service problems being a priority. However, a veteran of Room 40 took up the work and when one of the systems in use was identified (the OTP) in 1941, collaborative work with the Americans could begin. The Italian, Near Eastern, Balkan and Chinese Sections were reinforced as was the Japanese Section when linguists were found. The French Section had been disbanded in April 1940.

The Diplomatic Section benefited from the recruitment of the fifty-six seniors and thirty women linguists upon the outbreak of war. While the majority went to the Service Sections, some were sent to Elmers School and were immediately useful. Working space was barely adequate to house the peacetime staff, but this was solved temporarily by moving the Commercial Section back to London. This freed up an outbuilding but it was demolished by a stray bomb on 20 November 1940.

Italy's entry into the war allowed the Diplomatic Section to demonstrate that more than political intelligence could be obtained from the enemy's diplomatic and consular communications. It could reveal their military strength, intentions and plans for espionage and economic war. GC&CS had access to traffic from the Italian embassies in Moscow, Madrid, Lisbon, Washington and Tokyo. Legations in the Balkan capitals had military attachés who talked openly to Rome of German military movements until the Germans subsequently stopped their telegrams. Their representatives in the Near East, South America and Ireland along with their consuls at Lourenço Marques (now Maputo, the capital of Mozambique) and other strategic points, frequently reported on Allied convoys. Much of this traffic was now readable and by July 1942, twenty-five communications per day were being translated and issued. The Italian Section was placed on a 15-hour watch when Italy entered the war and on occasion this was extended to a 24-hour watch. The Section was reinforced to nineteen staff so that even low-grade traffic could be covered. Further traffic was obtained when the Admiralty cut the undersea cable running from Malaga to Genoa, forcing the Italian Embassy in Madrid to use W/T. This provided access to invaluable intelligence about the Spanish Government's relations with the Axis countries.

In September 1940, the Commercial Section moved to Wavendon House in the village of Wavendon near BP to avoid London bombing. By the end of December 1940, it had thirty-nine staff. In 1940 it circulated 135,000 messages either in code or as plain text to the Ministry of Economic Warfare (MEW) and to the Information and Records Branch of censorship. Many of these were also circulated to the Admiralty, War Office, Air Ministry and the Ministry of Shipping.

The success of GC&CS's diplomatic and commercial sections, under AGD's direct control, would prove to pave the way for events which played out later in the war. The academic David Alvarez has provided a comparison between the records of GC&CS and the US's SIS in reading foreign diplomatic codes.[57] It provides reasons why the US would stand to benefit significantly from any collaboration with Britain:

> British codebreakers for example had solved high-grade Italian ciphers while the Americans were struggling to master low-grade versions. GC&CS was reading several Vichy French diplomatic ciphers at a time when the SIS was hoping that the next staff increase

AGD's father, Dr James Denniston. (Denniston Family)

AGD with his parents and grandmother who lived until 103. (Denniston Family)

Above left: AGD with his parents at their home in Bowden, Cheshire. (Denniston Family)
Above right: AGD's family home in Bowden, Cheshire. (Denniston Family)

Below: AGD (sitting middle row, second from right) playing one of two villains in a production of *Dick Whittington* at the Royal Naval College, Osborne, Isle of Wight, in 1911. (Courtesy of the Britannia Royal Naval College, Dartmouth)

Above left: Sir Alfred Ewing, the 'Father' of Room 40 and the man who began AGD's Sigint career. (Ewing Family)

Above right: Admiral Sir Reginald 'Blinker' Hall. DNI for most of World War One and the man who brought the U.S. into it. He backed AGD's appointment as Head of GC&CS. (Crown ©. Reproduced by kind permission of Director GCHQ)

Left: Edward Bell, Second Secretary in the U.S. Embassy in London during World War One, played a key role in the release of the Zimmermann telegram. (Virginia Surtees)

Right: A young Dorothy Denniston, née Gilliat, AGD's wife. (Denniston Family)

Below left: AGD in naval uniform in 1918, aged 35 and shortly before he married Dorothy. (Denniston Family)

Below right: Admiral Sir Hugh 'Quex' Sinclair, Chief of the SIS from 1923-1939. He became Director of GC&CS and AGD's boss until his death in November 1939. (Public Domain)

AGD leaving Buckingham Palace after being invested with the insignia of the CBE on 2 January 1933. (Denniston Family)

AGD and Do with their children Robin and Margaret ('Y') outside their home at 48 Tedworth Square, London, Christmas 1936. (Denniston Family)

Left: AGD's wartime passport photograph. (Denniston Family)

Below: AGD's 1939 passport showing his Polish visa for the Pyry Conference. (Denniston Family)

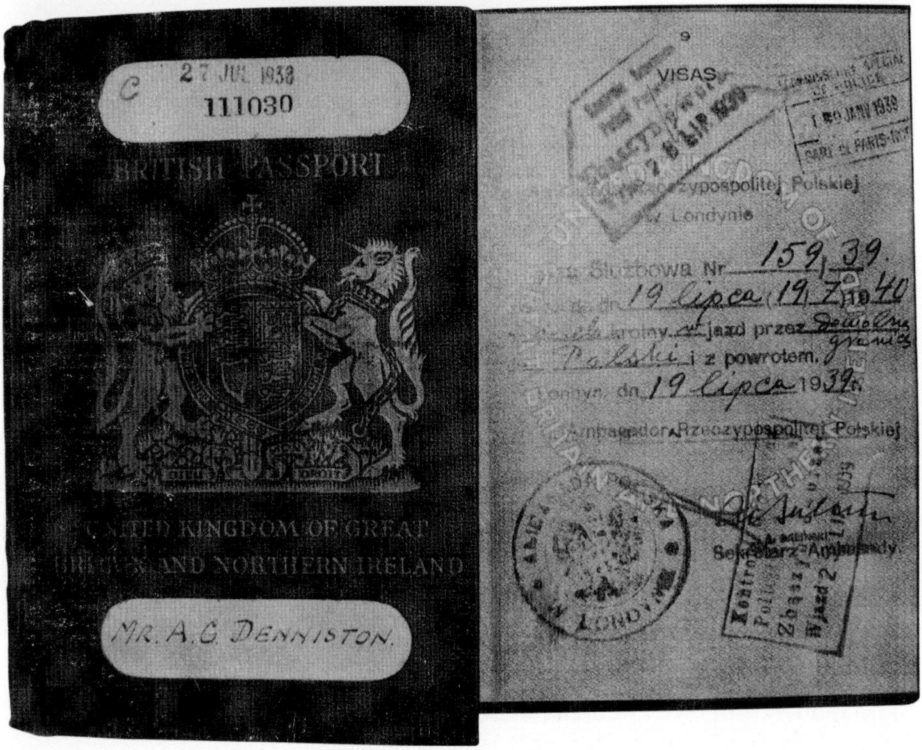

Above: Bletchley Park staff watching a rounders match circa 1940/41. Seated (left to right) are E.M. Smith, Edmund Green, Barbara Abernethy, Patrick Wilkinson, Alan Bradshaw; standing (left to right), Philip Howse, Stephen Wills, Captain W.H.W. Ridley, John Barns, George McVittie, Marjorie de Haan, AGD. (Bletchley Park Trust)

Below: AGD (left) during World War Two with Professor E.R.P. Vincent, Naval Section's Chief Italian cryptanalyst, and Colonel John Tiltman (right), Head of Army Section and BP's Chief cryptanalyst from mid 1941. (Crown ©. Reproduced by kind permission of Director GCHQ)

AGD with Dorothy and daughter 'Y' en route to Buckingham Palace on 12 June 1941 to receive his CMG. (Denniston Family)

William Friedman, Head of the U.S. Army's Signal Intelligence Service. (National Archives, Washington)

Left: AGD and family on holiday during World War Two. (Denniston Family)

Below left: Ernst and Angelica Vetterlein. The veteran Russian cryptanalyst worked in Room 40 in World War One and for AGD's Diplomatic Section in World War Two. (© Vetterlein Family)

Below right: Sir Stewart Menzies. He succeeded Sinclair as Chief of SIS and remained in post until 1952. His relationship with AGD was at best cordial, eventually removing him from BP and ultimately, the intelligence service altogether. (Public Domain)

AGD having a rare moment of relaxation during World War Two. (Denniston Family)

Berkeley Street, London headquarters of AGD's Diplomatic and Commercial Section. The arrow was drawn on the photo by William Friedman. (National Archives, Washington)

Above: AGD, Dorothy, Robin and 'Y' Denniston outside the family home in Burley, circa 1947. (Denniston Family)

Below: AGD (left) with a grouse hunting party in Upper Nidderdale, Yorkshire. He preferred to be a beater rather than shoot a gun. (Denniston Family)

Above: Three great Allied codebreakers in later life and friends of AGD until the end. Left to right they are William Friedman, John Tiltman and Josh Cooper. (Crown ©. Reproduced by kind permission of Director GCHQ)

Below: Members of the Denniston family at the opening of AGD's restored office at Bletchley Park on 4 December 2013. (Author's Collection)

> might free up one or two officers to open a French section. GC&CS routinely solved Balkan and Near Eastern systems that did not even appear on the cryptologic horizon of the SIS. Even in the matter of Japanese codes and ciphers (an American speciality) the British were reading more systems (including Red) than the Americans, although GC&CS had had no more luck with Purple than their cousins across the Atlantic. Only in the area of German and Russian communications were the prospective partners equal. In their efforts against Berlin's diplomatic systems neither had been able to advance beyond the reconstruction of the DESAB code. As for Russian systems, neither was studying Moscow's diplomatic ciphers, although GC&CS was reading a few Red Army and Comintern systems.

Throughout 1941 BP's Service Sections continued to expand. There were six separate naval sections four of which covered German, Italian, Spanish and French traffic. Hut 8 dealt with German Naval Enigma and Knox's section handled Italian Naval Enigma. Japanese naval Sigint had been passed to FECB and the staff had moved to the Japanese Diplomatic Section. Most of the French traffic was being read, but very little of the Italian traffic apart from Italian Naval Enigma, solved by Knox. For German naval work, there was an organisational division between Hut 8, which was tackling the Enigma problem and the German Naval Section, which was dealing with everything else. However, Hut 8 supplied the decrypts and German Naval Section, which became known as Hut 4, provided W/T cover, traffic analysis and relevant intelligence. At this time only two Bombe machines were operational although eighteen had been ordered. According to Birch: 'The sum total of cryptanalytic success on German naval systems of all grades and kinds cannot be said to have as yet achieved much operational significance.' Furthermore:

> The most significant achievement of German Naval Section in 1940 was the control it had over its own domain. At the beginning of the war, it did no cryptanalysis, because it had no cryptanalysts; no traffic analysis, because 'operational intelligence' was the monopoly of 8G; no general intelligence because there was none from Sigint sources. By the end of 1940 it had established a monopoly of all naval Sigint undertaken on German sources at G.C. & C.S. – even the raw products of Hut 8, the only exception, passed directly to it for processing and issue – and was already the champion of the 'one Service, one Section' principle as opposed to the interservice and the functional theories, for the proper organisation of G.C. & C.S.

While there was a considerable amount of operational intelligence coming from traffic analysis, the Admiralty was not convinced of its reliability. Birch, in his capacity as Head of the Naval Section at BP, had written to AGD on 20 October 1940:

> Apart from questions of efficiency and convenience here, there cannot, from the point of view of Admiralty, be several separate entities at B.P. independently responsible for supplying them with intelligence and its interpretation. The German Naval Section is the responsible body and Admiralty rightly holds it so. To them it's no excuse at all for me to say: 'Oh, yes, we're the German Naval Section, but this bit of intelligence is done elsewhere, so I'm not responsible.' It merely looks like a phoney alibi; it brings the Section into disrepute and makes B.P. look like a badly organised muddle.

The Military Section differed considerably from the Naval Section. It was part of 4 I.S. and controlled by MI8 with its head, Tiltman, responsible to DMI in the War Office as well as AGD. At this stage it had no Enigma traffic to work on as it had handed over Japanese work to FECB and Italian work to CBME. It devoted most of its staff time to the cryptanalytical problems of other Services. Tiltman was the leading cryptanalyst at GC&CS, although his role was not formalised until the following year and Military Section tended to become synonymous with his functions. Examples of this were the Russian Section created in March 1940, the setting up of an inter-service school for the training of cryptanalysts called Interservice Special Intelligence School (ISSIS) and a Research Section to tackle tough cryptanalytical problems.[58]

Air Section, like the Military Section was separated from Enigma traffic and under the control of a Ministry Section, AI1(e). However, it had had great success and could claim to read all GAF non-machine ciphers, including four German, five Russian and two Italian meteorological ciphers. It did not report or interpret the decrypts, as this was done in conformity with the Ministry's policy of decentralisation at Cheadle from where it was sent on to AI(e). Air Section was subordinate to AI1(e) whose view was that their function was purely cryptanalysis. Any effort to fill the many gaps in RAF intelligence from Sigint sources was discouraged and direct contact between them and AI3(b), Fighter Command and Bomber Command was denied as long as possible. A Fighter Intelligence Subsection had been formed in Air Section to study W/T traffic in December 1940, and the following month, a member of Hut 3 and a computer[59] from

Cheadle formed a subsection called SALU to tie up information between low and high grade sources. The work of both sections was ignored by the Air Ministry. Air Section also housed a meteorological service which provided weather data for British forecasting services in preparing weather forecasts for the RAF and, later in the war, the US Air Force.[60]

Another valuable source of intelligence for AGD's organisation was from the German military intelligence organisation, the Abwehr, headed by Admiral Wilhelm Canaris. They used a version of the Enigma machine to encrypt their communications with agents abroad. The system was broken at BP in 1940 by Oliver Strachey and his ISOS team. The intelligence was sent to SIS's counterespionage branch, Section V, which was located in St. Albans, about 26 miles from BP and the same distance from Whitehall in London. The intelligence war station in St Albans was headed by Captain Felix Henry Cowgill, who spoke about their work after the war:

> At first they were little more than fragments of German intelligence signals, in German, and either meaningless or almost so. But in a surprisingly short time, certainly less than a year, we were reading Canaris's traffic and that of the Sicherheitsdienst [the intelligence agency of the SS and the Nazi Party] too. From that basis we could, therefore, work towards first the control of the German intelligence service wherever and whenever it appeared, and then the liquidation of that service.[61]

Secret service communications were intercepted by the Radio Security Service (RSS) and worked on by the ISOS at GC&CS, although the cryptanalysts were working for SIS. By the end of the year, RSS had become the unit responsible for the breaking-down of the global communications of the enemy secret services. They relied on Post Office Y stations and amateur wireless operators throughout the country. They grew from 150 at the beginning of the war to 1,000 strong.

The internal organisation of GC&CS juxtaposed individual Service sections. This facilitated the sharing of experience, interchange of personnel, collaboration on common problems, pooling of research and machinery. The exception was the complete fusion of German Army and Air Force Enigma in Hut 6. They handed decrypted messages to Hut 3, who camouflaged the decrypts as agents' reports and by-passed the official Sigint sections MI8 and AI1(e), going directly to the Country Sections, MI14 and AI3. MI8 and AI1(e) did place staff in Hut 3 with a section called 3M advising on Military Intelligence and another section called 3A advising on Air Intelligence. Both of these sections disseminated material to ministries and commands.

Travis took charge of mechanical aids to cryptanalysis, and as the Bombes were used by the cryptanalysts of all Services, his command included Huts 6 and 8. Therefore, Hut 8 was divorced from Naval Section and Huts 3 and 6 became separate entities. Other variants of Service ciphers were attacked by a small and separate group led by Knox.

Knox persisted with his complaints throughout 1941 and AGD made one final attempt to explain the situation to him on 11 November 1941:

> My dear Dilly,
> Thank you for your letter. I am glad that you are frank and open with me. I know we disagree fundamentally as to how this show should be run but I am still convinced that my way is better than yours and likely to have wider and more effective results.
>
> If you do design a super Rolls Royce that is no reason why you should yourself drive the thing up to the house of a possible buyer, more especially if you are not a very good driver. I lost any confidence you had in me when I disagreed with you in Dec. 1939 and said that you could not exploit your own success and run huts 6 and 3. I was right – you broke new ground while the building in your foundation was carried on by Travis etc. who, I say, were better adapted to this process than you.
>
> our next big show was K. You alone among us found the way but the full value of <u>your</u> work could only be obtained by fitting results into the full picture in the Naval Section.
>
> And now comes your latest effort which only proves again that you are the right man in the right place. You told me of a side-line in Intelligence that you wanted to develop. I agreed but begged you to remember your real metier. So you produced this result which none other of our party could have done.
>
> You say you did it because you are a scholar who proceeds from his raw material to his finished text, well – who is preventing you – you have access to all past material and copies of all new.
>
> What are my grocer's window dressing. Eric Smith offers all productions in neat form to those who need them. Birch ties up information from every naval source and tells the story. Hut 3 collects and reports accurate information derived from the source you invented.

Do you want to be the inventor and the car driver? Do you want to be Eric Smith, Strachey, Birch and Wing-Commander Humphreys and De Grey wrapt into one which will include Knox who is the source? If so I don't agree and I don't mind at all what steps you take.

You are Knox, a scholar with a European reputation who knows more about the inside of an Enigma machine than anyone else. The exigencies of war need that latter gift of yours though few people are aware of it.

The exploitation of your results can be left to others as long as there are new fields for you to explore.

I do disagree with you.

Yours ever,

A.G.D.[62]

Alas, it was to no avail and, demonstrating an astonishing amount of arrogance, Knox wrote directly to Menzies. It is remarkable that AGD continued to treat Knox in a professional manner given the apparent contempt which Knox seemed to hold him:

Though it was not my business, since I was ordered to do something else, I devised a theory which reduced, often to a twentieth part, the time necessary to be expended on the solution of a day's messages, a method which, for at least nine months had escaped the Polish bureau. Having earned thereby still greater unpopularity with Commander Denniston, I was powerless to insist that the whole affair was still in an experimental stage, that watches should be constituted, that the best brains should be employed, and that we should be prepared when 'the war should begin'. The hut had, since Commander Denniston laid it down, to remain in charge of one officer physically unfit for night work, a very able worker of no marked push or originality. In consequence when the push came watches often possessed workers of the highest ability but unused to certain minutiae, and some early and vital keys were lost. For this Commander Denniston's mandate was responsible.

When a cipher is out Commander Denniston is willing to parade superiors round sections of whose work he understands literally nothing and to assume credit for achievements his mismanagement nearly ruined.

Two things remain to be said. As to my right to criticise I need only remind you that I am a Senior Cryptographer. At the end of the Great War Commander Denniston (with a staff of about 30) was administering one of the German Fleet Cyphers and I (with a staff of

> three) another. If memory serves me at the end of the war the smaller unit was supplying copious and accurate information, while the larger remained silent. Secondly, Sir, if you criticise me on the score that I have accepted money in peace time and desert during hostilities I need only say that neither Commander Denniston's friends, if any, expected, nor his many enemies feared that, on the outbreak of war such responsibilities should be left in hands so incapable.[63]

***

On 8 February 1941 a meeting took place in AGD's office at BP which many historians believe heralded the start of the 'Special Relationship' between Britain and the US. However, intelligence cooperation between the two countries can be traced back to WW1.[64] In July 1917, General John Pershing, commander of the American Expeditionary Force (AEF), decided that his intelligence staff (G-2) should follow the model of their British counterparts in the BEF. Pershing kept his distance from the British Army and its commander, Field Marshal Sir Douglas Haig, but did establish a good rapport with the French commander, General Philippe Petain. Major Dennis Nolan (later Brigadier General) was head of Pershing's intelligence staff. He established a good working relationship with the head of the BEF's intelligence staff, Brigadier General John Charteris. Charteris revealed details of the British intelligence system, including Sigint, and, after a presentation to the AEF by Charteris, Pershing approved the subsequent intelligence regulations on the British model without amendment. The British agreed to provide both document-based and training support.

The AEF's decision to copy from the British brought junior intelligence officers from both armies into close contact. In 1917 Major Stewart Menzies was responsible for counter-espionage at BEF GHQ, where he established close links with his opposite numbers. By 1941, he had become Major General Sir Stewart Menzies, head of the British SIS. In 1918, William Friedman was a cryptographer working for the AEF G-2. By 1941, he was head of the American Signals Intelligence Service and had established close links to AGD. As for AGD himself, while not directly involved in Room 40's work on the Zimmermann Telegram, he had witnessed first-hand how Admiral Hall and the American, Edward Bell, had worked closely together. The outcome of their collaboration had, in effect, brought the US into WW1. So AGD understood full well the potential benefits both to Britain and his own organisation, of a close working relationship with US intelligence services.

The 1941 meeting in AGD's office had its origins in an informal visit to London in July 1940 by William Donovan, a special envoy of President Roosevelt. His visit had been prompted by SIS's new representative in the US, William Stephenson, and his task was twofold: to assess Britain's determination and ability to continue with the war, and see whether closer collaboration could be arranged with the Admiralty on intelligence. At the end of August, the British Government invited the American Military Observer Mission to attend a meeting in London with the British Chiefs of Staff. While the purpose of the meeting was to discuss the 'Standardisation of Arms',[65] Brigadier General George Strong told the meeting about 'the progress his Service was making against the Japanese and Italian ciphers and formally proposed to the Chiefs of Staff that the time had arrived for a free exchange of intelligence'.[66] Interestingly, the US naval representative at the meeting, Admiral Ghormley, said nothing about cryptanalysis and the British offered nothing in return. Donovan returned to Washington and recommended a full and direct exchange of intelligence between the two countries' naval intelligence departments.

Within several months, the US Navy's position had changed dramatically and Ghormley attended a meeting in London on 22 October with DNI John Godfrey and Menzies. The following day in Washington, Secretary of War, Henry Stimson, met with Secretary of the Navy, Frank Knox, to discuss sharing of information with the British on 'the code methods of the Germans'.[67] By the end of December, an Anglo-American pact on cryptanalysis had been agreed with the intention of sharing with each other, information about the codes and ciphers of Germany, Italy and Japan.

On 7 February 1941, four passengers disembarked from HMS *King George V* after she had anchored in Scapa Flow, the Home Fleet's remote base in the Orkneys. Abraham Sinkov and Leo Rosen worked for the US Army Signal Intelligence Service, and Robert W. Weeks and Prescott H. Currier were US Navy communications officers. Sinkov was a late replacement for William Friedman who was unable to travel due to illness. They were greeted on the quay by a naval officer[68] and several drivers for the two staff cars and a lorry which were at their disposal. The equipment that they brought with them would not fit on the aircraft sent to meet them, so they were transferred to another dock where they boarded a Royal Navy destroyer. It took them south, along the coast of Scotland and England to the Thames and London, docking at Tilbury. They travelled through London and late on the evening of 8 February arrived at BP, becoming the first Americans to do so. Remarkably, they brought with them perhaps the greatest achievement of US cryptanalysis during WW2. Japan had developed a high-level cipher machine to encrypt its diplomatic traffic and, like the Enigma system, it was also used to decrypt messages. The American SIS team under William Friedman and Frank Rowlett had broken the system, *angoo-ki taipu b* (Type B Machine – codenamed 'Purple' by the SIS) and subsequently were able to build replica machines. Their gift to the British was one of their replica machines,[69] along with other codebreaking material

Before their departure, the Americans had been briefed on the importance of security in all aspects of their engagement with the British:

> All members of the Delegation were asked to pledge themselves to secrecy to the extent that the secret should only be told in the case of the Navy Department to the Director of their Cryptographic Bureau and the case of the War Department to their DMI, Director of Sigs., and their Chief Cryptographer, and moreover we disclosed them only our cryptographic methods of solution and asked them not to request to be shown the resulting intelligence.[70]

After arriving at BP, the American party was taken to AGD's office, where they were greeted by him along with Travis and Tiltman. AGD's personal assistant, Barbara Abernethy had been tasked with providing sherry for the guests and she managed to carry a large wooden cask from the Army and Navy Stores to the Mansion House at a spot adjacent to AGD's office,[71] from which she duly served sherry to all assembled there. They were then driven to their billet. According to Currier: 'Now our billet was the country home of the chairman of the board of the, at the time, Anglo-Persian Oil Company, an extremely wealthy man. He had turned over his entire house to these four travelling Americans, fully staffed, the larder full, with a butler and three upstairs maids and a cook to take care of us for the time that we were there.'

The Navy and Army groups were split up and never travelled together while visiting BP's outstations or parts of BP itself. Currier and Weeks spent much of their time in the Naval Section and visited naval intercept stations such as Scarborough. All four were given details of the Enigma machine and shown the Bombe machines in operation.[72] On 3 March, AGD informed Menzies that, 'Our American colleagues have been informed of the progress made on the Enigma machine.' Weeks wrote to AGD to assure him that all information about the Bombe machines would be treated with the utmost secrecy:

For: Commander Denniston
3/3/41
We are in accord with the purport of your memorandum of today. We undertake to vary out all instructions for the preservation of the secrecy of the work mentioned, informing by word of mouth only the head of our section, Commander L.F. Safford, USN.

In connection with the naval aspects of the above work we deem it advisable to obtain the wiring of interest to us (i.e. the device on which Turing is working), and to disclose that only when it is decided to work on the problem. In such an event we shall observe all precautions and keep you informed of our actions.

As far as is practicable we shall make arrangements for the forwarding of communications through our naval attaché, as mentioned by you.

Respectfully,
R.H. Weeks'

The Americans boarded HMS *Revenge* at Helensborough in the Clyde several weeks later for the journey home. On 19 March, Weeks wrote to AGD with a list of the materials that they had received from GC&CS.[73]

AGD had overseen the visit by the Americans despite serious health problems. On 27 February, he was X-rayed by a consultant called Shanks at 68 Harley Street and a gall stone was found in his bladder. Yet two days later, he invited the Americans to lunch where his family were billeted at Stapleford Mill Farm. On 10 March, he went for a further consultation in Harley Street and subsequently underwent surgery at Luton General Hospital on 13 March. He was not discharged until 14 April but shortly afterwards he had an attack of orchitis and he was again hospitalised on 20 April, this time at Ashridge Military Hospital at Ashridge Park, Berkhampstead, Hertfordshire. He did not return to BP until 27 May by which time his hospital bills had taken up a third of his monthly salary of £98.

One of the outcomes of the visit of the Americans to BP was that AGD agreed to visit the US and Canada to discuss further collaboration between the three countries. He cabled Washington on 28 July, informing them of his plans, which were to travel from Scotland on 11 August using American transport. He hoped to arrive in Washington on the 12th or 13th and following meetings there and in New York, he planned to visit Ottawa.[74] AGD duly departed for the US as planned and after stopping briefly in Newfoundland on the 12th, he eventually arrived in Washington. On 14 August 1941, Travis telephoned the

Denniston house (telephone number – Soulbury 7) to see if Mrs Denniston was okay. He subsequently cabled AGD that same night with a message that all was okay at Soulbury 7.

AGD met with William Friedman and members of his SIS team[75] in Room 3341 of the Munitions Building on 16 August at 9.00 am. The purpose of the meeting was to prepare a schedule for his visits to the various sections of SIS from 19 to 22 August. Apart from Friedman's own team, which consisted of Sinkov, Rosen, Rowlett and Kullback, also present were SIS Executives Lieutenant Colonel R.W. Winckler, Captain H.G. Hayes and Captain E.F. Cook. The schedule that was agreed included visits to SIS's German, Italian, Central and South American, Japanese Diplomatic and Army Sections. The final day would be spent visiting SIS's tabulating and machinery, intercept and school sections. AGD must have been reassured that SIS was keen to cooperate fully with him. During a three-hour meeting, he reciprocated by giving a brief report on the probable status of cryptanalytic work engaged in by certain other governments, in so far as the facts were known to him. He also reported that cooperation between GC&CS and the recently established Canadian cryptanalytic section in Ottawa, the Examination Unit, was wholly dependent on the removal of Herbert Yardley from that organisation. Yardley had written a sensational exposé of American and British cryptography in WW1, *The American Black Chamber*, in 1931. Despite Yardley's endorsement by General Mauborgne, the US Army's chief signals officer, his views were not shared by others officials in US intelligence services.[76] They also agreed on a more safe and direct forwarding and exchange of documents.

AGD hoped to convince Friedman that there were no spare Bombes to give to the Americans and that he should not waste valuable resources by commissioning one from IBM. He also wanted to persuade SIS that it should leave efforts against European military work to the British. When the American Army began to be involved directly in the European theatre, the British would reveal more about its methods and supply information where appropriate. AGD also offered to have some of SIS's mathematicians visit BP, despite his security concerns. One of AGD's key objectives was to persuade Friedman's team to concentrate on Japanese systems, given that he assumed they had vast technological resources to deploy against them. When he toured SIS facilities, however, he was disappointed to see how little space and equipment they actually had. But Friedman was receptive to AGD's advice, and accepted that a British Bombe was not available. Furthermore, the meetings between AGD and Friedman established what would become a lifelong friendship. In a letter to AGD's son Robin years later,

Friedman's close colleague in SIS, Frank Rowlett, said of the visit: 'I remember well your father's visit to Washington in 1941. It was his visit which laid the foundations for the collaboration between the cryptographic activities of the US and the UK which produced intelligence vital to the successful prosecution of WW2. We spent considerable time together discussing the technical activities undertaken by both countries and worked out some of the details of our early collaborative efforts.'[77]

AGD's diary shows that he dined with senior staff of the US Navy's OP-20-G group at 20.30 on 18 August and SIS on the 19th. While his dinner with OP-20-G was cordial, his reception when he arrived at their offices was anything but. He was shown around the OP-20-G offices by Currier before meeting with the leaders of the naval communications section. AGD was agreeable to providing more information about French and Italian systems and improving the security of naval communications with their British counterparts.[78] Several days later he had a more difficult meeting with OP-20-G's head Laurance Safford who had a history of Anglophobia. In 1937, the State Department had requested approval for a British engineer to spend four months with Bell Telephone Laboratories and the Radio Corporation of New York. Safford's reply on behalf of OP-20-G was: 'The Director of Communications can raise no specific objections to Mr. Gee's extended visit to the Bell Laboratories. However, it is considered an undesirable practice for this country to disclose its technical secrets to foreigners while getting nothing in return.'[79] Despite the fact that the American Navy was virtually on a war footing in the Atlantic, AGD urged Safford to restrict his team's efforts to nothing more than research when it came to European naval systems.[80]

When AGD met one of OP-20-G's top codebreakers, Agnes Driscoll,[81] it was clear that she was privy to some of the information that Currier and Weeks had brought back from their visit to Britain. It had been agreed that only Safford would have sight of British cryptographic secrets. One can only imagine AGD's thoughts when he met Driscoll, aged 53 and a 20-year veteran of cryptanalysis. Her attitude and approach to cryptanalysis bore startling similarities to that of Dilly Knox! She rejected BP's automated solutions based on mathematics and claimed to have developed a much better hand method based on intuition. Driscoll told him that she was evolving a method which would enable her to solve keys on a small amount of traffic. She went on to say that the American Navy did not want or need a Bombe machine and thought little of the British methods for attacking Enigma. She showed AGD a sample solution based on a short eight-letter crib and claimed that it would require only two dozen people a few days to find the Enigma settings using her soon-to-be completed 'catalogue'. AGD maintained his composure despite the insulting nature of Driscoll's comments. She could well have known of British successes against Naval Enigma in 1941. He offered to provide more information about the Bombe machines and Turing's methods and even offered to supply OP-20-G with a machine when one became available. Furthermore he invited her to BP, but a serious automobile accident she had suffered in 1937 prevented her from travelling long distances.[82] However, she did not offer to send a member of her team in her place, nor did she show any interest in a visit from a British expert.[83] AGD explained to Driscoll that the British and the Poles before them had explored the catalogue approach which she was proposing to use. It had had limited success against earlier versions of the Enigma system but would be of little value against the more formidable German naval Enigma system.[84] Finally, after further discussion, Driscoll conceded that she did not fully understand the Enigma system and she rather forcefully demanded that BP provide further information. AGD asked her to provide a list of questions which he would take back to his colleagues and he promised to provide answers to all of them. AGD, with only a limited knowledge of the Enigma system, must have been startled by how basic some of the questions were. She was clearly after just enough information to pursue her own methods.

AGD returned to England on 23 August. The family had had no news of him and as the Battle of the Atlantic was in full swing, all they knew was that he had flown rather than gone by sea. BP was worried as was the family. By 8 pm on the 23rd they were waiting, worrying and wondering. To quote his son Robin:

> There was a heart-stopping moment when we heard the crunch of car tyres on the farm track. Could it be? It was too much to hope. But it was. It had taken him 15 hours flying from New York to Gander, Newfoundland, across the North Atlantic to Prestwick in the bomb bay and thence to Hendon where he was collected and driven home. It was the best moment of all our lives. He had brought us presents, for me a green pullover with black and white borders. He had had an amazing week but he could not tell us anything about it. That did not matter, what mattered was that he was alive and okay.

AGD's health was still causing him problems and his diary for 26 August records 'neuritis returns', but around 30 August he was on his way back to North America by air. He flew to Washington and then on to Ottawa the following day to brief the Canadians about British cryptographic achievements against Japanese codes. In November 1939, Canada had offered to help the Allied intelligence effort by setting up its own cryptanalysis unit, specifically to attack German, Italian and Spanish traffic.[85]. AGD had told the Canadians that to get into the business of breaking ciphers, they needed a 'high-grade cryptographer of long experience' who would need at least three months of training in Britain.[86] They took his advice but, surprisingly, hired Yardley to set up and run their new cryptographic department, the Examination Unit. AGD arrived in Ottawa on 3 September to meet Canadian cryptographers and he was keen to press home the point that Britain wanted the US and Canada to concentrate on Japanese military ciphers while Britain looked after diplomatic material.[87] Having ensured that he would not have to meet Yardley, AGD told Lester Pearson, assistant to Norman Robertson, acting Undersecretary of State for External Affairs, that Yardley had to go or there would be no cooperation between Canada and Britain. AGD offered to provide one of Britain's best experts to replace Yardley, Oliver Strachey, a veteran of MI1(b) during WW1 and a member of GC&CS since its inception. Under pressure from Washington, Yardley's contract was not renewed and Strachey arrived in early 1942, having refused to go to Ottawa until Yardley left the city. He brought with him his personal assistant, Miss Rogerson and keys to high-level Vichy and Japanese diplomatic codes, which initiated close cooperation with Washington and London. Although he did not speak or read Japanese, he helped break the Japanese code, which was very complex, since it used variations of kanji, hiragana and Romanization

AGD flew back from Ottawa via Gander. He arrived in Ayr, Scotland, at 11.30 am on 13 September, went on to Hendon and then home to Bletchley. As soon as he arrived back in Britain, AGD sought from his experts the answers to Driscoll's questions. He also established detailed procedures to register and track all communications with OP-20-G and SIS. By October, GC&CS had provided answers to all of OP-20-G's questions and also dispatched the specifications of Enigma settings, details of wheel wirings and all relevant intercepts for 1941.[88] AGD also made enquiries about obtaining an Enigma machine for Driscoll and he then waited for her to honour her commitment to provide GC&CS with a description of her methods. While GC&CS cryptanalysts were extremely sceptical about these methods, AGD's view was that 'We are on a good wicket at present but can't afford to neglect any side lines.'[89] In the end, it was left to Turing to write a scathing critique in which he concluded that even if the majority of the settings of an Enigma machine were known, Driscoll's method would take far too long to find a solution.[90]

In mid-December 1941, Driscoll finally sent partial details of her special method to AGD. By now, GC&CS had concluded that her method had failed and AGD was reluctant to provide her with further information. Perhaps to hide its own failures, the US Navy suddenly claimed that AGD had never sent the material requested by Driscoll. Safford's superior, Leigh Noyes, sent a series of critical telegrams and seemed to support Driscoll and the power of her methods. AGD responded by saying that he had indeed provided the information and if the US had not received it, why had it taken so long to report this to GC&CS. Suddenly, in the days after the Japanese attack on Pearl Harbor, Noyes apologised and miraculously, the missing documents from AGD were discovered in the OP-20-G offices. However, friction between British and US intelligence agencies persisted and eventually reached the ear of higher authorities on both sides of the Atlantic. This would certainly play a part in events which would unfold at BP in the early days of 1942. Similarly, by February 1942, Safford had been replaced by Joseph Wenger and a new breed of US cryptanalysts began working in OP-20-G. It seemed that Anglo-American cooperation would at last be restored.[91]

***

Throughout 1941, administrative matters continued to occupy much of AGD's time. At the first meeting of the JCC on 6 April, Captain Ridley stated that GC&CS had asked for £500 for two full-size hard tennis courts on existing grass courts.[92] On 12 April, the JCC considered and approved a proposal from AGD to build a cafeteria to feed 1,000 at one sitting.[93] On 7 June, AGD was reporting to the JCC that:

> Owing to the course of events in the Mediterranean we have been asked to combine the German and Italian Naval Sections. Need has also arisen for a combined German-Italian Research Intelligence party. Birch to take charge of the Section and Clarke Research Intelligence. It will not be possible to amalgamate fully or to the best advantage until the new premises are ready.[94]

Accommodation issues continued to be a pressing concern and on 4 October, AGD commented at a meeting of the JCC:

> Priority must be given to the accommodation of the staff at Elmers and Wavendon within the perimeter. Nothing can happen until the new large huts (Naval and Military) are complete. Progress on these appears to be very slow. Elmers School are at present roughly 120 strong and Wavendon 60. These will therefore occupy at least Huts 10 and 5, leaving 4 and 9 vacant. When the Dining Room is completed two large rooms in the house will be available and suitable for offices. Is it possible that the Recreation Hut could be linked up with Hut 9 and that this joint building might be used for various amenities such as an enlarged coffee room which could be used as the general common room, a Senior common room, quiet rooms, etc?[95]

Interestingly, Travis, who has always been characterised as the 'hard man' at BP, responded to the suggestion that the rooms in the Mansion should be used for offices as follows: 'This has never been the view up to now and, although conversation on the subject has been desultory and indecisive, it has been generally hoped and assumed that those large and commodious rooms, which are not really suitable for offices, will be used for the social amenities of our community.'[96]

On 28 September 1941, AGD received a letter from Frank Birch denouncing Malcolm Saunders, the nominal head of Hut 3 as 'interfering, intriguing, creating and magnifying difficulties and misunderstandings, causing friction, undermining confidence and incidentally, making proper liaison impossible'.[97] Inter-Service rivalries had surfaced in Hut 3 between the senior liaison officer with the Air Ministry, Robert Humphreys, backed by C.R. Curtis, head of the military section and Saunders. Humphreys had lobbied effectively for BP in Whitehall but as a poor team player, he had caused great dissention in both Hut 3 and Whitehall. Nigel de Grey described the situation as 'an imbroglio of conflicting jealousies, intrigue and differing opinions'. In AGD's absence due to illness in April 1941, Travis issued the following orders:

> No. 1 of the watch will be in general charge and, working in collaboration with the Air and Military Watch officers, will report agreed renderings of such messages as are considered necessary. In case of disagreement as to rendering or the necessity to report, the Service Officer's version or decision is to be taken and the matter referred to Commander Saunders for the Head of GC&CS. The circulation both at home and abroad and the form in which reports

> are sent abroad will be decided by the Army and the Officers for their respective services.[98]

In October, the two senior intelligence officers, Humphreys and Curtis, demanded that the whole staff of Hut 3 should be subordinated to them for operational duties and to the GC&CS 'administrator' for 'purely administrative' purposes. In this they were supported by MI6 and AI1(e). They had exceeded their mandate and were in effect replicating the higher-level struggle for control of Sigint. On 7 November, a new conduct of work was issued which handed control to a triumvirate consisting of Saunders, Humphreys and Curtis. The intelligence officers were to be

> responsible to their Ministries for the Intelligence reported to their respective Ministries or Commands, resulting from the work of the GC&CS staff, ... for all Intelligence Reports and summaries issued from Hut 3, whether the reports have actually been compiled by an Intelligence Officer or by the staff of GC&CS and for any comment that may be added to the text or signals ... Decisions as to priority of the work of the watch rest with the Intelligence officers of the watch ... All emended material is to be passed directly to the Intelligence officer of the watch, who alone who will decide its disposal.[99]

This new arrangement didn't satisfy anyone involved and led to a breakdown in discipline. On 1 December, MI8 issued an inaccurate document on German Army and Air Force cooperation based on Enigma decrypts and traffic analysis without the knowledge of any part of GC&CS, contravening all rules of security. According to de Grey 'It was evident that the whole situation was getting out of hand and that GC&CS was unable apparently to control it.'[100] Eventually, Eric Jones, a RAF officer, was brought in to assess the situation. His report, dated 2 February 1942 and classified Most Secret provides a fascinating and objective commentary on the state of GC&CS at the end of 1941:

> The difficulties of the organisation of Hut 3 are manifold in cause, but the key lies particularly in the background and structure of the G.C. & C.S. The material which Hut 3 amends, edits and distributes, has first to be subjected to several stages before being finally broken. All the processes which the material undergoes at the War Station demand the application of great intellectual power with the result that there is as high a concentration of brain as has ever been achieved anywhere. That fact alone makes administration a delicate

matter, for such people tend to be unworldly: their task is fascinating, and they will continue until forcibly discouraged. They do not worry consciously about accommodation or facilities, and hence have tended to concentrate upon the immediate execution of the work than to provide for its more efficient execution in the future. Another strange factor works the same way. Luck enters into the whole process, and so cryptographers are apt to be superstitious to the extent of believing that if they make grandiose preparation for future output, nemesis will cut off the source as return for their presumption. Indeed it would have taken a very courageous man to have decided, say two years ago, to build a large organisation for coping with such a chance, albeit voluminous, flow of information. Hence G.C. & C.S. has lived a hand-to-mouth existence, always short of accommodation, nearly always overlooked (because cryptographers prefer to be overlooked) and always in the background is the fickle nature of the material. In addition, the general administration of accommodation, billeting, and general amenities, has become most incompetent, and would have not been suffered by more worldly personnel. The work is most exacting, demanding all patience and tenacity, and is being carried out against a background of inconvenience and irritation; it would therefore be amazing if tempers remained even.

The foregoing considerations apply to one aspect of the nature of the work, namely, its intellectual difficulty. There are two other aspects, the need for security and for an acute form of team spirit, which jointly mitigate against smooth running. For success, the work depends upon a chain, from the people who do W/I, through the crib constructors, and the breakers, to the amenders and editors. The chain carries on, in fact, through the Service Intelligence Sections, both at War Station and at the Ministries, to the Operational Staffs who finally use the information. Such a chain is, of course, not peculiar to MSS[101] nor even to less elaborate cryptography, but is characteristic of all Intelligence. The chain principle is, however, much more strongly developed in the case of MSS than in any other form of Intelligence. An inevitable feature of the chain is that each stage is regarded as the representative of the source to all stages on the user side, and as the representative of the user to all stages nearer the source. For efficiency, it is essential that each stage realizes this dual responsibility, for example, A.D.I (Science) represents the user of beam information to Hut 3, and the source to D. of S.

A further feature of the chain is that each stage will tend to regard its immediate neighbours as unnecessary middlemen. Hut 6 at one

> time looked upon Hut 3 in this light, but that feeling has now largely disappeared. The real work has to remain vitally secret, but at some point in the chain the information has to emerge as 'MSS'. The officer at this point must be a relatively public figure, and will be regarded by the Service Intelligence as (at minimum) the representative of the source. It is this officer who gains the glamour, and who in particular – if he is not scrupulously faithful – will come to be regarded as a profiteering middleman by all the others who have treated the material at an earlier stage. It would be the acme of unfairness for this officer to make capital from his privileged position: the achievements for those who remain secret should make any fair-minded man feel very humble.

Jones then went on to make the following recommendations:

> Apart from drastic reorganisation, which would be so dangerous that I would not care to advise upon it, there remains the possibility of cleaning up the present organisation, and MSS is sufficiently unique – even in cryptography – to justify ad hoc measures. The first thing is a change in the administration of working, billeting and general welfare facilities, so that no further time and energy be fretted away over irritation irrelevant to the work. Second, there should be confirmation or otherwise of the editing functions of Hut 3, and if possible the Admiralty should be induced to stabilise the arrangement by providing a competent Naval section in Hut 3. The Army Section ought to be strengthened by a change of Head: the present one is a charmingly naïve plagiarist who puts to the War Office as his own, interpretations borrowed from others: this can only end in trouble, for people will suspect him of capitalisation. In addition, his refusal to allow the letter 'G.L.' to appear in MSS reports, on the ground that they are secret, is characteristic. The Air Section, and indeed all the sections, needs a Head who is scrupulously honest, for the reasons I have given above. I consider it desirable that he should understand the principles of MSS cryptography and (essential) the academic mind, for then he will meet the worker as an equal – and through his appreciation – be less inclined to make personal capital out of the work. In addition, he must understand thoroughly the requirements of his Service. It is of less importance that he should be an expert linguist; this we have found from experience, that a good technical man working alongside a good linguist can nearly always bridge all the gaps. The Heads of the Service sections would fulfil the functions of Service

> editors; besides their direct editing, they would have to know what their readers wanted and hence what their reports, i.e. Hut 6 and the Y organisation, should cover. Above them, for the purpose of administration should be an Editor-in-Chief, who would exercise a supervisory control over general Hut policy. The Watch would be responsible to him, and the Service representatives on the Watch should be regarded as expert advisers to the No. 1, instead of Overseers. I believe that if the Services were to give a little in the matter of their rights, they would find an adequate return. Regarding the choice of an Editor-in-Chief, as the man who started it has obviously the most interest in the Hut's welfare, and it has yet to be shown that the present Head has been either prejudiced or incompetent, there is a good case for his remaining in office. The Research Section of Hut 3 needs expansion; this is already contemplated, but is held up through a shortage of people.

The outcome of Jones's report was the removal of Saunders from Hut 3, along with Humphreys and Curtis. They were initially replaced by a management triumvirate of the three senior officers in the Hut, but Jones was confirmed as overall head in July 1942. The 'Hut 3 affair' also brought further scrutiny of AGD's management of GC&CS at BP.

By September 1941, Sigint resources were stretched. According to DMI: 'Sigint is vital but at the present moment it suffers from two grave disadvantages: (a) lack of equipment; (b) lack of effective operational control.'[102] There were serious deficiencies in all three main branches of Sigint and subsequently, Navy and Air Sections had found and trained their own staff for low-grade cryptanalysis. While the Army had no low-grade material to work on, their training section ISSIS provided recruits to all Services. DMI complained that Typex facilities were insufficient 'to deal with even the present volume of traffic being sent home from abroad, with the result that much of this traffic is not seen by the cryptographers, much less broken'.[103] On 23 December 1941, at a Chiefs of Staff Committee meeting with the Directors of Intelligence, the Committee 'invited the Y Board to examine as a matter of urgency the organisation of Y Services generally and to submit proposals for the additional accommodation, equipment and staff that would now be required in the Y organisation and for the consequential increases in staff in the intelligence Directorates'.[104]

The Foreign Office stated that a 35 per cent increase had already been approved by the Treasury for GC&CS. This provided an increase in Temporary Senior Administrative Officers, Junior Administrative Officers, first, second and third grade Temporary Clerks, tabulating staff and typists. The Y Board set out a number of principles and recommendations to the Chiefs of Staff which were very significant for AGD's organisation.[105] In particular, the work of cryptanalysts would now be treated as a reserved occupation without question. Furthermore, there would be no prohibition against recruiting young men until the personnel requirements were met and absolute priority was to be given to demands for requisitioning premises in the neighbourhood of GC&CS.

In late October 1941, following a visit to BP by the Prime Minister the previous month, Welchman and some of his colleagues were becoming frustrated by the failure by senior BP management to deal quickly with urgent requests for vital equipment and personnel. Welchman drafted a letter[106] to the Prime Minister and signed it along with Turing and their two deputies, Stuart Milner-Barry and Hugh Alexander:

> *Secret and Confidential*
> *Prime Minister only,* Hut 6 and Hut 8, 21st October 1941
>
> Dear Prime Minister,
> Some weeks ago you paid us the honour of a visit, and we believe that you regard our work as important. You will have seen that, thanks largely to the energy and foresight of Commander Travis, we have been well supplied with the 'bombes' for the breaking of the German Enigma codes. We think, however, that you ought to know that this work is being held up, and in some cases is not being done at all, principally because we cannot get sufficient staff to deal with it. Our reason for writing to you direct is that for months we have done everything that we possibly can through the normal channels, and that we despair of any early improvement without your intervention. No doubt in the long run these particular requirements will be met, but meanwhile still more precious months will have been wasted, and as our needs are continually expanding we see little hope of ever being adequately staffed.
>
> We realise that there is a tremendous demand for labour of all kinds and that its allocation is a matter of priorities. The trouble to our mind is that as we are a very small section with numerically trivial requirements it is very difficult to bring home to the authorities finally responsible either the importance of what is done here or the urgent necessity of dealing promptly with our requests. At the same time we find it hard to believe that it is really impossible to produce quickly the additional staff that we need, even if this meant interfering with the normal machinery of allocations.

We do not wish to burden you with a detailed list of our difficulties, but the following are the bottlenecks which are causing us the most acute anxiety.

Breaking of Naval Enigma (Hut 8)

Owing to shortage of staff and the overworking of his present team the Hollerith section here under Mr Freeborn has had to stop working night shifts. The effect of this is that the finding of the naval keys is being delayed at least twelve hours every day. In order to enable him to start night shifts again Freeborn needs immediately about twenty more untrained Grade III women clerks. To put himself in a really adequate position to deal with any likely demands he will want a good many more.

A further serious danger now threatening us is that some of the skilled male staff, both with the British Tabulating Company at Letchworth and in Freeborn's section here, who have so far been exempt from military service, are now liable to be called up.

Military and Air Force Enigma (Hut 6)

We are intercepting quite a substantial proportion of wireless traffic in the Middle East which cannot be picked up by our intercepting stations here. This contains among other things a good deal of new 'Light Blue' intelligence. Owing to shortage of trained typists, however, and the fatigue of our present decoding staff, we cannot get all this traffic decoded. This has been the state of affairs since May. Yet all that we need to put matters right is about twenty trained typists.

Bombe testing, Hut 6 and Hut 8

In July we were promised that the testing of the 'stories' produced by the bombes would be taken over by the WRNS in the bombe hut and that sufficient WRNS would be provided for this purpose. It is now late in October and nothing has been done. We do not wish to stress this so strongly as the two preceding points, because it has not actually delayed us in delivering the goods. It has, however, meant that staff in Huts 6 and 8 who are needed for other jobs have had to do the testing themselves. We cannot help feeling that with a Service matter of this kind it should have been possible to detail a body of WRNS for this purpose, if sufficiently urgent instructions had been sent to the right quarters.

> Apart altogether from staff matters, there are a number of other directions in which it seems to us that we have met with unnecessary impediments. It would take too long to set these out in full, and we realise that some of the matters involved are controversial. The cumulative effect, however, has been to drive us to the conviction that the importance of the work is not being impressed with sufficient force upon those outside authorities with whom we have to deal.
>
> We have written this letter entirely on our own initiative. We do not know who or what is responsible for our difficulties, and most emphatically we do not want to be taken as criticising Commander Travis who has all along done his utmost to help us in every possible way. But if we are to do our job as well as it could and should be done it is absolutely vital that our wants, small as they are, should be promptly attended to. We have felt that we should be failing in our duty if we did not draw your attention to the facts and to the effects which they are having and must continue to have on our work, unless immediate action is taken.
>
> We are, Sir, Your obedient servants,
> A.M. Turing
> W.G. Welchman
> C.H.O'D. Alexander
> P.S. Milner-Barry

Milner-Barry was tasked with delivering the letter in person and upon arriving at No. 10 Downing Street, handed it to one of Churchill's staff. Remarkably, the Prime Minister read the letter and put an 'Action This Day' stamp on it with a handwritten note to his chief military assistant General Ismay, saying: 'Make sure they have all they want on extreme priority and report to me that this has been done.' Milner-Barry would later recall AGD's reaction to the letter: 'I by chance met Commander Denniston in the corridors some days later, and he made some rather wry remark about our unorthodox behaviour; but he was much too nice a man to bear malice.'[107]

Shortly afterwards, Menzies appeared at BP and according to Milner-Barry 'was very cross'. He personally rebuked Welchman for violating the chain of command and then met with AGD. It was not long, however, before the situation at BP started to improve. Staff requirements at BP were indeed given 'extreme priority' and on 18 November 1941, Menzies reported to Churchill that 'every possible measure was being taken'. While all of the new arrangements were not yet in place, BP's needs were being 'very rapidly met'.[108] However, in January 1942, when the spate of argument and recrimination was damaging efficiency and threatening a breakdown of discipline, 'C', in his capacity as Director of GC&CS, appointed an independent investigator, a former DDMI, to report not only on the dispute about the handling of the product of Air Force and Army Enigma and on the administrative control of GC&CS, but also on the functioning of GC&CS's Naval and Air Sections.[109]

***

By the end of 1941, the Diplomatic Section at BP, which AGD directly controlled, had grown to eighty staff which included sixty cryptanalysts (twenty-nine Senior and Junior Assistants, including temporaries and thirty-one Linguists or Clerical Assistants), and the remainder typists and other ancillary staff. The main country sections were Italian, Japanese, Near Eastern, Chinese, Balkan, Portuguese and a French Section enhanced by eight staff to work on Vichy government ciphers. In all, they worked on the traffic of twenty-six countries, received around 100,000 telegrams, read 70,000 and translated and circulated 8,495.[110] At least an additional fifty staff were required but working space was not available. So there was little change to the Diplomatic Country Sections apart from a small increase to the Italian and French Sections, bringing the establishment up to 100. Early in the year liaison was established with US Diplomatic Agencies and later a joint effort began to break and exploit German diplomatic traffic.

The America Army Security Agency (ASA) had more staff working on Italian diplomatic traffic, but GC&CS had more experience and knowledge, so it could provide them with codes more fully recovered than theirs along with information about enciphering tables. The Americans in due course provided help in recovering keys and had at their disposal more machine tabulating equipment. Regular exchanges of traffic registers, wanted material and code recoveries were in force by the beginning of 1942 and continued until the end of the war.

After the Americans had provided GC&CS with at least one replica 'Purple' machine in February 1941, there was joint collaboration in recovering the current settings of the machine. This work required both a specialised team of cryptanalysts and a greater number of linguist/translators. Once Japan entered the war, many former consular and diplomatic officials returned to Britain and were drafted in to help with the task.

Up until the Japanese attack on Pearl Harbor on 7 December 1941, GC&CS's Diplomatic Section had been reading US State Department cipher messages. On 25 February 1942, in a personal letter to Roosevelt, Churchill wrote:

> My Dear Mr. President,
> One night when we talked late, you spoke of the importance of our cipher people getting into close touch with yours. I shall be very ready to put any expert you care to nominate in touch with my technicians. Ciphers for our two Navies have been and are continually a matter for frank discussion between our two Services. But diplomatic and military ciphers are of equal importance, and we appear to know nothing officially of your versions of these. Some time ago, however, our experts claimed to have discovered the system and constructed some tables used by your Diplomatic Corps. From the moment when we became allies, I gave instructions that this work should cease. However, danger of our enemies having achieved a measure of success cannot, I am advised, be dismissed. I shall be grateful of you will handle this matter entirely yourself, and if possible burn this letter when you have read it. The whole subject is secret in a degree, which affects the safety of both our countries. The fewest possible people should know.
>
> I take advantage of the Ambassador's homeward journey to send you this by his hand, to be delivered into yours personally.[111]

While collaboration between Britain and the US was going well on the diplomatic front, AGD was becoming concerned that the Americans were going back on their promises to him in August. On 23 December, he wrote to Washington with his concerns:

> In a telegram from War Department, A. 16 of 18th December they raise the question of investigating the German Air-Army cypher. During my visit it was agreed that we should be responsible for this investigation and that when USA were in real need of this work we should invite their party to join ours.
>
> Could you find out if their views on this procedure have changed and if they wish to begin their own investigations now? It is devoutly hoped by all here that any such investigations will not interfere with their progress on Japanese work for which we count on them.
>
> We could send by bag two days of traffic and certain keys (all information on this being sent in cypher) but bag communication is very slow.

> Could you also find out if they are intercepting any of this material?
> I am sending by bag material for German air to ground traffic.[112]

This development prompted AGD 'to organise, without delay, an inter-service Japanese Section comprising all phases of Japanese work, ie, Diplomatic, Naval, Military and Air'.[113]

By the end of 1941, the pressure on AGD was growing with political battles continually being fought with the Service ministries and internal staffing and administration problems a constant concern. Inter-Service difficulties were also ever present and according to Birch:

> Throughout the history of Sigint in the Second World War there is noticeable the pursuit of satisfactory compromises between two pairs of alternative and mutually incompatible ideas: - Service versus inter-service structure of Sigint and centralisation versus decentralisation of cryptanalysis. In these early days, whenever the inter-service pooling of some Sigint function was mooted, one or other of the Services was apt to discover that its needs were different from those of the other two. When inter-service coordination of D/F was proposed, 'the Navy and Air Force had to deal with rapidly moving targets, whereas the stations the Army would try and place were either fixed or capable of only a small movement from day to day'.[114]' In the matter of 'Operational Intelligence', as we shall see, the Admiralty was 'different', in that it was 'an executive organisation' and therefore needs an O.I.C. inside itself, whereas the Army and Air Force need rapid dissemination from the source (GC&CS) to their executive commands.[115] So, too, when an Air Section was set up in GC&CS in 1936, Air Ministry felt that it had been 'formed for a somewhat different purpose to the other two'.[116]

In January 1942, DNI John Godfrey wrote:

> BP has grown in a haphazard way out of small body of research workers to a heterogeneous establishment numbering some 1,500 persons. I am urging 'C' with some success to put his house in order and to tackle the administrative problems involved, and what I hope to aim at is that there should be a Senior Officer in administrative charge of the whole establishment, who will look after administration, security, welfare, feeding, housing, etc. ... leaving Denniston and the technicians to pursue their highly important specialities.[117]

The problem according to Birch was that 'the Y expansion programme was out-of-date before it was fulfilled, and the Y communications plan was carried out only partially and tardily'. Furthermore, criticisms of GC&CS were driven by a paradox: 'The Services controlled Y, and GC&CS, under CSS, controlled cryptography, but Y and cryptography, although separate, were inseparable.'

The Army seemed to play the leading role in the battle for Sigint control. Enigma cryptanalysis was outside the jurisdiction of No. 4 IS, MI8's Military Section at GC&CS. The Enigma decrypts went from Hut 3 to MI14 in the War Office via MI6/SIS, bypassing MI8. Enigma traffic analysis was the function of MI8's No. 6IS but the major part of it was still at Beaumanor due to lack of accommodation at BP. While MI8 was responsible for all Army interception including Enigma traffic, it seemed sensible that interception policy should be driven by General Staff requirements. However, interception was, in practice, arranged by GC&CS and there was nothing in place for any sort of control by the General Staff.

DMI made a proposal in autumn 1941 concerning the operational control of Sigint. The Directors of Military Intelligence met weekly before seeing the Chiefs of Staff, and Sigint policy for the week could be set at that meeting. The Directors thought that they should be supplied with weekly reports and returns from GC&CS through the German Sections at the War Office and Air Ministry, supplemented by W/T reports from MI8.[118] However, the proposal was challenged by Welchman on behalf of Hut 6 and Hut 8:

> The operational control of the sets allotted for E work is an hour-to-hour business which should be left in the hands of experts, provided of course that these experts follow the general policy laid down by higher authority and report any emergency action that they have taken. This operational control could not be done efficiently by a body of men meeting only once a week and provided only with MI8 returns on which to base their decisions.[119]

Welchman's views were supported by the Y Board at their meeting of 24 September,[120] and there was no support from the other two Services. Naval Sigint in GC&CS worked well with NID and all naval decrypts and intelligence, either current or research, were passed by Naval Section to the Admiralty. As de Grey wrote 'The friction over responsibilities and divisions of labour which wasted so much time in the other Services, never occurred in the relations of GC&CS and the Admiralty.'[121] The Air Ministry also had few complaints, since almost the whole of the huge output of the Hut 6/Hut 3 operation concerned the GAF. There was, however, a very general Service dissatisfaction with GC&CS, based partly on the separation of Y and cryptography, the position of CSS between the Services and GC&CS, overall shortages of staff, equipment and facilities, and on what appeared to be managerial weaknesses at BP.

As Birch says:

> It had been intended to use Bletchley Park for a cryptanalytic bureau and, in the interests of security, to keep the bureau as small as possible. A great deal of the ensuing trouble may be ascribed to the retention of a parochial attitude long after the march of events had proved the inevitability of the development of 'the Park' into a global Sigint centre. The difficulties of recruiting civilians were common to many departments, but in GC&CS they were aggravated by abnormally low rates of pay and bad living conditions in the first years, and later by the operation of the call-up of women. Anomalies arising from the employment of many Service and civilian grades on substantially the same work needed constant reconciliation. The provision of working quarters, billets, meals and transport lagged increasingly behind requirements. At last, in July 1941, it was agreed as a matter of GC&CS policy to build two-storey brick buildings instead of the temporary wooden huts hitherto provided, but pending their construction, the limit of accommodation had been reached by the end of that year, and by the time they were ready for occupation, they were inadequate for the further expansion which had meanwhile become necessary.

The JCC had been set up in April 1941 to handle the general administration of BP. In effect, the administrative staff of CSS took over control of administration.[122]

According to historian Christopher Andrew, 'Without the expertise painstakingly built up at GC&CS on minimal resources by Denniston between the wars, Bletchley Park's wartime triumphs would have been impossible.' However, now others argued that AGD did not have a great vision, that he only wanted a restricted remit for GC&CS, i.e. cryptography, not the wider role of Sigint and all that entailed. The reality was that the two were inexorably bound together, but the Service Ministries insisted that it was their job to determine what intelligence was useful and what wasn't as well as evaluating it. If they sensed that they were being second guessed by the civilians at GC&CS, they would move to take over the cryptography role as well, making GC&CS a small research section. So AGD insisted, at least in any document that he produced, that the role of GC&CS should be restricted to cryptography pure and simple. In reality, he knew full well that their work was indivisible from other Sigint activities. His strategy would eventually win BP the right to be in total command of Sigint.

In early January 1942, Menzies, having received the report from his independent investigator, General K.J. Martin and in agreement with the DMI, invited Brigadier W.L. van Cutsem, formerly DDMI (I), 'To report to the Director and Head of GC&CS on any means of improving the military information derived from the cryptographic work and its flow to the military authorities interested. The report is only to deal with existing machinery, without suggesting any major change.'[123]

The Brigadier decided 'to extend the inquiry beyond the purely military side, in order to gain an insight into the organisation as a whole and to compare the systems in the Air and Naval Sections with that in the Military Section, with a view to seeing what features in the Naval and Air Sections might profitably be adopted in the Military'. He also decided 'to enquire into the administration of the GC&CS, for . . . it is evident that administration plays a direct and important part of the efficiency of the work carried out'. His report was presented on 30 January at a special meeting of the Director, ACSI and Travis.[124] Menzies acted quickly and, by 3 February, issued instructions for a radical reorganisation of GC&CS:

> **Reorganisation GC&CS**
> With the ever increasing work, I have found it necessary to carry out a reorganisation of the GC&CS.
> The posts of Head of the GC&CS and Deputy Head of the GC&CS have been abolished and the work of the GC&CS will henceforth be divided into two parts:
> Civil
> Services
> Commander Denniston and Commander Travis are appointed Deputy Directors to control the Civil and Services' sides respectively, with the titles of Deputy Director (C) and Deputy Director (S).
>
> <u>Civil Side:</u>
> The Deputy Director (C) (Commander Denniston) with headquarters at Wavendon, will control this side of the work, i.e. the Diplomatic and Commercial Sections.
> Mr. Earnshaw-Smith is appointed Assistant to Commander Denniston, with the title Assistant Director (C).

> Service Side:
> The Deputy Director (S) (Commander Travis), with headquarters at B/P, will control the Service Sections, including Hut 3, ISOS and ISK [Intelligence Services, Knox] , and will exercise general control at B/P and Elmers.
> Mr. N. de Grey is appointed Assistant to Commander Travis with the title Assistant Director (S).
> Colonel Tiltman, in addition to his duties as Commandant No. 4 IS, will act as Chief Cryptographer and will take charge of the Research Section.
> The Deputy Director (S) will represent the GC&CS at the Y Board and for the time being at the Y Committee. Colonel Tiltman will be responsible for Liaison with the FECB and the USA Bureaux. Mr. Cooper will be responsible for Liaison with the CBME.
>
> Administration:
> Administration will be unified under Paymaster Commander Bradshaw, who is appointed as Assistant Director with the title Assistant Director (A). He will be responsible to the Deputy Directors for meeting their requirements. The JCC is abolished.
>
> Effect is to be given to the above directions with the minimum of delay.
> Heads of Sections are to inform members of their sections of this reorganisation.
>
> (Signed) [S.G.M. Menzies, Chief of SIS]
> Director[125]

On 30 January 1942, AGD wrote to Tiltman, Bradshaw, Cooper, Birch, Malcolm Saunders, Denys Page,[126] Knox, de Grey, Eric Earnshaw-Smith[127] and Henry Maine:[128]

> In consequence of the great expansion of G.C. & C.S., the Director has decided to abolish the posts of Head and Deputy Head and to nominate myself and Cdr. Travis as Deputy Directors and to divide the organisation into two parts:
>
> The Civil side including Diplomatic & Commercial Sections.
> The Services side including Naval, Military, and Air Sections and ISOS and ISK.

> The Civil side will be under my direction with Mr. Earnshaw-Smith as my assistant. Cdr. Travis will control the Services side with Mr. de Grey as assistant.
> The Director will circulate his decision as to General Administration in a few days.[129]

New terms of reference were also approved by the Y Board for the Y Committee on 5 February 1942.[130] Birch later noted in his official history that:

> What strikes one most about comparing the old with the new is a change of outlook, a better understanding and a broader perspective of Sigint. It is, for instance, no longer 'the needs of the three Services, and of the GC&CS' that need co-ordinating, but 'the activities of the Y services', and increasing concern is shown with developments overseas, the Y services in the Dominions and the Y Committees now established in Cairo and at Gibraltar, liaison with the Allies and Sigint.

A number of factors led to the restructuring of GC&CS and AGD's subsequent removal from BP. The Service Ministries had continued to express concerns about GC&CS and in particular, AGD's view that all service cryptanalysis work should be centralised at BP. The problems within Hut 3 reflected badly on AGD as he was ultimately responsible for the smooth delivery of BP's 'product' to them. The Americans continued to apply pressure and it was proving difficult to secure agreement on the best division of labour in intelligence work between the two countries across multiple theatres of operation. The 'Action This Day' letter certainly would have been noted in Whitehall as further evidence of AGD's inability to effectively run the BP operation. Interestingly, Gordon Welchman, who had written the letter, believed that it was ill health that had forced him out.[131] According to the Official History of MI6, AGD's removal from BP by Menzies was a demotion.

In the years that followed, former colleagues of AGD began to give their views on his 'demotion'. Stuart Milner-Barry, who had co-signed the letter to Churchill and then personally delivered it to him at Downing Street, told the historian Ronald Lewin that by the winter of 1940, Denniston was a 'busted flush' and incapable of the organisational effort that was necessary if BP was to be put on a war footing. AGD was obsessed by secrecy and had a good relationship with Sinclair, who after all had appointed him in the first place. Sinclair's successor, Menzies, was a WW1 hero who conducted most of his MI6 business at White's

Club in St James's and was a different proposition. In his biography of Menzies, Anthony Cave Brown claimed that AGD and Menzies had remained in 'close and friendly association' between the two world wars. He also believed that AGD's removal from BP was one of Menzies's 'unhappier decisions'. However, during WW1, Menzies was an intelligence liaison officer between GHQ and the Directorate of Military Intelligence and MI1(c). While he was only a member of the Army in principle, he may well have felt that the Army's man, Malcolm Hay, should have been appointed as Head of GC&CS over the Admiralty's nominee, AGD. However, there is no evidence that Menzies knew about AGD being chosen over Hay for the role of Head of GC&CS. In any event, the view that he never fully supported AGD would be strengthened by events that transpired towards the end of WW2.

Harold Fletcher, who was in charge of administration in Hut 6, told Welchman in a letter on 26 October 1979 that, 'I have a clear recollection that you told me that Travis had had to tell C "Either he goes or I go"'. Peter Twinn, in correspondence with Welchman, wrote that:

> I do not regard him as a success. I think he failed between the wars to get GCHQ (GCCS as it was) the status & facilities it needed. And he was on a pretty good wicket in the years just before 1939. The organisation was having stunning success in reading the Spanish Civil War codes & had clearly demonstrated its potential trifling expenditure. Denniston's posting to London was clearly demotion. Indeed Denniston said to one of my colleagues, when his posting was arranged & Travis took over 'I am not jealous of Travis – what grieves me is the realisation that I didn't prove man enough for the job.'[132]

Others took a more charitable view of AGD's contribution to GC&CS's early success. Ralph Bennett, a former duty officer in Hut 3, said of AGD's removal:

> Denniston had spent his life in the time of the battle of Hastings dealing with hand codes and not much information that you could use militarily. Then he found himself in charge of a huge growing organisation, a lot of us younger and in some ways thinking along different lines, and he got a bit outdated in some ways and was shunted out. It was a bit of bad luck for him because he was a very good chap but he was overtaken by events.[133]

According to historians Michael Smith and Ralph Erskine:

> In contrast to the major difficulties that emerged in 1943 over the US Army's desire to attack Heer [Army] and Luftwaffe Enigma, cooperation between Britain and the United States on diplomatic codebreaking was remarkably trouble-free from its start in early 1941. Partly for that reason, and partly no doubt because of the range of countries potentially involved, no formal agreement about diplomatic Sigint was ever concluded between the US War Department and GC&CS. Inevitably there were misunderstandings from time to time, but they were resolved, in no small measure due to the wise approach adopted by Alastair Denniston, who was wholeheartedly in favour of Sigint cooperation with the United States. Denniston was a man of vision on this issue, just as he had been in 1939 when he recruited Alan Turing and Gordon Welchman to join GC&CS when war with Germany was declared. Sadly, there has been insufficient recognition of his vital role in laying the foundations of GC&CS's wartime successes and in paving the way for Britain's important Sigint alliances with the United States.

Another and more sinister view of AGD's removal was put forward by a former close colleague, Percy Filby. A Cambridge graduate, Filby was a captain in the Army Intelligence Corps from 1940 until 1945, first at BP then at Berkeley Street as AGD's official number two. According to him:

> Travis was deputy to Denniston and a crony of de Grey. They had endless talks in the crucial days and although they were held next door the walls were wooden and since we were almost always working in complete silence I couldn't help hearing the conversations sometimes. De Grey's voice was that of an actor and I knew ages before it happened that they didn't feel Denniston could cope with the enormous increase demanded of Ultra and other problems. AGD was headstrong and didn't like criticism; after all, he had carried the group throughout the 1930s, against criticism quite often, and now that war had actually occurred he wanted to be at the helm, in charge of the organisation he had created. Travis and de Grey were perfectly right.[134]

He went on to say:

> Obviously he [AGD] was disappointed and extremely bitter, but whenever I went to stay with him and with Dorothy he was relaxed. The villain of the piece was really a man named Freeborn, leader of the machine group from Letchworth. He was power hungry and

> realized that with AGD out of the way he could manipulate to his heart's content. Even Travis would generally address Freeborn: 'Mr Freeborn, we have a particularly difficult time in front of us. Do you think you could spare a few machines?' Freeborn would look at a board and ruminate, and would finally state that if he cut A and B he could accommodate Travis. Having got his own way he attacked AGD unmercifully, and because his Hollerith machines were now all powerful he virtually controlled all but Ultra. AGD was given the sop at Berkeley Street but to the horror of Freeborn it turned into a gigantic success for AGD. We used to work 18 hours a day, seven days a week as if to prove that AGD could control and direct. 'C' was always on good terms with AGD and one day in 1943 he was able to turn to AGD and congratulate him on a great success, with more to come. Freeborn called me into his office and he asked me to come back to Bletchley with my team. 'Travis will OK it if you wish'. I declined and he promised to stop further promotion.

GC&CS was under intense pressure at the end of 1941 and it appears that a number of people at BP blamed their problems on AGD. While he was comfortable in allowing creativity and innovation to flourish in the early days at BP, his non-combative personality made it difficult for him to fight the battle in Whitehall to get authority for the resources that would be needed for BP's expansion. Travis, on the other hand, was described by Welchman as a 'bulldog of a man' and would prove to be the ideal person to fight the ensuing battles for resources. For all of his qualities and huge personal contribution to the ultimate success of BP, it is unlikely that AGD would have been as successful in Whitehall.

While Travis' reputation was of one who was rough and burly, he was well respected by staff. He was visible through the Park during the war and knew many staff personally.[135]

Evidence of his management style compared to AGD is highlighted in a 1940 incident when Oliver Strachey had begun a petition about messing arrangements. Travis wanted to treat this as akin to 'mutiny'. AGD wrote to him saying:

> After twenty years' experience in GC&CS, I think I may say to you that one does not expect to find the rigid discipline of a battleship among the collection of somewhat unusual civilians who form GC&CS. To endeavour to impose it would be a mistake in my mind and would not assist our war effort, we must take them as they are and try to get the best out of them. They do very stupid things, as in the present case, but they are producing what the authorities require.

By the end of 1941, AGD must have been at the end of his tether. His nature prevented him from exploiting the unexpected success at BP under his control for his own advantage. Health problems and two arduous trips to the US and Canada had kept him away from BP for months and while he hadn't formally handed over control of BP to Travis, a lack of leadership was leading to quarrels within his organisation. Issues persisted between Menzies and the Service Ministries but he was out of touch with BP's day to day operation. Menzies' relations with AGD were not ideal and the two appear to have had little direct contact throughout the year. The Denniston family had just completed the move from their farmhouse accommodation to a small semi-detached house just outside the gates of BP called Friedenheim. Now AGD was to be stationed in London and quickly had to move the family back to their house in Ashtead. Fortunately, both for him and the country, he would soon find himself back in charge of an organisation more suited to his talents.

Chapter 5

Berkeley Street

The first three months of 1942 saw major offensives taking place on multiple fronts. The Soviet offensive was going well in January. The Japanese were advancing steadily down Malaya towards Singapore and British forces were trying to advance in North Africa. Naval battles were taking place along the French coast, in the North Atlantic and the Java Sea. In March, AGD and the main body of GC&CS's Diplomatic Section moved back to London. The German Section remained temporarily at BP along with the Commercial Section until its accommodation was ready in another building in London. The Diplomatic Section was housed in former flats at Numbers 8 and 9 Berkeley Street and took up four floors capable of housing seventy-five staff. The adjoining house, Numbers 6 and 7, also had floors available with capacity for around seventy staff. This expansion space would be needed as the Japanese Section (translating and codebreaking) was rapidly expanding along with the Italian, Near Eastern and some of the smaller sections.

The Commercial Section later moved to two floors of Aldford House in Park Lane, which were also previously residential flats. As the section worked closely with the MEW, this located them closer to that ministry. Only occasional contact took place between the country sections at Berkeley Street and the Commercial Section at Aldford House and little contact took place between them and the Naval, Military and Air Section at BP.

AGD, with his new designation of Deputy Director (Civil) (DD(C)), now found himself in charge of an organisation much the same size as the one he had brought to BP in August 1939. Percy Filby headed up the German Diplomatic Section when it moved to Berkeley Street later in March. According to Filby, while he never heard AGD comment on the move from BP, 'That he was crushed there was no doubt; he seldom smiled, showed unusual irritation and in general was far from his normal self.'[1]

However, AGD quickly threw himself into the work of his new section and was at his desk from 9.00 am until everyone else had left. He established a personal rapport with all ranks of his staff through regular visits to each country section, making suggestions but never interfering with the work. He never seemed to panic and almost all looked on him with considerable affection. AGD had recruited some excellent linguists and mathematicians. There were also several titled ladies and scholars such as Professor Adcock, Professor of Classics at Cambridge and Ernst Fetterlein. The latter was the top Russian cryptographer who had been brought out of retirement after invaluable service during WW1. He was only useful on book ciphers where insight was required. 'Fetty', as he was known, would arrive precisely at 9.30 am and read *The Times* newspaper until 10.00 am at which point he was ready to take on any task assigned to him. Filby continued to use Fetterlein when he was in his seventies, ill and at home.

Some of the older civil servants caused AGD problems as they demanded their rights which they believed to include having separate offices and other staff to do their bidding. They had worked on diplomatic material between the wars but didn't fit in with younger experts and translators recruited by AGD. They insisted on working 10.00 am until 4.00 am rather than 9.00 am until 5.00 pm like the rest of the staff. Filby, as head of the large German section shared a room with four colleagues. One of the old guard told him that if she didn't have a room of her own, she would not come to work. As Filby later recalled:

> How Denniston mollified her I will never know, but after a week's absence she meekly asked me if she could have a table and chair. She was an excellent translator, but with her status as the senior lady of the Foreign Office she insisted on translating only messages less than a week old! When there was nothing to her liking she brought from her drawer her manuscript of a definitive biography of Beethoven, which later became a classic.

Malcolm Kennedy worked as an intelligence translator in the Japanese Diplomatic Section from September 1939 to March 1942, and then moved to Berkeley Street until December 1942. In his diary, he offered the old guard's view of AGD's management style. In an entry for 4 March 1942 he wrote:

> Orders definitely issued for our branch of the F.O. to return to London next week. Feel very sore about it, as the move has been manoeuvred by certain 'interested parties' and by gross misrepresentation of the facts, while A.G.D. is so utterly spineless, that on his own admission, he has made no attempt to point out the serious snags and difficulties involved. No small portion of the personnel who, for one reason or another, are unable to go, have had to resign and for many of us, the move will entail 4 to 5 hours travel daily to and from work with an early start (from 8 a.m.) and a late return (9 p.m. or later). And yet A.G.D. has the brass to contend that efficiency will be increased 'in the tenser atmosphere of London'! We and others have sent in memos and made personal protests, pointing out how efficiency will be seriously affected rather than increased, but our warnings are simply brushed aside and we are censured by A.G.D. for having the temerity to question the decision. 'I never questioned it', he said, as though this were to his credit, though by his very admission he damns himself as utterly unfitted to be head of a show like ours. By failing to put forward his views and to point out the facts, he is guilty of negligence and incompetence and has failed deplorably in his duties as No.1.[2]

AGD never seemed to let such personal bitterness interfere with his efforts to drive the organisation forward. Kennedy's diary entry for 7 March 1942 shows how AGD tried to rouse his staff for the job ahead:

> A.G.D. has circulated an absolute masterpiece of fatuous 'pep talk' to those of us who are being sent back to London. In it he describes our coming return there as being 'in the nature of the adventure in the middle of the war' and says we shall be able to 'carry out our duties more in the front line' and that the 'tenser atmosphere of London will urge us on still further', though how he reconciles this with his assertion that we shall be 'more exposed to daylight raids' is somewhat mystifying! It is all in line however, with his remark to us the other day that, if we continued to work in the peaceful atmosphere of B.P. our work might suffer from 'dolci furviante'.

Not all of the old guard behaved in this way and E. Earnshaw-Smith, Frederic Catty and A.G.R. Rees, to name three, fitted in well with the new recruits such as Gerald Tomlins and Stanley White who worked in Filby's section. White, a bank official from Wallasey, near Liverpool, controlled the main linguists in the section while Tomlins, also a bank official, had a good knowledge of German knowledge.

Many of the more productive staff regularly worked fifteen-hour days, seven days per week. Few staff took leave and they rarely asked for a day off. Some were of high social status and included Dorothy Hyson (1942–5) who married the actor Anthony Quayle in 1947, Ela Beaumont (1942–5), later the Countess of Carlisle, and Sheila Thorpe (1942–5), who married Tomlins during the war.

AGD held few staff meetings but was always well informed about the work of each section While they were kept separate with little fraternisation, AGD began holding monthly Heads of Sections meetings also attended by the Head of the Commercial Section. He worked closely with Earnshaw-Smith, the head of the Distribution and Reference (D&R) Section, as his deputy, designated as Assistant Director (Civil) (AD(C)).

By the end of the 1942 AGD, along with his administrative, traffic-sorting staff and the D&R Section with typists, numbered twenty-five and occupied roughly one floor of the combined houses, joined by a door. The Axis sections staff numbered seventy-five, of which forty worked in the German Section and this grew to sixty by mid-1943. The Japanese and Italian Sections, comprising both cryptanalysts and linguists, each had twenty staff. The remaining country sections, of which the French, Portuguese, Near East and Chinese were the biggest, had fifty staff between them. During its first year of operation at Berkeley Street, AGD's organisation circulated 13,095 translations, compared to 8,485 in 1940. The recipients included the Foreign Office, which received all of them while the Admiralty received 6,901, the War Office 6,927 and the Air Ministry 6,158. MI5 received 9,315 compared with 1,166 in 1940.

According to Filby, 'unproductive' sections were sent to Berkeley Street believing that it would keep AGD occupied but have little impact on the war. However, AGD had increasingly more access to Menzies as the diplomatic and commercial output became interesting and attracted his attention. Menzies, along with Admiral Cunningham, the Commander-in-Chief of the Mediterranean Fleet, started to visit AGD on a regular basis. Travis also visited Berkeley Street and after a V1 flying bomb hit the Lansdowne Hotel in Berkeley Square and missed their rooms by a few yards, he tried to get some of the sections returned to BP on the grounds of security. This suggestion was, however, rejected by Menzies. From mid-1943, visits from the top brass were continuous and Anthony Eden gave them a dinner at the Café Royal along with a show, 'Crest of the Waves'. AGD had finally come into his own, with his full access to Menzies restored.[3]

***

In early 1942, there was an information exchange with Arlington Hall in Washington, home to the American Signals Intelligence Service (SIS), run by William Friedman. Filby visited Arlington Hall and Solomon Kullback[4] visited first Berkeley Street and then BP in April. Kullback brought with him some German diplomatic material, and AGD was able to reciprocate with his section's own material which included a work sheet used by a cryptographic clerk in the German embassy. He had apparently crumpled it up and thrown it into a wastepaper basket where it was recovered by a British spy in the embassy. Kullback spent two weeks at Berkeley Street.

Filby also visited Canada and discovered that tensions existed between US and Canadian intelligence agencies. The Canadians wanted to know why he was visiting the US, but Filby could only refer them to a contact in the US, as he was bound by secrecy. The Admiralty proposed an Allied wireless intelligence conference, and it took place in Washington from 6 to 16 April 1942. Unfortunately, the wireless intelligence agreement that AGD had secured with the US Navy's OP-20-G the previous year was not working. Canada was represented by Captain Ed Drake, head of several key Canadian listening stations, Colonel William Murray, head of the Canadian Army's wireless intelligence programme, and Commander John de Marbois, in charge of Canadian wireless interception. The Americans sent senior staff from both OP-20-G and SIS. Commander John Redman, Vice Chief of US Navy Operations, opened the conference. The British delegation was led by Humphrey Sandwith,[5] head of the Admiralty's Y service, and included Captain Roger Winn, head of the Admiralty's U-boat tracking room. There were also representatives from Britain's RSS and the British Foreign Office.

Sandwith proceeded to give a fairly detailed description of Britain's Sigint organisation:

> The Admiralty is responsible for reading every available intercepted and decrypted naval or naval air signal generated by Britain's enemies or potential enemies.
>
> The War Office is responsible for the intercepted signals of enemy military organisations.
>
> The Air Ministry is responsible for reading the intercepted signals of enemy air organisations, except those signals generated by aircraft over water.
>
> The Foreign Office is responsible for reading intercepted and decrypted commercial and diplomatic messages.

> The Radio Security Service (reporting to MI6) is responsible for illicit wireless transmissions in the UK, although it has recently expanded this responsibility to include illicit transmissions emanating from countries of the 'Empire' and neutral countries.
>
> Each of the five organisations cited above has its own wireless intercept or Y service and these are administered by a Y Committee composed of the heads of the 5 Y services plus certain senior intelligence officials. The head of this committee is an admiral [probably DNI].
>
> The cryptographic centre is 'Station X' [GC&CS at BP] and consists of about 2000 people drawn from the 2 services and the Foreign Office. It does both cryptanalysis and TA. The results are pooled.
>
> The wireless interception programme of the 5 Y services is determined half by the traffic needs of the cryptographers and half by the needs of the TA.
>
> Because the cryptographic centre is in England, the main intercepting stations, Scarborough and Flowerdown, are there also. For traffic that cannot be received in Britain, there are intercept stations at Freetown, Pretoria, Durban, Colombo, Melbourne, Bermuda, Alexandria, and several in Canada.
>
> The 65 receivers at Scarborough are all on German traffic whereas those at Flowerdown cover Italy, Spain, France, and any other countries heard in Britain.[6]

Sandwith also provided details of eighteen direction finding stations in Britain plus six in Australia, four in New Zealand, four in South Africa and fourteen in Canada. He provided details of successful operations such as the sinking of the *Bismarck* and the battle against the U-boats.

In late April, Lieutenant C.H. Little of the Canadian Navy was sent to London to confer with intelligence authorities there. His main task was to persuade the British to supply Canada with decrypts from non-naval Japanese traffic being sent to Britain from Canadian listening stations on the West Coast.[7] In mid-May 1942, Little visited Section V of MI6 in St Albans and met with Felix Cowgill, MI6's counter-espionage chief. He wanted to know why Canada was receiving so little South American espionage traffic. Cowgill in turn questioned whether any agreement to provide it was in place

However, AGD got on well with Little. He gave him a tour of the London offices and even invited him home for the weekend. AGD offered Canada the decrypts of high-grade Japanese diplomatic traffic. This included the 'Purple' encrypted messages from the Japanese ambassador in Berlin. In return, AGD asked that Canada continue to monitor Japanese traffic, concentrating specifically on the Japanese diplomatic and commercial messages being received by the Point Grey station near Vancouver.[8] AGD also supplied Little with a list of countries and call signs being monitored as of 3 June 1942. They included: Germany, Japan, Afghanistan, Argentina, Brazil, Bulgaria, Chile, Eire, France, Germany, Hungary, Iran, Italy, Japan, Portugal, Romania, Spain, Sweden, Switzerland, Thailand, Turkey, Russia and the Vatican.[9]

AGD made repeated requests that Canada concentrate on Japanese commercial traffic but Tommy Stone, the head of the Canadian Examination Unit, said that their work was for Canada, not as a service for Britain. On 6 June AGD wrote to Little, suggesting they try to work together so as to avoid duplication of effort:

> You will remember at our conference with the Director that he stressed the importance of your Japanese work and asked that steps to expedite this material should be taken. I therefore asked that the Admiralty (whilst you were at sea) arrange for the Japanese Government material obtained by Point Grey [Vancouver] to be wired home, and it is now possible to make use of the Ferry Command to transmit raw material, preferably unsorted frequently. Where the material is known to be either diplomatic or commercial it would save delay if you could address the package to DD(C) London. I believe it arrives via the Air Ministry.

AGD worked hard to build on the success of the visit to BP by representatives of SIS and OP-20-G in February 1941, known as the Sinkov Mission. The material that the Americans brought to BP included a copy of the German diplomatic code book *Deutsches Satzbuch Nr. 3* (called 'DESAB 3' by the SIS). His efforts led to full cooperation between SIS and GC&CS and ultimately to success against two very difficult German diplomatic cipher systems. The German Foreign Office used three different methods to encipher DESAB 3: OTPs (a system codenamed GEE by the SIS), a system using double encipherment (called GEC by SIS and 'Floradora' by GC&CS)[10] and reciprocal bigram tables, known as Spalierverfahren. Germany was confident about the security of OTPs and double encipherment systems, and lazy practices enabled SIS to recover part of the code book using cryptanalytic methods. A complete copy was obtained from the Army and FBI, taken from a German courier in July 1940, as he passed through the Panama Canal on a Japanese steamship. He was also carrying 3,500 OTP sheets. GC&CS had already reconstructed part of DESAB 3 and had made more progress than SIS on the method of encipherment being used.[11] It had also received a copy of the book from the east coast of Africa.

De Grey had been overseeing work on German Diplomatic systems in March 1941, along with Patricia Bartley[12] and several others including Filby. They had possession of material captured in Iceland in May 1940 from the German Consulate which was part of the 'Floradora' system. However, the absence of daily indicators had made breaks impossible, and work on 'Floradora' had almost been abandoned March 1941. As AGD would later note, 'Floradora' was broken because of three factors: 'The basic book fell into our hands; close cooperation with USA; and SS [Secret Service] work by an able ally who obtained first-hand information and one page of figures from a German cypher officer.'

Progress was slow but, by July 1941, considerable progress had been made with messages from 1940 and early 1941 being frequently readable.[13] In August, AGD was able to report that 'liaison with America has been conspicuously successful' and that ''Floradora' could not have been broken at all without an initial pooling of our resources'.[14]

***

By the end of 1942, AGD had a staff of around 200 and his organisation's primary responsibility was to break diplomatic messages for the Foreign Office. This could yield useful intelligence which would then be passed to Britain's Joint Intelligence Committee (JIC). It also processed plain-language and encoded commercial traffic for Britain's MEW, and AGD had considerable autonomy in this work. Information from both enemy and neutral nations, combined with that from Censorship, was used to plot the economic progress of the war and to set strategic priorities. While the German Section had been considerably enhanced, it was still not producing a consistent amount of decrypted material. The 'Floradora' cipher was not broken until August 1943, so work was concentrated on registration and key recovery.

As well as the 'Purple' machine, the Japanese used a transposition cipher on a code, of which 75 per cent had been recovered, along with 90 per cent of the code itself. This had resulted in some material of considerable intelligence value. The ten linguists involved needed to be well qualified to deal with the sometimes imperfectly recovered telegrams to and from the Japanese Ambassadors. The cryptanalysts working on the machine encrypted material collaborated with the linguists on some of the keys being used with the hand systems. While the main Italian systems had been changed in July and the new systems could have been difficult to master if used correctly, Italian misuse meant that messages continued to be read.

After the fall of France, the French Section targeted the traffic of the Vichy Government. Up to November 1942, they continued to use existing ciphers, which allowed the section to exploit its previous work. The Free French government was established in Algiers and also started to use old systems, but eventually both 'Governments' introduced some new systems towards the end of the year. Eastern European government traffic was also targeted, whether 'free', friendly, or hostile. Polish traffic was read when the code and keys used by the Polish General Staff in London and its military attachés in Berne, Washington and Stockholm were obtained. Work was carried out on Yugoslav, Bulgarian and Romanian traffic. As Germany advanced to Stalingrad and El Alamein, Near Eastern traffic became of interest, such as Persian, Turkish and Arabic, with sixteen staff covering the traffic of six governments. Sections in India and Sarafand had been reinforced, and an officer was sent to Baghdad and later Teheran to work on Persian Diplomatic traffic on the spot. Success was achieved with Saudi-Arabian, Iraqi, Afghan and Egyptian.

The Chinese Section had grown to five linguists and four supporting staff, and traffic was regularly being read. Given the vulnerability of the Chinese systems, a cipher expert was sent from India to Chunking (now Chongqing in south-west China) to improve their diplomatic and military ciphers. As new staff became available, the traffic of more neutral countries was covered if it was felt that the enemy may seek to exploit their strategic position or natural resources. A South American Section was established to cover Argentina, Chile and Mexico, all of which were of particular interest to American diplomatic agencies. Traffic was easy to break but a shortage of linguists over a number of languages hampered progress. By the end of the year, the section numbered twelve and systems in use were sufficiently recovered to enable most of the traffic to be read.

Swiss traffic was targeted for its 'economic warfare' value, and the Section was set up in January 1942 with two expert cryptanalysts with other ongoing work and a few linguists. By the end of the year about 1,000 messages had been circulated with most being of 'economic warfare' value, and others dealt with the affairs of a number of governments whose interests were represented by Switzerland in enemy countries. As the Italians might use Vatican representatives to seek peace negotiations, the Papal ciphers were also targeted.

In the first half of 1943 the Japanese Section was enhanced, along with a growth in both volume and interest in the translated messages issued.

In particular, the communications of the Japanese Ambassador in Moscow proved to be strategically valuable. The German Section was expanded to fifty and considerable progress was made, with current material on the 'Floradora' cipher being read from the beginning of the year. The Italians had made their new systems more secure by changing substitution keys daily. However, some posts continued to use old daily keys, thus neutralising the latest precautions. Mussolini was deposed in July, and in September the Royal Italian Government surrendered unconditionally. However, Mussolini was freed from captivity by the Germans and set up a Fascist government at Salo in northern Italy, supported by the Germans. Posts in various countries were reporting to and taking orders from Mussolini. As the Italian diplomatic service was always royalist by tradition, all major ambassadors and ministers in countries where they could safely do so, supported the King and handed all ciphering equipment over to the Allies. It was therefore assumed that these ciphers would be obviously compromised and never used again. However, when cipher traffic was intercepted it was clear that compromised ciphers were still in use. While the Italian Section had been dissolved when Italy surrendered, a small group remained to look at traffic. For seven months, most Fascist traffic was in plain text. Traffic was intercepted between Salo on Lake Garda and Berlin, Madrid, Tokyo and Budapest. Eight hundred messages were intercepted between September 1943 and January 1944, giving a picture of the Italian set-up at Salo and the attitude of the Germans. Given the vulnerability of Italian systems after their surrender, a joint Anglo-American Mission with Berkeley Street and ASA staff were attached to the Allied Control Commission in Italy from 1 October 1944.

On the American front, there continued to be problems over the ownership of diplomatic and commercial traffic. On 25 November 1942, John R. Redman had written to the Vice Chief of Naval Operations via the Director of Naval Communications. Redman was the Communications Officer on the staff of the Commander-in-Chief, US Pacific Fleet, Admiral Chester Nimitz, and in February 1942, had been put in charge of OP-20-G. His memo dealt with the current problem of cryptanalytical and decryption operations on diplomatic traffic.[15] He recommended that the Army be permitted to take over all of the diplomatic work rather than persisting with the current arrangement, which was inefficient and not desired by either OP-20-G or SIS. His proposal was approved by the Standing Committee for Co-ordination of Cryptanalytic Work on 25 August.

A joint British, Canadian and US conference was held at Arlington Hall on 15 January 1943 to formalise the sharing of diplomatic and commercial traffic. MI6 and GC&CS were represented by Kenneth Maidment and Tiltman, Canada by Drake, Tony Kendrick[16] and Murray, and the US by Colonel Frank W. Bullock, head of Signal Security Service (formally Signal Intelligence Service), Major Telford Taylor from Military Intelligence Service (G-2), Colonel Alfred McCormack, deputy chief of the Special Branch, and William Friedman. Remarkably, the US Navy's only representative was an ensign.[17] The US Army wanted total American 'self-sufficiency' in the worldwide monitoring of diplomatic traffic and wanted Canada and Britain to fill in gaps in their coverage. It was agreed that once a month they would exchange lists of what they were monitoring, and the exchange of data would be through Maidment's office in New York. Maidment worked for GC&CS and had been sent along with a small team to work with Benjamin Deforest (Pat) Bayly at British Security Coordination (BSC). Before the war, Bayly was a professor at the University of Toronto, and he had been hired by William Stephenson, the senior representative of British intelligence for the entire western hemisphere. Stephenson himself had been sent to the United States on 21 June 1940 to covertly open and run BSC, over a year prior to the US entering the war. The BSC office, headquartered in Room 3603 in the Rockefeller Center, became an umbrella organisation that by the end of the war represented the British intelligence agencies MI5, MI6/SIS, SOE (Special Operations Executive) and PWE (Political Warfare Executive) throughout North America, South America and the Caribbean.

In April 1943, new negotiations began between GC&CS and the US Army's Special Branch in London and Washington. William Friedman, Colonel Alfred McCormack and Lieutenant Colonel Telford Taylor arrived in London on 24 April. AGD paid a courtesy call on the American delegation at their hotel on 1 May. In the afternoon, Friedman, McCormack and Taylor made their first visit to Berkeley Street. AGD had already discussed the visit with Menzies, and a schedule of what the Americans wanted to see was agreed. They spent three days from 4 May going through the various sections at Berkeley Street.

On 2 May they met with Travis and other British officials and on 8 May Travis and Eddie Hastings[18] travelled to the US. Britain wanted the US to concentrate on Japanese Army and Air Force traffic. While there, Travis completed, on 17 May, an agreement in Washington with General George Strong, the US Army's Military Intelligence chief. The so-called 'BRUSA Agreement' was signed on 24 May and formed the basis of all subsequent Anglo-American Sigint cooperation. Travis returned to Britain on 11 June and met with Friedman and McCormack before they returned to the US the following day. McCormack would return to the

UK and he and Taylor subsequently produced detailed reports for the Army Intelligence Group at Arlington Hall about the Berkeley Street operation (see Appendix 11). While Travis had been in the US, Friedman and McCormack had met with various senior military figures in Britain, and visited BP as well as Berkeley Street. Friedman was effusive in his praise for British code breaking activities, many of which had been set in motion by AGD. He commented that:

> Their achievement is astounding not only because of the breadth of the concept upon which the operations are based and of the directness with which they are prosecuted, but also because of the manner in which the British tackled and successfully solved a cryptographic system which apparently presents insurmountable and impenetrable bulwarks against attack by pure cryptanalysis. It must be understood that the solution was attained not by cryptanalysis at all but by exploiting to the fullest degree possible the weaknesses injected into the system by the methodicalness of the Germans in their formulation and operation of the system, by studying and making use of the well-known German addiction to fixed habits, and by taking advantage of the occasional carelessnesses and blunders on the part of German cipher clerks. The margin upon which the British had and still have to operate in their solution is indeed a very narrow one, so far as technical cryptanalytic weaknesses in the system are concerned, but dogged British persistence, extremely painstaking attention to minute details, and brilliance in coordinating and integrating into one vast picture the many small operations involved, have brought about a success beyond the wildest expectations of any cryptanalyst's fancy.
>
> Moreover, the success the British have attained and continue to attain in this field is also astounding in that they have been able to keep the whole operation utterly secret from the enemy for so long a time, despite the hundreds of people who participate in the operations and despite the various tenuous threads upon which these operations rest – threads which might be broken by a mere whisper in the proper place at any moment.[19]

Friedman and McCormack visited AGD at Berkeley Street on 6 May and got a revised draft of a proposal for division of work on 'Floradora'. On 22 May, Friedman had a chat with AGD about a paper drafted by AGD which outlined the proposed basis of a talk with Taylor, McCormack and himself about the future relations in neutral and Allied fields. AGD had written that after McCormack had seen all of AGD's sections and knew 'all our methods', he wanted to draft a detailed plan for continued liaison, but that it would need to be submitted 'to our respective chiefs'.[20] There was already substantial cooperation on enemy diplomatic and commercial traffic which was just as well, since the BRUSA Agreement had avoided the issue of diplomatic traffic. In fact, it only called for full cooperation and complete exchange of cryptanalytical results and intercepts from the traffic of the German Army and Air Force, as well as the German intelligence service, the Abwehr. Even with this cooperation, the British were reluctant to share with Washington any diplomatic messages from neutral countries which were sent by cables controlled by Britain. The Americans in turn went to great lengths to conceal from the British their work at Arlington Hall on Russian diplomatic codes.

On 17 May 1943, the US Army agreed formally that Arlington Hall would concentrate on Japanese military traffic and leave the breaking of German and Italian military ciphers primarily to the British. Each side would be responsible for ensuring that the resulting intelligence got to Allied commanders in the field. AGD's 21 May paper attempted to address the existing problems:

> It has occurred to me and others here that your visit provides a good opportunity to define the scope and limits of the liaison which we are trying to build up between G.C. & C.S. (Civil side) and Arlington Hall and G2 (Diplomatic and Commercial).
>
> For my own personal part in this matter I have urged during and since my visit to Washington in August 1941 that Arlington's greatest contribution to the war effort is the effective and operational reading of Japanese military cyphers and that G.C. & C.S. was and is prepared to fill any intelligence gap in diplomatic work which may result from a supreme effort on Japanese Military by Arlington. I wish to repeat this and I know I shall have the support of my superior officers.
>
> Colonel McCormack's letter to me on his arrival gave me great hope that mutual misunderstandings were going to be cleared up and that we should straighten out the line of liaison. I have arranged that you should see every section and every detail in order that you may be familiar with 'our methods' and appreciate our aims, which are, in short, to provide our several customers with all possible intelligence derived by cryptography from telegrams from enemy and neutral sources. When you know all our departments who are in any way affected by our liaison, e.g. (in England) Foreign Office, M.E.W. and the Service Departments, whose efforts may be

influenced by the knowledge of our cooperation. The bases of the liaison between A and B are:

> Cryptographic documents i.e. code books and key tables obtained either by cryptography or by S.S. methods.
> Raw material, i.e. telegrams obtained by W/T interception, by cable censorship or by S.S. methods.
> The translated versions of the raw material.

Note: In London it is not the duty of G.C. & C.S. to extract intelligence from these translations: that is left to the Intelligence Sections in the receiving Ministries with whom G.C. & C.S. is in close touch.

> So far as enemy countries are concerned (Germany, Japan, Italy) it should be our aim to make the liaison absolutely complete and I believe we are already achieving this. If either A or B requires a telegram in cypher or en clair, it is passed without delay. It might be noted that Arlington helped us into the Japanese purple.

The immediate problem is the prosecution of the war and I consider it would be to our mutual advantage if G2 had their representative in London (Lt. Col. Taylor) as a liaison officer to G.C. & C.S. (civil side). He should have the entry to our D & R and all sections … As to the purely cryptographic part of the liaison, this should continue to be direct between Arlington Hall and the sections but Colonel Taylor would be available here to clear up questions hard to solve by letter or telegram.

> A.G.D. 21/5/43[21]

McCormack summed up their discussions as follows: 'Denniston says that if Arlington wants to divert any talent from present Japanese operations to turn them to JAC he is prepared to take up the full slack and to transmit finished translations of all material here. Second, he expresses a desire to give Arlington traffic and information of every kind that has to do with winning the war.'[22] Meanwhile, AGD and Friedman had become good friends and they subsequently spent a golfing weekend together at AGD's home in Surrey.

AGD was keen to give the Americans the benefits of British experience and of traffic obtained over many years. He was however, limited by a Foreign Office dictate forbidding the sharing of cable traffic into and out of London. He was also reluctant to share traffic in areas which he considered to be of prime British concern such as from various Near East areas. However, he did accept that given the American commitment in those areas, he may have to share information with them. He was prepared to share everything his team knew about methods of solution but he did not want to share so-called crypt documents such as code books, key tables, obtained either through cryptography or secret service methods. AGD thought it was more important to concentrate on liaison on the intelligence rather than the cryptography side of the work and he was annoyed by the interface role played by the BSC under Stephenson.

McCormack summed up AGD's views as follows:

> Denniston has said on several occasions that he did not like being unable to deal directly with Arlington on traffic exchange problems or on how exchanges should be handled. He also is very anxious to obtain good liaison with G-2 and has been going on the assumption that Taylor is to be quartered with him to function in that capacity. While there would be no point in trying to work out any revised traffic deal now, certainly not for us to try it, it appears to me that there is some value in pursuing discussions with Denniston along the above lines, so as to test his general ideas by specific cases, in order to carry back a fairly good idea of what sort of deals his authority permits him to make and what the general viewpoint here is on these various problems. His attitude, in my opinion, will permit all important intelligence problems along his alley to be solved satisfactorily, one way or another. Note also that Denniston, more than anybody else here, has turned his people over to us for questioning and given us a free run of his place.

According to McCormack, AGD was willing to let American staff in London read anything of interest and forward it on to Washington. However, in some cases, the Americans insisted on the material in its raw form and the appropriate keys to read it. He went to say:

> It [i.e. Washington] has just thrown Denniston into a state of bafflement by asking for Iraqi keys. This request would be roughly equivalent – if we still had the Philippines – to the British asking Arlington for Philippine keys, since Iraq is not only in reality part of the British Empire but the cornerstone, because of its oil, on which the whole Middle East and Eastern Mediterranean situation rests. Denniston however, wanted to put Arlington in a position to read

> whatever Iraq stuff it might intercept, insofar as he could do it without going to the Foreign Office for specific authority. Hence he authorized his people to explain the Iraq system to Taylor, and Taylor duly passed the information along, and Denniston felt that he had met Arlington's demands without having to create an issue here. If questioned by the Foreign Office, he could always say that Iraq uses simple substitution which any cryptanalyst who had an Arabic linguist at hand could solve in half an hour, and so he really only told Arlington what it could have found out for itself in a very short time.
>
> Now however, Arlington turns this matter into a major issue by a formal request for keys, forcing Denniston either to put himself on record as refusing something that Arlington specifically asked for or to create an issue by asking the Foreign office for permission. If Denniston is right about the difficulty of solving the Iraq system, what sense does all this make?

AGD had offered, through McCormack, to take on Japanese work and, according to McCormack, had expressed to him 'a desire to give Arlington traffic and information of every kind that has to do with winning the war, by which he means complete exchanges of all enemy traffic and crypt information plus anything that Arlington wants to get out of the non-enemy field where, as in the case of Turkey, we have asked for it and stated reasons connected with the war effort'. AGD also agreed that 'in the crypt field each country wants to establish for itself a position of independence so that it can get and turn its efforts toward any class of traffic that may interest it'.

On 21 May 1943, McCormack sent his first dispatch to Washington, describing AGD's organisation:

> Denniston's show, commonly called Berkeley Street, has none of the hectic atmosphere of Park but rather gives [the] impression of a well established operation that goes along through wars and peace. General impression is typified by the two ladies who receive and sort incoming traffic. [This was corrected in a later dispatch.] (They started as telegraph clerks in Post Office in reign of Queen Victoria and were fully familiar with general field when they joined present organisation in 1919.) These little birdlike old ladies receive and register incoming material and they have acquired such great familiarity with it that [they] can do everything except actually decipher it. Whole organization is very simple and they seem to accomplish a great deal with quite limited personnel. Whole outfit consists of two hundred.

The Americans assigned Taylor to work with the British on diplomatic traffic as the US liaison officer at GC&CS with full access to BP and Berkeley Street and their decrypts. However, he was ordered to confine himself exclusively to the diplomatic decrypts being produced by AGD's team.[23] His eventual replacement, Major Bancroft Littlefield became a close friend of AGD. He corresponded with his wife during his stay in Britain for the last few years of the war and his letters[24] provide a snapshot of the life enjoyed by American officers stationed in Britain.

The following extract is from a letter written on 26 March 1944:

> I had luncheon Friday with the British Major (ex school teacher) whom I went on the automobile trip with (I can't remember what I then told you his name was). He called me Thursday and (as one does over here) rather formally invited me to luncheon the following day – to meet him at a restaurant on Deane [*sic* – Dean] Street in Soho (Gennaro's Restaurant). When I got there I found he had brought along his brother and half brother – the former a private in the Medical Corps – the latter a clerk in the War Office. We had a most entertaining time – and I thoroughly enjoyed myself. After lunch I came back to work, en route seeing a February *Atlantic Monthly* in a bookshop window (quite unusual I think; at least the first time I've seen one) and buying it.
>
> Saturday (yesterday) was another social day. I worked all morning until about 2 pm – then had soup and a sandwich with Ed Kellog at a funny English Snack Bar near where he lives (Queen Street). Then we went together over to a performance by the French players here in town of the 'Paquebot Tenacity' – a very inconsequential 3 act creation whose chief merit was that it attracted a wholly French audience at the Institut Francais du Royamme-Uni on Queensway Place, Kensington, and that we soaked up a good deal of French during the course of the afternoon.

McCormack attempted to report on the amount of traffic being handled by Berkeley Street in a dispatch to Washington dated 21 May 1943:

> Records maintained at Berkeley Street do not include figures for total traffic and I did not ask them to go to geographical sections and add up all these figures, but they receive 'thousands' of messages per day. Their serial numbers of circulated diplomatic items crossed one hundred thousand early in 1942. Do not have present range of number.

***

By the end of 1943, AGD's Diplomatic Section now numbered 250 with his own office which directed administration, traffic sorting, the D&R Section and the typing section numbering forty-five staff. The main enemy country sections were the Japanese (dealing with hand and machine systems) and German Sections, each with fifty staff. The French and smaller enemy sections had thirty staff, while neutral and friendly country sections had seventy. Small research sections were being built up to deal with new developments such as the use of the Hagelin machine. The total number of translations issued in 1943 was 14,050, of which the Foreign Office received all, the Admiralty 5,481, the War Office 5,697, the Air Ministry 4,162, the MEW 1,702 and MI5 9,850.

Space became short at Berkeley Street, so smaller sections were moved to Aldford House. From October onwards, night raids gradually increased and the staff (serving by rota as part of the Fire Watch of the area) manned fire-fighting equipment through some noisy nights. Staff also contributed to the 2nd Home Guard Battalion of the City of London Regiment. By the autumn of 1943, old German traffic had been cleared and current traffic was being exploited. This allowed some resource to be freed up to look at the OTP system, some of which had been exposed.

The Japanese had introduced three new systems of encrypted code, so cryptanalysts and linguists worked together to produce an increased volume of translated decrypts of good quality which more than compensated for the loss of Italian intelligence. The French Section was working on both Vichy and Free French systems. The Vichy Government had only introduced new systems in Europe and the Near East, which were never identified. In the Far East, a mix of former systems being used or keys originally developed for one system being used with another, meant that the section maintained control of the Vichy traffic to some extent. Ethiopian traffic was investigated at the end of the year and read by April 1944, and the Syrian main system was also broken.

By the end of 1943 no action had been taken on Redman's proposal of the previous year. On 13 December, Frank Rowlett, now a Lieutenant Colonel in the Signal Security Agency (SSA, the new name of SIS), reported on a meeting between Army and Navy representatives to discuss the allocation of commercial traffic. It appeared that while the President had initialled an informal note to the Director of the Budget on 8 July 1942, no action had been taken by the Joint Chiefs of Staff. It appeared that there was confusion about whether or not the agreement was in force. One of the problems seemed to be the difficulty in separating Japanese commercial and diplomatic traffic, as Japan treated them as one and the same.

By the beginning of 1944, AGD's organisation was in full production with established procedures in place. Apart from material obtained from the US, the principal source was through the censorship measures put in place in telegram 'clearing houses' such as those in London and Ottawa. Foreign Office intercept stations in the UK, Canada, India, Australia and South Africa also provided material, as did secret intelligence services in neutral capitals. When all non-commercial material came into Berkeley Street, clerks routed it to the appropriate country section where it was registered under a number of headings. It was then passed to cryptanalysts for processing and if successful, results were passed to the Head of Section who decided which material should go to D&R.

All internal processing was done in longhand but typed before being distributed externally as GC&CS reports, and continued to be known as BJs. Copies of all distributed material were also sent to the Foreign Office, Menzies, the War Office, Air Ministry and Admiralty. Some material was not sent to service ministries if it revealed that a British diplomat abroad had been compromised in some way. Teleprinter links were available to Menzies's office, BP and the intercept stations at Denmark Hill and Sandridge. However, they were not used for circulating material, apart from some of exceptional importance to Menzies himself. Various government offices had liaison officers at Berkeley Street and most of them were senior figures. These included those of Menzies, the Prime Minister, the Foreign Office, the War Cabinet and SIS amongst others.

Distribution policy was simple; distribute everything that might have some intelligence value, however small. Berkeley Street was more a production organisation like Arlington Hall than an intelligence organisation with important operational functions like BP. McCormack noted in his report that 'In case of Berkeley Street as in case of BP, what impressed us was that they are taken to see that all information gets out to those who can make use of it.'

Berkeley Street was able to analyse the messages that it processed through its imaginative record-keeping system. A ledger or book contained sheets, roughly thirteen by sixteen inches, for every city which originated messages. Each of these sheets in turn catalogued messages by the city to which it was destined. Each city was then subdivided into nationalities and for each of these was recorded, the call signs of the originating and destination station, intercepting station or stations, estimated number of messages sent, number of messages sent, number missed and additional information to aid analysis. McCormack was very impressed with this system and recommended that his colleagues at Arlington Hall consider implementing something similar. He noted that it was possible 'to see what intercept stations produce important material and in what volume, to determine at a glance what sources of information there are in each principal city and how many of them are being tapped and of course to see how much of each type of traffic is being brought in'.

The CMY (Commercial Y) Section was moved from BP to Berkeley Street in 1944 and accommodated in the same building as the cryptanalytic sections. It controlled the intercept positions employed on international commercial W/T. Research sections were expanded to respond to monthly cryptanalytic reports from country sections on unsolved problems. A senior cryptanalyst coordinated these reports and kept AGD informed about developments. By the end of the war, the diplomatic sections had created a similar research-orientated structure to that which existed before the war began.

The cryptanalytical process at Berkeley Street started with the head of a country section (head of a subsection for larger country sections) deciding if a decrypt was sufficiently complete and reliable to be passed on. He would then decide if it was of sufficient interest to be submitted for issue and if the translation was accurate. Translation was not always necessary, as in the case of the Foreign Office which preferred to see French decrypts in their original text. The D&R section was crucial to this process as it ultimately decided which material should be circulated and supervised the mechanics of doing so. They in effect acted as a reference bureau for the cryptanalysts. The section was headed by Eric Earnshaw-Smith, who had been a member of MI1(b) before joining the fledgling GC&CS in 1919. He also acted as AGD's deputy. His assistant was Ore Jenkins, a Professor of Medieval History and Modern Greek at Cambridge. D&R kept indexes of all circulated material in longhand on cards. It had mainly a reporting function and never more than five staff. Its working model was to use the Heads of sections as outposts of a Central Distribution Office and, in effect, Intelligence Officers. The Head of D&R kept the Heads briefed so that they could deliver on this intelligence role. Information continually flowed to them and included directions received from 'user' departments for specific intelligence and valuations of recently circulated product, collateral material such as Foreign Office telegrams and dispatches, foreign newspapers, and press cuttings. While all collateral material was returned to D&R for filing, larger sections kept their own card indexes and other intelligence records. This was all coordinated by a Central Intelligence Officer.

D&R's first task was an editorial one, as it had to ensure that the judgment of the section heads was sound. In some cases, intelligence deemed worthy of distribution might already be in the hands of the user department from another source or known to the Central Distribution Officer but not yet to the Section. However, this never exceeded five per cent of submitted translations. Secondly, checks were required to judge the clarity of the translation, and the Section maintained a very high standard in this regard. The nuances which exist in Diplomatic material can be lost without precise translations in place. An example of this is a telegram from the Italian Ambassador saying: 'I believe that the Foreign Secretary was at some pains during our conversation to leave me with the impression that his government was uneasy about the course of events.' It was translated as: 'I think that at the end of our conversation what the Foreign Secretary was laboriously trying to say was that his Government was afraid of what might happen' – which misses the finer points of the message and would not be trusted by a Foreign Office reader. Continuity from pre-war experience enabled the Central Distribution Officer to press for more clarity in translation, even for languages such as Arabic. Finally, a check was needed for consistency with known facts. Subject matter of a day's traffic could be extremely varied and even, on occasion, quite technical.

The cryptanalyst/translator required an encyclopaedic knowledge of current affairs and to support them, a central library of reference books, card indices and records of unpublished information was built up under the Head of D&R. He was tasked with ensuring that nothing was issued which would not make sense to a user department. He was also able to refer failed decryption back to a Country section and his analysis usually proved to be correct. In one instance, a pilot from the Italian LATI airline reported details of an Allied convoy to Rome (this was standard and done twice a week). The Italian encoder mistakenly located the position by longitude and latitude in the middle of Spain. This was not picked up by the translator but by his section head. It would almost certainly have been picked up by D&R.

One D&R index was based on names, and over 19,000 were on file by mid-1943. One interesting name was that of the Japanese Ambassador to Berlin, Hiroshi Ōshima, who frequently sent messages in code from Berlin to Tokyo, containing information of great interest to the Allies. The largest index dealt with treaties, catalogued by country, and included details about treaties and negotiations for treaties among various governments. A 'Cabinet Book' recorded important officials in various governments, subdivided by country. It contained newspaper clippings and notes giving names of cabinet officials and elected officers. A file of ships recorded all ships which were named in intercepted messages. The 'Diary' was a large bound book which was assigned two opposite pages for each day. All events were recorded which might be of interest to anyone working on material and might involve such events. Each item was referenced to its source and thus fuller information if required. A 'Who's Who' file illustrated the thoroughness of the Section. It consisted of Foreign Office printed bulletins with details of foreign diplomats, supplied by British diplomats abroad. One diplomat was described as having a young wife who was very short-sighted and therefore wore very thick glasses!

D&R also kept a reference library for use by all Berkeley Street staff. It included a 'Geographical Handbook Series' published by the 'Naval Intelligence Section' of the Admiralty which contained considerable information about various countries. An annual publication of the Empire Parliamentary Association called 'Report on Foreign Affairs' gave a chronology of all important events during the year for each country. Foreign language press was also monitored with relevant articles sent to interested sections. All geographical sections kept their own reference material. McCormack summed up this part of the operations as follows: 'Whole key to this British operation lies in the infinite pains which they take with the files while never losing sight of their very practical objectives.'

D&R also graded and annotated diplomatic translation, and from 1942, user departments asked that all translations include both the grading believed to be attached by the sender to the cipher used by him for that message and their own rating of the security of the cipher used.[25] Accurate and consistent gradings proved to be difficult to achieve but user departments felt that they gave some indication of the secrecy desired by the sender and the likelihood of them being read by other governments. Ratings/gradings were supplied by Sections under the guidance of the D&R.

Pre-war experience had shown that for the diplomatic country sections, linguists could be trained as cryptanalysts and be responsible for translation. In some cases, they would even be tasked with the selection of decrypts for submission. The exception to this was the Japanese 'Purple' traffic. This differed from the model adopted for the Service sections because of the sheer volume of traffic faced by them and machine rather than hand ciphers in general use. The merger of cryptanalytic and linguistic skills was made possible by recruiting people of a very high intellectual standard with a good knowledge of international affairs.

The head of a country Section could, on his own discretion, translate and issue only part of a message. In some cases, this was driven by the subject matter changing and the remainder not being of interest. Summaries or digests of message subjects were not kept as it was found to be too labour intensive with little accrued value. More reliance was placed on the judgment and working relationship between the section Heads and Central Diplomatic Intelligence Officer. The diplomatic sections were part of a stable organisation at the beginning of the war with considerable experience. Once it moved to Berkeley Street, AGD was able to maintain and even enhance its efficient operation.

Diplomatic country Section work concentrated primarily on the systems of Germany, Italy and Japan. Secondary targets were China and France. In addition, some forty-five countries in Europe, South America and the Near and Middle East were targeted. Of the individual country sections, the Japanese and German were the biggest and most fruitful in terms of intelligence. The Japanese Section consisted of fourteen experienced and able staff who received all messages after they were logged by their clerks. One member of the Section handled liaison with the US and Australian Japanese intelligence sections dealing with diplomatic and commercial traffic. Head of the Section was Oswald White, who at the beginning of the war was Consul General in Tientsin and had long service experience in Japan and China. He, or a deputy in his absence, prioritised all messages before sending them for translation. The staff who under,took this work included W.B. Cunningham, formerly Consul to the Japanese Imperial Government (JIG[26]), Norman Roscoe who was Consul to JIG during WW1 and E. Hobart-Hamden, probably the world's leading JIG scholar and co-editor of the Standard Dictionary. They described themselves as the Translation Bureau and the leading lights included, Captain Rayment, an officer of Naval Intelligence and JIG expert and translator for the Navy, and Captain Harold Shaw, a civilian and ex-consul.

McCormack illustrated the effectiveness of this Section's work as follows:

> Lord Farrar, who sits as Economic Warfare Minister for purpose of handling most secret information in continental economic field and in fact for whole world, told us yesterday that 85 per cent of all important information about South Central economic picture has been built up from Berkeley Street production, the contributions by censorship, foreign press, radio broadcasts and agents being trivial in comparison with our material.

Most of the 1,000 JIG commercial messages which came into the section each day were in plain text so translation was the main task. Their sources included Point Grey and other west-coast Canadian stations and were sent over every week or ten days by bomber. Much of it was of little use, consisting of small financial and commercial transactions but about a dozen items per day were of interest. They might reference ships by name or routing and include the address of enemy military or naval units. The volume of this material was around 1,500 items per week. A second source was material in commercial code intercepted in Mauritius and a third came from UK stations picking up continental traffic. The output of the JIG Commercial Section went in longhand to Alford House where Berkeley Street's Commercial Section was housed.

The German Section dealt primarily with 'Floradora' and was headed from October 1939 until 1943 by 25-year-old Patricia Bartley, who had been recruited from Oxford at the beginning of the war by John Tiltman. She was assisted by Percy Filby, formerly librarian of one of the libraries attached to Trinity College, Cambridge. Staff numbers under Hartley reached thirty-seven and key members were Adcock and Fetterlein, S.A. Trantor, Pallinger, a former school master and Potter, a German Foreign Office expert on diplomatic English. Bartley left Berkeley Street to return to Oxford to complete her Ph.D. However, her health deteriorated and she never returned to London.[27] By early 1944, they were passing English versions of every message of importance in 'Floradora' with a delay of perhaps 24 hours, sometimes less. Progress was even made against OTPs, which should be unbreakable as settings are only used for one message. However, messages were being sent by Berlin (so-called Multex messages) to all posts in OTP but to Dublin in 'Floradora'. The messages were long and the same length in both systems, which could make tests productive. At the same time, several German pads were acquired from American sources. They could be assembled to work out the logical design of the machine that produced them. German diplomatic traffic of high importance was encrypted using OTPs. In collaboration with the Americans, the machine which produced these was reconstructed, but only one series of messages was read between Berlin and Madrid in March and April 1945.[28]

The Vichy Government traffic was read until the North African landings when they made belated cipher changes. They introduced three new systems which remained unsolved, but for Far East traffic they used improvised modifications of existing systems which GC&CS read.

The Near East Section was headed by Dr Thomas Thacker, Professor of Semitic Languages at Durham University. His team included

Raymond Thornhill, a clergyman and former pupil of Thacker's at Durham, Simpson, a geographer from the University of London, and Gungry from Cambridge University. They dealt with messages in Turkish, Persian and Arabic. The Persian sub-section was run by Frederick Humphreys, who was the Archivist for many years at the British Embassy in Persia. He was assisted by John Boyle who had learned Persian at the School of Oriental Studies. Thacker and Dr Bernard Lewis, who had lectured in the Islamic History School for Oriental Studies, ran the Arabic sub-section. Other code books were being read which were used by Turkey, Saudi Arabia, Iraq, Egypt, Iran, Afghanistan, Syria, Nepal and Ethiopia. The Turkish sub-section received about fifteen to thirty messages per day in 1943 and circulated on average six per day. Other traffic received by country per month was Saudi Arabia fifteen to twenty; Iraq four to five; Iran 1,000; and Afghanistan twenty to twenty-five.

The Italian Section was headed by Frederic Catty from the Spring of 1942 until September 1944. Two women handled Vatican traffic from April 1942. By 1 December 1942, the Section had read 550 out of 664 messages received but only sixty-four were considered worth translating and circulating as it was mostly of an ecclesiastic, charitable or personal nature. Italian diplomatic systems were strengthened at German instigation in July 1942, but misuse led to it being broken by the end of the year. Further innovations by the Italians in January 1943 were also overcome due to their carelessness in use.

The Portuguese and Brazilian Section was run by Arthur Exell, a botanist who had researched Portugal and its colonies. It had no permanent staff and the Brazilian side was handled by Exell's wife, Mildred, and an assistant. The Portuguese used a combination of book and machine ciphers, all of which were read by this Section.

Of the smaller European countries, a Romanian Section was run by R. Greiffenhagen, a former diplomat. Most of the traffic was commercial in nature, dealing with, for example, purchases of Spanish lead and blankets and Spanish demands for oil in exchange. The Bulgarian Section was run by Gabriel Woods but processed very little traffic. He also handled Yugoslavian and other Balkan country traffic.

Following the Nazi-Soviet pact in August 1939, GC&CS had broken the Soviet meteorological cipher and read a number of naval signals along with some 1,000 army and police methods. While useful as a source of tactical information, it yielded little of strategic importance. According to Hinsley: 'All work on Russian codes and cyphers was stopped from 22 June 1941, the day on which Germany attacked Russia, except that, to meet the need for daily appreciations of the weather on the Eastern Front, the Russian meteorological cypher was read again for a period beginning in October 1942.'[29] However, it does appear that Britain was working on Soviet traffic again by 1943. This had been decided at meeting that year between 'C' and the Director General of the Security Service in the US.[30] A covert section was set up at Berkeley Street under Professor David Bernard Scott, a senior administration officer and a Cambridge mathematician. It was tasked with breaking a system which appeared in late 1943 when the RSS picked up Morse code signals which was presumed to be a reinstatement of the Communist International or Comintern network (officially abolished in May 1943) and had been inactive for some time. Scott reported directly to AGD and the section had three to four staff. Scott broke the cipher being used in about a month. None of this traffic was shared with the US.

As the Soviet Army advanced, traffic increased on this network and the section was increased to around twelve staff. According to John Croft who worked in the section, they included 'the wife of a University of London professor, two 18-year-olds straight from school, one a classical scholar from Belfast, the other from Winchester College; the wife of one of the directors of J. Lyons and Co., the caterers; and a lady who asked for a transfer from MI5 in Curzon Street because she had had enough, so she said, of the society debs (who in wartime had been recruited to that outfit) gossiping about all the other society people under surveillance.' Croft was one of four or five cryptanalysts and a Russian expert.[31] He worked alongside one of the Fetterlein brothers who were brought out of retirement to translate the decrypts. These were then typed up, classified as top security with limited circulation such as the CSS and Churchill's assistant on security matters, Major Desmond Morton. Only AGD visited the section, and telephone communications with RSS or Berkeley Street was through scramblers. In early 1945, the traffic could no longer be broken as it was now being enciphered using OTPs.

In late 1944, a special section was working on non-Morse traffic on military and civil circuits. The Strong / Travis agreement of 1943 did not cover traffic from non-service enemy or neutral sources. Between August and September 1943, Roger Randolph of G-2 Special Branch visited Berkeley Street. He was shown almost everything and in his report he covered Russian issues under 'Miscellaneous matters'. His summary was: 'Prior to 1941 Russian diplomatic traffic was studied. The conclusion was reached that it was one-time pad and accordingly the research was abandoned. At the present time Russian diplomatic traffic is not being analysed and none of it is being read.'[32]

However, Randolph did not say that GC&CS had stopped collecting Soviet diplomatic traffic. Clearly, the whole issue was very sensitive and it may be that AGD was under instructions not to share this with the Americans. According to David Alvarez: 'Ironically, the Americans remained unaware that in late 1944 GC&CS established its own secret unit to study Russian internal traffic (civil and military) in Sloane Square, London.'[33] He went on to say that:

> By the end of the war, the United States had developed a large and productive signals intelligence organization that was reading the diplomatic traffic of almost every government in the world from Afghanistan to Yugoslavia. Much of this success was due to the diligence and skill of American cryptanalysts. No small part, however, was played by the British codebreakers at the Government Code and Cypher School. Throughout the war GC&CS provided timely advice and assistance that significantly advanced the American programme in diplomatic signals intelligence. The value of the British contribution was accurately summarized by the US Signal Security Agency (previously SIS) in a post-war review of operations: 'It is doubtful whether success in solution of certain diplomatic systems could have been achieved in time to be useful had not the British supplied the necessary information. The debt of the SSA to GC&CS in shortening the period between the beginning of study and the production of translations was in the case of the diplomatic traffic of certain governments very great indeed.' Without doubt, the British had been most helpful and cooperative.

A Research Section was headed by Norman Sainsbury and they were tasked with taking on new problems and making enough progress to be able to hand them over to the Language Section. Sainsbury could speak Finnish, Norwegian and Swedish, but Scandinavian countries used Hagelin systems, of which Berkeley Street had no expertise. By 1943, they were concentrating on the principal diplomatic system being used by the Free French. The bulk of the traffic was provided by Cable and Wireless Ltd.

The Commercial Section was based in Aldford House, a few streets from Berkeley Street. It was founded and led by G.L.N. Hope and the majority of his staff were women. They were dealing with some 7,000 messages per day by 1943 and almost all of them were in plain text. The German traffic dealt with things such as the sale of machinery or transactions in grain or mohair with Turkey and Spain. The traffic started to decline due to the restrictions placed on the use of codes by many governments and German occupation. The section did deal, however, with diplomatic codes which had commercial significance

All diplomatic traffic went by cable and wireless based on available routes. During WW1, the censorship organisation had provided all cable traffic. The small amount of wireless traffic was picked up by the Service intercept stations. While cable censorship ended in 1919, a Home Office order in 1921 required the Central Telegraph Office and the Cable Companies to submit all traffic handed to them to the Foreign Office for scrutiny. Censorship was re-imposed in September 1939 and at the same time, wireless traffic was steadily increasing. Traffic was picked up by Service Intercept stations kept active after WW1 by the Admiralty at Pembroke (later Flowerdown) and Scarborough, the War Office at Chatham and the Air Ministry at Waddington. The Metropolitan Police at Denmark Hill had also contributed German clandestine material from secret transmitters in embassies and legations, discovered during 1937–8.

With war looming, independent intercept stations were set up to take diplomatic traffic. These were staffed and maintained by the Post Office and operationally controlled by the Foreign Office. At the beginning of the war, two were operational, at Sandridge, Hertfordshire and Cupar (later closed down and replaced with one at Hawklaw), near Fie in Scotland. A third soon came into operation at Brora in the Scottish Highlands. They contributed Services traffic as well, being part of the Y Service. A special section, CMY (Commercial Y), was set up to centralise development and coordination, and evolved from WTC (W/T Coordination) in 1942. It eventually set up headquarters at Berkeley Street. Two more stations were set up at Whitchurch in 1943 and Wincombe in 1944.

Overseas sources were Mauritius, Ottawa, Delhi, Abbottabad, West Africa, Melbourne, Cape Town, Simons Town, Suez and Malta. Only the censorship and intercept post at Mauritius was under direct Foreign Office control, dealing with Japanese and French traffic. The rest were Service intercept centres, British and Dominion, which agreed to allocate a certain number of sets to diplomatic coverage. By July, 1945 the proportion of general traffic intercepted had reached 86 per cent and, of priority traffic, 96 per cent. Comprehensive arrangements with the US for the exchange of cable and wireless materials filled in any gaps in each side's coverage.

The total number of translations of diplomatic and commercial messages peaked in 1943 at 14,050. All went to the Foreign Office, two-thirds to MI5, one-third to the Service Ministries and 8 per cent to MEW. Staff numbers didn't increase after 1943 and when the Japanese Section was increased, it was mainly from other Sections. AGD and his organisation were now at the forefront of British intelligence gathering. In April 1944, they decrypted a Dublin message sent the previous day and subsequent events exemplified this. As Percy Filby later recalled:

> On Monday I went to see Commander Denniston and handed him the Dublin message. It was an innocuous message and Denniston appeared to wonder why I had troubled to show him it. But when I asked him to look at the date he was startled and when I told him of the results of the weekend work, he shook hands, dialled his scrambler phone and said, 'Denniston here, may I speak to C?' C came on the line and Denniston said, 'C, I have some good news for you, may I come over?' Denniston put on his hat, carefully folded the message and placed it in his inner pocket and almost ran from the building.

The Foreign Office allowed the messages from the German Consul in Dublin, Hempel, to go through the Leicester Square office for transmission to Berne, on the basis that it was a neutral to a neutral. This did allow the messages to be delayed for seven days so that AGD's section could read the contents before the intended recipient. As D-Day approached, Dublin was passing possible dates and places for the landings in France. While no one at Berkeley Street knew the exact date, they were given a number to ring for any dates that were suggested in decrypted messages. This message did exactly that.

Staff numbers in AGD's organisation in London eventually peaked at between 250 and 275 with only the Japanese Section seeing significant expansion. Translated decrypts issued in 1944 totalled 13,153 and in 1945 up to Japan's surrender, 8,512. The Admiralty, War Office and Air Ministry received only one-third of the total product available. However, the Intelligence Exchange at BP was receiving all material and therefore intelligence from diplomatic attaché and commercial intercept was being received by Military Commands overseas by both signal and courier. A total of 72,624 decrypts were distributed to the Foreign Office between 3 September 1939 and 15 August 1945. It received, with only a few exceptions, all of the material, while thirteen other Departments each received a portion of the total, based on their particular interests. In general, ten major cryptanalytic country sections with between five and twenty-five staff produced a weekly average of 233 decrypts during the period above.

Life at Berkeley Street continued to be hazardous and the offices there were narrowly missed by V1 and V2 attacks on London as the work was relentless through 1944 and 1945 until VE Day. Suddenly, at the end of December 1944, AGD gathered his staff together. He informed them that he intended to retire and wanted to thank them for their work and loyalty to him personally. He was to be replaced by his deputy, Eddie Hastings. AGD held a dinner for some of his section heads and wished them well. He advised those that planned to stay in GCHQ, the post-war GC&CS organisation, that their lives would be different. 'Before the war you came home and discussed the day with your wives, but now never again will you be able to share your life with your family. Some wives will not mind, but most do have some disappointment, so do think carefully before you decide.'[34]

Was this the speech of a bitterly disappointed man or just realistic advice from an experienced intelligence officer? In any event, AGD simply put on his hat and walked out of Berkeley Street to the Green Park Underground Station, saying nothing to his fellow workers. There was no official thank you or goodbye from GCHQ or the Foreign Office. It is not known if he was asked to nominate any of his staff for decorations but it appears that not one award was given to the 250 individuals who contributed to the success of AGD's Berkeley Street organisation.

Chapter 6

Cut Loose

During the early months of 1945, Allied Sigint organisations began to seek new tasks as German military ciphers were continually mastered. On the night of 23/24 March, Field Marshal Montgomery led his British forces across the Rhine, and the Americans followed suit the next night. In the East, the Soviets completed the taking of Vienna on 13 April and three days later began their advance on Berlin. Military Enigma decrypts became less important and the emphasis of GC&CS shifted from BP to Berkeley Street and to diplomatic and commercial W/T traffic. AGD's organisation processed the messages of the German Foreign Ministry, the Japanese military attaché in Berlin and Japanese diplomats in neutral countries around the world. They were also reading the ciphers of Spain, Nationalist China, the Free French and many other non-belligerents. There was also the commercial traffic processed for the MEW.[1] All of the incoming and outgoing cipher telegrams, intercepted by Canada, were being sent to AGD at Berkeley Street.

The success of AGD's Berkeley Street operation and its invaluable contribution to the war effort was significant and, in the last few years of the war, may even have equalled that of Travis's at BP. While documents providing official reports of the impact of the diplomatic product are not available, some assessment of it can be made. After June 1941, Berkeley Street revealed the authentic views of neutral countries such as Turkey. The Japanese ambassador in Berlin, Lieutenant General Hiroshi Ōshima, was admired by Hitler, and both Berkeley Street and SIS in the US were reading his traffic right through until May 1945. Berkeley Street provided the Allies (apart from the Soviet Union) with reliable and up-to-date information on the state of the German armed forces and the thinking of their high command. While other Japanese diplomats in Europe such as Yakichiro Suma in Madrid and Kurihara in

Ankara provided a volume of reports equal to that of Ōshima, regular Berkeley Street weekly dispatches, discriminatingly read, provided a vital source for Allied war planners from 1943 on. Useful intelligence was also obtained from the Turkish ambassador, Tugay, and the Italians, Peppo and Quaroni.

Berkeley Street continued to read Japanese traffic even after the BRUSA agreement which allocated this work to the Americans. Many BJs were sent to Washington by Churchill, some of which were annotated by him, for the personal attention of Roosevelt. Japanese decrypts from their Naval Attaché gave estimates of Germany's total monthly production of front-line aircraft, which could then be compared with Allied intelligence estimates.[2] The BJs remained important until early 1944, when it became clear that there was no possibility of an Axis victory.

Berkeley Street's primary job was to provide BJs for Churchill, the JIC and the Foreign Office as well as processing plain language and encoded traffic for the MEW. This information was used to plot the economic progress of the war and to set strategic priorities. In 1943, up to a third of 'C's' daily delivery to Churchill consisted of BJs. When he was away, they were sent to him in summary form but were available on his return. While Enigma traffic continued to serve the needs of the military and COSs, BJs served geopolitics and war strategy. Diplomatic intercepts reported the changing course of the war.

In mid-1944, discussions were initiated about a future peacetime GC&CS, and Travis set up a small planning group to make recommendations. It was led by Gordon Welchman, one of AGD's early 'professorial' recruits in 1938 and included Harry Hinsley, who had worked on Naval Enigma and would play a key role in post-war Anglo-American-Commonwealth Sigint discussions, Edward Crankshaw, who had been responsible for wartime Sigint discussions with the Soviets, and Hugh Foss, a GC&CS veteran who had been in Washington working with US naval cryptanalysts on Japanese ciphers. Welchman's group produced a paper on 17 September 1944, which recommended the creation of a more centralised 'Foreign Intelligence Office'. They also called for a comprehensive body dealing with all forms of Sigint, including a modern signals organisation which exploited the latest communications technology. It would in effect become a modern 'Intelligence Centre' controlling all British interception work.[3]

Not all senior figures at BP agreed with Welchman and his group. John Tiltman produced a paper in October 1944 arguing for GC&CS to be absorbed into SIS under Menzies to create a single intelligence-producing service.[4] However, in January 1945, the Chairman of the JIC,

Victor Cavendish Bentinck, suggested that GC&CS should remain under the overall direction of the Chief of SIS while remaining a separate organisation. It would be provided with its own budget along with the other secret services as part of the 'Secret Vote', the strangely named intelligence budget.[5] In the end, it was Travis who would decide on the shape of GC&CS after VJ Day. His new organisation would be divided into five groups, Technical, Traffic Analysis, Cryptanalysis, Intelligence and Cipher Security, each run by his key subordinates with a total staff of around 1,000 civilians and 100 military staff.

Meanwhile, the legacy of AGD's Berkeley Street organisation lived on and in October 1945, an Allied Mission was sent to Rome to ensure security of the Italian Diplomatic Ciphers. It consisted of the Head of the Italian Section at Berkeley Street, a secretary and an officer from the ASA's Italian Section in Washington. It operated as a subsection of the Allied Control Commission until the end of the war in May 1945. Its brief was to keep a watch on Italian diplomatic communications and their security and ensure that the appropriate intelligence and government departments in both Britain and the US were kept informed about Italian ciphers and lines of communication.

On 22 October 1945, Travis arrived in Ottawa to meet with the JIC on his way to Washington to discuss post-war management of Ultra and other forms of special intelligence. According to Canadian sources, he reported that GC&CS was being absorbed into a General Signal Intelligence Centre and it would manage the product of all intercepts.[6] Travis also reported that he believed that commercial codes and ciphers (those of business and industry) were not seen as legitimate targets for peacetime Sigint. While Menzies' position was always secure under Churchill's stewardship, after Churchill lost the election of 26 July 1945, his control over Ultra was loosened. While remaining as Director-General of Sigint (as did his successor, Sir John Alexander Sinclair) he had increasingly less time to be involved in it. In January 1945, post-war planning was taken over by William F. Clarke, a veteran of Room 40 and GC&CS's naval sections. He argued for a separate organisation under either the Chiefs of Staff or the Cabinet Office, operating as a third secret service.

Group Captain Claude Daubeny was tasked with finding a new home for GC&CS and he recommended recombining the remnants of the staff at BP with those at Berkeley Street. The move to Eastcote in London took place in early 1946 in four main groups, and was completed by April.[7] Between 1945 and 1948 the name 'GCHQ' was used interchangeably with both 'London Signals Intelligence Centre' and 'Station X', although the first was preferred as it gave nothing away about the nature of the organisation.[8] By November, British defence chiefs argued for increasing the expenditure on intelligence, with particular emphasis on Sigint, and it was granted.[9] With a larger budget approved, GCHQ staff began the move to its new base in Cheltenham in late 1952 at two locations. By now Travis, who had been fighting poor health throughout the late 1940s,[10] had been replaced by Wing Commander Eric Jones. He had taken over Hut 3 after its internal problems had bubbled to the surface, in July 1942. GCHQ's existence became widely known in the 1970s and 1980s as a result of several trials over leakage of Sigint secrets and the sacking of a number of employees as a result of industrial action.

With Travis, rather than Menzies in charge in 1945, it is hardly surprising that AGD had no role to play in a future GCHQ. He was 'encouraged' out of the organisation before VJ Day and officially retired on 1 May on an annual pension of £591,[11] considerably smaller than what he expected. Eventually, the Sigint organisation that AGD had created no longer required BP and perhaps fittingly, it was left to his faithful personal assistant during his days there, Barbara Abernethy, to shut the now abandoned site: 'I and a guy called Colonel Wallace closed up the place. We just closed down the huts, put all the files away and sent them down to Eastcote. I was the last person to leave Bletchley Park. I locked the gates and then took the key down to Eastcote.'[12]

***

After years of secrecy and intense work pressure, AGD returned to his original profession of teaching to supplement his meagre pension. He taught French and Latin for a while at Downsend Prep School near Leatherhead, but now in his 60s, he found it too strenuous. So he retired completely and, with his wife, settled down to family life in the New Forest while continuing to play golf and squash. While his years of public service were over, friendships established during that service were not. He had befriended the American liaison at Berkeley Street, Telford Taylor, and his successor, Bancroft Littlefield as well as another American, Lou Stone. Robin Denniston remembered both men spending weekends at Ashtead during the V1 and V2 raids on London. Bancroft picked and ate the Denniston's soft fruit, while Taylor played piano duets with Robin and beat everyone at tennis. In the evenings, Taylor and AGD drank whiskey and no doubt confided in each other about intelligence matters.

AGD was a meticulous and careful man, noting his expenses, however small, in his diary. He was generous and gave all his women friends a diary at Christmas. He got quite bad depression (which his wife called Scottish blight) which disabled him for hours. After he left BP, he didn't get depressed or turn to drink but developed an uncontrollable lower lip quiver. He was irritable and had seemingly lost confidence in himself, perhaps even feeling betrayed by close former colleagues. Furthermore, he did not trust the bureaucrats at the Treasury or the rich and privileged who circulated on the edge of and sometimes in the middle of the Secret Services.

In late 1944, after he retired, AGD became aware of a classified memorandum by Eric Jones[13] titled 'Post-War Intelligence'. Jones' comments were intended to inform discussions about a new post-war GC&CS. One remark in particular compelled AGD to respond: 'It would indeed be a tragic and retrograde step for intelligence as a whole, and therefore – this is not putting it too high – for the future of the country, if GC and CS were to sink back into its pre-war position.'

He decided to document his personal thoughts on the origin and purpose of the 1919 GC&CS, its establishment under Treasury control and its development. He did so completely from memory, and Dorothy typed the manuscript on her old typewriter.[14] He felt there were few who knew the true history or anything of his early work to prepare GC&CS for war. The perceived wisdom was that GC&CS was completely unprepared for war, had failed to take on the mathematical needs of machine decryption and was run by amateurs unable to cope with the officials in the Treasury, the needs of the Armed Forces or the requirements of BP's enhanced wartime capability. AGD had kept in touch with Birch, Tiltman, Cooper and De Grey and to some extent Travis and eventually with the new Head of GCHQ, Eric Jones, who he had appointed.

Another old friend made contact with AGD on hearing of his retirement. On 12 April 1945, William Friedman wrote:

> As the date of your retirement from active service approaches, I want to tell you how much I personally have enjoyed our friendship and how highly I regard the cordial relationship which existed between us from 1941 to the present moment.
>
> Words are often poor things to express the deep feelings one has at times like these, but I do want you to know that there are many of us here who realize the exceptionally valuable contribution which you made toward bringing the war in Europe to a successful conclusion. This added to what you did in the last war makes a target for those who will follow you to shoot at, and it will take some very good shooting to come near it.

AGD and Friedman had immediately struck up a friendship when they met first in the US and then in Britain. In October 1943, Friedman had sent AGD some golf balls, as both were keen golfers. On 5 January 1944, Friedman replied to a letter from AGD and talked about exchanging daughters on what he jokingly referred to as 'a Lend-Lease basis' He went on to say that: 'We are anticipating another expansion to go into exploitation on a much wider scale as regards the Pacific Theatre. Things look pretty good in that direction and we have great hopes of "making a kill".' But they were able to mix business with pleasure, as he goes on to say: 'It seems to me about time for you to be thinking of making another visit in this direction, say some time this spring or early summer. I would like to try you out again on that Army-Navy golf course and see if I could not make up for that drubbing you gave us in 1941.'[15]

Freidman wrote to AGD again on 19 June, 1945, informing him that he too had left government service. He formally retired on 12 October 1955 to work on 'civilian' cryptographic problems. AGD's daughter 'Y' was working in Washington at the time, and Friedman assured him that she was well and happy. The following month, AGD was able to update Friedman on some of their old colleagues:

> My dear Friedman,
>
> Some weeks ago I was very grateful to receive an invitation from the Director to be present at a ceremony marking your return to private life. I wish I could have been present to have shaken you by the hand & congratulated you on your very successful active life & have welcomed you to the world of the 'has beens'. I was glad to see that at least two of your leading pupils are still with you, Sinkov and Kullback – please greet them for me. I am sad to have to tell you that not many of my old party still survive.
>
> I did see Travis in his home in the early spring, also on the retired list, but alas there are not many others. I exchange news once a year with Telford Taylor and Bancroft Littlefield &, we heard McCormack's voice on the phone while he was visiting England. Since I retired, now 10 years ago I have kept quite clear of the old office. I know nothing of it & its activities for obvious reasons. Oddly enough a biography of Admiral Hall has just appeared which hints at the work of 1914-18. I believe an American edition is now thought of – it might amuse you as I know you once had a long collection of such books. Its title is 'The Eyes of the Navy'. All personal allusions have been avoided but I fancy you may be able to read between the lines. I hope life has been kind to you & all your family. No doubt

> you are now a proud grandfather as I am, now attending to my garden & my golf in the depths of the New Forest. Will you please give my warm greetings to any of my old friends should you happen to meet them & accept my warm congratulations.[16]

Friedman replied and said that the intelligence agency was still keen on him doing work for them, albeit from home. He was also attempting to catalogue all of the items in his cryptographic collection.[17]. By the end of 1957, AGD told Friedman that he was not as mobile as he once was and 'am inclined to stay put in this forest village'. The following year, AGD's health was no better and he updated Friedman in a letter dated 18 January: 'Since those days at the end of 1957 when we nearly met & when you sent me your book, I have alas been in the hands of doctors who, kindly but firmly, tell me I am now an old man whose works require careful treatment. I must not try to do too much. After weeks in bed I am now allowed up for some 3 or 4 hours a day & feel I am really a nuisance to my overworked wife.'[18]

By May, AGD was able to report that he was feeling better and becoming more mobile. The two old friends had initiated a discussion about the old days and, in particular, Edward Bell and the Zimmermann Telegram. On 4 May, AGD wrote: 'You may remember the name Bell, he was the link with that distinguished man whose life we were looking at on Saturday & he dealt personally with our people who were engaged in that affair.'[19]

By this point, Friedman had decided to produce a definitive account of the Zimmermann Telegram episode, and AGD was probably the only living survivor of the halcyon days of Room 40 that he knew. He had acquired a copy of *The Eyes of the Navy*, a 'biographical study' of Admiral Sir Reginald Hall by Admiral Sir William James. Not surprisingly, it included the story of the Zimmermann Telegram. He told AGD that he was mentioned in the book but not listed in the index. He thought that it was 'a good piece of work; so far as I have dipped into it and the account appears to be quite factual and I haven't encountered any glaring misstatement'. Friedman asked Prescott Currier, who was visiting Britain, to deliver a copy of the telegram by hand to AGD.[20] AGD and Friedman then proceeded to get into a discussion about how many routes were used to transmit the Zimmermann Telegram. It gives a fascinating insight into the difficulty of recalling historical events from years before without recourse to documents of the day. Some of the letters can be found in Appendix 12.

AGD's beloved wife Dorothy was diagnosed with breast cancer in the autumn of 1957. She had supported him throughout his career and, while she knew about his work, had been as secretive as her husband. She had an operation in January the following year but sadly died on 7 February 1958. AGD moved to New Milton where 'Y' lived with her husband, Geoffrey Finch, the local vicar. 'Y' looked after her father as he became frail, inactive and, in the words of his son, 'distraught'. He died in hospital in Lymington, Hampshire, on 1 January 1961 aged 79, and was buried in Burley in the New Forest. He left his children £2,000 each in his will but his wife, a shrewd investor in stocks and shares, left them £10,000 each. No official representative of the intelligence services attended his funeral and it went unreported in national newspapers.

The following month, 'Y' wrote to Friedman, informing him of her father's death:

> Feb 7th 1961
>
> Dear Mr Friedman
>
> I hope this letter reaches you only I have lost the letter I had saved up with your address on it.
>
> This comes to tell you that my father died very peacefully on January 1st aged 79. He was really only ill one week though he had been very frail & inactive for the last 3 years. He missed my mother who died in February last year very much & was really only waiting to join her. I think he had been reasonably happy with us & enjoyed the company of the grandchildren. He knew that we were expecting No. 3 in May & was pleased as our first two are adopted. I miss him very much but realise that really his death was a blessing.
>
> With greetings to you all
> 'Y' Finch (nee
> DENNISTON)[21]

Friedman's reply reflects the great esteem with which AGD was held in the intelligence community:

> Dear 'Y',
>
> Your letter was forwarded quite promptly by my friends at the American Branch of the Cambridge University Press.
>
> The news of your father's death had been communicated to us and other friends of your father, by Brigadier Tiltman, who as you probably know, is still in Washington.
>
> Your father was a great man in whose debt all English-speaking people will remain for a very long time, if not for ever. That so few of them should know exactly what he did towards achievement of

victory in World War I and II is the sad part of the untold story of his life and of his great contribution to that victory. His devotion to the supremely important activities to which he gave so much of himself unstintingly, and with no thought to his own frail strength and physical welfare will never be forgotten by those of us who had the pleasure of knowing, admiring and loving him.

You probably know that on each of my visits to London after the war I journeyed into the country to renew acquaintances, to further cement our long-standing friendship, and just chat with him. During my last two visits I was sad to see him physically so frail, but glad to find that his mind was as keen as ever. When I learned in January of 1960 of your mother's passing, I felt that he would not be long in joining her, for on my last visit I saw that she gave him the strong support which was what probably kept him alive. Her pre-deceasing him was so unexpected by me and it was then all the sadder for me to contemplate how much he would miss her. I was relieved to learn from your letter that he was really only ill for a week and that he died peacefully.

Mrs. Friedman joins me in thanking you for your letter and in offering you and your band our very best wishes in regard to the soon anticipated addition to your nice little family.

Very sincerely
William F. Friedman

So Alastair Denniston, the forgotten man of British Sigint, was gone, along with his knowledge of its evolution from a small group crammed into a room in the Admiralty to the beginnings of modern-day GCHQ. While he documented some of his thirty years in intelligence for posterity, it would in the end be left to others to properly assess his contribution to the world of signals intelligence.

Epilogue

A close examination of Alastair Denniston's thirty-year career in Sigint still leaves many questions unanswered. Given the inherently secret nature of his work, it is not surprising that key documents relating to it remain classified,[1] and opinion about the significance of his contribution is divided. Frank Birch, the official historian of British Sigint and former colleague of AGD both in Room 40 and at BP, showed little interest in AGD's Berkeley Street organisation in his post-war history. While acknowledging the breadth of the work undertaken there, he was quite dismissive of its use in the war effort:

> The work of the Diplomatic Sections was primarily concentrated on the systems of the Axis powers, Germany, Italy and Japan, and secondarily on those of China and France, but some 45 other countries – in Europe, South America and the Near and Middle East – also received attention. The Section's fundamental function had been to spread research over the communications of all countries in readiness to intensify the attack on any in which the Foreign Office might, from time to time, show particular interest, and in the last months of war, the structure of the 'Civil' side of GC&CS tended to revert to type.

After AGD left BP, colleagues there seemed to look down on the work at Berkeley Street and considered it to be easy and unexciting. It is curious that they took this view, as did Birch, in the absence of any real understanding of its true value. Their criticism appears to have been driven by the fact that AGD had simply recreated the pre-war GC&CS without its military sections. The implication was that while the rest of BP had been transformed into an intelligence agency, AGD was stuck in the past. Ironically, it was AGD's strategy in the interwar years which had consolidated all British Sigint under GC&CS and by 1944 facilitated this transformation.

In 2011, his grave was rededicated and GCHQ was represented to finally honour its first Director. Despite the attendance of GCHQ Departmental Historian, Tony Comer, at the rededication service and AGD's contribution to Sigint being publically acknowledged for the first time, doubts persisted within the intelligence community. Only several years ago, I told a former head of GCHQ that I was writing AGD's biography and his response was 'Why would you write a book about him?' One suspects that even such a senior figure would have known little of the true value of AGD's contribution to Sigint over a thirty-year period.

It is hard not to come to the conclusion that any public acknowledgement of AGD's work at Berkeley Street from 1942 to 1945 might have drawn unwelcome attention to a part of GC&CS that the British intelligence community prefers to pretend never existed. Even the award of a knighthood to AGD might have raised questions about British diplomatic Sigint, both during the war and immediately afterwards.

However, GCHQ have, for the first time, provided an opinion on the legacy of diplomatic and commercial Sigint during WW2:[2]

> The point is that being exiled to Berkeley St made Diplomatic and Commercial seem like second class work in comparison to the military tasks carried out at BP. Furthermore, Denniston's re-creation of pre-war GC&CS led most famously to the Eric Jones comment[2] which spurred AGD into producing 'The Government Code and Cypher School Between the Wars'. It wasn't Sigint for the experts: it didn't require the same talent. This differentiation was largely carried on into Eastcote even though the nationality of the military target had changed. It was generally thought that the best talent ought to work Soviet military. Right up to the end of the Cold War we talked about Soviet and NSWP (Non-Soviet Warsaw Pact) on the one hand, and, (almost dismissively) of 'Rest of the World' on the other. Denniston didn't get his Knighthood because Menzies didn't recommend him, and the source of the antipathy is the events of late 1941 when 'C' himself almost lost control of BP owing to AGD's poor management of an increasingly complex organisation.[3]

The one person who would never challenge decisions which would affect the rest of his life and legacy was AGD himself. According to his son Robin:

> My father was the most secretive man I knew. I learned more about his work from his colleagues than I did from him. Our whole family life was dominated by the fact that my father could not and would not talk about his job. 'The less said the better' was the ruling principle of his life.[4]

By 1973, Robin Denniston had become increasingly frustrated by the failure of the intelligence community to acknowledge his father's many achievements. A career in publishing[5] gave him a professional as well as a private perspective on the true history of Sigint over two world wars. He was particularly concerned about the circumstances of AGD's removal from BP as he later wrote:

> He got quite bad depression, which my mother called Scotch blight, in which he found it impossible to say anything for hours. After he was fired from Bletchley, he suffered enormously. He was very irritable. He had lost confidence in himself, betrayed as he saw it, and so did many, by his friends – by Travis, his subordinate for so many years who now took his job – no evidence at all that he behaved badly – by de Grey. The privacy of his temperament, the secretness of the job meant not only total security but no delegation. He found delegation very difficult not because he was possessive (I don't think he was), he was a good and experienced cryptographer, but others like Knox and Cooper and Strachey might have been better and he knew it, and of course he readily acknowledged and supported the recruitment of the great mathematicians and chess players – areas in which he did not pretend to compete.[6]

Robin also felt that he knew very little of his father, who was 45 when he was born and spent much of his time working in London as head of GC&CS. He had gone to boarding school aged 13 in 1939, and thereafter was only home in the holidays when the war was all-consuming for AGD. Robin subsequently went straight to university from school aged 19 when AGD retired, and then married in July 1950 when he was 23. After that he was not at home and tensions between Robin's first wife, Anne, and AGD had inevitably affected his relationship with his father. It no doubt contributed to his later effort to restore his father's reputation to its rightful place in Sigint history. His role in the publishing world would help considerably in his efforts to, in the words of his daughter Candy, 'finish unfinished business'. He had already learned that he needed to tread carefully when it came to the security services. As a young editor at Collins, he had told a publishing friend a little about Bletchley Park while his father was still alive. After his friend made a few enquiries, 'within days GCHQ (the successor of GC&CS) had descended on my father's retirement cottage asking him how he, the most discreet of all civil servants, could have become a security risk in his old age. Remarks were made about withholding his pension. He was furious, I was apologetic. There the matter rested.'

During the war, MI6's counter-espionage Section V underwent an effective expansion. With a responsibility for the security of signals intelligence in the field, the section successfully exploited the use of what was known as ISOS reports, the generic term for decrypted German Abwehr signals intelligence traffic. MI6 had no history of counter-espionage work and learned how to use double-cross agents and mount *'l'toxication'* or deception operations, designed to confuse the enemy as to its true intentions, from Paul Paillole, deputy of the French counter-espionage section of the pre-war Deuxième Bureau. Much had depended on the abilities of the section head, Felix Cowgill.

Cowgill had been recruited in March 1939 from the Indian Police, for whom he had made a special study of communism. He brought years of counter-espionage experience to bear on his post, but had no experience of Europe, having spent the previous twelve years running penetration agents in the Comintern's network in Bengal, most recently as Deputy Commissioner of Special Branch. It had been understood that he would eventually succeed the Deputy Chief and former head of Section V, Valentine 'Ve-Ve' Vivian, as the resident MI6 expert on communism and director of a new operational department dealing with the subject. Cowgill's ablest student within the Section was the successful head of its Iberian subsection, Kim Philby, who would eventually become the British secret service's favourite son.

It was not until 1961 that senior intelligence officials such as Menzies had to acknowledge the bitter truth of Philby's treachery. Philby defected to the Soviet Union in 1963, and several years later was living in Moscow and writing his memoirs. Clearly, the publication of such a book could damage the reputations of both Menzies and his service during the war. At the same time, the *Sunday Times* began a major examination of the Philby affair and assigned to it an experienced team of reporters, Bruce Page, David Leitch and Phillip Knightly. Their subsequent articles caused quite a stir and were subsequently published in 1968 by Andre Deutsch in the UK and Doubleday in the US.[7] The book described the 'British tradition of cryptographic skill' and provided some detail of the activities of Room 40 and GC&CS at BP. It named AGD as a veteran of the former and the head of the latter organisation.

The Foreign Office tried to stop Kim Philby from publishing his memoir, *My Secret War.* No publisher wanted to take it on but Robin, a director of Hodder & Stoughton at the time, according to the *Sunday Telegraph*, 'felt so strongly that the book ought to be published that he took the unusual step of offering to act as London agent for the book in his private capacity and on a no-commission basis'. He gave no reason for his support for the book, which could damage the reputation of 'C' and SIS. According to Menzies' biographer, Anthony Cave Brown, 'Robin Denniston believed that it was "C" who had been incompetent, not his father. He became a determined enemy of Stewart Menzies by ramming through the publication of Frederick Winterbotham's memoir *The Ultra Secret* despite the threats of the British Government. And it was Robin Denniston who found Philby's book a home at MacGibbon and Kee, a small but respected London publisher.'

It does seem that Menzies supported Philby far too long, having mistakenly reached the conclusion that he was innocent. MI5 informed him of their suspicions of Philby after interviewing him for the first time on 12 June 1951. Despite this, Menzies took Philby to dinner at the Travellers' Club on 1 April 1952 and asked him 'whether he wished for any advance of the bonus that was given to him at the time of his resignation'.[8] Philby eventually confessed to being a Soviet spy on 13 January 1963 and on the 24th he was smuggled out of England by his Soviet handlers on the Russian freighter *Dolmatova.* All of this would have been known to Robin and Philby's book was duly published in 1968. According to Robin's daughter Candy: 'I think Dad was keen to see the truth be revealed and hence his choice of a publishing career. Getting the Philby Memoirs was for him a coup because it was telling the truth about what he (Philby) had done.' Robin's son Nick believes that his father wanted the true story of AGD's wartime activities to be told but at the same time was not averse to 'putting right a few wrongs'.

A year before Winterbotham's book, generally considered to be the first authorised account of GC&CS's activities at BP, was published, another book appeared. *Philby: the Long Road to Moscow* by Patrick Seale and Maureen McConville included a fifteen-page chapter titled *The Golf Club and Chess Society.* This was apparently a jokey name coined by early recruits to GC&CS in the late 1930s. The chapter summarised the whole story of British Sigint, starting with the creation of Room 40 and ending with William Friedman's letter to 'Y' Denniston on learning of AGD's death. It also included personal details about the Denniston family, from AGD and Dorothy's daily assault on *The Times* crossword puzzle to 'Y' and Robin playing rounders in the grounds of BP. Both 'Y' and Robin were thanked by the authors in the Acknowledgements.

Given his character and strong religious beliefs,[9] it seems unlikely that Robin Denniston saw Menzies, as Cave Brown claimed, as an enemy. While he did show great animosity towards GCHQ near the end of his life, it is more likely that he was trying to set the record straight and establish his father's true legacy. His support for Gordon Welchman's book *The Hut Six Story*, the first to provide technical details of GC&CS's work, was another example of this. He subsequently arranged for the publication of Welchman's paper *From Polish Bomba to British Bombe*, which gave the true history of the Polish contribution to the breaking of the Enigma system. In a 1992 paper, Robin described the process which led to the publication of the Philby, Winterbotham and Welchman memoirs.[10]

According to Robin, Philby's memoir was dismissed as a 'plant' by the British authorities, with the sole intention of creating division between the British and American secret services. Robin had never met Philby, but his parents had been on good terms with him and his sister 'Y' had, for a time, worked at MI6 headquarters in Ryder Street as a secretary for Philby and others. Robin had read the complete typescript in the offices of Percy Knowles, an American literary agent. It appeared to Robin to be a genuine account of key events in Philby's career as a Soviet spy. He was completely convinced when he read Philby's casual description of the move of the diplomatic and commercial Sigint traffic work from BP to its new headquarters in Berkeley Street. Over twenty years after Philby wrote his memoir, the activities and existence of Berkeley Street had not been officially acknowledged!

Rather cryptically, Robin responded to Cave Brown's comments on his part in the publication of Philby's book in a footnote:

> He believes that its chances of publication would have been slender, given the Foreign Office's campaign to prevent the book ever appearing, and attributes my own efforts on its behalf to a family dislike of Menzies, who, some may think, emerges rather badly from Philby's pages. I, on the contrary, think he gets surprisingly kind treatment. It is true that my father never got on so well with Menzies as with his predecessor, 'the admiral', Hugh Sinclair, who was warmly admired by all his staff. Yet my father and Menzies remained in regular touch until the former's retirement.

Robin began the process of planning his father's biography, and in April 1982, met with Rear Admiral W.N. Ash, Secretary of the Defence, Press and Broadcasting Committee. Aware of the sensitivities within the intelligence community about such a book, he had put forward a more modest proposal. He suggested that he would collect information on a privileged basis and prepare a draft biography, not for publication but for submission to the appropriate authority. He would only begin discussions with Lord Weidenfeld about publication when the authorities gave him approval to do so. By July, Admiral Ash confirmed that he had put the proposal 'into the machine' but was still unable to let Robin have 'a reaction' to it.

Robin pressed on with his research and began by trying to contact the very few survivors of Room 40. He spoke to Patrick Beesley, who had just published an account of Room 40. Beesley told him that the only surviving member of Room 40 that he had found was W.H. Bruford. He also thought it would be difficult for Robin to find anything new about AGD's work in WW1 or that 'there would be sufficient fresh information to produce a book about your father's working life'. One Berkeley Street veteran was more than happy to provide Robin with everything he could remember. Percy Filby had arrived at BP on 8 September 1940 and was assigned to Tiltman. He eventually ended up at Berkeley Street as head of the German section. He wrote to Robin on 15 April 1981 and gave him details about AGD's removal and his strong views about those who had 'plotted' against him.[11]

While British post-war reports about the Berkeley Street operation were still classified, as they are to this day,[12] he was able to acquire a copy of the McCormack Report (see Appendix 11) which provided an American description of the operation. He also obtained all of the war and post-war correspondence between AGD and William Friedman. He continued to accumulate a considerable amount of information about his father's life, but a coherent structure for the book was still not in place.

In 2006, Robin was introduced by his daughter to the publisher Jerry Johns. Jerry agreed to work with him to put the book together. By this time Robin was nearly 80 and not in the best of health. Jerry recalls being 'summoned' to Robin's house in Malvern where he lived alone, surrounded by piles of books, papers and other documents in somewhat chaotic circumstances, and he would be handed some material to work on. Robin continued to struggle with the book but eventually, in 2007, Polperro Press published *Thirty Secret Years, A.G. Denniston's work in signals intelligence 1914-1944*.

On 4 October 2012, Iain Lobban, the Director of GCHQ, gave a speech at the University of Leeds called 'GCHQ and Turing's Legacy'. It was one of a number of events held to commemorate the centenary of the birth of Alan Turing. In his speech, Lobban publically acknowledged AGD's role in the creation of GCHQ. He began by noting AGD's recruitment of mathematicians:

> It was this information which crystallised a crucial insight by Alastair Denniston, the Director of the Code and Cypher School, and a veteran of cryptanalysis in the First World War: he had already worked out that the forthcoming war and the profusion of mechanical encryption devices needed a new sort of cryptanalyst to complement the existing staff. He decided to look out wartime colleagues who had returned in 1919 and 1920 to the Universities (well, to Oxford and Cambridge) and asked them to identify what he described as 'men of the professor type', academics engaged in mathematical research who could be persuaded to turn their hands to cryptanalysis. In the first list of names drawn up in response to his request we can see the hint of what was to come: Alan Turing, Gordon Welchman and Max Newman.

He went on to say that:

> One of the reasons for the success of Bletchley Park, and something that I and Alastair Denniston's other successors have striven to maintain in GCHQ, is the organisation's ability to make space to allow individuals to flourish, both in isolation, and within teams. I will be talking more about the importance of recognising and making space for the unique and different contribution that each person makes, but part of that recognition can often involve a leap of faith by the manager.

He concluded his remarks by drawing a clear line from AGD's pioneering work to his own:

> Let me conclude, though, by looking at Denniston, the Director in 1938 who saw Turing and accepted him as a new type of cryptanalyst for a new era. Obviously my job, like his, is to make sure that all of the wonderfully talented people we have retain their focus on the task set out for GCHQ by the government. But what drives me, what will make me feel that I have in a small way achieved a little of what he did, comes from focusing not just on the outputs and achievements of GCHQ, but on fostering, protecting and developing a culture which prizes passion and dedication, in which today's and tomorrow's Turings can achieve as much as the genius, the man Alan Turing, did.

In the end, the last word is probably best left, not to politicians and administrators, but to those who actually produced the signals intelligence which so dramatically affected two world wars. Writing in his personal memoir, the Head of the Air Section at BP, Josh Cooper, said of AGD:

> He understood the wider problem of Sigint better than he was credited for. When he made me head of the Air Section he gave me a charge which I never forgot that I was to use cryptanalysis as one of the tools for obtaining intelligence by interception. But later when I asked for additional staff to build up an intelligence card index he became agitated and warned me earnestly not to 'confuse cryptography with intelligence', and said that the intelligence departments in Whitehall would object to this kind of thing.[13]

The two dominant figures in British and American signals intelligence of the twentieth century, John Tiltman and William Friedman, remained close friends with AGD for the rest of his life. In a letter to Robin, Tiltman said: 'I had a great respect for your father . . . and remember him as a very good director and personal friend. I think I can claim that together with Josh Cooper I was about his [AGD's] best supporter in a job which was by no means easy and I have always considered that he was quite unnecessarily roughly treated when Travis took over in 1942.'

Friedman, in his poignant letter of condolence to 'Y' Denniston, perhaps best summed up AGD's career: 'That so few of them should know exactly what he did towards achievement of victory in World War I and II is the sad part of the untold story of his life and of his great contribution to that victory.'

Appendix 1

Charter Document for Room 40

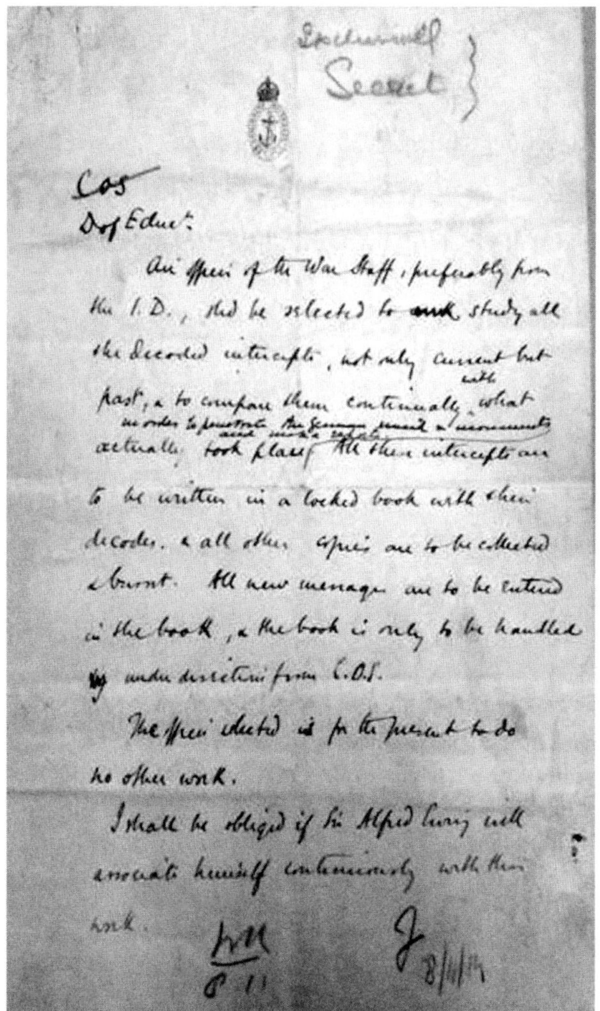

Exclusively
Secret

COS
D of Educ:

An officer of the War Staff, preferably from the I.D., shd be selected to study all the decoded intercepts, not only current but past, & to compare them continually with what actually took place in order to penetrate the German mind & movements and make reports. All these intercepts are to be written in a locked book with their decodes, & all other copies are to be collected & burnt. All new messages are to be entered in the book, & the book is only to be handled under direction from C.O.S.

The officer selected is for the present to do no other work.

I shall be obliged if Sir Alfred Ewing will associate himself continuously with this work.

WSC 8.11   J 8/11/14

Churchill College CLKE1&2

Appendix 2

GC&CS Staff, November 1919

Name	Age	WW1 Department	Background	GC&CS 1939[4]
Head				
Denniston, Alexander Guthrie[1]	38	Room 40	Master at RNC[2]	Yes
Assistant Head				
Travis, Edward Wilfred Harry[3]	31	Admiralty	RN Officer	Yes
Senior Assistant				
Fetterlein, Ernst Konstantin	46	Room 40	Tsarist cryptographer	Yes[5]
Fryer, Sydney Ernest	38	MI1(b)	Egyptian Civil Service	No d.1924
Knox, Alfred Dillwyn[1]	35	Room 40	Academic	Yes
Strachey, Oliver	45	MI1(b)	Various	Yes
Turner, James	34	MI1(b)	Academic	Yes
Junior Assistant				
Aitken, Robert	37	MI1(b)	Academic	No r.1920/1
Anderson, Emily	28	MI1(b)	Academic	Yes
Carew-Hunt, Robert Nigel	29	MI1(b)	Academic	Yes
Clarke, William Francis[1]	36	Room 40	Lawyer	Yes
Earnshaw-Smith, Eric	26	MI1(b)	Academic	Yes
Ford, Hugo Robert	57	Room 40	Unknown	No
Hanly, Edward Dudley	33	Room 40	Former Army Officer	Yes
Hayllar, Florence	51	MI1(b)	Academic	No r. 1920
Hobart-Hamden, Ernest Miles	55	MI1(b)	Consular Service	Yes

Hooper, John	40	Room 40	Master at RNC	No d. 1924/25
Hope, George Leonard Nelson[1]	35	Room 40	Master at RNC	Yes
Jopson, Norman Brooke	29	MI1(b)	Academic	No r. 1922/23
Maine, Henry Cecil Sumner	34	MI1(b)	Royal Household	Yes
Mayo, Mark Poole	41	MI1(b)	School master	No r. 1938
McGrath, Edward Henry	40	MI1(b)	Unknown	Yes
Montgomery, William	48	Room 40	Academic, Clergyman	No d. 1930
Rees, Alfred George Rickard	34	MI1(b)	Mining Engineer	Yes
Lady Translator				
Carelton, Jeanetta Frances	27	MI1(b)	Unknown	No r. 1920
Lunn, Helen Clara	–	–	Unknown	Yes
Spurling, Claribel	44	MI1(b)	Schoolmistress	No r. 1920
Wireless Expert				
Lambert, Leslie[1]	36	Room 40	Magician	Yes
Editor of 'Wireless News'[6]				
Somers-Cocks, Charles Sebastien	9	Room 40	Foreign Office	No

1 Individual regarded by the Admiralty as liable to transfer to the Admiralty control in wartime.

2 Royal Naval College at Osborne in the Isle of Wight.

3 Graded as Senior Assistant but as Deputy Head, received an extra £100 per annum.

4 d – died in service; r – retired/resigned.

5 Fetterlein retired in 1938 but rejoined GC&CS on the outbreak of war.

6 Post dispensed with 1923/24

Appendix 3

Code Text of the Zimmermann Telegram

Edward Bell's copy of the decode made at the American Embassy (US National Archives, Foreign Affairs Branch, State Department Decimal File 862.202 1 2/81 ½). English translation by Barbara Tuchman.

The following has Bernstorff's slight alterations at the beginning and is the same as the text obtained by Hall in Mexico City and which he gave to Ambassador Page.

130	(number of telegram)	–
13042	(Code identification number)	–
13042	Auswärtiges Amt	Foreign Office
8501	telegraphiert	telegraphs
115	Januar 16	January 16
3528	colon (:)	colon (:)
416	number 1	no. 1
17214	ganz geheim	strictly secret
6491	selbst	yourself
11310	zu	to
18147	entziffern	decipher
18222	stop(.)	stop(.)
21560	Wir	We
10247	beabsichtigen	intend
11518	am	from the

23677	ersten	first
13605	Februar	February
3494	un-	un-
14963	eingeschränkt	restricted
98092	U-boot	U-boat
5905	Krieg	war
11311	zu	to
10392	beginnen	begin
10371	stop(.)	stop(.)
0302	Es wird	It will
21290	versucht	attempted
5161	warden	be
39695	Vereinigten Staaten	United States
23571	trotzdem	nevertheless
17504	neutral	neutral
11269	zu	to
18276	erhalten	keep
18101	stop(.)	stop(.)
0217	Für den Fall	In the event
0228	dass dies	that this
17694	nicht	not
4473	gelingen	succeed
22284	sollte	should
22200	comma(,)	comma(,)
19452	schlagen	offer
21589	wir	we
67893	Mexico	Mexico
5569	auf	on
13918	folgender	following

8958	Grundlage	terms
12137	Bündnis	alliance
1333	vor	(prefix of verb vorschlagen – to offer
4725	stop(.)	stop(.)
4458	Gemeinsam	Together
5905	Krieg	war
17166	führen	make
13851	stop(.)	stop(.)
4458	Gemeinsam	Together
5905	Krieg	war
17166	führen	make
13851	stop(.)	stop(.)
4458	Gemeinsam	Together
17149	Freidenschluss	peace
14471	stop(.)	stop(.)
6706	Reichlich	Generous
13850	finanzielle	financial
12224	unterstützung	support
6929	und	and
14991	einverständnis	understanding
7382	Unserer Seits	our part
15857	dass	that
67893	Mexico	Mexico
14218	in	in
36477	Texas	Texas
5870	comma(,)	comma(,)
17553	New	New
67893	Mexico	Mexico

5870	comma(,)	comma(,)
5454	AR	AR
16102	IZ	IZ
15217	ON	ON
22801	A	A
17138	frühen	former
21001	verloren	lost
17388	Gebiet	territory
7446	zurück	back
23638	erobern	conquer
18222	stop(.)	stop(.)
6719	Regelung	Settlement
14331	im	in the
15021	Einzelnen	details
23845	Euer Hochwohlgeboren	Your Excellency
3156	überlassen	To be left
23552	stop(.)	stop(.)
22096	Sie	You
21604	woollen	will
4797	vorstehendes	of the foregoing
9497	dem	the
22464	Präsident	President
20855	streng	in strictest
4377	geheim	secrecy
23610	eröffnen	inform
18140	comma (,)	comma (,)
22260	sobald	as soon as
5905	Kriegs	war's
13347	Ausbruch	outbreak

20420	mit	with
39689	Vereinigten Staaten	United States
13732	fest	certain
20667	steht	is
6929	und	and
5275	Anregung	suggestion
18507	hinzufügen	add
52262	Japan	Japan
1340	von	by
22049	sich	himself
13339	aus	from
11265	zu	to
22295	sofortig	immediately
10439	beitretung	join
14814	einladen	invite
4178	(setze infinitiv mit zu – i.e., einzuladen)	(form the infinitive – i.e., to invite)
6992	und	and
8784	gleichzeitig	at the same time
7632	zwischen	between
7357	uns	us
6926	und	and
52262	Japan	Japan
11267	zu	to
21100	vermitteln	mediate
21272	stop(.)	stop(.)
9346	Bitte	Please
9559	den	the
22464	Präsident	President

15874	darauf	of this
18502	hinweisen	point to
18500	comma(,)	comma(,)
15857	dass	that
2188	rücksichtslos	ruthless
5376	Anwendung	employment
7381	unserer	our
98092	U-boote	U-boats
16127	jetzt	now
13486	Aussicht	prospect
9350	bietet	offers
9220	comma(,)	comma(,)
76036	England	England
14219	in	in
5144	wenigen	few
2831	Monat-	month-
17920	en	s
11347	zum	to
17142	Frieden	peace
11264	zu	be
7667	zwingen	compelled
7762	stop(.)	stop(.)
15099	Empfang	Receipt
9110	bestahigen	acknowledge
10482	stop(.)	stop(.)
97556	Zimmermann	Zimmermann
3569	stop(.)	stop(.)
3670	Schluss der Depesche	End of despatch
	BERNSTORFF	

Appendix 4

Examples of Room 40 Decrypts with AGD's Initials

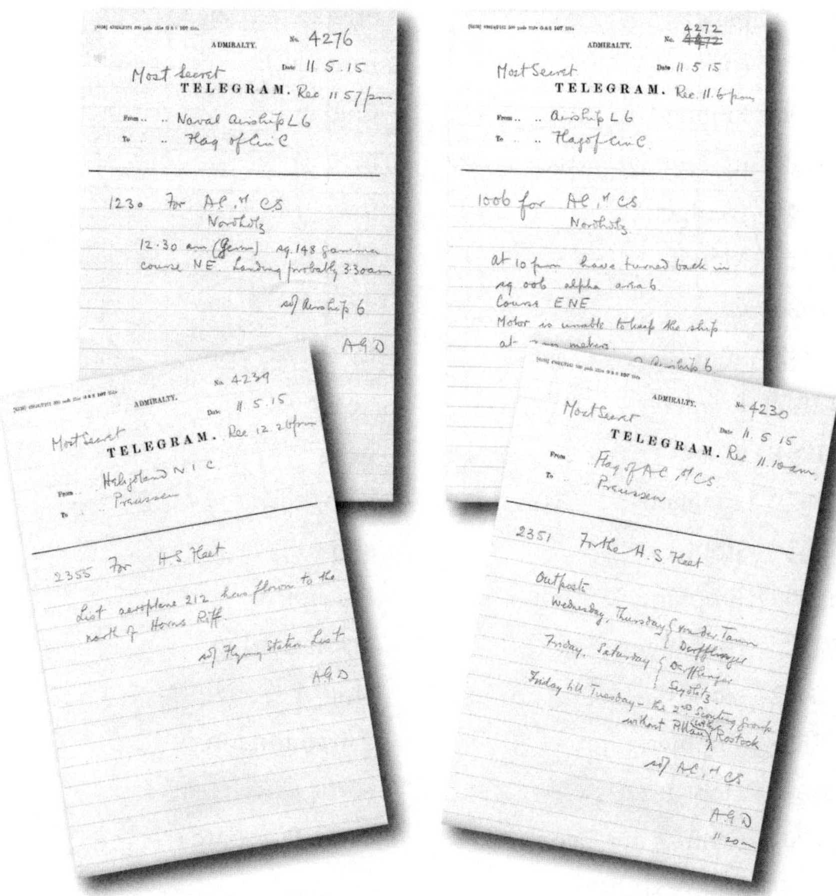

ADMIRALTY. No. 4276
Most Secret Date 11.5.15
TELEGRAM. Rec 11.57 pm
From .. Naval Airship L6
To .. Flag of C in C

1230 For AC, II CS
Nordholz
12.30 am (Germ) sq. 148 gamma
course NE. Landing probably 3.30 am
sd Airship 6
AGD

ADMIRALTY. No. 4272
Most Secret Date 11.5.15
TELEGRAM. Rec. 11.6 pm
From .. Airship L6
To .. Flag of C in C

1006 for AC, II CS
Nordholz
At 10 pm have turned back in
sq 006 alpha area 6.
Course ENE
Motor is unable to keep the ship
at ... metres.

ADMIRALTY. No. 4239
Date 11.5.15
Most Secret TELEGRAM. Rec 12.26 pm
From .. Heligoland N I C
To .. Preussen

2355 For H.S. Fleet
List aeroplane 212 has flown to the
north of Horns Riff.
sd Flying Station List
AGD

ADMIRALTY. No. 4230
Most Secret Date 11.5.15
TELEGRAM. Rec 11.10 am
From Flag of AC, II CS
To .. Preussen

2351 For the H.S. Fleet
Outposts
Wednesday, Thursday { von der Tann, Derfflinger
Friday, Saturday { Derfflinger, Seydlitz
Friday till Tuesday – the 2nd Scouting Group without Pillau, Rostock
sd AC, II CS
AGD
11.20 am

Appendix 5

How News was Brought from Warsaw at the end of July 1939

This is AGD's personal account (and the only British first-hand account) of the famous July 1939 meeting between British, French and Polish intelligence personnel. It was written on 11 May 1948 from memory and using his pocket diary to check dates (TNA HW 25/12):

> Before attempting from memory a description of the visit of July 24–27 it is necessary to outline previous events which led up to the visit. The hero or mystery man or *deus ex machine* was undoubtedly the French officer Bertrand alias Godefroi. I never really grasped how G.C. & C.S. came to be involved in this liaison.
>
> From 1937 onward it was obviously desirable that our naval, military and air intelligence should get in very close touch with their French colleagues for political and military reasons. The Admiral had always wished and worked for a close liaison between SIS and G.C. & C.S. but I have always thought that Dunderdale, then in Paris, was the man who brought Bertrand into the English organisations. Menzies it is true, had a close liaison with Rivet under whom Bertrand worked but I think it was Dunderdale who, entirely ignorant of the method of cryptographers, urged the liaison on the technical level. Bertrand was his man in the French military branch. The French had no interservice organisation. In fact all four (including Quai d'Orsay) thoroughly disliked and distrusted each other. Bertrand was no cryptographer and never pretended that he was. Any technical staff under him must have been very second rate but he had a genius for making use of others. By July 1939 he certainly was obtaining cryptographic results from us and from the Poles and he also salvaged five Spanish republicans who had

worked at Barcelona & installed them in Paris as his party working on Spanish and Italian material.

Bertrand was, no doubt inter alia, a peddler & purchaser of foreign government codes and I think that, as he never had an opportunity in his own organisation of obtaining results from crypt he had decided to concentrate on careful purchase as the surest method. I would say he did not have access to very much cash and frequently asked us to go 50-50 in a possible deal. We were averse to this as we already read most telegrams except the Russian and German neither of whom was among Bertrand's customers. But the Admiral thought that occasionally it was well spent money to keep in with Bertrand. He must have been useful to SIS in other ways as I well remember an official lunch in '38 or '39 at which Menzies presented Bertrand with a gold cigarette case engraved with the royal arms.

It should be noted as of some ultimate importance that in the course of some of his visits to us in Broadway we arranged for Bertrand to have conferences with certain sections such as the Spanish and Italian. He heard explanations of our methods and saw results and with the Admiral's permission received a regular supply of certain results.

I think he was impressed by our success and by the ability of certain officers and it might well be that this had an important bearing on his subsequent actions.

The Spanish war had rekindled our interest in the German Enigma as, at last, we were intercepting a considerable volume of German Naval material and a little Military or Air traffic. Knox was working on the naval material with intermittent assistance from Foss. Tiltman was in the background but was really fully occupied with the military section and the solution of the Japanese military cyphers. In addition to this we had found that the Italian Navy were using the commercial Enigma. This was cracked by Knox and a small section was formed with Bodsworth in virtual charge to handle the current traffic, leaving Knox clear for the German machine.

So far as I can remember this was the position in January 1939 when Bertrand asked me to come over to Paris as he wanted us to meet certain Polish experts. We assumed that such a meeting could only concern German & Russian work on both of which we were so weak that we felt we might well profit by such a meeting. So I went over with (I think) Tiltman, Knox and Foss. We met in an atmosphere of secrecy and mystery. One of the Poles, a Major Ceski [*sic*], gave us the alleged results of their research into the Enigma machine as used by the German services. He had no English and his French and German were only fair but it was clear that he was describing the results of his work on the 'message setting' which at that period appeared as the first group in all messages in all services. (It was only in May '39 that the German Navy adopted the bigrammatic indicator which Knox quickly diagnosed & found himself to drop the Naval & concentrate on the Military / Air). The Poles gave us a long and pedantic description of what Tiltman had spotted and learnt in an hour namely that the message setting was soluble because no letter could by cyphered by itself and the German operators were simple souls with childish habits. The Poles finished by saying that they were obtaining a lot of material and pursuing their research and it would keep us informed of any results. At that time we had to regard the meeting as a flop and that the Poles were no great find. Since then I have thought that it was our party who were being vetted by the Poles who were at the time reading the traffic and only wanted to know what progress we had made. Bertrand himself let it be understood on this occasion and always when the question was raised that he himself was ignorant of the ability of the Poles, or of what they could read. He was aware, he said, that they obtained some results. Later he admitted that he had to visit Warsaw once a month at least to exchange raw material and results and further he considered them exceptionally well-placed to do 'business', as he understood it, with treacherous Germans & Russians.

For the next six months we heard nothing more from the Poles probably because they felt that they did not require any help from us. In the middle of July however we received an invitation, through Bertrand, to pay them a visit in Warsaw. The international situation was now tense. England was pledged to go to the assistance of Poland if attacked by Hitler. Each party knew that the other had an active cryptographic organisation. So it appeared quite natural that the Poles should invite us. But it must not be forgotten that the German Navy had changed in May. The Polish invitation specifically included Knox who was known both by the French and Poles to be working on this subject. I do not think though now I cannot be sure that they were aware of our success on the commercial Enigma as used by the Italian Navy.

However, the Admiral instructed me to take Knox with me. I could well wish now that I had added others of our party but everyone was fully occupied and could ill spare the time to travel to another flop as in January. D.N.I., in close touch with the Admiral, suggested that Sandwith should go also, why I don't know as Sandwith was not a cryptographer and the Poles had no navy. Bertrand was of course of the party, Knox and I went by train as we wished to see Germany probably for the last time, the other two separately by air. We left on the 24th & were met by the Poles & Bertrand and lodged at The Bristol. We were there for work on the 26th & 27th & leaving on the 28th. I was back in London by Sunday the 30th. Knox, whose passport had been wrongly stamped for his return transit through Germany, had to go back from the frontier to Posen and get the visa from the British Consul in that town. The 26th (Wednesday) was THE day. The Poles called for us at 7 am and we were driven out to a clearing in a forest about 20 kilometres from Warsaw. Here we found a new, strongly built and strongly guarded office with some underground accommodation and here we met the Polish cryptographers some of whom luckily spoke some French or German.

A prolonged full dress conference with the Polish senior officer in the chair (I have forgotten his name). Colonel Langer was in charge of the organisation in the Forest. Major Ceski with the stecker Enigma now described in full detail the steps they had taken to break down the cypher and obtain the wheel order and to read the messages; we followed him each to the best of our ability. Knox, as our expert, was alongside Ceski and in the best position to follow his explanation. He, however, reacted very badly to the explanation which took about three hours with a break for a cup of tea. I confess I was unable to understand completely the lines of reasoning but when, as [the] second part of the conference, we were taken down to an underground room full of electronic equipment & introduced to the 'bombs' I did then grasp the results of their reasoning and their method of solving the daily key. Knox accompanied us throughout but maintained a stony silence and was obviously extremely angry about something.

It was only when we got back into a car to drive away that he suddenly let himself go and assuming that no one understood any English, raged and raved that they were lying to us now as in Paris. The whole thing was a fraud he kept on repeating. They never worked it out. They pinched it years ago and have followed developments as anyone could but they must have bought it or pinched it.

Our position became increasingly difficult as even Bertrand, who knew no English, was aware that Knox had a grudge against the Poles, who, so far as Bertrand knew, had only been successful where Knox had failed.

I assume that he did not believe that they had constructed the order on the wheels and he may have been correct in his surmise. Ceski's explanation was very lengthy and involved and in a language which he knew only fairly well and I was not competent to judge of the possibility of complete success. So far as I was concerned they were reading messages up to the previous May and were now quite sanguine as to the reading of current messages again by means of their 'bombs'. I have since thought that they were finding considerable difficulty especially with the naval and knowing Knox's reputation and ability, felt it was a good moment to come clean and gain his assistance especially in view of the political situation.

The rest of the day remains a nightmare to me. Knox remained aloof and alone. Bertrand, Sandwith and I discussed the situation at length and decided to get away as soon as possible. The next day had been allotted to personal contacts with their technical and intelligence officers. Knox had cooled down considerably and spent a long morning with their technical staff examining the machine and their methods. Language was of course still a difficulty but he now seemed to understand their reasoning and in his conversations with me never referred to his outburst after the disclosures.

I was shown the mass of telegrams they had read, the naval traffic being practically only between Berlin and their fleet in Spanish waters, which formed the bulk of their material. They undertook to send us copies and a model of the machine through Bertrand as we, of course, had no line of communication with them. The machine did arrive during August but I doubt if any messages arrived. As the situation was now clearly war and service sections had already gone to Bletchley we were not interested in back material but were naturally concentrating on current air/army traffic.

I should add that on the second day Knox was really his old bright self and won the hearts and admiration of the young men with whom he was in touch.

If only that first day of formal disclosure could have been avoided and pompous declarations by senior officers had been omitted, Knox's mind and personality in touch with men who really knew their job would have made that visit a very real success. They were all simple and straightforward.

To me Bertrand's attitude remains a mystery. I still believe that he knew all about their work and feigned the surprise which he manifested at the Polish success.

For a full set of notes to AGD's document, see Erskine's paper.

Appendix 6

Approximate Strength of GC&CS on Move to War Station, August 1939

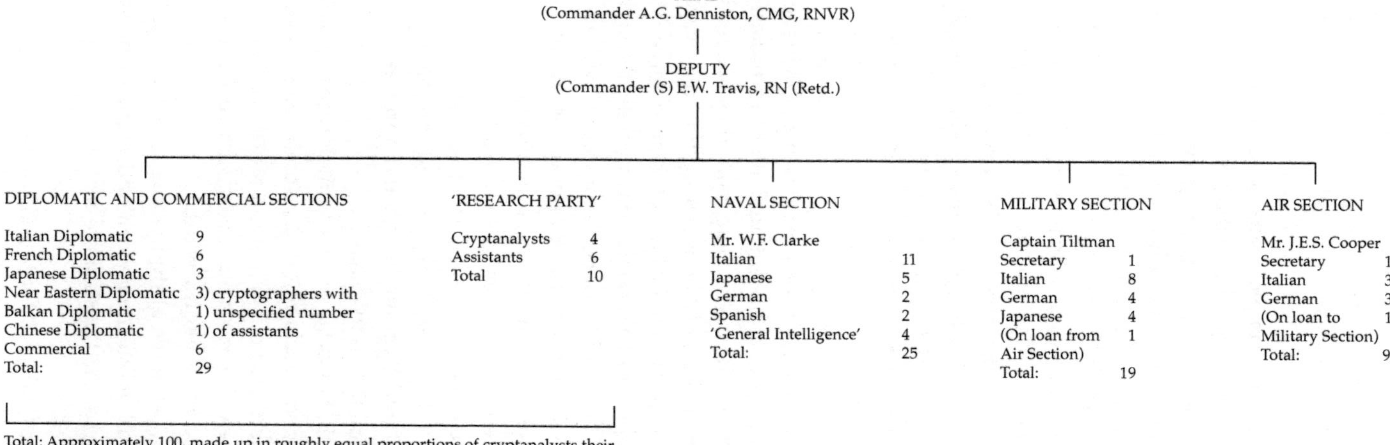

Appendix 7

Naval Sigint in the UK, December 1940

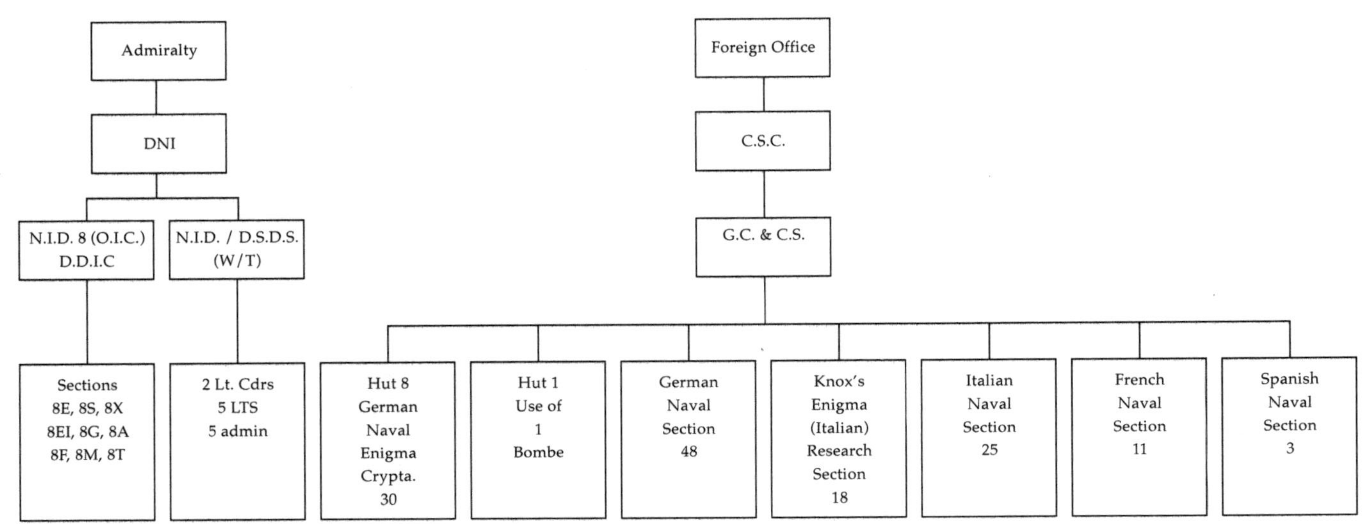

Appendix 8

Military Sigint in the UK December 1940

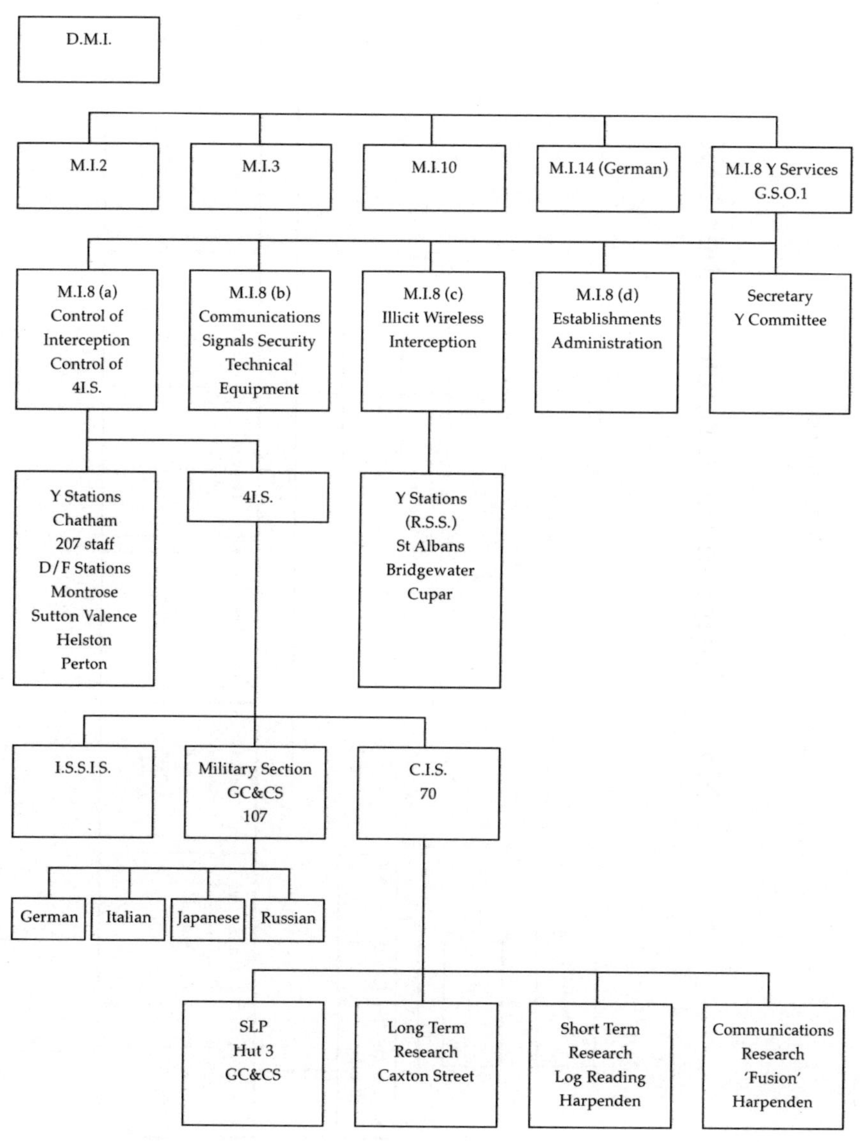

Appendix 9

Air Force Sigint in the UK December 1940

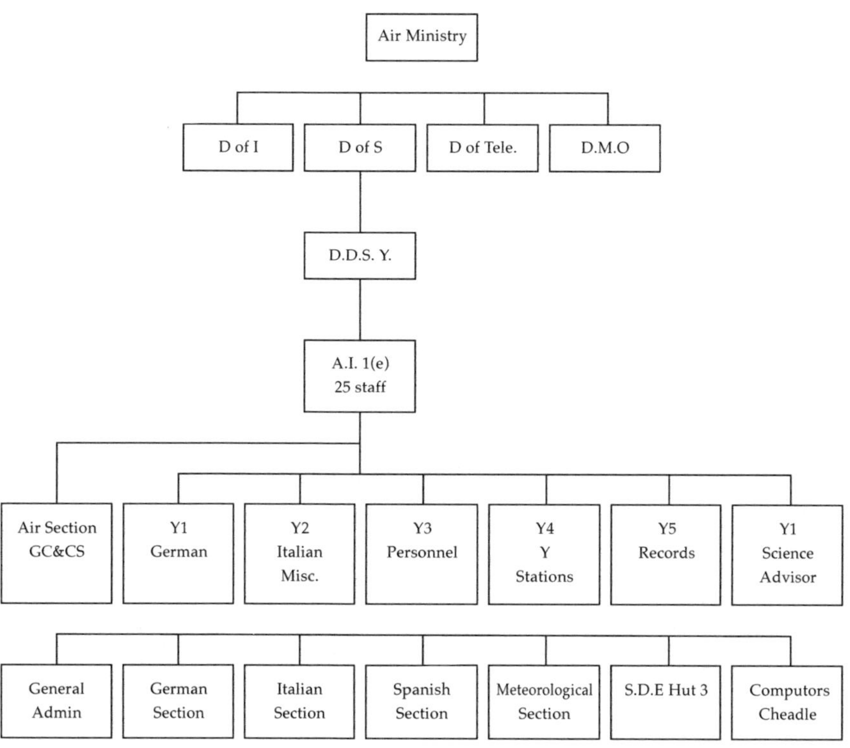

Appendix 10

GC&CS Diplomatic and Commercial Sections (Civil) Structure in 1944

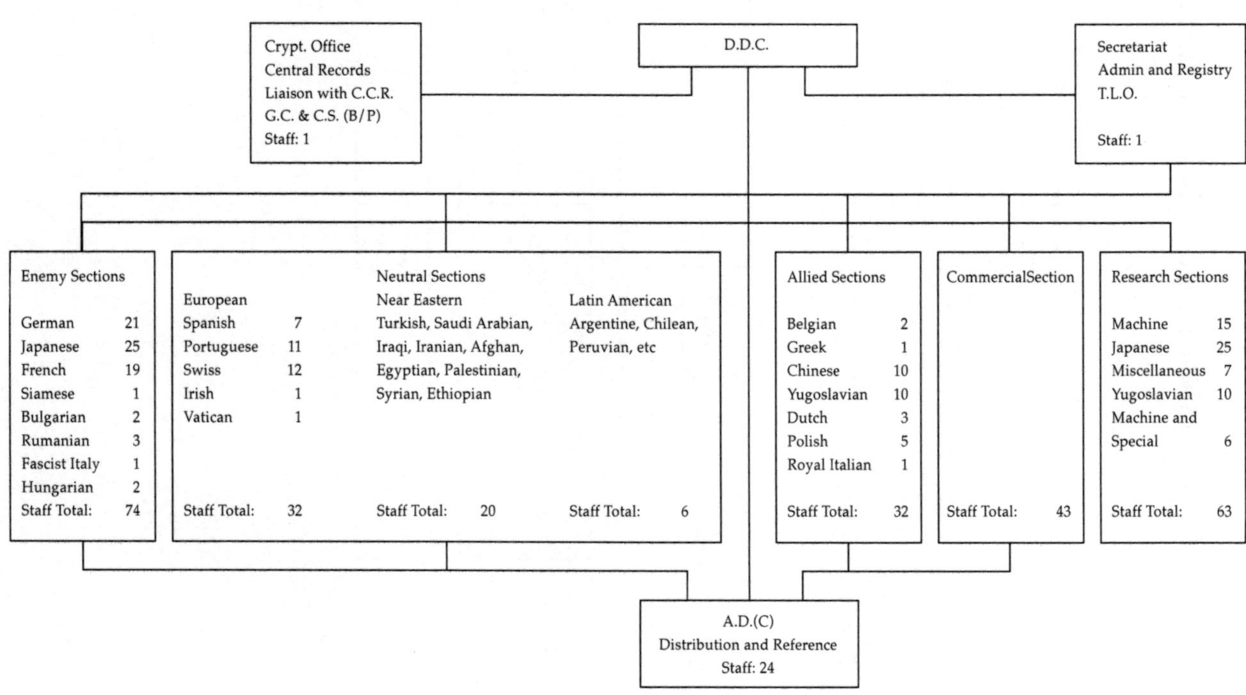

Appendix 11

The McCormack Report

Colonel Alfred McCormack was deputy head of the US Army's special branch which supervised signal intelligence in the US War Department. He visited GC&CS in 1943 with William Friedman and Lieutenant Telford Taylor, who rose to the rank of colonel in the Office of Strategic Services, and spent most of his time at BP, where he served as a liaison between American and British intelligence. After the war he served as an American war crimes prosecutor at Nuremberg.

The report consists of a series of signals (messages) sent by McCormack and occasionally others, to the US Army Arlington Hall Station Message Centre in Washington via the American Embassy in London. The messages were for the attention of General George Strong, the US Army's Military Intelligence chief, and Colonel Carter Clarke, Strong's deputy. They were sent between 21 May and 1 July 1943. The standard signal specific information has been removed for ease of reading and each is a separate section. The actual text of each message has not been edited.

***

> Denniston's show, commonly called Berkeley Street, has none of the hectic atmosphere of Park but rather gives [the] impression of [a] well established operation that goes along through wars and peace. General impression is typified by the two ladies who receive and sort incoming traffic. (They started as telegraph clerks in Post Office in reign of Queen Victoria and were fully familiar with general field when they joined present organisation in 1919.) These little birdlike old ladies receive and register incoming material and they have

acquired such great familiarity with it that [they] can do everything except actually decipher it. Whole organization is very simple and they seem to accomplish a great deal with quite limited personnel. Whole outfit consists of two hundred.

38 bodies divided, subject to some doubling up, as follows:

Deputy Director and admin staff – 5
Distribution and reference section – 2
Sorting section – 2
Typing – 14
Teleprinter clerks – 2
Geographical sections – 155
Commercial sections – 50
Research section – 5

Geographical sections are divided into enemy countries, neutral countries and allies.

Personnel in enemy country sections are:
German – 26; Italian and Vatican – 19; Japanese – 36; French (which now overlaps enemy and allied groups) – 14; Siamese – 1 (who in off moment doubles up on Irish); Bulgarian – 2; Roumanian and Hungarian – 1; Finnish is now being worked on in Research Section.

Neutral countries are divided up as follows:

Spanish – 6 bodies; Portuguese – 10; Swiss – 4; Irish – (see above); Latin America, Spanish language – 5; Near East (which covers Turkey, Saudi Arabia, Iraq, Iran, Afghanistan, Egypt, Palestine and Syria) – 17.
All Scandinavia is handled in off moments by Rees who is Chief Administrator Officer.

Allied countries account for full time personnel of 11, of whom eight work on Chinese, two on Belgian and one on Greek. Dutch is done by people who work in Near Eastern section, Brazilian by Portuguese section, Polish, Jugoslav and Czeck [*sic*] by the man who handles, with a clerk assistant, Bulgarian material, and Mexican of course is done by Latin American section.

Taylor will report later on composition of commercial subdivisions. Principal sources of material, other than by exchange with United

States, are censorships at London, Ottawa, Mauritius, Barbados, Gibraltar and Middle East. (Where there are joint censorships at Cairo, Baghdad, Teheran and possible elsewhere). Foreign Office intercept stations in United Kingdom (Denmark Hill, Sandridge, Saint Albans, Whitchurch, Cupar, and Brora) and, through BP, other intercept stations at Ottawa, New Delhi, West Africa and Mauritius. You will observe what extensive coverage this adds up to. Other source of material is secret intelligence service in neutral capitals. General outline of workings of outfit follows: sorting clerks route material to proper geographical section, where it is registered in appropriate book in which notations are made under following headings:

First serial number,
Second cipher,
Third signature,
Fourth reference (that is, to cipher keys),
Fifth subject (briefly indicated),
Sixth remarks and distribution number (this is inserted if material is distributed, so that by looking at any page you can tell what has been distributed and what not),
Seventh source (that is, intercept station or other point which it was picked up).

Traffic then goes to crypt people and if successfully processed results are passed to Head of Section, who sets aside what he thinks not important enough to give to anybody and the rest to distribution and reference section, which is heart of organization and which I will report on in more detail in another message. This section decides whether material is worth circulating and if so gives each item to be circulated its proper serial number and sends uncirculated items back to geographical sections for filing or destruction. Up to this point everything is done in longhand. Only what is going outside is typed up. Note that commercial material does not go into this section but processes along another routing which Taylor will describe.

Everything that is circulated goes to the Foreign Office and Director, that is C, and except in very special cases everything goes to the War Office and Admiralty (will have to check further what goes to Air Ministry). The very special cases that service ministries do not get are such cases as where material shows that some British diplomat abroad has 'dropped a brick'. Policy is to recognise that especially in time of war service ministries have their own views on matters of foreign policy and are entitles to be kept fully informed on all diplomatic developments. In case of Berkeley Street as in in case of Park, what impressed us was the pains that are taken to see that all information gets out to those who can make use of it.

There are liaison officers from various governmental offices who are assigned to Berkeley Street and have access to the material, although this is not the full time job and most of them are high personages. In this manner the following are directly represented in Berkeley Street operation:

> C's office; BP; Winnie himself; Foreign Office; all three services; Ministry of Economic Warfare; Treasury; War Cabinet; Colonial Office; Military Intelligence Five, which is counter espionage; India Office and Secret Intelligence Service, which is Charlie in another form but this last named liaison officer does not serve C but serves other branches of the government, including Board of Trade; Department of Overseas Trade; Petroleum Board; Home Office and Minster of War Transport. There is some form of liaison to everybody who might be able to act on information coming in.

Through BP liaison is maintained with Washington, New Delhi, Melbourne and African Force Headquarters. Please make following correction at beginning of message: Elderly ladies do not register and record all incoming material, but only material from certain sources, when there is some reason to keep such records in order to evaluate source or keep track of source for some reason. At present they are keeping register of incoming traffic only from Mauritius, Port Sudan, Cairo, Gibraltar, Khartoum and Jerusalem. Khartoum is not mentioned above and I believe this is censorship point. Note however that complete register of all traffic by nationalities is kept by geographical sections.

***

Records maintained at Berkeley Street do not include figures for total traffic and I did not ask them to go to geographical sections and add up all these figures, but they receive 'thousands' of messages per day. Their serial numbers of circulated diplomatic items crossed one hundred thousand early in 1942. Do not have present range of number.

But monthly average has been running at from eight hundred to one thousand. Generally speaking I would say that their policy of what to distribute is same as Arlington's, the difference in numbers distributed being accounted for by fact Arlington covers wider field and that here they have been going for much longer and have learned over period of time what is new information and what is not; and they also have had much more guidance as to what to put through and what to discard than Arlington gets from its distributors, naturally in view of short time that operation has been going on present scale.

Basic principle is same however, namely, to distribute everything that might have any intelligence value, however small.

Great difference between BP operation and Berkeley Street is that BP is essentially an intelligence organization with important operational functions whereas Berkeley Street is production organization like Arlington. However they do seem to have the intelligence side of their operation, functioning as aid to crypt people, very well set up. It centers in the distribution and reference section, headed by Earnshaw Smith, a youngish looking man who nevertheless has been in this work since 1917. His assistant is Ore Jenkins, Professor of Medieval and Modern Greek at Cambridge, who has been in it since war started. They have three girls in theory but two in actuality, one of whom has been fourteen years at Berkeley Street and six years in this section. The other has been in the section for five years. These people are in effect a reference bureau for crypt people, and in addition they determine what shall be circulated and to whom it shall go in cases of doubt, and they supervise mechanical operation of getting it out.

Nothing goes out by teletype, other than exceptional material for Chief, the four teletype connections being with BP, Chief's office and intercept stations at Denmark Hill and Sandridge. Earnshaw Smith's section has most simple filing system imaginable. Material is simply laid in folders in serial number order, unbound. There are three files – one is master file and another is spare file, both in straight serial number order. The third and important file is called 'Subject and Country' but in fact it is only country and not subject, since all material bearing on any particular country is laid in a folder in order of dates and there is no subdivision of country files by subjects. Most startling fact about this section is that it receives daily, shows to geographical sections where interesting to them and then puts in its files all incoming and outgoing communications of Foreign Office, Dominions Office, Colonial Office and India Office, and all but purely operational material of the three service ministries. More later.

***

One of the most illuminating documents in Denniston's show is book showing net results of all British intercept activities in diplomatic field for second half of 1942. It consists of one sheet or set of sheets for each city in which traffic originated. On each sheet:

The first column shows alphabetically the cities to which traffic was destined.

Column two further breaks down traffic for each city according to nationality, all subsequent columns following the breakdown of column two.

Columns three and four show by call signs the originating station and, station of destination.

Column five shows station or stations which did Interception. Column six shows estimated number of messages sent. This is based on message numbers. In some cases exact number of messages is known; in others estimate is based on numbers intercepted up to late date in month; in others it may be guess based on small numbers of interceptions not running to end of month. In cases where senders do not number messages this column is left blank.

Column seven is number of messages intercepted

Column eight is number missed, being difference between column six and column seven, where six has been filled in.

Column nine is number of messages intercepted in cases of unnumbered series.

Column ten is the usual remarks. Remarks include information necessary to understand figures, such as note that traffic only started in June or that interception commenced in August or that diplomatic relations were broken in May and traffic discontinued. Remarks also include information to guide users of book, such as note that traffic is important and that further efforts should be made to get it, or that at actual places of interception it is hard to get legible copy, or that because only slow means of relaying are available it arrives too late to be used, etc.

Pages are thirteen plus by sixteen plus inches and triple spacing is used, leaving plenty of room for notes. Such a book would be of great use to us and over the past year if information of this kind had been available in this readily usable form it would have saved innumerable inquiries to Arlington and would have made answers to many inquiries more accurate. From such a book it is possible to take off totals of material by origin and destination, by nationalities etc, and to see what intercept stations produce important material and in what volume, to determine at a glance what sources of information there are in each principal city and how many of them are being tapped and of course to see how much of each type of traffic is being brought in.

Recommend that you and Corderman consider setting up this kind of a record and keeping it up month to month, which British are now starting to do.

It is impossible to exaggerate how many surprises you would get from looking at these records or how many subjects that we have discussed it would illuminate. To mention one, you will recall our discussion of possibility of stopping Axis traffic to and from Portuguese African points. You may be surprised to learn that Portugal, which governs the colony, sent 122 messages to Lourenco Marques during second half of nineteen forty two whereas the Italian Embassy in Lisbon send 1295, and that figures in other direction are comparable. Had we had these figures in our mind at time of our discussion we would have seen this picture in very different light.

Pages for Tokyo give clear and extremely interesting picture of whole Japanese diplomatic communications picture. They reveal that 498 diplomatic circulars were intercepted out of 936 sent out, but unfortunately figures for interceptions does not in any instance include traffic received from United States and therefore that side of picture is incomplete.

Tokyo figures show that German communications to and from Berlin are much more numerous than Japanese (almost four times as large).

I cannot carry in mind all striking examples which I noted but one other is that Italian traffic to and from Bangkok is much larger than I had imagined and that much the largest item in Irish Government traffic was to and from Vichy. I give you these to illustrate how much information you can spot quicker from such a schedule and how useful it would be in various ways, including setting up of traffic priorities (Special Friedman System)

***

Japan Section of Berkeley Street is most impressive because of experience and ability of personnel. Traffic coming in is classified and registered by three girls who have had long experience and is then passed to proper crypt people who number 14. Those who actually do crypt work at present are not prewar employees but have been in this work most of war.

One girl handles crypt side of Purple while two men in middle thirties or thereabouts do all work of recovering JIC keys and are now complaining of lack of work. Head of Section was away when we visited and name escapes me.

One young man handles liaison with us and Australia and balance of section consists of decoders and clerks. This young man and two men handling JIG Nineteen keys are typical of selection methods here. Before war one was history teacher in public school, one was detective story writer and third was seller of odd books to American collectors. All were called up and all were selected for Intelligence Corps and after six months in Army sent to Tiltman's school. On finishing course they had privilege of taking commission or being returned to civil life in assignments in this work. Two took commissions and are now Captains, the third chose to serve as civilian. All wear civilian clothes.

You can see that these realistic British know that men working on JIG Nineteen are not really in Army and they do not have to pretend that they are unless they want to. JIG Translation Section is much higher form of animal life than Crypt Section and includes people who have done crypt work and might be doing JIG crypt now if it were not so easy. Head of Section is White, who at beginning of war was Consul General in Tientsin and had long service in Japan and China. All work coming from Crypt Section passes over his desk and is examined by him or whoever is acting during his absences, in original language, and is marked with one to four symbols meaning high priority, priority, unimportant, or please look over to determine whether it is worth translating. High priorities must be translated at once, priorities must be translated when translators get around to them, unimportant ones are not translated. Result is that eighty per cent of color material and fifty per cent of JIG Nineteen's are translated. Lousy Annie material is not normally translated. It is looked over in original language and watched for items referred to in higher class material, to circulars, for identifications OK persons etc, and in certain special cases, such as Kabul, where it has proved to be source of information, it is followed with more care.

This is based upon study of Lousy Annie* material made last year.

Translation staff (working on DIP and not including those on Commercial) consists of retired Colonel (who was Military Attaché in JIG in twenties and has been in his present work since 1927), and seven civilians: Cunningham, formerly Consul in JIG, Roscoe, who was Consul in JIG during last war, thereafter lived and worked there and returned here for present work in nineteen thirty one after seventeen years of residence there, Hobart-Hampden who they say is probably world's leading JIG scholar and coeditor of Standard Dictionary recently reprinted in Washington, two recently retired Consuls, who were Consuls General at two JIG commercial cities, one Consul on active list, who when war started was serving at Taiwan and, finally, one Braithwaite, who was brought up in JIG, got his advance education there during last war, went into business and resided there up to present war. As White remarked, his section's standard of scholarship in JIG is very high.

We did not have chance to inspect closely the files of this section or aids used in its work. While general impression is of men steeped in knowledge of their special field, and who carry most of what they need in their heads, we did see a lot of dictionaries and reference books and two complete looking files, one of personal names and one of geographical names, the latter apparently considered very important in their work. They of course keep files of their own material, and I got impression that they more or less specialize, one man dealing with material relating to one part of world and another man another part, and that these men are not merely translators but are experts on the areas with which they deal, and that they are consulted by Foreign Office people for their opinions on information coming out or material.

All of which leads me to this suggestion: Arlington is plugging away at very difficult work which is largely for use of State Department [and] that Department must have JIG experts who are spending their time at much less important work than getting this JIG diplomatic material out when Army can very properly say that, with JAC material to handle, it cannot do State Department's job unless such people are furnished to handle DIP translation work.

This leads me to another thought: when you get some idea of economic warfare picture that has been built up here from continental commercial material, by process of just getting every tiny item and putting them all together by most painstaking labor, you cannot fail to think that we ought to be doing same thing for areas involved in JIG material. It would take many months of most intensive work to start building up picture, and no time ought to be lost in starting it, because at some point in this war important decisions in JIG area are going to be affected vitally by what we know and do not know about the details of economic matters in those areas.

Lord Farrar, who sits in Economic Warfare Ministry for purpose of handling most secret information in continental economic field and in fact for whole world, told us yesterday that 85 per cent of all important information about South Central economic picture has been built up from Berkeley Street production, the contributions by censorship, foreign press, radio broadcasts and agents being trivial in comparison with our material.

There is evidence that people here, who already are reading and translating around a thousand JIG repeat JIG commercial items per day, are beginning to build up JIG economic picture.

Here is another case in which, unless we approach this problem with imagination and energy, they are going to steal the show.

Problem is principally one of translation, since large part of stuff comes in clear and code problems are either not serious or can be licked. When sure that with help of State Department, with vigorous efforts to find personnel without being scared by shadows (and security problem could be taken care of easily by putting this translation operation in place away from Arlington) and with MSVCL selling job that should be easy in light of evidence of what British have been able to do, this JIG commercial picture could be built up into one of best intelligence sources available. Whole job except decoding could be handled by Special Branch if translating talent were found, and translators of ability might be willing to participate in work that would involve both translating and adding up the produced intelligence. Strongly recommend that you consider this in prayerful conference with powers, including Adolph Berle.

JIG commercial part of White's section describes itself also [as a] Translation Bureau and consists of six translators and two lady clerks. Principal translators are Captain Rayment and Captain Shaw, both of Navy, and a civilian who I believe is an ex-consul. When war began Shaw was serving as Chief Cryptographer at Singapore. Rayment was officer of Naval Intelligence and JIG expert and translator for Navy. Note quality of personnel assigned to this commercial field.

Believe their traffic comes from Point Grey and other west/coast Canadian stations and is sent over every week or ten days by bomber. Great majority of items are in plain language. Material in four figure code thought to be mercantile marine code, in which page start with 111 or 110 are of interest to Park and are sent up there. Some of material is in NYK RPT or OSK RPT OSK codes, and occasionally there are items in one of the other MITS RPT MITS. Some messages are in public commercial codes. In cases of both MITS, both old and new books are used, old ones for Europe. I understood them to say that in both cases they have old books and have made progress in building up new ones.

Large part of traffic is inconsequential, such as small financial remittances and even greetings. Rest of it concerns mainly commercial transactions, mostly offers to buy or sell, conditions on obtaining licenses. There are however about ten or twelve items per day in ship material from Canada which are important enough to circulate. Examples of these as given were references to ships by name or routing, reports or large financial transactions or of specific completed commercial transaction, messages which give address of military or naval unit or ask for personnel for such purposes as building ships, putting up power house, or contain information or clues to progress of dock repairs, restoration work on mines, refineries or something of the kind. Their rough guess on volume of Canadian material is fifteen hundred items per week.

An important source of material is intercept station at Mauritius, which sends it only code or cipher material. Plain language stuff taken down at Mauritius is apparently translated there and sent directly to Economic Warfare Ministry. What Berkeley gets from Mauritius is mainly in commercial codes, and 80 per cent of stuff of both MITS is picked up there. Much of it involves Indo Chinese peninsula but it covers all areas of interest to us, perhaps twenty-five per cent of material is worth circulating. The two Navy Captains were very vague of figures, but they finally produced traffic register covering the four syllable MIT form, for periods from last August to this May 15, and I counted up four hundred fifty five recorded messages. Could not count number circulated, but my guess would be around one fourth.

Third source of JIG commercial is what is picked up in England, mainly stuff from Continental points. Output of JIG Commercial Section goes in longhand to Alford House, where 'Commercial Section' of Berkeley Street is housed.

The material is typed up and routed to consumers. Taylor will give you in later message important facts re Alford House. Note that principal consumer, Economic Warfare Ministry, gets not only what is produced in White section but also what comes from New Delhi, where as you know considerable work is done on commercial stuff, and also whatever Mauritius turns out from its plain text interceptions. End of story re JIG at Berkeley Street.

Finally got two letters

Note to code clerk: after third, repeat, in part seven text should read 'output' of JIG Commercial Section goes in longhand to Aldford House, where 'Commercial Section' of Berkeley Street is housed etc.

***

Continuing with Denniston's distribution and reference section: this section keeps indexes of all circulated material.

This work is done in longhand, mainly by the two girls, but it may interest Huddleston to know that Foreign Office officials and Cambridge professors, unlike Harvard Law School graduates, are not above putting pen to paper in order to produce good indexes. I have examined a number of index cards and hereby pronounce that a good workable index can be maintained in longhand and that it would not be any great intellectual feat, though it would take time, to devise system under which what our girls do not now index could be indexed in our own geographical sections by men who follow the material and without occupying many of their minutes during any day.

***

One of the indexes is a name file of all name references in special material, in which important events in lives of senders of messages are noted and also all references in messages to individuals, on cards under their names. In cases like those of our favorite oriental author* [FN Hirohashi, Japanese ambassador in Berlin] his trips and important interviews are noted. Collateral information is also noted, in much the way Durant's section … job, though job is keyed on lower scale and they have advantage of working with file that goes back before last war. They now have 19,000 names in file, of course after eliminating those who are permanently dead. Subject indexes are kept, based not only on Berkeley Street material but also on cables of various government officers.

By far the largest subdivision in index is Treaties and under it, by countries, are set forth all details about treaties and negotiations for treaties among various governments.

By all details I mean dates and important subjects dealt with, but of course cards do not attempt to cover any whole subject further that is necessary to refer index user to underlying material. Index cards give references by dates and serial numbers to source material. Next to treaties the largest headings are 'Conventions – Economic' and conferences. While it may seem like going into too great detail I believe that it would be useful for our people to have exact idea of subjects considered important index headings, and I therefore set them forth:

> Air Associations and Federations; Banks; Budgets; Churches; Commissions and Committees; Communists; Anarchists; Espionage Plots Outrages etc (we were told confidentially that this elaborate heading is really designed to cover subject of enemy spy organizations in various countries); Concessions and Contracts; Conventions; Coups D'Etat; Ciphers; Debts; Delegations and Missions; Disarmament (including sub-headings for disarmament conferences); Economic (under which subject headings are almost all names of commodities, with oil comprising by far the largest amount of material, but with some non commodity subjects such as 'mergers'); Economic Number Two under which information is indexed by countries; Exhibitions; Expeditions; Finance; Frontiers and Frontier Incidents; Jews; League of Nations; Loans; Mandates; Military and Military Missions; Naval; Opium; Press; Propaganda; Railways; Refugees; Revolutions, Plots etc; Shipping; Slavery; Supply of Munitions; Tariffs and Customs; Telegraph, Telephone Lines and Wireless; Traffic in Arms and Trials.

Please have Huddleston meditate in more prayerful attitude than usual on lessons to be learned from these headings.

Note that under Treaties headings they put not only treaties and negotiations as such but also all relations between governments not otherwise classifiable. Whole impression is that, like everything else that these very practical people do, index is designed to serve its purpose as neatly as can be achieved with minimum waste of effort. Note also that, while they try to keep track of all material for sake of whatever information readily available in indexes, their primary purpose is to supply crypt people with preference file in which they may locate quickly whatever information may be helpful to them in solution work.

Another important reference item is what they call the Cabinet Book. This is [a] record of important officials in various governments throughout [the] world, but it is very different thing mechanically from what Durant keeps. It is big ledger with subdivisions by countries in alphabetical order. When you turn to pages devoted to any particular country you find clippings and longhand notes giving names of cabinet officials and elected officers in order of dates, and you may trace through pages for any country and see very quickly what governments it has had for years covered by book. It is all somewhat disorderly in appearance, but when you examine it you find that, what with clippings from *Times* and *Telegraph* and longhand notations, there is a surprising amount of information in a form where it is quickly usable.

They also maintain a file of ships referred to in material, but here you may doff my hat to brother Snow, because this is the only thing I have seen in England in this general field where we have done a better job. One of the most interesting records that they keep, and from what they say one of [the] most useful, is what they call the Diary. This is a very large bound book in which each day is assigned two opposite pages, on which notations are made in longhand of all the events of that day that might be interesting to one who is working with material that might involve such events. The important subjects are mainly country classifications, and for every day the information about any country or other subject classification is set down at the same place on either the left hand or right hand page. For instance everything about Turkey is always to be found, say, in column five on the left hand page, three quarters down the column, so that a crypt man who wanted to know what was going on in Turkey over a period of two weeks last year can see at a glance what was happening in Turkey everyday, as gleaned from intercept material, government communications, or news reports in [the] London *Times* or *Telegraph,* which are the two newspaper sources that are relied on. Note that these two newspapers are clipped daily for all news of possible diplomatic importance for each country and the clippings put in country file with intercept material and government cables, all in order of dates.

Nothing is filed twice. If an item affects Russia and Japan it is filed under either Russia or Japan but not both. According to rules of thumb evolved over the years they decide which country; but if the same subject involves communications between the opposite Ambassador and his country, they file it under that country.

You can see how little they permit duplication of effort and building up of cumbersome files.

Incidentally, coming back to the Diary, let it also be noted that Diary contains after each item entered the reference to where full information may be found in the various sources on which it is based. Another file maintained is the Who's Who file, which appears to consist almost entirely of Foreign Office printed bulletins which identify diplomats in various parts of the world and other important personages. It seems that British diplomats report periodically to [the] Foreign Office on all important diplomatic and local personalities in their respective countries, giving not what might be called official information but also whatever else may contribute to

Foreign Officers store of useful knowledge. For example, of one diplomat it was stated that he had a youngish wife whose myopia required her to wear very thick glasses and of another it was intimated that his wife was on the frivolous side and 'is not interested in the community problems on which her husband works so indefatigably'. I mention all this as further evidence to the thoroughness with which these Britishers do their jobs.

[The] same section also keeps reference library for use of Berkeley Street personnel. Among books that they have published weekly which deserve note is a manual of current events, known as Kensing's Contemporary Archives, subtitle Weekly Diary of Current Events. This is published in England and covers all events of note in the world. I understand that it is difficult to get a subscription to it now, but please ascertain whether Arlington and Gee Two get it, because I think they should if they do not now get it. There is a library of Who's Who and various reference books of the sort that you would expect, and where they are out of date and more recent editions are now available the staff annotates the books as new information comes in. For instance the German encyclopedia of newspapers of the world *Handbuch der Weltpress*, compiled in 1934, has been kept up to date by staff following all information about newspapers in various countries. Staff seemed to feel that one of their most useful books was *Annual Pontifico*, the Vatican yearbook, though it seemed to me to be no more than a catalog of Vatican representatives throughout the world.

One very interesting set of books is a series that is being published by the 'Naval Intelligence Section' of [the] Admiralty about various countries of the world. This was started in nineteen forty two. I had brief look at books on France and [the] Iberian Peninsula and they appear to cover every conceivable subject that would be interesting to one interested in the particular countries. They are called 'Geographical Handbook Series' and if Gee Two does not have them immediate steps should be taken to get on [the] circulation list. They are not to be sold publicly but are for use within British Government. However Earnshaw-Smith said he was sure that any United States agency could get on [the] list if it wanted to. Another excellent reference book that Gee Two should take steps to get if they are not getting it is an annual publication of the Empire Parliamentary Association called 'Report on Foreign Affairs'. This gives for each country of [the] world a chronology of all the important events during the year. It has a good index and would make [an] excellent reference book, especially for Arlington. Another publication that [I] noticed, and I think Foreign Office gets it out every so often, is *Q Book of Geographical Names*. They say that it is much used in identifying places referred to in messages.

Smith's section also receives foreign language press of various countries and (this is interesting) sends it to interested sections where it is read by crypt people or translators in order that they may keep up with developments in the respective countries. They do not cover German press, which is very thoroughly covered by other Government agencies, but they read at least one newspaper from principal cities in each other country in which they are interested. Note: I now have figure for present message numbers in Denniston's outfit to wit 117,000 odd, indicating that in last fifteen months some 17,000 messages have been circulated.

Continuing: in addition to files and indexes kept up by distribution and reference section, each geographical section maintains whatever files it may think helpful. We did not get a chance to see what files are kept, but have impression that long organized sections have built up [a] substantial amount of reference material.

All foregoing may seem to you too detailed to justify use of cables, but we are anxious to give you as full a picture as possible in order that you and Corderman may ask any questions that occur to you or suggest what further lines of investigation we should pursue.

[The] whole key to this British operation lies in the infinite pains which they take with the files while never losing sight of their very practical objectives.

***

Herein report on Near Eastern Section of Denniston's show. Understand you have had through Johnson full information on cryptographic method which I am including cryptographic information given me for what it is worth. Section comprises eighteen people of whom seven are linguists and do the book breaking and translating, ten are decoders and clerical, and one is keybreaker for Turkish traffic. Section handles Turkey, Saudi Arabia, Iraq, Egypt, Iran, Afghanistan, [and] as minor sidelines Syria, Transjordan, Nepal and Ethiopia. Head of Section Dr Thacker is Professor of Semitic languages at Durham University and can do all three languages involved to wit Turkish, Persian and Arabic but specializes in Arabic PYIOT KISH. Most important branch comprises one keybreaker, five decoders and clerks and three translators and bookbreakers; Thornhill, a clergyman and former pupil of Thacker's at Durham has learned Turkish in last two years, Simpson, geographer at University of London has learned Turkish since war began, Gungry learned Turkish recently at School of Oriental Studies formerly in London now in Cambridge.

Persian section three decoders and two translators; Humphreys, elderly and only permanent employee, was Archivist [at the] British Embassy Persia for many years and knows other Near Eastern languages as well as Hindustani, Russian and many others, Boyle learned Persian at [the] School of Oriental Studies.

Arabic section two decoders and two translators, Thacker and Dr Lewis lectured in Islamic history School for Oriental Studies.

Turkey uses Turkish except for one code book in French for treaties etc, Saudi Arabia and Iraq use Arabic, Egypt uses French, Iran and Afghanistan use Persian, Syria has not started code yet because has no diplomatic posts but will be in Arabic, Transjordan has no diplomats but Emi Abdullah has private cipher in Arabic which British read but Emir has not yet said anything worth circulating.

Nepal uses simple substitution cipher in English and three messages have been circulated in last eighteen months, Ethiopia has five figure book for traffic between London and Adis Ababa, British have twelve messages but cannot read them.

Turkish section receives fifteen to thirty messages per day, slightly more to Ankara than from Ankara, and circulates from two to twelve per day – perhaps six would be a fair average; majority of circulated messages are to not from Ankara. Principal circuits covered are London, Kuibyshev, Teheran, Budapest, Lisbon, Rome, Madrid, Stockholm also some Berlin, Washington, Vichy, very little South America, Helsinki, Bucharest, Sofia, good coverage Tokyo but very little traffic. Two principal secret diplomatic code books introduced [in the] middle of nineteen forty one called CANKARA and ISMET INONU, both ten thousand group two part codes.

***

In order to comply with instructions in your 2734, I will have to discontinue all discussions with Denniston, since there are no intelligence problems to discuss except those which have to do with crypt and traffic exchanges. Since Denniston is willing to let somebody here read, and if interesting to forward to Washington, all decodes not in special reserved series, the only questions that have been involved have related to whether the Government of the United States was willing to take particular classes of intelligence that way, or whether as to some or all of them it wanted to process the material itself. I will tell Denniston that these problems will be worked out directly by Corderman or perhaps through Taylor. It is disheartening, however, to work hard on getting the facts for Arlington and to get this kind of response.

While you prepare Washington Monument for appropriate part of my anatomy, I will say flatly that Arlington does not (repeat does not) understand the problems involved in crypt and traffic exchanges. For instance, it has just thrown Denniston into a state of bafflement by asking for Iraqui [*sic*] keys. This request would be roughly equivalent – if we still had the Philippines – to the British asking Arlington for Philippine keys, since Iraq is not only in reality part of the British Empire but is the cornerstone, because of its oil, on which the whole Middle East and Eastern Mediterranean situation rests. Denniston, however, wanted to put Arlington in a position to read whatever Iraq stuff it might intercept, insofar as he could do it without going to the Foreign Office for specific authority. Hence he authorized his people to explain the Iraq system to Taylor, and Taylor duly passed the information along, and Denniston felt that he had met Arlington's demands without having to create an issue here. If questioned by the Foreign Office, he could always say that Iraq uses simple substitution which any cryptanalyst who had an Arabic linguist at hand could solve in half an hour, and so he had really only told Arlington what it could have found out for itself in a very short time.

Now however, Arlington turns this matter into a major issue by a formal request for keys, forcing Denniston either to put himself on record as refusing something that Arlington specifically asked for or to create an issue by asking the Foreign Office for permission. If Denniston is right about the difficulty of solving the Iraq system, what sense does all this make?

Some of these Britishers, I think perhaps including Denniston, think we in Washington are a little bit at loose ends, and what do you suppose I would think, if my thoughts made any difference, when I get three cables in short succession, one of which says that cables were omitted because nobody asked for them, the second says they were omitted because the parties were exchanging them through censorship, and the third says they were omitted by common consent. Jesus. Taylor has been talking to Denniston about the Iraq matter and he is holding it in abeyance until Taylor gets back and has further talks, after which Taylor will communicate with Corderman.

***

Iranian principal diplomatic book has been photographed and was sent today to Baker Peter for transmittal to Washington. Have been discussing smaller enemies and will have further information next week. Reference FLORADORA agreement Berkeley Street has sent off two batches for you and are sending specially about eight Dublin items at my request; they are interested to know how Arlington is coming on its share of back traffic, which is to be interchanged on fortnightly basis enciphered with forty figure subtracter. Washington does not figure subtracter, Washington does not hold ISMET which is perhaps the more secret of the two except at London which treats CANKARA as more secret, Tokyo has neither and uses one of three older books of same type enciphered with five to forty figure subtracter and used except at Tokyo only for administrative traffic. Subtracter changed at frequent intervals. In addition Turks have French book for treaties, obsolete consular book, and military attaché book held at all capitals one part thirty thousand groups enciphered with short subtractor or by switching order of figures within the groups.

Saudi Arabia intake fifteen to twenty messages per day, circulate two or three per day. Capital is at Riyadh but King nomads around and traffic may center at Taif summer residence, Mecca during pilgrimages, or Jedaah where foreign diplomats are kept. Circuits are to Ankara, London, Baghdad, Cairo, Damascus, Jerusalem and Vichy (now defunct). Principal code is two years old three letter two thousand random groups used unenciphered, also two new books used at Ankara two letter seven hundred fifty random groups. For administrative financial and less secret political use simple two figure cipher.

Iraq traffic intake four or five per day circulate perhaps one a day. Circuits are between Baghdad and Aleppo, Alexandria, Beyrouth, Bombay, Cairo, Damascus, Jeddah, Jerusalem, London, Kabul, Teheran, Washington and Sanna (defunct). So far this year 21 messages Baghdad to Washington of which British have four, and 34 messages Washington to Baghdad of which British have all but one. Iraq messages are really in clear, they have arbitrary Roman letter equivalents for Arabic alphabet and only element of cryptography is that letter equivalents vary from post to post; also use cover letter combinations for names of people, places, dated etc.

Iran traffic intake about 1,000 messages per month, circulate about one hundred per month. Circuits covered are between Teheran and Ankara, Baghdad, Baku, Basra, Berne, Beyrouth, Bombay, Bucharest, Cairo, Hamburg, Herat, Istanbul, Jerusalem, Kabul, Karachi, Khanegin, Kuibyshev, London, Mosul, Quetta, Rome, Simla, Smyrna, Soleynanieh, Stockholm, Tokyo, Trebizond, Vichy and Washington. Washington traffic about ten per cent of total. One diplomatic and one military book each alphabetical 12,500.

Afghanistan intake five or six messages per day circulate about every other day. Circuits are between Kabul and Ankara, Bombay, London, Teheran, Meshed, Berlin, Rome, Geneva, Tokyo and Vichy, traffic with Tokyo very infrequent and purely administrative. One book which closely resembles the Persian.

I spent several hours reading nineteen forty three output of Near East section. While the Iraq, Saudi Arabia, Afghanistan and Egypt output is picturesque and occasionally interesting I think it is a safe assumption that we can live happily without reading this mail immediately and in any event I will probably be able to send you decodes of anything of interest. Iran for the most part is dull stuff but contains some significant material in view of our present special interests in Iran and I think we should read this as soon as possible. Turkey is definitely an important line; it is disappointing in that messages from Ankara are largely administrative and do not substantially reflect leanings of the government, but traffic to Ankara contains a fair number of very important messages such as interview with Molotov, or with JIG gents in Far East; furthermore a great many messages from smaller European capitals seem quite as important as those of familiar ministers at same points whom we frequently honor with an item in the Bugle. Thacker tells me that since April all Turkish traffic has been sent to Washington, if Arlington has not been getting it please let me know promptly. Subject to your approval I propose to make photographing and mailing to you of important Turkish books matter of first priority and that of Persian books second priority and Chinese books third priority.

***

Friedman and myself have seen Italian section Denniston's show, Friedman will report on personnel headed by Mr Catty and cryptanalytic features. British coverage includes hosts at Madrid, Lisbon, Tetuan, Tangiers, Tenerife, Lobito, Dublin, Stockholm,

Oporto, Seveille [*sic*], Barcelona, Raima, Helsinki, Bratislava, Vienna, Budapest, Sofia, Bucharest, Belgrade, Athens, Rhodes, Istanbul, Izmir, Adana, Mersina, Kabul, and Sanna now quiescent. According to my recollection our coverage of above circuits has been poor or nonexistent. I am told that since April first they have been sending us copies of all their traffic; if traffic is now reaching you I assume it can be read at Arlington as well as here if not please let me know. Cryptanalytic exchange appears to be going smoothly and no pressing problems in this quarter, however I propose to read back files of decodes on above circuits and send you anything of real interest.

This section includes two ladies who handle Vatican. Work started on this line April 1942 after lapse of two years in continuity. Up to December first nineteen forty two British had received six hundred sixty four messages in all ciphers and read five hundred fifty or eighty two per cent. Only sixty four were found worth translating and circulating and these are made to be of little interest; I plan to read these as well as later and current traffic and send you if important. Most traffic is ecclesiastical charitable or personnel. Apparently stuff goes by bag. One system in use London, Vichy, Berlin, Madrid, Lisbon and Washington is not yet cracked because of traffic shortage.

***

Herewith some miscellaneous information on Berkeley Street Brazilian and Portuguese sections, Friedman will report in detail on crypt observations.

Section comprises ten people of whom five are decoders and clerical and five are linguists bookbreakers of whom two do cryptanalysis. No permanent employees. Head of section -ELL is a botanist who has researched on Portugal and colonies. Brazilian largely handled by his wife and one assistant. Enterprise started February nineteen forty at which time all continuity had been lost. As in case of Italian. British have been covering several Portuguese continental circuits inaccessible to us, I will run over these old decodes and send you nuggets. I am told that since April first they have been sending us all Portuguese DIP traffic, but not Portuguese colonial traffic, which can be read here. One basic book for all colonial with variety keys. Am told colonial traffic is most uninteresting but will look it over. Portuguese military use PLAYFAIR at Lisbon and Lourenco Marques, simple substitution at

Atlantic islands, British read both kinds. At end of March this year the Portuguese bought some Swedish HAGELIN repeat HAGELIN machines and have them at Air, War and Colonial Ministries, some Azores traffic in Hagelin has been observed. Portuguese security police in Azores at Ponta Delgada are using ten alphabet substitution, I am told British have sent us the keys for this.

***

Herein the smaller European enemies. Hungarian not read and continuity lost but Denniston expecting return of someone who will soon undertake it; however Hungarian commercials in clear are translated by member of Swiss section and circulated if important.

Paragraph two. Roumanian section consists of Griefenhagen former diplomat and one secretary started nineteen forty having lost continuity and started reading nineteen forty one. Intake zero to twenty messages per day perhaps twelve average. Principal circulation a day perhaps twelve average. Principal circuits covered are to Lisbon, Madrid and Rome, also get some Stockholm, Helsinki, Tokyo and Buenos Aires. Highest grade code not read, is in early stage of reconstruction. Bulk of traffic in two large two part codes called Roger Forty Two and Roger Forty Four, some of the traffic is enciphered. Roumanians follow French practice of numerous and voluminous two part codes. Bulk of traffic which is circulated is commercial in nature, for instance purchases of Spanish lead and blankets and Spanish demands for oil in exchange. So far as is known there is no Roumanian exiled government traffic.

Bulgarian section Woods elderly permanent and one secretary. Continuity since 1934. Small traffic intake circulate perhaps one per week. Principal circuits covered are Berlin, Kuibyshev, Roge, Vichy, Budapest and Bratislava; Tokyo which has new book can't be read and Stockholm can't be read. No Bucharest traffic. Coverage on all circuits very poor; for instance between Sofia and Berlin they got only twenty four out of 450 messages. For administrative purposes an old one part code is used unenciphered, pagination changes twice per month. Secret stuff in newer books used unenciphered.

Woods also handles Jugoslav traffic; diplomatic books not yet read, Jugoslav Army Chief Cairo named Pretnik talks to London and Istanbul in double transposition but British switch the keys. Jugoslav intelligence organization headed by Piritch is housed at Istanbul and is in touch with Mihailovitch, apparently using same system. Three or four Jugoslav messages per day are procured and about seventy five per cent of the intake is circulated. Friedman will I hope supplement crypt data herein. Will look over old decodes of all this stuff. Please advise have sent dozen letters home hope some received.

***

Research section Berkeley Street, four men, two women, headed by Sainsbury. Main job is to take problems about which nothing is known and penetrate far enough so that problem can be turned over to language section for bookbreaking etc, and secondary job is to handle odd sticky problems for language sections. Sainsbury speaks Finnish and his section theoretically handles Finnish Hagelin but in fact is doing little on it; Norwegian Hagelin was dropped long ago and Swedish Hagelin has been dropped as impossible because of excellent Swedish use. In fact Hagelin activity at Berkeley Street appears to be at complete standstill, possibly because best Hagelin man is at 'Baker Peter'. Main current occupation of this research station is Free French; they appear to have made a considerable penetration of principal diplomatic system, but I was told there has been no interchange of cryptanalytic data on Free French with Arlington as yet. System in question is based on four figure code groups, the first figures are reinciphered on a table into three figures producing five figure groups, and this result is transposed on a key derived from the magazine *France Libre*. Bulk of traffic perhaps ninety per cent is furnished by Cable and Wireless Ltd.

Next job scheduled for research station is Dutch about which nothing is known.

***

Continuation of my message on Commercial Section number four eight seven six. Extent of shift from commercial code to clear is most surprising; excluding JIG, out of some 7,000 intake per day only about one hundred are in code all the rest in clear. French and English branch of commercial section comprises four people, intake about two thousand per day, circulate in Charlie Sugar series about two hundred per day. No translation done in this branch, British assume everyone can read French and circulates French messages in French.

German branch ten people, circulates from one hundred fifty to two hundred per day; small amount is MOSSE repeat MOSSE but the bulk is in clear, HISROWAK traffic not handled by this branch in considerable German traffic to Far East, some of which reflects

German sales of machinery; other traffic deals with transactions in grain, mohair etc with Turkey and Spain, seems to be an important line of traffic. Italian section five people, all the traffic they handle is in clear; circulate about one hundred per day, covering BARFDV* with Turkey, special articles, list of other MEW papers which can be procured on request, etc; MEW Far Eastern weekly intelligence summary classified secret ten pages covers broadcasts and other information including Charlie Sugars, arranged by geographical areas within Far East with special sections on shipping and trade with Europe; MEW monthly statement of action taken secret twelve pages arranged geographical sections special sections on relief, contraband control, enemy transactions. MEW also furnishes secret daily Lloyd's Shipping Index showing sailings and locations of merchant ships. MEW also puts out short weekly list most secret summary of comm. Series which has very limited circulation.

I examined March file of comm. Series covering serial numbers 7540 to 8500 about thirty per day. JIG messages averaged perhaps twelve per day, usually two to four each German, Portuguese, Spanish and Swiss, scattering French, Italian, Turkish, Belgian, Persian and South American. Also included occasional Spanish Naval Attaché messages between Berlin and Madrid sent down to Hope from Baker Peter called 'XIP Series' dealing chiefly with German naval supplies to Spanish Navy.

Also hastily examined two days output of Charlie Sugars each about important trade with Spain, and most important purchases of Roumanian and Hungarian oil by Italian companies such as AXSP (Axienda Generate Italiana Petrol) and Sterava Romana. Portuguese Charlie Sugar circulation about fifteen per day, Spanish forty, miscellaneous (comprising Hungarian, Roumanian, Bulgarian, Finnish and Japanese) one hundred per day. Cryptanalytic section five people headed by Hooker, whose routine job is to handle HISROWAK KRYHA traffic but also do other commercial ciphers; for example Italian 1STCAMXI cipher based on Mengrini code used Rome to Lisbon, German MELCHERS cipher used Bremen to Tientsin and Mukden, Italian commercial attaché cipher used by Angelone, and a cipher which lay on top of JIG OKURA book was pulled off and book was turned over to Berkeley Street for breaking.

The six thousand messages rejected by Hooker are sent to Information and Records branch of censorship which re-examines them and sends about five hundred per week to MEW.

Relations between Hope and MEW very close and MEW gives Hope lots of stuff to assist his work as follows: MEW weekly intelligence report classified secret ten to twelve single space legal size pages contains notes covering week's developments, long term five hundred messages. Single messages rarely meaningful and it seems clear to me that either we must rely on British and accept their intelligence summaries based on this mass of material and other related material from other sources, or else we must start a very substantial operation of our own. It would be impossible for us to process or digest the Charlie Sugar series even with several assistants, may be twenty.

***

Iranian principle diplomatic book has been photographed and was sent today to Baker Peter [Bletchley Park] for transmittal to Washington. Have been discussing smaller enemies and will have further information next week.

Reference Floradora agreement Berkeley Street has sent off two batches for you and are sending specially about eight Dublin items at my request. They are interested to know how Arlington is coming on its share of back traffic, which is to be interchanged on fortnightly basis.

***

SECRET

<u>G- Section ('Floradora').</u>

The G Section is primarily Floradora. It started out as strictly an amateur show under the present section head, who is attractive 25-year old Patricia Hartley, whom Tiltman took at the beginning of the war fresh from Oxford and trained in his school. Assisting her in the central direction of crypt work are Lt. Filby, Librarian of one of the Cambridge libraries attached to Trinity College, and 2 civilian men who formerly worked for Barclay's Bank in Germany. The total personnel of the section is 37, of whom 3 are registers of traffic, 17 are code clerks, who are proficient in German, and the 13 not included in the above figures are the following: Key breakers, Fett Erlien [*sic* Fetterlein], dean of crypt people and a permanent employee of great age, who was the leading figure in this work in Russia during the last war and has been with the British ever since, Adcock, Professor of Classics at Cambridge, and Trainor, another permanent employee; three who comprise the liaison section and do practically everything except break keys, depending where the heat is on; and 7 top-flight translators. Including a schoolmaster named Pallinger, and one Potter, who before the war was the German [*sic*] Foreign Office expert on diplomatic English.

Conversations with Denniston

Certain gleanings from conversations with Denniston may be of interest to you, in case you are discussing with Arlington any of the problems involved in diplomatic and commercial.

First, as to Japan, Denniston says that if Arlington wants to divert any talent from present Japanese operations to turn them to JAC (?) he is prepared to take up the full slack and to transmit finished translations of all material here plus anything that Arlington wants to send him for that purpose.

Second, he expresses a desire to give Arlington traffic and information of every kind that has to do with winning the war, by which he means complete exchange of all enemy traffic and crypt information plus anything that Arlington wants to get out of the non-enemy field where, as in the case of Turkey, we have asked for it and stated reasons connected with the war effort.

Third, he agrees that in the crypt field each country wants to establish for itself a position of independence so that it can get and turn its efforts toward any class of traffic that may interest it.

Since in the European field the British have been in the game much longer than we, and can supply both traffic and solution information, he agrees that it is only fair for them to give Arlington the benefits of their experience and also traffic if they want it. The only lines that he appears to draw are these. He has express instructions from the Foreign Office which prevent him from giving cable traffic into or out of London. He is not enthusiastic about giving us traffic on areas which are considered by the British as their primary concern, such as various Near East areas, but nevertheless admits that we are now so committed in those areas in their war aspects that, if we ask for that solution information, he will have to furnish it though not including traffic to and from London by cable. As you know, the British have a cable running around Africa and of course have their own communications net over which they can permit the Shah of Persia or whoever else it may be to communicate with his representatives in London or elsewhere. Finally, he distinguishes between information as to solution methods and crypt documents (defined to mean code books and key tables obtained either by cryptography or by S.S. methods). While he is prepared to give everything that they know about methods of solution, so far as Arlington may now or hereafter want them, he does not want to commit himself to give crypt documents except where required for immediate jobs related to the war. It is not clear how much in this case he is influenced by the difficulty of copying some of the books that Arlington might want, though he stresses that point, and his facilities for copying are rather limited; and he mentions some instance of a year or so ago where he had some stuff copied for Arlington which was valuable only as library material and not for current use connected with the war.

In general, he would like to employ liaison on the intelligence side of those cases where liaison on the crypt side does not seem to him desirable. He is willing to let Taylor and another properly vested officer look at all material which is circulated by Berkeley Street, including all material into and out from London which is thus circulated. There is a limited class of material that his office sends to C instead of circulating, just as in the case of Park. He illustrates these by the case of some British diplomat 'dropping a brick' but very likely any case where, from the British standpoint, a delicate subject was involved would fall into this reserve class, and with an American officer reading the material it would only be natural that a new class of reserve material would arise, to wit, those that it might be unwise to let an American officer read. However, Denniston's whole approach is very reasonable and he says he has great hopes that all mutual misunderstandings will be cleared up and the line of liaison straightened out. While the basis for his feeling is not yet entirely clear to us, it is plain that he has been annoyed by the way Bailey and Maidment have handled the exchange problem, without consulting him as he thinks they should, and without giving his people any clear idea of just what the exchange is supposed to cover. Taylor found that Waterfield, the man in charge of traffic, had no list to guide him on material to be interchanged and that he was sending what the various geographical sections gave him. Taylor then went around to the geographical sections and found that they had no very precise idea of the problem and that the section heads were deciding what to send on their guess as to what might be wanted.

This situation needs clarification, and Denniston has said on several occasions that he did not like being unable to deal directly with Arlington on traffic exchange problems or on how exchanges should be handled. He also is very anxious to obtain good liaison with G-2 and has been going on the assumption that Taylor is to be quartered with him to function in that capacity. While there would be no point in trying to work out any revised traffic deal now, certainly not for us to try it, it appears to me that there is some value in pursuing discussions with Denniston along the above lines, so as to test his general ideas by specific cases, in order to carry back a fairly good idea of what sort of deals his authority permits him to make and what the general viewpoint here is on these various problems. His attitude, in my opinion, will permit all important intelligence problems along his alley to be solved satisfactorily, one way or another. Note also that Denniston, more than anybody else here, has turned his people over to us for questioning and given us a free run of his place.

TOP SECRET
ULTRA

Appendix 12

Denniston / Friedman Correspondence

In this correspondence, William Friedman questioned AGD's memory over the Zimmermann Telegram and how it was transmitted.

On 4 May 1958 AGD claimed that 'there were 4 (not 3) ways of transmission &, as you say, 2 bases'.[1] Friedman wrote on 26 May, still uncertain about how many routes were used:

> I note that you feel sure that there were four and not three ways of transmission. This would make it appear that our deduction with regards to the non-use of the Nauen-Sayville route is incorrect. Unless, of course, there is one additional route which we don't mention.[2]

In June, Currier was able to give AGD a copy of the telegram as well as a new book dealing exclusively with it by Barbara Tuchman. Both AGD and Friedman subsequently questioned claims made in the book that code No. 13040 was found by Hall amongst papers belonging to Wilhelm Wassmuss, German Vice-Consul at Bushire on the Persian Gulf. As well as the James and Tuchman books, a BBC radio broadcast on 26 May talked about the Zimmermann telegram and gave a 'very full & accurate details of 40 OB & the methods employed and even the names of the actual performers'. AGD assumed that James has advised on the programme, and both wondered how James had gotten clearance for his book. In July, Friedman and his wife attended a summer symposium for a specially-selected group of mathematicians, including two from GCHQ, and he has given talks on the telegram and other 'certain classified matters'. In a lecture on 27 June 1958, Friedman had read from one of his letters from AGD.[3]

On 23 August, AGD sent his recollections about Room 40 to Friedman:

> But do remember also the origins of '40 OB' – a collection of amateurs with a good knowledge of German and no experience of cyphers collected by Sir A. Ewing in Aug 1914 to study the vast amount of W/T material which was coming into the Admiralty. Within a few weeks, NAVAL material was sorted out & the First Lord (Churchill) instructed us to make a profound study of the methods of the German Admiralty. We carried this out successfully & the staff grew & by the middle of 1915 we began to seek fresh fields where we could tackle the Germans. But we all had to learn the technical side of our job! Not easy work even for enthusiastic amateurs. Out of that small body & a similar party in the W.O. studying the German Army, & you know as well or better than I what has grown up from these sections![4]

On 30 August, Friedman wrote to AGD and queried his assertion that the Zimmermann Telegram had been sent via the 'main line' Nauen-Sayville route. AGD replied on 5 September:

> I know that we received the Z.T. by 4 routes, one by W/T Nauen-Sayville & three by cable of which one was procured by M. W/T interception was then in infancy & results often garbled. Cables were only available to us after delays as they were controlled by censors & not directly by us. I only remember that we did receive a lot of W/T traffic on this 'main line' route but I cannot confirm that we did hear the Z telegram accurately on this route.[5]

Friedman replied on 19 September:

> You make a categorical statement that the 'main line', the Nauen-Sayville route was used. Permit me to say, for your information, that I am troubled by your statement, because in a good deal of research I find no evidence that this route was used. Whenever that radio channel was employed, the messages were carefully examined and decoded by means of a copy of the 'Englischer Chiffre' which was deposited with the State Department by Ambassador Bernstorff. I do not see how a message such as the Zimmermann Telegram would have escaped the censorship which was imposed on the radio route. I know, of course, that a radio route from Nauen to Mexico City was being established but there was so much difficulty in communication via that channel that it was not until months or perhaps years after the Zimmermann Telegram episode that it could be used in a practical manner. Of course, it is possible that Nauen

may have transmitted the message in 13040 via that channel to Mexico City and this was what was intercepted in London. Do you remember anything to this effect? Could this serve as an explanation of your recollection that the radio route was used? Do you recall whether German Government official messages, transmitted via the 'main line', were at any time disguised by 'phoney' addresses and signatures intended to make it appear that they were strictly business messages between business men in Germany and in the United States.

I know that three other (cable) routes were used but it is important for my official story about the Zimmermann Telegram (a revision of the brochure you had and which you returned) to be accurate with regard to whether or not the radio route was actually used.[6]

AGD replied on 5 November:

As to the routing of the telegram, I said in the final paragraph of my long note of recollections that you were in a position to disprove any of my views if you have access to the records either in the State Department or in the Cable & Wireless companies though I greatly doubt if Sayville has preserved copies of all the traffic they received from Nauen. But I am surprised that you consider that all traffic on this route was in the Englisher Chiffre. You say that traffic between Bernstorff & Berlin was in 7500 & you thought that possibly Z Tel. was so sent. Now I make another suggestion which I will develop if you wish – if the German F.O. had the 'nerve' to use the good-will of your Ambassador in Berlin to send dispatches by his bag why should they hesitate to include 'unreadable' cyphers amid the telegrams or radiograms sent in the Englisher Chiffre. Again my memory fails me but I think they did.[7]

Friedman sent his final letter on the subject to AGD on 29 December:

About the Zimmermann Telegram and whether it was sent by radio in addition to having been sent by cable over more than one route: I now have a Photostat of the records of that episode as they appear in documents of the German Foreign Office. A soon as I get an opportunity I'm going to read a long memorandum in those records, dealing specifically with how the telegram was sent, speculations as to how the plain text fell into American or British hands, and so on.

In answer to AGD's 'other suggestion', Friedman goes on to say:

> The answer to your question is that <u>every</u> message sent via the radio route Nauen-Sayville or Nauen-Tuckerton was carefully scrutinized by our communications censorship imposed long before the date the Zimmermann telegram was sent. No, I'm pretty sure the telegram couldn't have gotten through that way. I think I know how the theory that the telegram was sent by radio came to be held but it would take too long to explain it in a letter. When and if we come to England next autumn I'll hope to visit you again and tell you.[8]

Notes

Chapter 1: A Life in Signals Intelligence

1. Attributed to a comment by Garnett Wolseley in discussion about a lecture by Major C.F. Beresford, 'Tactics as Affected by Field Telegraphy', *Journal of the Royal United Service Institute,* Vol. 31 (1887), p. 591.
2. Memorandum by G-2, GHQ, undated but *c.* 1945, 'The Use of Ultra by the Army', WO 208/3575.
3. National Army Museum (NAM), Leith-Ross papers, 8312-69, 'The Strategical Side of 1(a)', undated and unsigned but Spring 1919 according to internal evidence and presumably by Leith-Ross.
4. Intelligence Corps Museum (CM), Kirke papers, Accession Volume 58, notes for lecture by Kirke, 27 November 1925.
5. Friedman's lectures were also published by the NSA for the first time in 1963 and reprinted in 1965 to help provide an authoritative history of the subject. The latest version was published in 2006 by the NSA's Center for Cryptologic History – see bibliography.
6. James Thurloe had been granted control of both Inland and Continental postal offices through a so-called farming system at an annual rent of £10,000 per year in 1655 and retained control after his appointment. He was Secretary of the Council of State from 1652 to 1659 and MP for Ely from 1654 to 1655 and 1656 to 1658.
7. Isaac Dorislaus was the son of the ambassador to Holland and served in the post from 1653 to 1681 and possible until his death in 1688. He was paid £200 per year as Solicitor to the Admiralty from 1653 to 1660 and afterwards, £220 per year, issued to the Secretaries of State from the Post Office revenue.
8. John Wallis was born in 1616 and started his career in cryptography by deciphering the King's dispatches for parliament in 1643. He was appointed Secretary to the Westminster Assembly in 1644 and Savilian Professor of Geometry at Oxford in 1649. Together with his work on conic sections, Wallis published the book on which his fame as a mathematician is based, *Arithmetica infinitorum,* in 1656.
9. Commons Debates lxxv (1844), 1291. Similar sentiments were expressed by the US Secretary of State, Henry Stimson, who closed down the US Army's codebreaking section, the Black Chamber. Years later in his memoirs, Stimson made the frequently quoted comment, 'Gentlemen do not read each other's mail.'
10. In the latter part of WW2, Hitler's cryptography experts wanted to replace the Enigma en masse with the more secure SG-41 cipher machine. However, by that time there were tens of thousands of Enigmas in service. In mid-1944, the German Supreme Command ordered a procurement of 11,000 SG-41 machines for the Armed Forces. Despite these large orders, only about 500 units of the SG-41 were delivered, mainly due to the production problems experienced during the last two years of the war and operators finding the machine difficult to use. See Klaus Schmeh, http://www.heise.de/tp/artikel/17/17995/1.html

11. ADM 137/4701, Intelligence E(C) to G.S.I. e., 10 October 1918.
12. See Ferris, 'The British Army and Signals Intelligence in the Field During the First World War'.
13. The British Red Cross is part of the International Red Cross and Red Crescent Movement, the world's largest independent humanitarian network. The Red Cross and Red Crescent Movement is made up of three parts: the International Committee of the Red Cross (ICRC); the International Federation of Red Cross and Red Crescent Societies; 190 National Red Cross and Red Crescent Societies around the world, including the British Red Cross.
14. He was awarded the Star of the Third Order of the Osmauli and the Star of the Third Order of the Medjidie and with the war medal for the Serbian campaign.
15. Merchiston Castle was the former home of John Napier, the inventor of logarithms.
16. James Alfred Ewing was born in Dundee in 1855 and went from Dundee High School on a scholarship to Edinburgh University in 1872. He studied engineering under Fleeming Jenkin, Professor of Engineering. Jenkin was remarkable for the versatility of his talent. Known to the world as the inventor of Telpherage (a transportation system in which cars [telphers] are suspended from cables and operated on electricity), he was an electrician and cable engineer of the first rank, a lucid lecturer, and a good linguist, a skilful critic, a writer of and actor in plays, and a clever sketcher. Jenkin sent Ewing to South America in 1874 to work on a cable to Montevideo and while doing this work, Ewing became interested in devising telegraphic codes. He returned to Edinburgh in 1876 to take his degree and two years later accepted the new Chair of Mechanical Engineering in the University of Tokyo. In 1887 he returned to Dundee as Professor of Engineering at the new University College and in 1890 went to Cambridge as Professor of Mechanism and Applied Mechanics.
17. Fisher was appointed First Sea Lord at the end of October 1914 even though he was in his seventies. He had previously served in the role from 21 October 1904 until 25 January 1910. He served until 15 May 1915 when he was replaced by Admiral Sir Henry Jackson who served until 30 November 1916. Jackson in turn was replaced by Admiral of the Fleet Sir John Jellicoe who served until 10 January 1918. His successor, Admiral of the Fleet Sir Rosslyn Wemyss, served until 1 November 1919.
18. By the end of 1919 the Admiralty had decided to abolish Osborne, take in boys at 13, give them three years at Dartmouth, then a year in a cruiser. The winding down of the college began at the end of 1920 and it finally closed on 20 May 1921.
19. See Partridge, p. 17.
20. The Osborne Lists are a record of staff at the College and some of these are held in the Archive of the Britannia Royal Naval College in Dartmouth. The Navy Lists are of naval personnel including those at educational establishments. The latter are also held in Dartmouth.
21. A selection of the Osborne College magazines are held in the Archive of the Britannia Royal Naval College in Dartmouth.
22. See Partridge, p. 53.
23. Custance Committee, Fourth Report, 20 September 2012, Inclosure 9, The National Archives (TNA) ADM116/1288.
24. Godfrey's brother John would serve as DNI from 1939 to 1942.
25. A series of figures, numbers or letters which are used in the encryption/encipherment and decryption/decipherment of messages in a given cipher system.
26. A Watch usually consisted of a group of men (watchkeepers) tasked with translating and analysing incoming enemy traffic. The term originated in the Royal Navy system which linked a group of personnel to a period of time.
27. Treasury file T1/11937.
28. DENN 1/2, Churchill College Archive, Cambridge.
29. A group usually of three or more letters and/or figures, sent either in clear or in cipher, either in the preamble or in the body of a message, and serving to identify the sender and/or the recipient.

30. DENN 1/2, Churchill College Archive, Cambridge.

Chapter 2: British Sigint in World War One

1. Two hundred and fifteen wireless stations have been documented in an English Heritage report as follows: eighty-seven coastal wireless (W/T) and/or intercept sites; twenty-two Royal Flying Corps (RFC) home defence sites; forty-one Royal Naval Air Service(RNAS) aerodrome sites; fifty-two RFC aerodrome sites; seven lightship sites; six experimental/portable sites. See *First World War Wireless Stations in England.* English Heritage Report, January 2015.
2. This is generally considered to be a fable of Churchill's.
3. See Hammant.
4. All three German systems: the naval code proper (the three-letter *Signalbuch der Kaiserlichen Marine*); the four-letter *Handelsverkehrsbuch,* used by both naval and merchant vessels; a five-figure naval attaché cipher (the *Verkehrsbuch*) fell into British hands early in the war but their successors were broken through cryptanalysis. All code books were alphabetical until 1917 when the *Signalbuch* was replaced by the three-letter 'hatted' *Flottenfunkspruchbuch* (FFB). While other complications were introduced, Room 40 gradually mastered most German naval cryptographic methods. The main limitation was the volume of messages which could be intercepted at the Y stations at Hunstanton (HQ), Mercar in Aberdeen, Stockton-on-Tees and Cambridge.
5. DENN 1/2, Churchill College Archive, Cambridge.
6. This view was taken by historians because MI1(b)'s contribution to diplomatic Sigint had been forgotten.
7. This is probably Admiral Sir Sydney Fremantle, who was assigned to the Signal Division in the Admiralty and responsible for compiling secure code and cipher books. See Fremantle, p. 172.
8. See Ewing, *The Man of Room 40.*
9. Oliver had been Director of the Intelligence Division (DID), the senior Division of the Naval Staff. His taciturn manner resulted in the nickname 'Dummy' and he was apparently very poorly dressed. He was a hard worker and former Admiral of the Fleet who lived to the age of 100. His principal deputy was Captain Thomas Jackson, Director of the Operations Division (DOD).
10. Admiral Sir Arthur Wilson, a former First Sea Lord and before that, Commander-in-Chief of the Channel Fleet. Retired in 1912 at 70 but returned in an unofficial and unpaid capacity in November 1914 to help his friend, Oliver. Dedicated and tough, he was known on the Lower Deck as 'Old 'Ard 'Art'.
11. See Churchill, Vol. 1, p. 361.
12. Hall was born at Britford, Wiltshire, on 28 June 1870. He was the elder son of Captain William Henry Hall, RN, the first Director of the Intelligence Division at the Admiralty. The Admiralty Board decided to set up a section under Hall Sr. in 1882 to collect and sift reports from abroad and to provide them with up-to-date information about foreign fleets in the event of potential conflict. Hall Jr signed on in 1884 and after rising through the ranks, was promoted to Commander in 1901 and appointed to HMS *Magnificent,* flagship of the Second-in-Command, Channel Fleet. He was promoted to captain in 1905 and installed by the First Sea Lord, Sir John Fisher, as Inspecting Captain of the new Mechanical Training Establishment. In 1913 he was appointed captain of the new battlecruiser *Queen Mary.* The British naval historian Patrick Beesly met Hall once and provides a colourful description of him. See Beesly, p. 36.
13. Ewing had been made a Commander of the Bath in 1906 and Knight Commander of the Order in 1911.
14. GCHQ is in possession of two 1907 reports from Simla dealing with Russian ciphers which provide a useful insight into modern Sigint. They were distributed to headquarters in India and via the India Office to the War Office and possibly the Admiralty.

15. This system was probably the German training cipher known from the discriminant used in exercise traffic as ÜBCHI (Übungschiffrierung). MO5 had obtained a German army staff manual before the war and it was studied for 'many weary hours' by Major Walter Kirke, Macdonagh's assistant in the 'Special Section'.
16. John Ferris, 'The British Army and Signals Intelligence in the Field during the First World War,' *Intelligence and National Security*, 3/4 (1988).
17. Intelligence E (c) to G.S.I.e, 10.10.18, TNA ADM 137/4701.
18. The only primary sources available are: three folders of MI1(b)'s own papers, a few MI1(b) diplomatic decrypts and information on its 1919 work and staffing recorded in the course of the discussions about establishing GC&CS; History of MI1(b), HW7/35 written between November 1919 and January 1923 (it is quoted in a War Office paper of that date 'History of the Cryptographic and Wireless Intelligence Organisation', HW 3/39) possibly by Maj. G.L. Brooke-Hunt); Hay's notes and his wife's book.
19. The War Office destroyed the relevant records after the end of the war. It is likely that as in Aden, cryptanalysis was used to detect attempts to evade censorship.
20. This was the so-called ADFGVX cipher, a complicated combination of substitution and transposition with frequently-changing keys.
21. Macdonagh would later serve as DMI from January 1916 until September 1918.
22. The MI1(b) files were destroyed during the Blitz, along with the rest of the War Office's intelligence archives, and those of other arms of service as well.
23. Hay would later contest with AGD for a new post which would head a combined army/navy intelligence section. He would also go on to be an eminent historian, publishing a number of major historical works. Hay was admired by his staff and considered to be a good chief and was given charge of constructing codes and ciphers for British forces early in 1917.
24. A 'crib' is a guessed word or phrase contained within an encrypted message.
25. See Alice Hay.
26. History of MI1(b), TNA HW 7/35, written between November 1919 and January 1923 (it is quoted in a War Office paper of that date (History of the Cryptographic and Wireless Intelligence Organisation, TNA HW 3/39)).
27. Hay made notes for much of the war which were published in a biography by his widow in 1971, together with some of her own views. See Alice Hay. The earliest surviving American telegram is from their Ambassador in London to Washington, sent on 23 January 1916. (TNA HW 7/17)
28. History of MI1(b).
29. Ibid.
30. Regrettably, while the Admiralty preserved the archives of Room 40, the Army chose to destroy most of the original intelligence files of MI1(b). Only twenty-five of the 3,330 (at least) files of codebreakers at GHQ France survive. Only four of the 400 weekly reports of the codebreakers in the Middle East on traffic analysis and cryptanalysis survive.
31. DENN 1/3, also DENN 1/2, Churchill College Cambridge Archive Centre (CCAC). Some messages dated between August 1915 and January 1916 are available at TNA (HW 7/5, HW 7/6). Around five of the thirty staff were working on German diplomatic messages (similar to MO6(b)'s effort against American telegrams).
32. TNA HW 3/184.
33. Ibid.
34. See Hay.
35. One of the most skilled MI1(b) cryptanalysts was Captain G.L. Brooke-Hunt. He solved the so-called FürGOD cipher in early 1917 which was used for messages sent around three times a week from a powerful German station at Nauen outside Berlin to German wireless stations with the callsign GOD. A message arranging for a submarine to bring rifles and ammunition to a Moroccan nationalist was passed to Hall at the Admiralty and the submarine was duly intercepted and sunk.

36. A hatted code is arranged in other than numerical (or alphabetical) order. A 'hat code-book' is characterized by the fact that when the plain-language terms are arranged in alphabetical order the code groups are not in numerical (or alphabetical) order; i.e. a two-part code. A recipherment conceals the true character and figures or letters of an encoded message by applying a key or subtractor (usually by non-carrying addition or subtraction) or by any system of transposition or substitution.
37. These were standard in format throughout the armies and similar to those still used in WW2, but easily modified locally by changing meanings or by encryptment. They consisted of trinomes or trigraphs together with encipherment tables. Similar codes were used for air-to-ground communications.
38. DENN 1/2, Churchill College Archive, Cambridge.
39. See Appendix 1. GCHQ regard this as their own charter document.
40. Admiral of the Fleet Sir Henry Oliver, 'Recollections', National Maritime Museum, OLV 12.
41. The Heligoland Bight is a stretch of water off Germany's main North Sea naval base of Wilhelmshaven, a coastal town in Lower Saxony.
42. DENN 1/2, Churchill College Archive, Cambridge.
43. Ibid.
44. Churchill, Vol. I, p. 115
45. DENN 1/2, Churchill College Archive, Cambridge.
46. Ibid.
47. 'Dilly' Knox was one of four sons of the Bishop of Manchester. Of his brothers, Edmund became editor of *Punch* magazine, Wilfred was a Church of England theologian and Ronald was a Catholic clergyman who translated the New Testament for Catholics.
48. See Fitzgerald on the Knox brothers.
49. Frank Birch had enlisted in the RNVR at the outbreak of war and served at sea in the Atlantic and at the Dardanelles. He was a Fellow at King's from 1915 to 1934 and a lecturer in History from 1915 to 1928. In the 1930s he left Cambridge to work in the theatre. He worked in Room 40 from 1916 to 1919 and was Head of the Naval Section at BP during WW2 from 1942 to 1945.
50. Frank Adcock had become a King's Fellow in 1911 and held the Chair of Ancient History from 1925 to 1951. He came from a Methodist background and excelled academically.
51. Montgomery was 44 and the author of studies of St Augustine and a translator of Albert Schweitzer.
52. De Grey was a favourite of Hall, and went on to take charge of the Mediterranean Section. He had studied languages and was fluent in French and German.
53. Clarke is the source of much of the information about recruits to Room 40. See CLKE 1 ,2 and 3, Churchill College Archive, Cambridge.
54. DENN 1/2, Churchill College Archive, Cambridge.
55. See Churchill, Vol. 1, p. 414.
56. Ibid., p. 500.
57. The Dogger Bank is a large sandbank in a shallow area of the North Sea about 100km off the east coast of England.
58. See Churchill, Vol. 1, p. 559.
59. Ibid., p. 560.
60. Ibid., p. 264.
61. Ibid., p. 175.
62. See Ewing, *The Man of Room 40*.
63. AGD and Clarke, the two chroniclers of Room 40, never offered a complimentary assessment of Ewing's contribution and it appears he was not held in the highest regard. He presided over Edinburgh University until his retirement in 1929 and died in 1935.
64. Clarke papers, Churchill College, Cambridge.
65. The Zimmermann Telegram has been written about by numerous authors. James claimed his account was the first, probably followed by Hendrick. Friedman and Mendelsohn's

account is considered by most historians to be close to definitive. Barbara Tuchman wrote an entire book on the subject and more accounts have been provided by Beesly, Gannon and Ramsay. Friedman was still querying aspects of it with AGD in the 1960s.

66. Code 7500 was one of a series of two-part codes used by the Germans. The two parts consist of 1) a set of 10,000 phrases in alphabetic order and numbered from 0000 to 9999, the numbers being entirely mixed up so that they have no numerical sequence; and 2), the same phrases fitted with the same numbers as before, but this time with the numbers in sequence and the phrases mixed up. The first part is used for encrypting, i.e. sending a message, the second for decrypting, i.e. reading a message.
67. This route was revealed during an elaborate investigation by the German Constituent Assembly in 1919-20 into the responsibility for the war and the part played by the Zimmermann Telegram. Among its published documents is a note which reveals the other route used by the German Foreign Office (Vol. II, p. 1337, 'Official German Documents Relating to the World War'. Translated under the supervision of the Carnegie Endowment for International Peace, Division of International Law). 'Instructions to Minister v. Eckardt were to be taken by letter by way of Washington by U-Boat on the 15th January; Since the U-Boat *Deutschland* did not start on her outward trip, these instructions were attached on January 16 to telegram No. 157, and through the offices of the American Embassy in Berlin telegraphed to Count Bernstorff by way of the State Department in Washington'. The German Government frequently used the American State Department to send messages to its Ambassador Bernstorff as it had no cable links to the US. They went through British cable facilities and the British didn't mind as they could read all of the traffic. The messages should have been handed to the American Embassy in plain text to be enciphered with an American code before transmission. However, President Wilson, who was in effect, his own Secretary of State, allowed messages to be handed in already in code on the basis that they were in aid of peace initiatives. The Zimmermann telegram was attached to a message which did pertain indirectly to peace efforts in a very indirect fashion. The German Government was informing its Ambassador that it 'promises the early termination of the war and the restoration of that peace which the President has so much at heart'. It proposed to bring about this peace by the institution of unrestricted submarine warfare!! Bernstorff was sent the message on 16 January and told not to inform Washington until 1 February. The Zimmermann telegram was attached to this message (No. 157), put into German cipher and handed to US Ambassador Gerard in Berlin. He telegraphed it to Copenhagen, it then went on to London and finally to the State Department in Washington from where it was delivered to Bernstorff.
68. Code 13040 was an old German diplomatic code which was partially mixed up. The alphabetic vocabulary was broken up into fractions and these in turn into smaller fractions before numerical code groups were attached. However, the original alphabetic sequence of the words and phrases was only partially destroyed. This provided helpful clues when decrypting messages encrypted with the code.
69. A third possible route for the Zimmermann Telegram was by radio between the German station at Nauen and one of two American radio stations at Sayville, Long Island and Tuckerton, New Jersey. See Hendrick, Ewing, James and Tuchman who supported this. While now generally dismissed by historians today, it would be the subject of lengthy discussions between AGD and William Friedman fifty years later.
70. TNA HW 3/177 p. 2
71. HALL 3/6, p. 10, Churchill College Archive, Cambridge.
72. Walter Page was born on 15 August 1855. He worked hard to maintain close relations between the US and Great Britain while the US remained neutral. From an early stage of the war, he urged US intervention on an unwilling President Woodrow Wilson. When the British liner *Lusitania* was sunk by a German submarine (7 May 1915), with the loss of more than 100 American lives, Page called for a US declaration of war. He insisted then and later that US intervention at that time would have resulted in a swift victory for the Allies. In April 1917, when Wilson did ask Congress to declare war on Germany, he used the

arguments that Page had been using for two-and-a-half years. Page became ill in August 1918 and retired. He died shortly after returning to the US on 21 December 1918.
73. Wiseman was a member of the Purchasing Commission of the British Ministry of Munitions. His duties also included intelligence and counter-espionage. (See Hyde, p. 63.)
74. The decoded message actually changes handwriting after a few groups, presumably from Bell's to that of de Grey's.
75. Edward Mandell House was an American diplomat and confidential advisor to President Woodrow Wilson. He played a key role in formulating the conditions of peace to end WWI.
76. According to a biological sketch, published by the NSA: 'William Frederick Friedman (1891–1969), the dean of modern American cryptologists, was the most eminent pioneer in the application of scientific principles to cryptology and laid the foundations for present-day cryptologic concepts. He retired from the National Security Agency in 1955 after thirty-five years of service with US cryptologic activities.
77. See Kahn's paper in *INS* which provides the only source of biographical information on Bell.
78. Harrison was partly educated at Eton and considered to be an anglophile. He was Secretary in the Diplomatic Service and assigned to the State Department. He became Assistant Secretary of State in 1922.
79. Correspondence of Leland Harrison with Edward Bell, 12/154/1916 – 7/8/1918, Department of State, Office of the Counsellor 1909-1919, Record Group 59: General Records of the Department of State, 1763 – 2002.
80. See Yardley.
81. See for example Beesly, *Room 40*.
82. NID Vol. 26. The memorandum is reproduced in facing p. 18.
83. 'A Contribution to the History of German Naval Warfare, 1914-1918', Vol. I, pp. 39, TNA H/W 7/1.
84. 'Thus was built up in the end a system by which momentary or 'action' Intelligence could go hand in hand with cumulative or 'deferred' Intelligence, and both be singly or together at the immediate disposal of the authorities.' (A Contribution to the History of German Naval Warfare, 1914-1918, Vol. I, pp. 48, TNA H/W 7/1).
85. Roskill, pp. 145–6; Churchill, Vol. I, p. 466.
86. CLKE 3, Churchill College Archive, Cambridge.
87. See Fraser.
88. See Clarke.
89. James' biography of Sir Reginald Hall in 1955 is one of the earliest published accounts of the activities of Room 40.
90. Navy List for October 1917. Even though the seniority of the rank is listed as temporary, AGD is still listed as a Commander in the RNVR in January 1920.
91. Hall was elected to Parliament in 1919 and took his seat on 13 March as the MP for the West Derby Division of Liverpool. In October 1919 the University of Cambridge conferred on him the degree of LLD and later Oxford University conferred on him the Honorary Degree of DCL. He died on 22 October 1943.
92. See Churchill, Vol. I.
93. See Scheer.
94. Lecture by Major General D.E. Nolan, 20.3.33, Curriculum Archives, 392-A-19, United States Army Military History Institute, Carlisle Barracks.
95. Barker, p. 180.
96. Memorandum by I9e, 'Enemy Codes and their Solutions', I.18, TNA ADM 137/4660.
97. Memorandum by Second Army Intelligence, 1.12.18, AIR 1/2268/209/70/200; memorandum for Chief, Intelligence Section, AEF, 1.1.18. A.L. Conger papers.
98. WO 157/164. 3rd Army Intelligence summary, 14 Aug. 1918 (including order by Ludendorff, 19 Dec. 1917).
99. *Notes and Records of the Royal Society of London*, Vol. 34, No. 1 (July 1979).

Chapter 3: Between the Wars

1. DENN 4/2, Churchill College Archive, Cambridge.
2. An Anglo-French author, journalist and diplomat who wrote a number of books involving international intrigue.
3. Thwaites to Hall, 14 November 1918; Hall to Thwaites, 26 November 1918; Thwaites to Hall, 28 November 1918, WO32/21380.
4. Field Marshal Sir Henry Wilson was Chief of the Imperial General Staff in 1918, the professional head of the British Army.
5. See Alice Hay.
6. Ibid.
7. TNA HW 3/1.
8. Sinclair was a career sailor who had been educated at the Britannia Naval College at Dartmouth, entering the navy as a midshipman in 1888. His service record indicated that his ability and professional knowledge was 'very good' and other positive comments included: 'steady and trustworthy'; 'zealous & capable'; 'Excellent tact & temper'; 'Very discrete & loyal; exceptional powers of administration' (Sinclair service record, TNA ADM 196/43). He served in the Mobilisation Division of the Admiralty during WW1 and by its conclusion, was chief of staff of the Battlecruiser Fleet. In January 1919, he succeeded Hall as DNI. Hall was pleased and told Sinclair that it was 'not often given to men that they see their job filled by the only man who can do it'. (Hall to Sinclair, 18 December 1918 and 14 January 1919, Sinclair papers MS 81/091, scrapbook vol. 1). His stay in Naval Intelligence ended after eighteen months when in August 1921 he was appointed to a three-year post as Rear Admiral 'S' (commander of the Submarine Service). However, by the late Spring of 1923, it was decided that he should take over from Cumming, whose health was failing, as Chief of SIS in September of that year. Following Cumming's death on 14 June, he took up his new post on 3 September.
9. Rotter and Hope had better claims to be the Admiralty candidate but both were moving on. Other civilian members of Room 40 were keen to return to life outside the Service.
10. Curzon to Walter Long, First Lord of the Admiralty, 24 March; minute by Sinclair, 28 March; minutes of conference held at the Foreign Office, 29 April1919, TNA, ADM 1/8637/55.
11. TNA HW 3/35. Notes of Formation of GC&CS TNA HW 3/33.
12. It seems highly unlikely that the Admiralty would have accepted a non-Room 40 candidate.
13. See Alice Hay.
14. Hay's OBE was actually gazetted, i.e. announced in a Government publication.
15. Establishment of GC&CS covered in TNA HW 3/34 and ADM 1/8637/55.
16. Edward Wilfrid Harry Travis was born on 24 September 1888 in Kent. He was known as Wilfrid to his family and 'Jumbo' to friends due to his rather rotund build. He joined the Royal Navy in 1906 and passed to Paymaster in 1909. On the first day of WW1 he was posted as Secretary's Clerk to the Commander-in-Chief, Admiral Sir John Jellicoe, on the flagship HMS *Iron Duke*. His 1918 report signed by Jellicoe refers to his zeal, ingenuity and ability. He was lent to the Admiralty's Signal Division in 1916 at Jellicoe's request 'for the compilation of cyphers for use in the Fleet'. It is said that he got this posting because he had personally broken Jellicoe's ciphers to show their vulnerability.
17. TNA HW 12/1-3.
18. Code and Cypher School memo by Lord Curzon (C.P. 3105), 3 July 1921 (Curzon papers, Mss Eur/ F.112/302).
19. The 'Geddes Axe' refers to proposals for spending cuts in Britain, made by Sir Eric Geddes who had been Director-General of Munitions and Railways in WW1, and later Minister of Transport (1919–21). In 1921, He chaired a committee which would suggest reductions in public expenditure of £86 million. The eventual reduction in the 1922 budget was £64 million and Geddes specifically targeted the armed forces, whom he had successfully portrayed as profligate spenders
20. By the late spring of 1923, it was decided that Sinclair should take over from Cumming,

whose health was failing, as Chief of SIS in September of that year. Following Cumming's death on 14 June, he took up his new post on 3 September. Sinclair was a *bon vivant* whose nickname 'Quex' was given to him as a young man and taken from a play by Arthur Pinero called *The Gay Lord Quex*, in which the hero was described as 'the wickedest man in London' who subsequently became a reformed character. According to Jeffrey's *Official History of MI6*, he was 'one of the most imperturbable of men' and was 'always appreciative of good service in a subordinate'. He had a stormy private life and had violent rows with his wife in the captain's cabin while serving as captain of HMS *Renown*. Much to his embarrassment he was divorced in 1920, soon after becoming naval aide to the King (Andrew, *Secret Service*, p. 295 and Sinclair service record, TNA ADM 196/43, p. 368, ADM 196/53, p. 199).

21. See Appendix 2 for GC&CS staff list for 1919 (Curzon to Lee, 25 April; and reply 23 May; minute by Lee, 2 May 1921, TNA, Foreign Office 366/800).
22. Report of Inter-Service Directorate Committee, 9 April 1923; note on 'control of interception', n.d. [*c*. 1924] TNA, WO 32/4897.
23. The wartime WOGs had in effect become local Sigint organisations, capable of providing a service to the local commander.
24. The Government Code and Cypher School: A Memorandum by Lord Curzon, CAB 24/126.
25. DENN 1/3.
26. Sinclair to Crowe, 3 November 1923, TNA, Foreign Office 366/800.
27. See Jeffrey, pp. 213–14. His source referenced as 'Denniston, "Government and Code Cypher School", 49'.
28. GC&CS 'Historical Notes'.
29. TNA HW 42/1, HW 42/2, HW 42/30.
30. TNA HW 62/20, HW 62/21.
31. H.C. Kenworthy , 'A Brief History of Events Relating to the Growth of the 'Y' Service', 11 June 1957, TNA HW 3/81.
32. See Clarke's memoirs at Churchill College and 'Naval Section 1927-1939 – Mr W. Bodsworth's account', n.d., TNA HW 3/1.
33. Menzies was born on 30 January 1890 in London. He joined the Life Guards in 1910. He served on the Western Front and was decorated for gallantry before being gassed. He was then appointed to a security intelligence position at GHQ and by 1918 he was a liaison officer between the Directorate of Military Intelligence and MI1(c). While in principle a member of the army, who paid his wages, he was a part of 'C''s organisation and formally transferred from the War Office to the SIS payroll on 1 April 1923 as Head of Military Section IV. He represented SIS in collaboration with the main French intelligence agency in the 1920s, the Deuxième Bureau. Menzies was fluent in French and this would stand him in good stead in the years leading up to WW2.
34. DENN 1/4.
35. A One-Time Pad disguises the numerical codegroups of a diplomatic or military code by adding them to a long numerical key. The German diplomatic system consisted of pads of fifty numbered sheets, each with forty-eight five-digit groups, distributed in eight lines of six groups. All the digits on each sheet were random, no sheet was duplicated and each sheet was used only once. For example, the code 3043 9710 3964 3043 might have the key 7260 0940 5169 4174 added to it yielding 0203 9650 8023 7117 (no carry over or tens digits are carried or written down so for the first digit in the example above, 3+7 = 10 becomes 0).
36. A slip is a sheet of paper containing a short description of a particular code or cipher system with details of its external characteristics (e.g. call-signs, preamble, etc.), users and period of currency.
37. John Tiltman could lay claim to being one of the greatest cryptologists of his generation. Born in 1894, he was offered a place at Oxford when he was 13 but as his father had recently died, he left school at the end of 1911 to become a teacher. Following a distinguished career

in WWI, he was sent on an elementary Russian language course which would change his life. On 1 August 1920, he was seconded for two weeks to GC&CS to help with a backlog of translation work. He took to decryption work so well that the War Office posted him to GC&CS initially for a year but he never returned to conventional regimental duties. A biography of Tiltman is long overdue and his accomplishments are too numerous to cover here. He continued working for GCHQ after the war until his retirement in 1964. He was immediately asked to join the NSA as he was living in the US, and served until 1980 when he was 86! He was honoured by the directors of GCHQ and NSA for his 'uncountable contributions and successes in cryptology' and for setting 'exemplary standards of professionalism and performance in cryptology'.

38. The correct spelling is Vetterlein but official British Government documents of the day use Fetterlein.
39. TNA HW 25/6. Some authors have mistakenly credited 'Dilly' Knox with purchasing the machine in the 1920s.
40. Dorothy Denniston's pass, providing access to the Anglo-French decryption unit at the Paris Peace Conference, is on display at Bletchley Park.
41. 'Experience 1920-1939', Brigadier John Tiltman, NSA website, DOCID: 3868631.
42. DENN 1/4.
43. Ibid.
44. DENN 1/4.
45. A small Metropolitan Police wireless unit was initially based in the attic at Scotland Yard and, from the mid-1930s, in the grounds of the Metropolitan Police Nursing Home at Denmark Hill, South London.
46. This was the commercial Enigma with (IIRC) rewired rotors and could be solved using the notes left by Hugh Foss, who had investigated the commercial machine.
47. The steckerboard was in effect a plugboard at the front of the Enigma machine which had twenty-six sockets, one for each letter of the alphabet. By the 1930s, ten pairs of letters were pugged together adding 150.7 million, million additional possible configurations to the machine.
48. TNA HW 62/21, 62/20, (previously called Q/2000).
49. TNA N.I-XV – GC&CS Naval Sigint History, Vols. I–IV (previously Documents Relating to Naval Section, 1915-1939, No. 21, 16.11.27).
50. TNA HW 62/19 (previously called Q/2000, paper dated 'End of 1927', para. 4).
51. TNA HW 62/19 (previously called Q/2000, 29.4.32).
52. TNA HW 62/10 (previously called Q/2062, 21.6.32).
53. TNA N.I-XV – GC&CS Naval Sigint History, Vols. I–IV (Naval Special Intelligence, 1.10.32, also NID Vol. 26, 9.12.36).
54. TNA HW 62/19 (previously called Q/2064, 21.6.32, 7.11.34).
55. TNA HW 62/21 (previously called Q/2020, 11.1.38).
56. A series of figures or letters (or a group or single unit of such) which is added non-carrying figure by figure or letter by letter to the figures or letters of code groups in the process of re-enciphering or to the letters of plain language in the process of enciphering, and subtracted from the cipher in the processes of stripping and deciphering.
57. TNA HW 62/21 (previously called NID 00714/39 (Q/2000. 30.6.39)).
58. TNA HW 62/21 (previously called Q/2000, 1.7.38).
59. TNA HW 62/20 (previously called Q/2000, 20.11.36).
60. TNA HW 62/21 (previously called Q/2000, 17.7.39).
61. TNA N.I-XV – GC&CS Naval Sigint History, Vols. I–IV (previously Documents relating to Naval Section, 1915–1939, No. 1, pp. 8).
62. TNA N.I-XV – GC&CS Naval Sigint History, Vols. I–IV (previously Documents relating to Naval Section, 1915–1939, No. 65, 17.10.38).
63. TNA HW 62/21 (previously Q/2064, 14.2.38, W.F. Clarke to AGD in a covering letter enclosing letter from one of his staff, Lieutenant Commander M.G. Saunders).

64. TNA HW 62/10 (previously Q/2064, 28.4.38, pp. 13, 15).
65. DENN 1/4.
66. E.R.P. Vincent, unpublished memoirs, pp. 77–8.
67. Peter Twinn was the first mathematician to be recruited by GC&CS between the wars and arguably, was the first person in Britain to break a message encrypted by an Enigma machine which included a plugboard.
68. BP had been bought by Sir Herbert Leon, a wealthy London stockbroker and his second wife Fanny around 1882, along with 581 acres of land. They had added servants' and domestic quarters and further extensions. The mansion was described by one former GC&CS employee as ghastly and another as indescribably ugly. Apparently, the Leons travelled abroad extensively, would see some architectural feature which they liked and would return home with a sketch of it for their builders to implement. Sir Herbert died in 1926 and his wife carried on running the estate until her death in January 1937. Sir Herbert's heir, his son, George, duly sold off the bulk of the estate at auction by splitting it into lots. Lot 1, which initially didn't sell and consisted of 55 acres including the mansion, stable yard and lake, was bought by a consortium of local builders and developers headed by Captain Herbert Faulkner.
69. Property transfer documents from Land Registry (Leicester Office), Bletchley Park, Title no. BM677; Sinclair's will, 4 Nov. 1938.
70. HW 3/83 (Josh Cooper Reminiscences, written in 1975).
71. The Munich Agreement was a settlement reached by Germany, Great Britain, France, and Italy that permitted German annexation of the Sudetenland in western Czechoslovakia.
72. Conduct of Work No. 46, 15.11.39. 'Army Interception History, Chapter II, pp. 1–3'.
73. See Kahn.
74. System by which the starting position of the Enigma machine is encrypted or concealed before being sent to recipients of specific encrypted messages.
75. The Reichswehr was the German Army from 1919 until 1936, when it was renamed the Wehrmacht.
76. TNA HW 25/12.
77. Ibid.
78. Ibid. See also Foss, 'Reminiscences on Enigma' in Erskine and Smith, p. 45. Foss joined GC&CS in 1924 and was tasked with examining an Enigma machine in 1927 by Travis.
79. Knox memo, 13 January, 1939, TNA HW 25/12.
80. 'The breaking up of the German cipher machine "ENIGMA" by the cryptological section in the 2nd Department of the General Staff of the Polish Armed Forces', S.A. Mayer, memo, 31 May, 1974, TNA HW 25/12.
81. DNI at this time was Rear Admiral John Godfrey. A number of authors who wrote about this meeting years later, mistakenly believed that it was not Sandwith who attended the meeting, but the future head of MI6 Stewart Menzies, in disguise as a distinguished British professor.
82. The ring around each Enigma wheel had 1–26 (Army/Air Force) or A–Z (Navy) embossed on it and could be set to any one of twenty-six positions. Thus there were 26 x 26 x 26 = 17,576 possible ring settings.
83. TNA HW 25/12.
84. See Rejewski, 'How Polish Mathematicians Deciphered the Enigma'.
85. TNA HW 25/12.
86. The task was assigned to a team led by John Jeffreys and a machine was built to punch out the holes. It was a monumental task and apparently a small party was held to celebrate the punching of the two-millionth hole. The Poles were doing the same work by hand with razor blades! The Zygalski sheet method was called the Netz method (or just Netz) at BP and because Jeffreys led the work, some authors have subsequently confused the Netz with another perforated-sheet method which he developed. The Jeffreys sheet method was actually a catalogue of the effect of two wheels and the reflector. The Netz method was reinvented by Gordon Welchman in his early days at BP.

87. The German military ciphers adopted a new indication system on 15 September 1938 which the Poles attacked with their bomba machines. The reference to Mrs B.B., who has never been identified, refers to Knox's failure to deduce the wiring to the entry disc. In (c) 'machine' probably refers to the bomba, SSD to Sicherheitsdientst (the intelligence service of the Nazi party), and O.S. & n.s. to old and new indicating systems used before and after 15 September 1938. Knox's reference to Polish failure (d) is harsh as the Poles were working with limited manpower and resources. This was stretched further when the German Enigma operators were given two additional wheels, thus increasing the number of wheel configurations from six to sixty.
88. Up until May 1940, the sending operator would choose a message setting and encrypt it twice with the daily setting of his machine. The resulting six encrypted characters would appear as the first six characters in the body of the encrypted message.
89. AGD is probably referring here to Dunderdale.

Chapter 4: Bletchley Park

1. TNA HW 3/1.
2. Foreign Office 366/1059.
3. Due to a shortage of office space at BP, Elmers School, a private school for boys located nearby, had been acquired for the Commercial and Diplomatic Sections.
4. TNA HW 14/1.
5. Knox to AGD 29 September 1939, TNA HW 14/1.
6. Welchman was asked by Knox to analyse Call Signs and Discriminants. The former revealed the designation of the sender and intended recipient of the message; the latter revealed the designation of the specific Enigma setting or key that had been used to encrypt the message. See Welchman and Greenberg.
7. Enigma settings were known as 'keys' at BP.
8. See Welchman.
9. TNA HW 14/7.
10. Official History of MI6, p. 329.
11. Major General Sir Stewart Menzies served as head of SIS/MI6 until 1952. He died on 28 May 1968 at the age of 78.
12. TNA HW 14/2.
13. No copy of Welchman's original proposal to Travis has survived but he documented it again in his own book and other writings. See Welchman, and Greenberg.
14. See Greenberg.
15. TNA HW 3/107.
16. TNA HW 14/3.
17. Ibid.
18. Ibid.
19. The 'Phoney War' was the name given to the period of time in WW2 from September 1939 to April 1940 when, after the blitzkrieg attack on Poland in September 1939, there was little military engagement between opposing forces in Europe. The term 'Phoney War' was first used, allegedly, by an American senator called Borah. Winston Churchill referred to the same period as the 'Twilight War' while the Germans referred to it as 'Sitzkrieg' – 'sitting war'.
20. Admiralty Hydro and Ultra series, 5.1.40–2.7.40.
21. See Chapter 3, Note 78.
22. A Watch was like a shift in the modern workplace.
23. SIS Communications was known as MI6 Section VIII and was based at Whaddon Hall in the village of Whaddon during WW2.
24. TNA HW 3/33.
25. IV LN Versuchs or Luftnachrichtenversuchsregiment.
26. TNA HW 62/21 (previously called Q/2006, 29.9.40).
27. TNA HW 62/21 (previously called Q/3261, 29.12.39).

28. TNA HW 62/21 (previously called Q/2006, 28.5.40).
29. GC&CS Naval Sigint History, Vol. IV, pp. 29–41. Also see Batey.
30. The Foreign Office officials were Miss Emily Anderson, who would later work at Berkeley Street, and her chaperone.
31. TNA HW 62/21 (previously called Q/2006, 22.7.40).
32. TNA HW 62/21 (previously called Q/2065 13.11.40).
33. Q/3213, 1.2.42.
34. Q/2006, 20.5.41.
35. TNA HW 62/21 (previously called Q/2022, 11.4.40).
36. TNA HW 62/21 (previously called Q/2006, 6.10.40).
37. The French party included: Capt. Roger Baudouin, at BP 12 June 1940 to 9 March 1942 then Liaison Officer between Free French Sigint and BP. Died in April 1944 in an aircraft accident while en route to Algiers (by then a Commandant). Wartime pseudonym R. Baldwin; Capt. Bracquerie (believed to have returned to France at some point after the Armistice); Lt. Graverand (returned to France after the Royal Navy attack on the French Fleet at Mers-el-Kébir); Capt. Hutter (believed to have returned to France after the Armistice); Kiefe (believed to have joined the Free French in London summer 1940); Capt. Felix Meslin (at BP 27 April 1940 – 9 March 1942, then Wavendon, then London. Wartime pseudonym F, Miller); Lt. André Mirambel (at BP 27 April 1940 – 9 March 1942, then Wavendon, then London. Wartime pseudonym M.M. Merry); De la Pierre (returned to France after the Royal Navy attack on the French Fleet at Mers-el-Kébir); Roger (Believed to have joined the Free French in London summer 1940); Lt. Jean Emile Royer (arrested in Nov 1940 for a major security breach – no further information. Interned. 'C' ruled in September 1944 that he was not to be expelled to France until after VE Day); Lt. Claude Schaeffer (at BP 1940. Officially joined the Free French Naval Force in London. At BP 27 April 1940 – 9 March 1942, then Wavendon, then London. Brought his whole family to the UK so no pseudonym); Lt. Marc Vey (at BP 27 April 1940 – 9 March 1942, then Wavendon, then London. In 1944 replaced Baudouin as Free French liaison with BP. Wartime pseudonym M.A. Volney).
38. Government Code and Cypher School Report for 1940, TNA HW 14/11.
39. TNA HW 14/9.
40. Q/412, 23.11.40.
41. Q/412, 25.11.40.
42. Q/312, 24.11.40.
43. TNA HW 62/21 (previously called Q/2068, 13.12.41).
44. TNA HW 62/21 (previously called Q/2068, 14.2.41).
45. TNA HW 62/21 (previously called Q/2006, 25.2.41).
45. TNA HW 62/21 (previously called Q/2067, 17.3.41).
47. TNA HW 62/21 (previously called Q/2067, 18.11.41).
48. Sixta History, Section A, p. 16.
49. Q/3175, 5.2.41.
50. Q/3648, 8.2.41.
51. Q/516, 20.4.41.
52. History of I.E. (Intelligence Exchange), pp. 1–2.
53. N.S. Misc., 21.4.41.
54. Allied Sigint – Policy and Organisation, Chapter III, Part 1, pp. 84–5, TNA HW 43/75.
55. N.S. Misc., 8.3.41.
56. History of I.E., p. 8.
57. See Smith and Erskine.
58. TNA HW 62/21 (previously called Q/2006, 31.8.40).
59. People working on calculating machines were known as 'computers'.
60. A network of observing stations had been set up covering Europe and the rest of the world. At certain agreed hours the observers at all stations made a note of the weather and incorporated it into a numerical international code message. This was typically of the form

$IIIC_LC_MwwVhN_hDDFWN$, where III was the number assigned to the observing station; C_L and C_M were the types of low and medium cloud; ww was a 2-figure number describing the weather at the time of observation, from '00' which meant cloudless to '99' which meant heavy thunderstorm with hail; and so on for the other meteorological elements. This taken from an *Autobiographical Sketch prepared by G.C. McVittie for the Royal Society of Edinburgh during 1976/77.*

61. Interview in April 1983. See Cave Brown's book on Menzies.
62. TNA HW 14/22.
63. Hugh Alexander, who became head of Hut 8 and remained in GCHQ after the war, wrote to the Director of GCHQ, Sir Clive Loehnis, in 1963. Margaret Rock had left GCHQ in 1963. She 'bequeathed' Hugh Alexander, as he went on to say in a covering note, 'a fascinating series of memoranda from Dilly Knox written about 1940-41. Dilly was head of the original Enigma party and I suppose the senior cryptanalyst at the time. I enclose for your interest a letter written to the then Director [Menzies] … just so that you can appreciate how well behaved we analysts are nowadays!' Loehnis' reply: 'and you of course can appreciate the advantages obtained from working with an enlightened and sympathetic Directorate'.
64. Jim Beach, 'Origins of the Special Intelligence Relationship? Anglo-American Intelligence Co-operation on the Western Front, 1917-18', *Intelligence and National Security*, Vol. 22, No. 2 (April 2007), pp. 229–49.
65. This involved talks about supply and defence programmes and staff plans. Churchill and Roosevelt had agreed in principle to the pooling of information on these subjects.
66. See Hinsley, Vol. 1, pp. 312–13.
67. Henry Stimson diary, 23–24 October 1940, Yale.
68. In an interview after the war, Sinkov said that the officer who greeted them was John Tiltman. In Currier's account of the trip to England, he thought the officer was Humphrey Sandwith.
69. Accounts by Currier (Prescott Currier, 'My 'Purple' Trip to England in 1941', *Cryptologia,* Vol. 20, Issue 3, (1996), pp. 193–201) and by the head of OP-20-G, Commander Laurance F. Safford (L.F. Safford, in Dundas P. Tucker, 'Rhapsody in Purple: A New History of Pearl Harbour – Part I' (Greg Mellen (ed.), *Cryptologia*, Vol. 6 (1982), p. 216) claimed that the Americans brought two machines with them. Ralph Erskine has argued that based on the weight of the items shipped to Britain, only one machine could have been included (Ralph Erskine, 'From the Archives. What the Sinkov Mission Brought to Bletchley Park', *Cryptologia*, Vol. 27, Issue 3 (2003), pp. 111–18).
70. TNA HW 62/21 (previously called Q/2049, 6.5.43, AZ/393.
71. According to GCHQ, the Roll of Honour in a wood and glass cabinet now stands on the spot where the sherry cask was placed.
72. Sinkov and his group were shown the Bombe machines as their names appear in the Hut 11 Visitor Book, held today in the BP Archive. Apparently this was done with the express approval of Churchill.
73. Ralph Erskine, 'What did the Sinkov Mission Receive from Bletchley Park?', *Cryptologia,* Vol. 24, Issue 2 (2000), pp. 97–109.
74. TNA HW 14/45. AGD's made it clear that his visit to Ottawa would only take place if he could avoid meeting Herbert Yardley, a former US cryptanalyst now working in Canada.
75. Denniston Report, TNA HW 14/45. See also Burke.
76. Pearson to Massey, 23 Sept. 1942, CSE doc. 000221-22.
77. Rowlett was the first of William Friedman's original employees, hired for the Army's Signal Intelligence Service (SIS) in 1930. From 1939–40, he had played a major role in solving a much more sophisticated Japanese diplomatic cipher machine, nicknamed 'Purple' by the US. Friedman and Rowlett also had crucial roles in protecting American communications during WW2. Working with the US Navy, they helped design the SIGABA, the cipher machine which was never solved by the Germans during the war. After the war, Rowlett eventually served in a number of senior roles in both the NSA and CIA.

78. TNA HW 14/45 'Notes on Conference Held August 14/15, 1941'.
79. United States Navy File of Correspondence with Department of State, 1919-1950, SRH-281, CCH Holdings, 74.
80. TNA HW 14/45 'Interrupted Conference with Commander Safford', 18 August 1941.
81. Agnes May Meyer was born on 24 July 1889. She graduated from Ohio State University in 1911 and on 22 June 1918, she enlisted in the US Naval Reserve. After initially being assigned to the Office of the Chief Cable Censor, she on 18 June 1919 she moved to the Code & Signal Section with Naval Communications. After leaving the Navy, she was reemployed as a civilian and worked within MI-8, the 'American Black Chamber'. She learned her trade at Riverbank Laboratories, where Willian Friedman had trained. In 1924 she joined the Research Desk of the Navy's cryptographic section, OP-20-G. She married Michael Bernard Driscoll on 12 August 1925 and after WW2, she worked within the NSA until her retirement on 31 July 1959 at the age of 70. She died on 16 September 1971.
82. TNA HW 14/45 'Interrupted Conference with Commander Safford', 18 August 1941, Para. 6.
83. Safford was informed that as soon as Driscoll's work proved 'in any way successful' that GC&CS wanted to send out one of its best men. TNA HW14/45 'To Washington December 1 1941, 'Your CXG 105 of 27.11.41'.
84. It seems that the Germans also considered a catalogue method. TICOM-I-38 – Report on Interrogation of Lt. Frowein of OKM/4 SKL III, On His Work on the Security of the German Naval Four-Wheel Enigma, June 21, 1945. Frowein had been assigned to check the security of the naval system in the summer of 1944 after the German naval authorities discovered a suspicious pattern of U-boat sinkings. In his interview with Allied investigators, he claimed that he had found a method to read the four-wheel Enigma using rather traditional methods of determining the fast-wheel, then, using a large catalogue of the other possible settings of a machine. As a result, the Germans ordered that only double turnover wheels be used in the fast position because his method would not work with a multiple turnover wheel in the fast position. However, his method demanded a very long crib, an enormous catalogue (some 4,000,000) entries and forbidding amounts of human and tabulator time if it was to be turned into more than a theoretical exploration.
85. National Archives of Canada (Ottawa), RG24, 12,324,s.4/cipher/4D.
86. Col. D.A. Butler (mI8) to DDMI(O), 27 December 1939 as above regarding remarks by AGD.
87. AGD memo of May 1943 in Virginia Military Institute, William Friedman papers, 110, SRH-153.
88. TNA HW 14/45 'Dispatch of Packages for US Authorities at Washington', 28 August 1941.
89. TNA 14/45 'Dear Eddie', 9 October, 1941.
90. Turing deduced that even if the wheel order and ring settings were known, it would take 72,800 hours of work to find a solution; National Archives and Records Administration (Washington), RG38 CHSG, Library, Box 104.
91. TNA HW 14/48, GC&CS memorandum of 16 August 1942.
92. TNA HW 14/74.
93. TNA HW 14/14.
94. TNA HW 14/16.
95. TNA HW 14/20.
96. Ibid.
97. TNA HW 8/23.
98. TNA HW 62/21 (previously called Q2006, 4.4.41).
99. TNA HW 62/21 (previously called Q2006, 7.11.41).
100. Allied Sigint – Policy and Organisation, Chapter III, pp. 109–10.
101. BP's output was known as Most Secret Source and later, ULTRA.
102. TNA HW 62/21 (previously called Q/2006, 10.9.41).
103. The Typex machine was developed initially for the Air Ministry and following successful trails, 350 machines were ordered in June 1938, of which thirty went for trials with the

Army. By October 1939, the War Office had ordered 207 machines while the Admiralty had ordered 630, of which around 350 were intended for use on ships. There was a shortage of machines throughout the war, given slow production. The total cumulative production of the two main models, Mk. II and Mk. VI was 500 by June 1940, 2,400 by the end of 1942, 4,000 by December 1943 and 5,500 by May 1944. The total built by the end of the war was around 12,000.

104. Q/3647A, 23.12.41.
105. Q2073, 19.1.42, Q/2065, 5.1.42.
106. Both the letter and Churchill's minute appear in Hinsley, Vol. 2, Appendix 3, pp. 655–7. A facsimile of Churchill's minute appears on p. xiii of Erskine and Smith. The letter and minute are in TNA HW 1/155. They are Crown copyright and are reproduced with the permission of the Controller of Her Majesty's Stationery Office.
107. P. S. Milner-Barry, '"Action This Day": The Letter from Bletchley Park Cryptanalysts to the Prime Minister, 21 October 1941', *Intelligence and National Security*, 1 (1986), pp. 272–3.
108. Hinsley, Vol.2, p. 657.
109. Ibid., p. 26.
110. All were sent to the Foreign Office, the Admiralty – 4,526,; the War Office – 3,767; the Air Ministry – 4,212; MI5 – 1,166; MEW – 3,639; nine other departments and authorities received a smaller selection.
111. Kimball, *Roosevelt and Churchill,* Vol. 1, item C-32/1: letter from WSC to FDR, dated February 25, 1942
112. TNA HW 3/33.
113. Q/2022, 20.2.41.
114. TNA HW 62/20 (previously called Q/2000, 11.3.38).
115. NID Vol. 21, 1.3.47.
116. TNA HW 62/20 (previously called Q/2000, 18.6.36).
117. TNA HW 62/21 (previously called Q/2006. 23.1.42).
118. TNA HW 62/21 (previously called Q/2006, 10.9.41).
119. TNA HW 62/21 (previously called Q/2006, 9.9.41).
120. TNA HW 62/21 (previously called Q/2068, 24.9.41).
121. Allied Sigint – Policy and Organisation, Chapter III, p. 120.
122. TNA HW 62/21 (previously called Q2006, 1.4.41).
123. TNA HW 62/21 (previously called Q/2006, 30.1.42).
124. Ibid.
125. TNA HW 62/21 (previously called Q/2006, 4.2.42).
126. Head of ISOS and then combined ISOS and ISK from March 1944.
127. Head of Diplomatic Section until the move to Berkeley Street.
128. Responsible for communication lines and all GPO liaison with GG&CS.
129. TNA HW 14/27.
130. TNA HW 62/21 (previously called Q/2068, 6.2.42).
131. Welchman later told Robin Denniston that he had good reason to feel that his father was badly treated: 'It was utterly disgusting – far, far worse than the way I was treated, which was bad enough.' See Greenberg.
132. See Greenberg.
133. See Smith.
134. Paper written for Robin and 'Y' Denniston by Filby on 15 April 1981. He also made the point in a letter to Ronald Lewin on 11 April 1979.
135. Travis was formally appointed Director of GC&CS in March 1944 and knighted in June of the same year. GC&CS was renamed GCHQ and Travis remained as its director until 15 April 1952.

Chapter 5: Berkeley Street

1. Filby letter to Robin Denniston, 15 April 1981.

2. Kennedy's diaries are held by the library of the University of Sheffield. See Ferris.
3. Filby letter to Robin Denniston, 15 April 1981.
4. Kullback was recruited to SIS, based in Washington in 1930. He was responsible for breaking many Japanese codes, ciphers and machine systems during WW2. After the war he became Chief of the Research and Development effort at the NSA, retiring in 1962. See Oral History Interview with Kullback, NSA OH-17-82.
5. Sandwith attended the Pyry conference with AGD and Knox in Poland in July 1939.
6. Discussion paper presented by Captain H.R. Sandwith, 6 April 1942, NAC, RG24, 3806, NSS-1008-75-20. This is a rare contemporary description of British Sigint.
7. Little to Denniston, 18 April 1942, Canadian Security Establishment (Ottawa) doc. 300.
8. Shortly after returning from Britain, Little was promoted to lieutenant commander and appointed Director of Naval Intelligence.
9. AGD to Little with list attached, 6 June 1942, NAC, RG24, 8125, NSS-1282-85(1).
10. In this system, the code groups were enciphered by additives in the usual way, but the resulting superenciphered groups were then enciphered a second time using additives from the same book, but with a different starting point. This method enabled the additive book to produce several million 'double additives'. (A complete book of Floradora additives covered a range from 0000 to 9999 (page 00, row 00 to page 99, row 99, with six groups of five additives in a row). The first half of a book (pages 00 to 49) was used for encipherment, while the second half (pages 50 to 99) covered decipherment. The second part consisted of the digital compliments of the first half (so that additive group 43642 in the first half would be 67468 in the same relative place in the second), to allow addition rather than subtraction to be used when deciphering messages. Unusually, addition was chosen for both operations because it gave rise to fewer errors by the cipher clerks.)
11. 'Report of Cryptographic Mission 0 Maj. Sinkov 1941', 8-10 (HCC, Box 1296, Nr. 3873). GC&CS Report, 1940, German diplomatic section, TNA HW 14/11.
12. Head of the German Diplomatic Section from 1939 to 1942 when she left due to ill health.
13. GC&CS (civil section), 'Report on present position of legibility of foreign ciphers', 25 May 1942, TNA HW 14/38.
14. German diplomatic section minute, 8 August 1942, TNA HW 14/48; AGD memo of 31 October 1942, para 24 TNA HW 14/45; AGD to Tiltman, minute of 8 March 1942, item 7, TNA HW 14/4. According to Filby: 'Denniston received a message from the British Consul in Lourenco Marques, the capital of Portuguese Mozambique on the east coast of Africa. The German Consul's primary job was to report shipping passing the port. Denniston received a letter and a pouch. "Dear Alastair", the message read, "this was dropped in my letter box by a sailor, thinking it was the German Consulate. Are the contents of any use to you?" Remarkably, they contained the daily keys for the next three months which enabled the section to work out the additive lines used in every message sent by the German Foreign Office. With the help of SIS at Arlington Hall, the system was effectively broken. The main break was based on a message from Berlin to Dublin that said that new instructions for the use of 'Floradora' between Berlin and Dublin were being sent in a message which would be like an OTP message. The new 'Floradora' system would then become the principal form of communication between the two centres. Further information about the operation of the system gave the Section all it needed to break 'Floradora'.

See also Phillips.

15. NSA declassified document (SC)A6-1(8)(C) A-N Collab.
16. Tony Kendrick had been an early recruit to Dilly Knox's team at BP and was thus, an experience cryptanalyst. In 1942, he was sent to Canada to take over the running of Canada's Examination Unit from another BP veteran, Oliver Strachey.
17. A junior commissioned officer rank in the US Navy.
18. Hastings was SIS's Head of Codes in Washington from June 1941. He returned to Britain in 1943 and from May he was Head of the Diplomatic section at Berkeley Street. AGD appointed him Deputy Director in March 1944.

19. Mr Friedman's Report of his activities in England during the period Apr.23–June 13, NSA Report Ref ID:A4146452.
20. Informal memorandum by Commander Denniston outlining his original concepts of the American liaison, 21 May 1943: Liaison Activities in the UK, p. 16, NARA RG 457, Entry 9002, SRH 153.
21. Informal Memorandum by Cmdr. Denniston Outlining His Original Concept of the American Liaison – May 1943 and handed to Colonel Alfred McCormack.
22. Berkeley Street, p. 59 in 'Conversations with Denniston': 'Col. McCormack's Trip to London, May-June 1943', NARA HCC Box 1119, No.3600.
23. NAC, RG2(14), 5758, DC135.
24. Kindly provided to the author by the Denniston family.
25. The Section graded and annotated diplomatic translation as follows:
    Explanation of reference: e.g. My No. 249 [Departmental Note. Issued as our BJ No. 105279] or [Departmental Note. Not yet decipherable].
    Textual Comment: e.g. [two groups indecipherable] or [remainder not received].
    Elucidations: e.g. To M. Anastasiadis' [Departmental Note: The new Foreign Under-Secretary]. These were normally inserted by the submitting section (in the third case sometimes initiated by D. and R).
26. There is some confusion about the term JIG. McCormack and Birch seem to use it to refer to the Japanese Government. However, JIG also refers to the letter J in the US Phonetic Alphabet, a radio alphabet used in WW2.
27. Correspondence between William Friedman and Filby, 25 April 1944. In the same correspondence, Friedman tells Filby about a chance encounter he had with 'Y' Denniston on a train and after renewing acquaintance with her, planned to look after her while she was in the US.
28. A Lorenz machine had been offered to GC&CS for producing pads in 1932 and while the Foreign Office declined, documentation and illustrations had been retained. The pads consisted of eight lines of six five-figure groups, each group emerging from a set of five wheels, each bearing around its circumference ten digits in hatted (not numerical) order. The wheels were notched like Enigma wheels to prevent cyclic repetitions.
29. *British Intelligence in the Second World War*, Volume 1, pp 199. This is the official GCHQ line at this time.
30. Lou Maddison, GCHQ archivist. Discussions with R.L. Benson at GCHQ, 6 May 1992.
31. In late 1943, John Croft had been assigned to Scott's team. Croft's description of the system illustrates the sort of systems AGD's team were dealing with: 'It turned out to be a substitution cipher in which the 36 letters of the Russian alphabet transposed as numbers, the message was set out in a sort of three line grid: to this was added the key, and the result transmitted to the recipient. The key, the indicators of which were sent at the beginning of each encryption, was a text which was taken from an edition, in English, of Shakespeare. The indicators gave the page and line with which to start both the encipherment and decipherment.' See Croft.
32. Verona collection, box D101, in a folder marked NSA Technical Library S-7289, a series of papers on individual target desks at Berkeley Street.
33. See Smith and Erskine, Chapter 9.
34. Filby letter to Robin Denniston, 15 April 1981.

Chapter 6: Cut Loose

1. Virginia Military Institute, William Friedman papers, SRH-153, TNA FO371/50209.
2. See Hinsley, Volume 3, Part 2, pp. 616–7.
3. Welchman, Hinsley and Crankshaw, to Travis 'A Note on the future of G.C. and C.S.', 17.09.44, TNA HW 3/169.
4. Tiltman (GC&CS), 'Note by the Chairman: Brigadier Tiltman on Mr Welchman's Statement', 04.10.44, TNA HW 3/130.

5. Bentinck, 'The Intelligence Machine', CAB 163/6.
6. JIC meeting, 22 Oct. 1945, NAC, RG24, 2469, S715-10-16-1-3(4-5).
7. Director's Order 89, 'Eastcote', 24.01.46, TNA HW 14/164.
8. The proposal was that the organisation would be GCHQ in public (at UNCLASSIFIED and RESTRICTED) and LSIC at CONFIDENTIAL, SECRET and TOP SECRET. It dropped out in 1948 partly because it was so cumbersome, and partly because GCHQ was leaving London.
9. COS (52) 152nd mtg (1) Confidential Annex, 04.11.52.
10. Wenger (NSS) to Travis (GCHQ), 05.03.46, Box 101, CSG records, RG 38, NARA.
11. AGD's monthly salary was £80 in 1939, £161in 1942 and £100 in 1943.
12. See Smith, p. 177.
13. Group Captain Jones was Head of Hut 3, 1942–5 and later Sir Eric Jones, Director of GCHQ, 1956–60.
14. DENN 1/4 and also see Denniston's INS paper.
15. William Friedman Papers, Box 3, Folder 16, Geo. C. Marshall Research Library, Lexington, VA.
16. Ibid.
17. In May 2015, the NSA declassified and released to the public an enormous trove of documents from the William F. Friedman collection. Copies have been given to the Marshall Library in Lexington, VA, where they are being digitised and catalogued.
18. William Friedman Papers, Box 3, Folder 16, Geo. C. Marshall Research Library, Lexington, VA.
19. Ibid.
20. Ibid.
21. Ibid.

Epilogue

1. GC&CS Diplomatic and Commercial Sigint Volume I, 1 November 1919 – 30 August 1945, TNA HW 43/4. GC&CS Diplomatic and Commercial Sigint Volume II, 1 September 1939 – 30 August 1945, TNA HW 43/5
2. Jones wrote that 'it would indeed be a tragic and retrograde step . . . if GC&CS were to sink back into its pre-war position'.
3. Kindly provided by Tony Comer, the GCHQ Historian.
4. Personal letter to Patrick Seale and Maureen McConville.
5. Robin Denniston started his publishing career when he joined the Collins publishing house in Glasgow. Within 18 months he had been promoted to head office, and become a close friend of the Collins family, for whom he worked as editor, for nine years, before leaving to head a small religious publishing house, Faith Press. He was then recruited by Hodder and Stoughton, where he was to build a formidable reputation, becoming successively editorial director and managing director. In 1973, he joined George Weidenfeld as deputy chairman, and was then recruited by Thomson Publications to head a string of firms, including Michael Joseph, Thomas Nelson, George Rainbird and Sphere Books. He ended his publishing career in the academic division of the Oxford University Press, where he brought an acute business mind to bear on a department that was struggling, and succeeded in transforming its fortunes.
6. Robin Denniston personal papers.
7. The UK and US versions had different titles. See Page, Knightly and Leitch.
8. Guy Liddell *Diaries,* TNA KV4/466.
9. Robin's spiritual life was ultimately as important to him as his publishing career. Ordained first as a deacon, then as priest in the Anglican church, he became an honorary curate in the late 1970s, before taking on the assignment that he was to grow to love more than all others – as stipendiary minister at Great Tew in Oxfordshire. So loved was he by his parishioners that they persuaded him to return for an unprecedented second term of office after a five-year break.

10. See his *INS* article.
11. Filby subsequently published his account of his days at Berkeley Street. See Filby.
12. GCHQ have given the following reason for not releasing the documents: 'The retention (subject to periodic review) of "Diplomatic and Commercial Sigint" is that it is entirely a cryptanalytic history: it is cryptanalytic techniques that we are protecting.'
13. J.E.S. Cooper, 'Personal notes on GC&CS 1925-1939', n.d., TNA HW 3/83.

Appendix 12: Denniston/Friedman Correspondence

1. William Friedman Papers, Box 3, Folder 16, Geo. C. Marshall Research Library, Lexington, VA.
2. Ibid.
3. SCAMP III LECTURE, SECTION 1 AND 2; ZIMMERMANN TELEGRAM https://www.nsa.gov/public_info/_files/friedmanDocuments/LecturesandSpeeches/FOLDER_021/41700089073941.pdf.
4. William Friedman Papers, Box 3, Folder 16, Geo. C. Marshall Research Library, Lexington, VA.
5. Ibid.
6. Ibid.
7. Ibid.

Bibliography

Aldrich, Richard J., *GCHQ* (London: Harper Press, 2010).
Andrew, Christopher, *Secret Service* (London: Heinemann, 1985).
Andrew, Christopher, *Defence of the Realm: The Authorized History of MI5* (London: Penguin, 2009).
Barker, Wayne G., *The History of Codes and Ciphers in the United States During World War I* (Laguna Hills, Ca: Aegean Park Press, 1979).
Batey, Mavis, *Dilly: The Man Who Broke Enigmas* (London: Dialogue, 2009).
Beesly, Patrick, *Room 40: British Naval Intelligence 1914-1918* (New York: Harcourt Brace Jovanovitch, 1982).
Beesly, Patrick, *Very Special Intelligence* (London: Hamish Hamilton, 1977).
Bertrand, Gustave, *Enigma, The Greatest Riddle of World War II* (Paris: Plon, 1973).
Birch, Frank, *The Official History of British Sigint 1914-1945, Volume 1, The Bletchley Park Archive, Volume III* (Milton Keynes: The Military Press, 2007).
Birch, Frank, *The Official History of British Sigint 1914-1945, Volume 1 (part 2) and Volume 2, The Bletchley Park Archive, Volume IV* (Milton Keynes: The Military Press, 2007).
Boyle, Andrew, *The Climate of Treason* (London: Hutchison, 1979).
Bruce, James Alan, *The Most Important Branch of our Confidential Work: The Government Code and Cypher School, 1919-1927*, Dissertation presented to the University of Salford, 2 October 2009.
Bryden, John, *Best Kept Secret* (Toronto: Lester Publishing, 1993).
Burke, Colin, *Agnes Meyer Driscoll vs. the Enigma and the Bombe*, http://userpages.umbc.edu/~burke/driscoll1-2011.pdf.
Cave Brown, Anthony, *The Secret Servant, The Life of Sir Stewart Menzies, Churchill's Spymaster* (London: Michael Joseph Ltd, 1988).
Churchill, Winston, *The World Crisis*, Volumes I and II (London: Odhams Press, 1938).
Ciechanowski, Jan Stanisloaw, Garbowski, Jaroslaw, Maresch, Eugenia, Piechocka-Lipka, Halina, Sowin'ska, Hanka, Sylwestrzak, Janina, and Rejewski, Marian (eds), *Living With The Enigma Secret* (Bysgosczc City Council, 2005).
Clark, Ronald, *The Man Who Broke Purple* (Boston: Little, Brown, 1977).
Clarke, William, *From the Dreadnought to Scapa Flow: Vol. III Jutland and After* (Oxford University Press, 1966).
Copeland, B. Jack, *The Essential Turing* (Oxford University Press, 2004).
Copeland, B. Jack (and others), *Colossus* (Oxford University Press, 2006).
Croft, John, 'Reminiscences of GCHQ and GCB 1942-45', *Intelligence and National Security*, Vol. 13, No. 4 (Winter 1998), pp. 133–43.
Denniston, Alastair, 'The Government Code and Cypher School Between the Wars', *Intelligence and National Security*, Vol. 1, Issue 1 (1986), pp. 48–70.

Denniston, Robin, 'Three kinds of hero: Publishing the memoirs of secret intelligence people', *Intelligence and National Security*, Vol. 7, Issue 2 (1992), pp. 112–25.

Denniston, Robin, *Thirty Secret Years* (Polperro Heritage Press, 2007).

Dilks, David, *The Diaries of Sir Alexander Cadogan, 1938-1945* (London: Cassell, 1971).

Ellis, Kenneth, *The Post Office in the Eighteenth Century* (Oxford University Press, 1958).

Erskine, Ralph and Freeman, Peter, 'Brigadier John Tiltman: One of Britain's Finest Cryptologists', *Cryptologia*, Vol. 27, No. 4 (2003).

Erskine, Ralph, 'The Poles Reveal their Secrets: Alastair Denniston's Account of the July 1939 meeting at Pyry', *Cryptologia*, Vol. 30, Issue 4 (2006).

Ewing, Sir Alfred, 'Some Special War Work', lecture given by Sir Alfred Ewing to the Edinburgh Philosophical Institution, 13 December 1927.

Ewing, A.W., *The Man of Room 40, The Life of Sir Alfred Ewing* (London: Hutchinson & Co., 1940).

Fitzgerald, Penelope, *The Knox Brothers* (London: Macmillan, 1977).

Garlinski, Jozef, *The Enigma War* (New York: Charles Scribner's Sons, 1980).

Ferris, John, 'The British Army and Signals Intelligence in the Field During the First World War', *Intelligence and National Security*, Vol. 3, Issue 4 (1988), pp. 23–48.

Ferris, John, 'From Broadway house to Bletchley Park: The diary of Captain Malcolm. D. Kennedy, 1934-1946', *Intelligence and National Security*, Vol. 4, Issue 3 (1989), pp. 421–50

Ferris, John, *The British Army and Signals Intelligence During the First World War* (Stroud: Alan Sutton for the Army Records Society, 1992).

Filby, P. William, 'Bletchley Park and Berkeley Street', *Intelligence and National Security*, Vol. 3, Issue 2 (1988), pp. 272–84.

Filby, P. William, '"Floradora" and a Unique Break into One-Time Pads', *Intelligence and National Security*, Vol. 10, Issue 3 (1995), pp. 408–22.

Fitzgerald, Penelope, *The Knox Brothers* (London: Macmillan, 1977).

Fraser, William Lionel, *All to the Good* (London: William Heinemann, 1963).

Freeman, Peter, 'MI1(b) and the Origins of British Diplomatic Cryptanalysis', *Intelligence and National Security*, Vol. 22, Issue 2 (2007), pp.206–28.

Fremantle, Sir Sydney Robert, *My Naval Career* (London: Hutchinson & Co., 1949).

Friedman, William F., and Mendelsohn, Charles J., *The Zimmermann Telegram of January 16, 1917 and Its Cryptographic Background* (Washington, DC: War Department, Office of the Chief Signal Officer, GPO, 1938: Laguna Hills, CA: Aegean Park Press, 1976 and 1994).

Friedman, William, 'The Friedman Legacy, A Tribute to William and Elizabeth Friedman', *Sources in Cryptological History*, No. 3 (NSA 2006).

Friedman, William, *Solving German Codes in World War 1* (Laguna Hills, Ca: Aegean Park Press, 1977).

Greenberg, Joel, *Gordon Welchman: Bletchley Park's Architect of Ultra Intelligence* (Barnsley: Pen & Sword, 2014).

Hammant, Thomas R., 'The Magdeburg Incident: The Russian View', *Cryptologia*, Vol. 24, Issue 4 (2000), pp. 333–8.

Hay, Alice Ivy, *Valiant for Truth: Malcolm Hay of Seaton* (London: Neville Spearman, 1971).

Hendrick, Burton J., *The Life and Letters of Walter H. Page* (London: William Heinemann Ltd., 1925).

Hinsley, F.H., *British Intelligence in the Second World War*, Vols 1–5 (HMSO, 1979).

Hyde, H. Montgomery, *The Quiet Canadian* (London: Hamish Hamilton, 1962).

James, Admiral Sir William, *The Eyes of the Navy* (London: Methuen & Co. Ltd., 1955).

Jeffrey, Keith, *MI6: The History of the Secret Intelligence Service 1909-1949* (London: Bloomsbury Publishing Plc, 2010).

Johnson, John, *The Evolution of British Sigint 1853–1939* (GCHQ History Document, 1997).

Kahn, David, *The Code-Breakers* (New York: Scribner, 1967, 1996).

Kahn, David, *The Codebreakers* (London: Weidenfeld & Nicolson, 1968).

Kahn, David, *Hitler's Spies* (New York: Macmillan, 1978).

Kahn, David, *Seizing the Enigma* (New York: Barnes & Noble, 1991).
Kahn, David, 'Edward Bell and his Zimmermann telegram memoranda', *Intelligence and National Security*, Vol. 14, Issue 3 (1999), pp. 143–59.
Kahn, David, *The Reader of Gentlemen's Mail: Herbert O. Yardley and the Birth of American Codebreaking* (Yale University Press, 2004).
Kozaczuk, Wladyslaw, *W Kregu Enigmy, Ksiazka I Wiedza* (Warsaw, 1979).
Kozaczuk, Wladyslaw, *Enigma – How the German Machine Cipher was Broken and How it was Read by the Allies in World War Two, with Appendices A to F* (edited and translated by Christopher Kasparek) (London: Arms and Armour Press, 1984).
Lewin, Ronald, *The American Magic* (New York: Farar Straus Giroux, 1982).
Mackinnon, Colin, 'William Friedman's Bletchley Park Diary: A New Source for the History of Anglo-American Intelligence Cooperation', *Intelligence and National Security*, Vol. 20, Issue 4 (2005), pp. 654–69.
Macintyre, Ben, *A Spy Among Friends* (London: Bloomsbury, 2014).
Madeira, Victor, *Britannia and the Bear* (Woodbridge: Boydell Press, 2014).
Mathews, Peter, *SIGINT The Secret History of Signals Intelligence 1914-45* (Stroud: The History Press, 2013).
Montague, Ewan, *Beyond Top Secret ULTRA* (New York: Coward McGann and Geoghegan, 1977).
Page, Bruce, Leitch, David, and Knightly, Phillip, *The Philby Conspiracy* (New York: Doubleday, 1968).
Page, Bruce, Leitch, David, and Knightly, Phillip, *Philby: The Spy Who Betrayed a Generation* (London: Andre Deutsch, 1968).
Parrish, Thomas, *The Ultra Americans* (New York: Stein and Day, 1986).
Partridge, Michael, *The Royal Naval College Osborne, A History 1903-21* (Stroud: Sutton Publishing, 1999).
Phillips, Cecil, 'The American Solution of a German One-Time-Pad Cryptographic System (G-OTP)', *Cryptologia*, Vol. 24, Issue 4 (2000), pp. 324–32.
Pincher, Chapman, *Their Trade is Treachery* (London: Sidgwick and Jackson, 1981).
Pincher, Chapman, *Treachery: Betrayals, Blunders, and Cover-ups: Six Decades of Espionage Against America and Great Britain* (New York; Random House, 2009).
Pincher, Chapman, *Treachery: Betrayals, Blunders, and Cover-ups: Six Decades of Espionage Against America and Great Britain* ('Updated and uncensored UK edition' Edinburgh: Mainstream Publishing Company, 2012).
Ramsay, David, *'Blinker Hall' Spymaster* (Harrow: Spellmount Limited, 2008).
Rejewski, Marian, 'An Application of the Theory of Permutations in Breaking the Enigma Cipher', *Applicationes Mathematicae*, 16, No. 4 (1980).
Rejewski, Marian, 'How Polish Mathematicians Deciphered the Enigma', *Annals of the History of Computing*, Vol. 3, No. 3 (July 1981).
Rejewski, Marian, 'Mathematical Solution of the Enigma Cipher', *Cryptologia*, Vol. 6, Issue 1 (1982).
Roskill, S.W., *Admiral of the Fleet Earl Beatty* (London: HarperCollins, 1980).
Rowlett, Frank, *The Story of Magic* (Laguna Hills, CA: Aegean Park Press, 1998).
Scheer, Reinhard, *Germany's High Seas Fleet in the World War* (London: Cassell and Company, 1920).
Seale, Patrick, and McConville, Maureen, *Philby, the long road to Moscow* (London: Hamish Hamilton Ltd, 1973).
Sebag-Montefiore, Hugh, *Enigma, The Battle for the Code* (London: Weidenfeld & Nicolson, 2000).
Smith, Michael, *Station X* (London: Channel 4 Books, 1998).
Smith, Michael, and Erskine, Ralph, *Action This Day* (London: Bantam Press, 2001).
Stengers, Jean 'La Guerre des Messages Codes (1930-1945)', *L'Histoire* (February 1981).
Stengers, Jean, 'Enigma, the French, the Poles and the British, 1931-1940', in Andrew, C., and

Dilks, D. (eds), *The Missing Dimension: Governments and Intelligence Communities in the Twentieth Century* (London: Macmillan, 1984).
Stubbington, John, *Kept in the Dark* (Barnsley: Pen and Sword Aviation, 2010).
Tuchman, Barbara, *The Zimmermann Telegram* (Edinburgh: Constable & Co. Ltd, 1958).
Welchman, Gordon, *The Hut Six Story, Breaking the Enigma Codes* (New York: McGraw-Hill Book Company, 1982).
West, Nigel, *MI5: British Security Service Operations, 1909-1945* (New York: Stein and Day, 1982).
West, Nigel, *The SIGINT Secrets, The Signals Intelligence War, 1900 to Today* (London: Weidenfeld & Nicolson, 1986).
West, Nigel, *GCHQ* (London: Weidenfeld and Nicolson, 1986).
Winterbotham, F.W., *The Ultra Secret* (London: Weidenfeld & Nicolson, 1974).
Yardley, Herbert O., *The American Black Chamber* (Indianapolis: Bobbs-Merrill, 1931).

Index